AFTER THE FIRST DEATH

AFTER THE
FIRST DEATH

A JOURNEY THROUGH CHILE, TIME, MIND

LAKE SAGARIS

A Karen Mulhallen Book
SOMERVILLE HOUSE PUBLISHING
TORONTO

Canadian Cataloguing in Publication Data

Sagaris, Lake
After the first death : a journey through Chile, time, mind

"A Karen Mulhallen book".
Includes bibliographical references and index.
ISBN 1-895897-63-7

1. Chile – History – 1973-1988.
2. Chile – History – 1988- . I. Title.

F3100.S3 1996   983.06'5   C95-932966-8

Cover and text design: Reactor/Nick Trentadue
Author photograph: Barbara Cole
Cover photographs: Patricio Lanfranco and Jose Fuste Raga/First Light

Printed in Canada

A Karen Mulhallen Book

Published by Somerville House Publishing,
a division of Somerville House Books Limited,
3080 Yonge Street, Suite 5000, Toronto, Ontario M4N 3N1

Somerville House Publishing acknowledges the financial assistance of the Ontario Publishing Centre, the Ontario Arts Council, the Ontario Development Corporation, and the Department of Communications.

This book is for Patricio without whom it would never have existed for the music he has never stopped hearing and playing

For Jaime, Camilo, Daniel
For the Battens, Agnes & Archibald, Lois & Don,
Mike & Susan, Dave & Barb

TABLE OF CONTENTS

ACKNOWLEDGEMENTS viii
CAST OF CHARACTERS xi
INTRODUCTION xviii
1. AFTER THE FIRST DEATH 1
2. GOING TO ISLA NEGRA 9
3. ESCAPES FROM PARADISE 34
4. PRONOUNCEMENTS 62
5. THE RICH VILLAGE 90
6. OPERATIONS 97
7. MURDER AMONG STRANGERS 117
8. IGNACIO 138
9. SOWING THE WIND 164
10. OF DWARVES AND GIANTS 183
11. LA VICTORIA 201
12. TINQUILCO 226
13. NGUILLATÚN 233
14. ALVARO VALENZUELA/JULIO CORBALÁN 253
15. CAMILO'S FIRST DAY AT SCHOOL 269
16. THE LITTLE RIFTS 288
17. THE DRAGON PINCHOT 309
18. A ROOTED SORROW 331
19. WHERE WE START FROM 343
TIMELINE 359
GLOSSARY 366
SOURCES / BOOKS 371
NOTES 375
INDEX 390

ACKNOWLEDGEMENTS

I wish to express my thanks to the Canada Council for giving me two price-less years to prepare and initiate the journey through time and landscape that began this book and saw it almost to completion. I would also like to thank Mark Abley, author of *Beyond Forget*, Steven Hume, author of *Ghost Camps*, and Patricia Politzer, author of *Fear in Chile* whose absorbing books made me think that this one might be possible.

I am grateful to Lesley Krueger for providing some otherwise unobtainable sources, particularly the Yamana-English dictionary prepared by the British missionary Thomas Bridges, and Joan Simalchik, for her support and her thesis, with its practical information about the Chilean coup's short- and medium-term impact on Canadians.

I also owe special thanks to other writers who have researched and written some extraordinary books about Chile past and present, in both English and Spanish. These have served me well. They are listed under Sources at the end of this book. I offer them many, many thanks, and, of course, no blame for what I have done with what I discovered within their pages.

When I came to Chile I felt accompanied by many people I had known and loved in Canada. Their affection and their strength helped me through some of the harder moments. Among them I remember and would like to thank Brian Mason, Karin Olsen, Morna Ballantyne, Donna Baines, Jim Stanford, Patty Gibson, John Doherty, Blair Redlin, Jim Payne, Gene Long, Robin Breon, Nick Smirnow, without whose demands and encouragement, I might never have felt tempted to stray into journalism.

Of those who have helped along this pilgrimage of sorts, I would like to thank Paul Knox, Frances Lowndes, Paul Mylrea, Imogen Mark, Raul Sohr, Sergio Sanchez, the indomitable Yadranka, Paul Mably, Lydia Casas, Pato Mason, Barbara Moon, Cecilia Jadue, Bernarda Contreras, María Inés Arribas, Bob Carty, Bill Fairbairne, Gary Geddes, Jan Geddes, among, many, many others.

I am particularly grateful to all those who were willing to sit down for the rather lengthy interviews that formed the basis of many of these chapters. For some this was a difficult and painful process; to them I offer a special thanks. I know my book differs from many of the opinions expressed to me, but I have tried to give each voice fair play.

Hard work, the willing support of my sons and Patricio Lanfranco, and the quiet refuge of Renato Cárdenas's and Catherine Hall's comfortable house in Chiloé, and the kind offices of Karen Mulhallen, my editor, have made it possible for this journey to culminate, if not in exorcism, at least in an unquiet peace.

A previous version of "Tinquilco" originally appeared in *Saturday Night*, Toronto, and an earlier version of "Punta Arenas, A Rooted Sorrow" appeared in *Matrix* magazine, Montreal.

In addition, the author makes the following acknowledgements: W. H. Auden's poem, "Epitaph on a Tyrant", from *Collected Poems* by W. H. Auden, edited by Edward Mendelson, quoted by permission of Faber and Faber. Jose Cayuela, interview with Nelson Lillo, Laura Soto: una Dama de Lila y Negro, quoted by permission of the author. La Ciruela, quoted by permission of Patricio Lanfranco. Ariel Dorfman, *The Last Song of Manuel Sendero*, quoted by permission of the author. T. S. Eliot's poem, "Little Gidding", from *Collected Poems 1909 - 1962* by T. S. Eliot, quoted by permission of Faber and Faber. Rolf Foerster, Vida Religiosa de los Huilliches de San Juan de la Costa Conjunto Wetchemapu quoted by permission of Rolf Foerster. Gero Gemballa, Colonia Dignidad, quoted by permission of Cesoc. Eduardo llanos, "Goodbye", quoted by permission of the author. Dylan Thomas' poem, "A Refusal to Mourn the Death, By Fire, of a Child in London", quoted by permission of David Higham Associates. Jorge Vergara and Ana Cecilia Vergara, "Justice, Impunity and the Transition to Democracy: a challenge for human rights education", quoted by permission of the authors. W. B. Yeats' poem, "Easter 1916", quoted by permission of AP Watt Literary Agents Ltd. There are a few quotations whose copyright owners have not been located after diligent inquiry. The publisher would be grateful for information enabling it to make suitable acknowledgements in future printings.

CAST OF
CHARACTERS

IN ORDER OF APPEARANCE

CHILE ~ a long serpentine country, winding its way down the bottom half of the west coast of Latin America.

PABLO NERUDA ~ Chile's Nobel-prize winning poet, a teacher by training, from the rainy south.

AUGUSTO PINOCHET ~ Army general who leapt to world fame after the military grabbed power from the elected government of Dr. Salvador Allende.

GENARO ARRIAGADA ~ A Christian Democrat, political scientist who studied the military, co-ordinated the anti-Pinochet campaign during the 1988 plebiscite, and became a minister in the cabinet of President Eduardo Frei.

THE RETTIG COMMISSION (THE NATIONAL COMMISSION FOR TRUTH AND RECONCILIATION) ~ a mixed panel of respected lawyers, historians, individuals, created to investigate human rights violations during the military government.

THE "DEGOLLADOS" CASE ~ Manuel Guerrero, president of Santiago Teachers' Association; Jose Manuel Parada, human rights worker, father of four; and Santiago Nattino, a retired commercial artist, were kidnapped and their throats slashed so they bled to death, at the end of March 1985.

RODRIGO ROJAS (THE "QUEMADOS" CASE) ~ During a two-day national strike in July 1986, a military patrol commanded by Lieutenant (now captain) Pedro Fernández Dittus captured Rodrigo Rojas, a young photographer, and Carmen Gloria Quintana, a student, set them on fire, then dumped them on a deserted street outside the city. Rodrigo Rojas died. Carmen Gloria Quintana survived.

IGNACIO VALENZUELA ~ an economist and one of the founders of the Manuel Rodríguez Patriotic Front, an armed resistance group formed mostly by Communist Youth in the early eighties.

THE AGRUPACION CULTURAL UNIVERSITARIA ~ a university-based cultural association known affectionately by its acronym, ACU (pronounced A-COO).

JUANCHO PEREZ (DR. JUAN MANUEL PEREZ) ~ an active participant in the ACU and editor of the ACU's magazine, *La Ciruela,* he became a psychiatrist working with child victims of repression.

PATRICIO LANFRANCO ~ head of the musical branch of the ACU, later he was elected president. We married after his forced disappearance for five days in 1981.

DIEGO MUÑOZ ~ an Engineering student and active leader of the ACU.

CECILIA CARVALLO ~ a librarian at the University of Chile with a difficult family life; through ACU she met, and fell in love with, Ignacio Valenzuela.

LINARES ~ a small farming community, about four hours' drive south of Chile, in the fertile folds of Chile's Central Valley.

COLONIA DIGNIDAD ~ a controversial German settlement or "colony", located in the foothills of the Andean mountains, near Linares. The Colony's main ideologue and leader is Paul Shäfer (see separate listing), often recognized because he has one glass eye. Other spokesmen include: Herman Schmidt (who served as a Luftwaffe pilot during World War II) and Dr. Hartmut Hopp.

WILHEMINE LINDEMANN ~ one of the few women to escape from Colonia Dignidad, Lindemann eventually returned. She is believed dead.

KIKA SANINO ~ wife of Hector Taricco, regional governor of Linares when the first scandals surrounding Colonia Dignidad broke out, Kika

Sanino became friends with Wilhemine Lindemann and tried to help her.

HECTOR TARRICCO ~ regional governor of Linares when the first scandals surrounding Colonia Dignidad broke out, was sympathetic to the beleaguered Colony initially, but as he learned more about their dealings he became of it most powerful enemies. In 1966 he was the subject of a Congressional investigation for his "persecution" of Colonia Dignidad, but he continues to live near and maintain an office in Linares.

PAUL SCHÄFER ~ Colonia Dignidad's legendary leader, originally fled post-World War II Germany to avoid being charged with sodomy and sexual abuse of minors. In the sixties, when local authorities attempted to control the Colony, he faked his own suicide, but was seen on several occasions win the seventies and eighties.

OSVALDO MURAY ~ one of the Chilean journalists, working for the magazine *Ercilla,* who first covered the stories and charges about Colonia Dignidad.

JORGE OVALLE ~ A Chilean lawyer who represented the government in its cases involving the Colony 1990-1994.

HEINZ KUHN ~ a former leader and defender of Colonia Dignidad, he eventually escaped and now lives in the city of Los Angeles, in southern Chile.

THE ESCAPEES FROM COLONIA DIGNIDA ~ After Heinz Kuhn (see separate listing), Franz and Teresa Wohri escaped, leaving one of their four children in the Colony, and, in 1970, Peter Packmor (now dead) escaped. Fourteen years later in December 1984, Hugo Baar, one of the Colony's founders, fled, leaving wife and children behind (he was later able to have his wife join him) and then (March 1985) George and Lotty Packmor, all of whom had worked closely with the Colony's leader, Paul Schäfer, successfully escaped, leaving their adopted son behind. The last known escape occurred in April 1988, but Jürgen Szurgelies was recaptured.

MANUEL CONTRERAS ~ retired Army General, founder and head of General Pinochet's secret police (1973-1978), convicted for the killing in Washington in 1976 of Orlando Letelier, a former minister in the Allende government, and Ronni Moffit, an American colleague.

ALEJANDRO MEDINA LOIS ~ retired Army general, Black Beret, artillery commander, professor in the National Academy for Political and Strategic Studies.

RAÚL VERGARA ~ retired Air Force Captain. He was arrested after the coup and taken to the new Air Force Academy, where his former companions-at-arms tortured him.

MARIO MORALES MONDACA ~ retired Carabineros (uniformed police) General, who did not play an active role in the coup or the military government that followed.

THE MAPUCHE ~ Chile's largest group of Native people, about 1 million out of a total population of 13 million. They speak Mapudungun.

VILLARRICA ~ a small frontier town about ten hours' drive south of Santiago, near Temuco.

THE DINA ~ Decree Law no. 521 officially created the Dirección de Inteligencia Nacional DINA, on June 14th, 1974. Articles 9, 10, 11 of the law were secret. They give the governing military Junta the power to involve Army, Navy and Air Force Intelligence departments in DINA or DINA-type activities, including searches and arrests. DINA agents became infamous for their participation in torture and forced disappearances. In a televised interview in May 1995, Osvaldo Romo, a former DINA agent, boasted about his prowess as a torturer in great detail, the main techniques he and his companions used. He also listed the names of government and other political leaders he planned to personally strangle, upon his release, at that time expected to occur later in the year.

THE CNI ~ Central Nacional de Inteligencia, the military intelligence group, responsible directly to General Augusto Pinochet, that carried out many of the military government's more violent operations. created to replace the DINA in 1977; dissolved in January 1990, with most of its members being passed on to the DINE, the Army's Intelligence department.

THE DINA AND CNI AGENTS WHO HAVE SPOKEN OUT PUBLICLY ~ include Osvaldo Romo (DINA) Michael Townley and Mariana Callejas (DINA), Luz Arce (DINA), Andrés Valenzuela (DINA/ CNI), Juan Muñoz Alarcón (DINA). Alvaro Corbalán (CNI) has talked a great deal, but not revealed very much.

MONICA GONZALEZ ~ a Chilean journalist who stubbornly pieced together information about officers involved in human rights violations, author of several books.

RODRIGO ANFRUNS ~ a young boy who was kidnapped and murdered in 1979, apparently to punish his grandfather, a retired Army Colonel, for revealing theft in the post office.

NELSON LILLO ~ the police commissioner who solved the crimes of the "Viña Psychopath" and was fired for his pains.

LUIS GUBLER ~ the man who confessed twice to being the "Viña Psychopath", but was later released.

JORGE SAGREDO AND TOPP COLLINS ~ two former Carabineros, arrested, sentenced and executed for the crimes of the Viña psychopath.

TUCAPEL JIMENEZ CASE ~ the case of a union leader, knifed to death in February 1982.

THE POLICE FORCES ~ Aside from the secret police, that is, the DINA (1973-1977) and the CNI (1977-1990), Chile has Carabineros, a national police force of about 30,000 officers; Investigaciones, a small contingent of civilian police detectives. Each branch of the Armed Forces has its own intelligence department, as does Carabineros. The Joint Command was an initial attempt at coordination between the different intelligence services.

ADRIANA POHORECKY ~ mother of Ignacio Valenzuela.

MANUEL RODRIGUEZ ~ a hero of Chile's wars of Independence from Spain, Manuel Rodríguez was a kind of Chilean Robin Hood.

WAR ~ the military's justification for human rights violations (the military calls them excesses) "the continuation of politics with the admixture of other means," wrote Karl von Clausewitz; "the source of all arts ...", according to one Chilean officer.

"EDUARDO" ~ a member of the Communist Youth at the time of the coup, he eventually signed up with the Manuel Rodríguez Patriotic Front.

THE MEMBERS OF THE MANUEL RODRIGUEZ PATRIOTIC FRONT ~ include José Joaquín Valenzuela, Raúl Pellegrín, its top leader, often known as "José Miguel", Cecilia Magni, César Bunster (who worked for the Canadian Embassy, for a brief but memorable moment).

ORLANDO LETELIER ~ a former minister in the Allende government, he was arrested, imprisoned on Dawson Island and later exiled by the military government. On September 21, 1976, a car-bomb, organized by DINA agent Michael Townley and set off by two Cuban exiles, destroyed his car, killing him and Ronni Moffit, his colleague and passenger. Her husband, Michael, survived the blast.

THE LETELIER CASE ~ Because the killing of Orlando Letelier, in Washington in 1976, was not covered by the 1978 Amnesty Law, it became virtually the only opportunity for trying and convicting those responsible for human rights violations. On May 31, 1995, the Chilean Supreme Court convicted General Manual Contreras and Brigadier Pedro Espinoz for ordering the killing of Orlando Letelier. They were sentenced to seven and six years, respectively.

TINQUILCO ~ a small lake on a mountain top in southern Chile, in the midst of a spectacular National Park.

QUINQUEN ~ a small embattled indigenous community high in the mountains, south of Santiago, just north of Tinquilco.

VICTOR PAINEMAL ~ director of the Special Commission for Indigenous People's Office in Temuco, in southern Chile.

ALVARO CORBALÁN ~ a.k.a. Julio Castilla, Alvaro Valenzuela, a CNI agent who became well-known when he tried to begin a political career in 1988.

RAQUEL CORREA ~ a tough Chilean interviewer, working for the conservative newspaper, *El Mercurio.*

CLAUDIA DUEÑAS ~ a specialist in creating curricula for human rights education in the schools.

ANDRES DOMINGUEZ ~ a Chilean lawyer, active member of the Chilean Human Rights Commission during the military government; then worked for the Corporation for Truth and Reparation, which replaced the Retting Commission in 1991.

JUAN PABLO LETELIER ~ son of Orlando Letelier and Isabel Morel, born in Washington, DC in January 1961 and brought up mostly in the United States. He returned to Chile and was elected to the House of Deputies in both the 1989 and the 1994 elections.

COPPER ~ probably the greatest single reason for the United States' extraordinary interest in Chile throughout the twentieth century.

LAURA NOVOA ~ a corporate lawyer, she grew up in the north, in Viña del Mar and Santiago. When she graduated in 1954, no one really wanted to hire a woman lawyer and her first job was a favour to her father, a

Carabinero general. The head lawyer at Anaconda's Chile Exploration Company hired her and from then on she was at the centre of the debates over foreign ownership of Chile's huge copper resources. In 1990-1991, she sat on the Retting Commission.

HARRY BARNES ~ the US Ambassador to Santiago, from November 1985 on, he presided over US policy that encouraged the opposition to unite, excluding the Communist party, and fight the military regime through the plebiscite scheduled for October 5, 1988.

LA VICTORIA ~ *a población,* or poor, working-class community on Santiago's southside, said to be the first land occupation of Latin America's homeless. La Victoria became one of the leading *poblaciones* in the almost monthly protests against the military regime, which began in May 1983 and continued until the 1988 plebiscite campaign.

MARIA NÉLIDA SANCHEZ AND HER SON RENATO ~ two generations, two perspectives on life in La Victoria, before, during and after military rule. She grew up in the Coya camp, near what is today the El Teniente copper mine.

JOAQUÍN LAVÍN ~ an economist, author of *Revolución Silenciosa,* published in 1987, celebrating the successes of the military government's economic policies. A member of the Unión Demócrata Independiente, Lavín was elected mayor of the wealthy Las Condes district of Santiago in municipal elections in 1992.

EUGENIO TIRONI ~ a sociologist, author of *Los Silencios de la Revolución,* written in response to Lavín's enthusiastic evaluation of the military's policies.

FERNANDO LANFRANCO ~ an engineer (and my brother-in-law), arrested, tortured, tried and exiled, in the southern city of Punta Arenas, after the 1973 coup.

HUMBERTO PALAMARA ~ a Naval Captain, expert in intelligence, whose book on ethics and intelligence was seized and confiscated in 1993.

INTRODUCTION

I have consistently followed one idea through all of my life. I preyed upon the weak, the harmless and the unsuspecting. This lesson I was taught by others: might makes right.

CARL PANZRAM, MULTIPLE MURDERER

Los hombres normales han matado quizá unos cien millones de semejantes normales en los últimos cincuenta años. [Normal men have killed about 100 million normal men in the past fifty years.]

R.D. LAING

"Human", my dictionary tells me, "belonging or pertaining to man or mankind: having the qualities of a man"; "humane, having the feelings proper to man: kind, tender, merciful, benevolent"; "humanize, to render human or humane: to soften"; "humanitarian, one who denies Christ's divinity and holds Him to be a mere man: a philanthropist".

After more than a decade living in Chile, I find it hard to view our species, male and female, as synonymous with kindness and mercy. Cruelty, collective cruelty, has been an integral part of our social institutions: the cruelty expressed in the Romans' predilection for crucifixion, the bloody lessons of the Inquisition and the way these lessons influenced the Conquest of the Americas. In the twentieth century, Hitler's Third Reich and World War II were perhaps the worst of this "tradition", but not the only expression. The granite face, incapable of empathy, has risen again and again, masking our torturers and dictators, as we slide toward the edge of the twenty-first century.

The conflict between our humane aspirations and our human practices is sharply etched in Chile, a country with a democratic tradition and an overweening respect for legality.

I was in my late teens, studying Creative Writing at the University of British Columbia, when I first picked up a copy of the Chilean poet Pablo Neruda's *Song of Protest*. Thematically, the book is about Central America, but even in translation Chile lives and breathes through the poet's images, as if the landscape had become his language. In 1979, I visited Chile as a representative of Canada's National Union of Students. Chile became a world symbol in 1970, when it became the first country to elect a Marxist-inspired, Socialist government; and, after the military seized power three years later, it became a source of news stories, all springing from the same source: the impact of living under, and sometimes trying to resist, one of the world's most brutal military regimes. I fell in love with the country, the people and the tortured poetry of their resistance to the military government headed by General Augusto Pinochet.

In 1980, I lived in Chile for three months. In January 1981, I moved there indefinitely. I eventually found my feet, working as a foreign correspondent, even as I realized that many of the best stories did not fit into the format of a daily or nightly news report.

Chile is a long serpentine country, winding its way down the bottom half of the west coast of Latin America. Until the Pacific War in 1879, it was a poor, basically agricultural land. By the time the war with Peru and Bolivia was over, Chile had added a huge stretch of territory that included the world's driest desert, the Atacama, and, more importantly, some of the world's richest copper and nitrate reserves.

With the Pacific Ocean on the west, the Andean mountains extending from the North, all the way down the country's eastern limits, and Antarctica to the south, Chile has lived an island existence for most of its history. In the words of Pedro de Valdivia, founder of Santiago in 1541:

This land is such that life here cannot be equalled. It has only four months of winter ... and the summer is so temperate and has such delicious breezes that men can walk all day in the sun and not suffer for it. It is abundant in grass, and can support any kind of cattle or livestock and plants that you can imagine; there is plenty of very beautiful wood for building houses, great quantities of wood for fuel for heating and working the rich mines. Wherever you might dream of finding them, there is soil to sow, materials for building and water for the animals, so that it seems as if God had created everything so that it would be at hand.

From its beginnings in 1541, as an impoverished colony of the Spanish crown, through the legends and adventures of Chile's War of Independence in the early 1800s and its development as an important mining country during the 1900s, to its bursting onto the world stage as the first country to freely choose a socialist government and economic system in national elections, followed by the brutal smashing of the constitutional democracy by the military in 1973, Chile has very much cut its own path through history. This reflects its geographic isolation, but also the rich cultural and intellectual tradition that isolation helped to engender.

For hundreds of years before the Conquest, among the northern communities of the Atacameño and Diaghuita peoples, who travelled the Atacama desert and its oases, cultural expression took the form of brilliantly dyed and finely woven fabrics and baskets, ceramic pots and pitchers, whose designs continue to be copied by modern ceramicists, and elaborate preservation of the dead through mummification. To the south of what is today Santiago, the Mapuche created wonder-filled stories, songs and a complex mythological world. Still further south, the Chilotes in the southern archipelago of Chiloé, themselves a mixture of Spanish and native Huilliche (southern Mapuche) stock, developed a rich tradition of music, dance, weaving and story-telling.

Even today, it is easy to see native traits in the straight, dark hair and eyes of many Chileans. But the higher you climb on the totem pole of Chilean class structure, the blonder the hair and skin of its people become, testimony to the immigration of German and Yugoslavian "colonists" in the late eighteen hundreds, to the British, who played an influential role in the 1879 war Chile fought against Peru and Bolivia, to the Americans, who have been the dominant foreign influence in this century.

Education, whether through the oral tradition of Chile's original peoples or the formal institutions of the West, has always been a crucial theme in Chilean society. The University of Chile, founded in 1843, was one of Latin America's first universities. By 1860, with only 17 per cent of the population literate, primary education became not only free but the responsibility of the Chilean State. Sixty years later, half the population could read and write. In 1920, primary education became obligatory and public schools became increasingly accessible to children from all walks of life. By the early seventies, the public educational system covered most of the population, although under considerable stress from this hefty demand, like educational systems elsewhere in the world.

Today, with a small population of less than 14 million people, Chile has made its presence felt in the world through two Nobel prizewinners, both of them poets, Gabriela Mistral and Pablo Neruda; the renowned painter Roberto Matta; the folk artists, singers and composers Violeta Parra and Victor Jara; the pianists Claudio Arrau and Roberto Bravo; the musical groups Inti Illimani and Quilapayún; the film-maker Miguel Littín (*Sandino*); and others.

How did a country with a rich cultural and political tradition like Chile's become synonymous with some of the worst brutality of our century? How is it that some countries, some peoples, manage to "get it right" and live a long and peaceful existence? And how is it that some, who "get it right" for so long, the way Chile seemed to from 1925 to 1973, begin a downward slide into extremes of conflict, characterized by violence and the wholesale brutality of torture applied as central elements of state policy?

Racism was a factor, the permanent existence in Chile of peoples and social groups whose rights have been trampled since the country's founding. The ultra-conservative character of many of those who have traditionally monopolized political power is another element, as is the power wielded by the military and the military's need to divide the world into friends – and enemies who must be killed. Hypocrisy and its role in the breakdown of the justice system, as shown by the experience of Colonia Dignidad, are other elements.

Each time humanity's capacity for cruelty has reared its head, it has been treated as something from our distant, more barbaric past; as anomaly; as exception or even insanity. But its constant repetition through oral and written history, its most recent manifestation in Latin America over the past twenty years, indicates this capacity for cruelty is as much a part of the human as the humane. What happened in Chile, the daily, nitty-gritty details of dictatorship, of pain, of the wilful cruelty of social institutions toward individual men and women, and resistance to all of these, happened in Rome, in America during and since the conquest, in Europe during World War II. Watch the news. It is happening somewhere today.

The *Encyclopedia Encarta* (1994 edition) defines torture as "infliction of severe bodily pain either as punishment or to compel a person to confess to a crime". It was a standard element in the judicial process in Greece and Rome, where torture was an integral part of examination. In 1252, at the start of the Inquisition, Pope Innocent IV officially required the use of torture in trials for heresy, thus opening the door for its use within the legal systems of Europe, starting with Italy and then France (thirteenth century) and every other European country except Sweden and England, although in the latter it could be practised as a royal pre-rogative. Torture was illegal in the American colonies. During the 1700s, it was gradually eliminated in each of the European countries, and the Roman Catholic Church officially banned its use in Catholic countries through a papal bull issued in 1816.

Genaro Arriagada, a Chilean political scientist who studied the military and went on to co-ordinate the anti-Pinochet campaign during the 1988 plebiscite, and then took on a post as a top adviser in the cabinet of President Eduardo Frei, wrote that torture, "in a perverse way, is a personal and human relationship. It is one person acting on another, directly. It is one human being with wounded flesh, naked, shivering from cold and terror, covered with blood, sweat and vomit, and another, causing that pain, laughing at it, calculating at what point the other's resistance and dignity will finally give way." The goal of torture is to destroy the person who is subjected to it, but it also horribly damages those who learn to inflict the pain.

The seeds of violence or brutality lie in each individual, a capacity for callousness or cruelty which is an integral part of human nature because it can be useful – when a surgeon cuts into a patient or a mother pulls a sliver from her child's foot. It is human society, our collective being, which sets limits on our own capacity for coldness, creates incentives for kindness, teaches empathy. There is nothing more dangerous than a society that declares, through its main institutions, that it is all right to kidnap, torture, kill – that one particular set of human beings have lost their right to belong to our society. The spiral of violence thus unleashed quickly develops the raging force of a tornado, cutting a swathe of desolation through any community that spares no one the anguish of being, or knowing or fearing one might become a victim.

The methods used have grown more sophisticated, as knowledge of human biology, psychology and social bonding has developed, along with pharmaceuticals influencing the mind and perception. There are several accounts of torture in this book, so I won't repeat them here. The point is that the wholesale practice of torture by legal bodies representing the State affects not just the particular victim, or survivor, but the whole fabric of a society. Torture is practised as much against the body politic of a nation as it is against the soft and vulnerable flesh of the individual. For torture to exist, there must be complicity – from the judicial system, from the media, from the people, or even from the country next door. When the complicity starts to break down, the system begins to falter and eventually loses its grip.

That is why it would be a mistake to leave Chile, as if it were nothing more than a synonym for Pinochet or dictatorship, torture or disappearance. Quietly, painfully, in the tremendous solitude that followed the destruction of the public meeting place, individuals found their own consciences putting them on trial. Slowly, imperceptibly, they began to react, family members at first, friends, lawyers, priests and layworkers, congregations, physicians, nurses, psychologists and social workers, students, workers, the unemployed, women, native people. The accusing silence of the first march of relatives of the disappeared in 1978 was echoed by songs and poems, reports abroad, the endless clauses of the inevitable habeas corpus. The monotonous drumming and the shuffling of military boots, the crack of clubs, the endless babble of official versions met with the clamour of pots and pans, a maelstrom of protest.

What happened in Chile put other countries to the test as well, among them my homeland, Canada. Until the 1973 coup, Canadian immigration policy had no special category for refugees of any kind. Humanitarian concerns did not count among the criteria used to decide who could cross the border and who could not. In fact, Canada did not remove the colour bar from its legislation until 1962 and it did not sign the 1951 UN Convention on Refugees until 1969. Thirty years earlier, Canada had refused entry to a ship full of Jews fleeing Nazi Germany. They were eventually forced to return and most were killed.

"Chile posed a challenge for Canada," writes Canadian historian Joan Simalchik. "While previous refugee movements were consistent with Canadian foreign policy considerations or with Commonwealth commitments, Chilean would-be refugees were by definition left-wing opponents of United States political and corporate interests who were fleeing a military coup supported, if not engineered, by the Americans. Canadian interests in Latin America were ill-defined and insignificant as illustrated by its nonmembership in the Organization of American States. Neither the Canadian government in Ottawa nor the Embassy in Santiago believed that Canada had any responsibility with regard to events following the 1973 coup in Chile."

Five confidential cables by Andrew Ross, the Canadian ambassador in Chile at the time of the coup, reveal the Canadian government's official complacency in the face of bloodshed: "With almost the entire leadership dead or in custody Chile's Marxist Left is decapitated and on the run. Country nonpolitical activity is returning to normal progressively and quite rapidly. But curfew is still imposed 8 PM to 7 AM. Reprisals and searches have created panic atmosphere affecting particularly expatriates including riff-raff of LatAm left to whom Allende gave asylum. Hopefully UN will be able to arrange refuge although some of these quote activists unquote are running out of countries willing to accept them. Hopefully brutalities and witchhunting perpetrated by ultras and all too reminiscent of Nazi methods will soon be curbed by the junta. There seems to have been considerable diminution in horror rumours during the past few days and there should be comensurate [sic] lessening of pressures on us and other embassies for refuge or asylum."

Concerned Canadian churches, many with lay and religious workers in the field in Chile and other Latin American countries, formed the nucleus of a coalition of unprecedented breadth that included the Canadian Association of Latin American Studies, Canadian Association of University Teachers, Canadian Labour Congress, Confederation des syndicats nationaux, CUSO, National Union of Students, Oxfam-Canada, SUCO, World University Service and various solidarity and settlement organizations. Together these groups presented a brief to the federal government. Their views met with support from many quarters, including the Conservative MP from Edmonton-Strathcona, Douglas Roche, (I was living in his riding at the time!) who said in parliament, "the situation in Chile is not normalizing ... All of this should be of great concern to the Canadian government which could provide more help than just support of a UN resolution. If we are not going to reappraise our economic relations with Chile so that we could get out of the invidious position of supporting repression, could we at least open our doors a bit wider?"

During early meetings, the churches' representatives met with a frigid response from the Department of External Affairs. "For the longest time the government was saying that 'they're hotblooded down there, they have these revolutions, it doesn't really amount to very much and there is nothing we have to do,'" Fred Franklin, who participated in these meetings, told Simalchik in 1989.

Along with citizens' groups around the world, the Canadian churches did not give up. On September 15, 1973, the United, Catholic and Anglican Churches signed a joint statement, protesting the coup and urging the government to provide safe conduct and refuge to its victims. Within weeks, the government's lack of response led the Anglican Church of Canada, the Religious Society of Friends, the Canadian Council of Churches, the Lutheran Church of America (Canadian Section), the Presbyterian Church in Canada, the Canadian Catholic Conference, the Scarborough Foreign Mission Society, the Toronto Passionist Community and the United Church of Canada to form the Interchurch Committee on Chile.

The efforts of Canadians triggered by the Chilean coup have institutionalized a strong, humanitarian strain in Canada that it is in all our interests to nourish. The Inter-Church Committee on Human Rights in Latin America (ICCHRLA), continues to monitor and act upon rights violations in many countries, now with more than twenty years' experience in helping refugees. A number of non-governmental organizations have acquired similar experience abroad, aiding in the rebuilding of human rights organizations and democratic practice. The Canadian Centre for Victims of Torture, initially set up to assist Chilean refugees, now contributes to the healing of victims from regimes around the world. Many of those who led the first charge to help those suffering from the Chilean military coup continue to work for the same humanitarian goals in organizations around the world.

"The grassroots diplomacy undertaken by Canadian churches with regard to Chile as a reflection of spiritual and social understanding has provided genuine achievement in the development of public policy," writes Simalchik. Since those early days, when many Canadians worked day and night to have Canada give asylum to Chileans threatened by imprisonment, torture and death, national immigration laws have been modified to include official refugee status and Canada has gone on to accept refugees from many countries.

By 1975, governments around the world were echoing the concerns of citizens' groups like Canada's church people, often expressed in tandem with Chilean exile communities. In January of that year, Australia detained wheat shipments to Chile; in February, England demanded an improvement in the human rights situation before carrying on foreign debt renegotiations. From 1974 on, the United Nations published annual reports on the human rights situation in Chile, urging respect inside the country, urging action from abroad, urging support for the regime's surviving victims. Each time there was an arrest, a kidnapping, a disappearance, an avalanche of telegrams could and did save lives. They made resistance easier and they taught the dangers of complaisance.

In April 1990, the newly elected government of President Patricio Aylwin appointed the Rettig Commission, a mixed panel of respected lawyers, historians, individuals, to investigate human rights violations during the military government. Some members had supported the military government, others had defended its victims, while still others worked quietly for democracy. In its conclusions, the Commission observed that under democracy, freedom of the press and particularly the weight of public opinion and debate prevented major violations of human rights by balancing out the many flaws in Chile's political, legal and social structures. When the military swept away these controls, claiming to be the country's moral conscience and therefore above reproach, the contradictions shot to the surface. Like hidden landmines, they were indifferent to the suffering they caused and often mortal. Chileans eventually lost not only their freedom, their right to be informed, their right to participate, they also saw their public health and public education system slashed and privatized, their shared value system of material support and aid abruptly replaced by the cold principle of extreme competition.

Chile's experience is worth more than an absent-minded glimpse. Its lessons are valid far beyond its borders, not only because, given the right circumstance, "it might happen here", but also for the reasons highlighted by Canadian church-workers, who struggled so hard for Canadians to respond humanely, rather than humanly, to what was happening in a small country that many had never heard of.

As Canada and the United States follow up on Mexico's inclusion in the North American Free Trade Agreement, NAFTA, by looking south toward further hemispheric integration, it is worthwhile for Canadians and Americans to look beyond the often illusory figures of macroeconomic success and the cold currency of what is to be pocketed or lost, at what these numbers have cost in terms of human suffering, of what, besides good macroeconomic indicators, has brought celebration. Independent of the world of agreements and trade, the endless traffic of commodities, there is something more here to be exchanged.

In our classrooms, we learn that North and South America are two separate continents, while Chileans study that we're each halves of one whole. In the North, only citizens of the United States are called "Americans", whereas in the South, "Americanos" refers to citizens of both continents. There is a lot to be said for the Chileans' perspective. Canadians and "Americans" enjoy a fine standard of living. Chileans have historically enjoyed a rich and diverse culture that has contributed two Nobel prize-winning poets, Gabriela Mistral and Pablo Neruda, to the world. More knowledge of each other can offer us more insight into ourselves. This alone would be useful, especially to Canadians, given Canada's agonies over its own collective identity and future. In an increasingly integrated world, we must all learn to look beyond our own horizons – and the "elephant" to our South where our gaze so often seems to stop – for references, roles, ideas, for doing things differently and to offer our own experience where it may be useful.

In the Timeline, at the end of this book, I've charted the costs to Chileans of rebuilding a democratic country. Hundreds were killed during national protests, many of them children, many of them passersby, or even people huddling in the illusory safety of their own homes. These costs could be our own.

The Chileans are ordinary people, who have been capable of extraordinary feats. They are worth knowing, and well, for their own history, their own writers, their own brilliant ideas and practical experience, and not just for the taste of their summer fruit purchased off supermarket shelves during our harsh winters, not just as the glint of their copper lining the wires in our homes and cars.

The Rettig Commission concluded that "The true cause of the human rights violations ... was the insufficiency of a national culture of respect for these rights." In the wake of the atrocities committed by Canadian soldiers in Somalia, we must ask if we are really any different.

Throughout this book I've tried to explore Chile – geographically, historically, psychologically, intuitively as well as rationally – to discover the roots of these fatal contradictions. One of my conclusions is that any society's excessive dependence on a rational approach to truth, divorced from intuitive, mythological or other "primitive" methods, is an essential ingredient in this kind of tragedy.

Chile is Chile. It could be Somalia or ex-Yugoslavia or Iran. It is our world both New and Old. Our time. And perhaps our future. We need to reflect and act on these experiences in our own time, in our own lives, with an eye to what social institutions and personal qualities can prevent them. And what we can do to help, when they occur.

The people who flee from lands in strife bring those conflicts with them. Many of the refugees trying to build new lives in Canada or other countries have been tortured or suffered the trauma of humanity's failure to be "humane". Our treatment of them, as individuals and communities, as friends or states, can renew the trauma or help to heal it.

It is we who learn the most from that healing.

Chapter one

AFTER THE
FIRST DEATH

SANTIAGO 1989

After the first death there is no other

DYLAN THOMAS

Palm-lined Peace Avenue stretches from the bustling central market area, past the morgue with its pompous official title, El Instituto Médico Legal, to the triumphal arch of Santiago's General Cemetery. Through that gateway lies another world, an eerie but faithful reflection of the living city that surrounds it.

In more than a decade here in Chile, I have walked Peace Avenue alone and with crowds, in silence and surrounded by cheers and chants for the newly dead. One warm March evening in 1985, I huddled with a group outside the morgue, all nerves focused on the door, which remained stubbornly shut. Hours later, a man popped out just long enough to mutter two names and the information that a third body remained unidentified, and had been labelled NN in the Chilean fashion. Someone else had to assume the painful task of shouting those names aloud: Manuel Guerrero, president of the Santiago Teachers' Association; Jose Manuel Parada, human rights worker, father of four. The identity of the third man puzzled the city for days. His name turned out to be Santiago.

Unidentified armed civilians had snatched Manuel Guerrero from the door of a public school and, when Jose Manuel Parada ran to help him, both disappeared into the back seat of a fast car. Two days later a farm-

1

worker found their bodies, along with that of a third man, their heads almost severed from their necks. It took months to discover why Santiago Nattino had been kidnapped. He was a commercial artist with no public political affiliation. The military regime announced immediately that all three had been leaders of Chile's illegal Communist Party.

Parada's wife, Estela Ortiz, had already experienced the arrest of her father in 1976. When an anonymous caller reported her father was in a secret prison, she went to the president of the Supreme Court, José María Eyzaguirre. He refused to act on her information and she never saw her father again. That night outside the morgue, braced by friends, her voice choked but charged with passion, Ortiz said: "The day will come when each one of them will pay for these crimes. ... This is too horrible. How long will this dialogue with murderers go on! How long will they go on killing our people! How long are we going to permit so much killing, so many crimes, so much torture? Chileans, companions, compatriots, please, rise up! Let us demand justice once and for all."

During a meticulous investigation conducted by Judge José Cánovas, airline attendants reported hearing the men's bloodcurdling howls in a solitary field on the way to Santiago's international airport, during curfew hours, just before dawn. Like Judge Carlos Cerda before him and Judge René García, who would come later, Cánovas unwound the tangled threads of a police intelligence service involved in kidnapping and indicted several top officers. The Supreme Court temporarily closed the case, arguing it could advance no further. Cánovas resigned.

At those funerals in 1985, tens of thousands of people shouted and laughed and marched their defiance. It had become a habit, turning the funerals of the regime's victims into protest marches, making every death a political liability with unforeseeable consequences.

The first time I visited the General Cemetery I got totally lost and so did my Chilean guide. It was 1980 and we were on the way to a *romería* for Pablo Neruda, Chile's Nobel-prizewinning poet, the man who painted Chileans' defeats and victories with words that reached across worlds.

When you enter, as we did that day, through the Peace Avenue arch, you are immediately surrounded by luxurious mausoleums, the mansions of Chile's wealthy dead. Here, as in life, they spare no expense to flaunt their taste. Elaborate marble stairways, stained-glass windows, arched entrances and multi-roomed palaces house the velvet-lined coffins of

Chile's ruling classes. The family names repeating themselves in expensive script on these walls still resound on nightly news reports.

Shadows and sunlight played along the tree-lined avenues, filled with chirping birds and wildflowers, as we wandered further and further into the cemetery. Small chapels, gargoyles and monuments stole our attention; we forgot the original purpose of our visit and became lost in a timeless maze, where the living are mere visitors, kneeling, heads bowed, before the dead.

Further on, we found the middle-class neighbourhoods: concrete walls resembling apartment buildings, where the dead are layered in neatly labelled niches, each one with a code discreetly carved in a corner, to indicate the date the rent runs out and cemetery personnel remove the remains, so a new tenant can be moved in.

These niches, with their flowers, occasional pictures, inscriptions, crosses standing straight or lying balanced on one tip, stretch in all directions. It's hard to believe that somewhere there is a boundary, a wall, flanked by streets filled with honking cars and people hawking dark-leaved wreaths and bouquets of carnations. Their persistent perfume, which once delighted me, has blended now, inextricably, with the mild, sour stench of putrefaction.

But the niches end, or at least pause, in the poorest part of the cemetery. Here green grass spills relentlessly over the dark soil, interrupted by wooden and iron crosses, graves with miniature fences that look like cradles, each with an attempt at a name, scrawled or pinned or pegged in place. Navigating the orderly paths which separate these graves, you reach a patio dotted with hundreds of anonymous labels, with only the initials NN (No Name) and the date, 1973, to distinguish them from the rest.

For almost two decades, nobody knew how many of those who were killed after Chile's military coup lay in this patio of the General Cemetery. Rumour, that great authority where people trust no other, said each grave held several bodies and that many were removed for burial elsewhere, in fear of changing times and the truths the earth would reveal when those in power chose to turn it over.

Our path led us finally to the back of the cemetery. We turned and walked between the anonymous graves on our left and a row of apartment-like niches on our right. One familiar name, enveloped in red carnations, stood out: Victor Jara. The man who sang "I remember you Amanda, coming from the factory"; the man who sang, imprisoned in

3

the National Stadium, badly tortured, threatened with death; the man who sang, even after his fingers had been broken, even after they'd aimed their machine guns at him and begun to fire; the man who sings still, in festivals around the world.

At last we came upon a small crowd of perhaps two hundred people. Children and posters had sprouted on bare branches; flowers and verses overflowed from Neruda's grave, covering the compressed earth, the stones around him, even some people's faces. Poets read poetry, singers sang, politicians made speeches, the crowd chanted. In a country which had once known (and would again know) demonstrations of more than a million people, this was a modest attempt at a political gathering. Even so, there were clubs, tear-gas and imprisonment waiting for all of us when we emerged again into the living city.

That was my first demonstration in Chile. Looking back on those years, before the protest movement exploded in 1983 and perhaps especially after, I see an endless procession of funerals, subverted by their participants into protests and homages to an unending stream of victims, martyrs, leaders, or simply ordinary people in the wrong place at the wrong time, whose hearts or minds couldn't hold up under the beatings, the electric shock, the small animals forced into orifices.

For some reason, the police were more careful about the cemetery. But they occasionally tried to steal the hearse and spirit the body away, as they did in the case of Rodrigo Rojas, burned alive by soldiers in 1986. And they sometimes used their clubs and tear-gas inside those thick, high walls. I remember one funeral where every tombstone seemed to hide a police officer in full riot gear and the tear-gas made everyone cry in spite of their rage.

But times changed. Even the funerals became more "normal". One unusually warm day in 1989, I found myself standing in front of those great sand-coloured arches, waiting for yet another procession. As usual, parked around the entrance gate were three buses of police in riot gear and several of the small, armoured jeeps that race along sidewalks, squirting gases and occasionally bullets at their human prey.

We mourners stood in awkward groups, unsure of our roles. The rituals which had become routine did not fit here. The four people we were burying, all of them young, all of them involved in the opposition, had not died for their political beliefs. They had survived the worst years of the repression, only to die on a lonely mountain, when one of their number miscalculated the strength of a support, hurtling them all into a last, white abyss.

A friend whispered under his breath: "I can't believe they died this way. It's such a waste!" Another was disgusted by what he called "this cult of death". He refused to carry flowers, to bow his head, to idealize our dead friends.

We could not understand accidental death. For sixteen years, fatal illnesses, death by misadventure, the ordinary, everyday ways of dying, had not existed. We had grown accustomed to dead contemporaries, dead children, dead friends. We believed death always had a reason. And we were wrong.

As we stood waiting, a few blocks away in the city centre pro- and anti-regime politicians were trying their rusty hands at electoral debates and promises and winning public support. The press, muzzled for years, shouted its truths to the world, although biases hadn't changed. In the modern cement-and-glass skyscrapers which are the regime's legacy to Chileans, human rights became a campaign issue. Estela Ortiz and others like her ran for seats in the House of Deputies (she lost, but her mother-in-law, María Maluenda, was elected). The government's presidential candidate accused the opposition of defending "terrorists". The opposition promised that justice would be done – through the same legal system that had administered justice during sixteen years of military rule.

Everyone agreed that human rights were a good thing.

Nevertheless, somewhere in those same anonymous buildings which ruled Chile so secretively for sixteen years, someone had ordered riot police to attend our friends' funerals, because although their deaths were accidental, they belonged to the opposition. When the hearses arrived, we formed a hushed river of friends that flowed behind them, past the mausoleums, the niches and on to the crematorium.

Somewhere in the General Cemetery lies another friend of ours, but I have never visited his grave. Intelligent, impassioned and impatient, Ignacio was shot down in a police ambush in 1987. One winter, we visited his widow and their son for the first time since he had been slain. Their apartment hadn't changed much. His photograph smiled from the wall. His son played the guitar. Cecilia talked, simply, openly, a small catch in her voice that hadn't been there before. It was easy to think he'd just been delayed, that any minute he'd come through the door with a kilo of mussels, some white wine and a welcoming grin, as he did the last time we were there. Her words rushed on through phrases, ideas, feelings that she'd been pondering for two years. She was caught in a terrible contradiction: the need to escape that feeling of his impending return, without obliterating their years together.

The political issues sparking debates in living rooms throughout the country could not penetrate her small apartment. We've filed charges against the secret police, Cecilia said. We're hoping that someday there'll be results.

The regime had its own victims and martyrs too, and they are represented among the neat rows of the General Cemetery. In August 1983, General Carol Urzúa, shot by an armed commando of the Left Revolutionary Movement (Movimiento de Izquierda Revolucionaria), MIR, was buried with full military honours, to strains of the funeral dirge, the first time I had heard it anywhere but in films or Disney cartoons. In April 1991, the public outcry caused by the Rettig Commission report on human rights violations was abruptly silenced by two fatal gunshots, which buried themselves in the chest of Jaime Guzmán, one of General Pinochet's most trusted friends and brilliant advisers.

In the 1989 elections, Chile's first after the military government, Jaime Guzmán ran for Senator against a major opposition leader, Ricardo Lagos. Lagos won 29.2 per cent of the votes, but Jaime Guzmán was elected, with only 16.4 per cent, thanks to the peculiar electoral system which he played a major role in creating. Many of those Chileans who favoured the regime during the 1988 plebiscite and feared the advent of a genuine, elected government, felt reassured by Guzmán's presence in the Senate. A tearful neighbour, who described herself as "a fascist through and through", managed to congratulate my husband for Patricio Aylwin's victory over General Pinochet's dauphin, Hernán Büchi.

"Under the Popular Unity I used to hate them [the left] so much," our neighbour blurted out. "But the hate was awful, it was destroying me. I'm over that now. I don't want to hate any more," she said, her voice choked with tears. "And we're happy with Guzmán," she went on. "As long as he's there everything will be all right."

General Pinochet himself had barely announced Guzmán's death to supporters crowded around the gates to Santiago's military hospital, when cries of "Pinochet!" arose and stones and blows rained down on the government's representatives – and on a moderate military leader, Air Force General Fernando Matthei.

Days later, student leaders denounced the kidnapping and torture of the vice-president of the University of Chile students' union. Although he was released alive, fears of a new round of political violence grew.

Salvador Allende himself now lies in state in the General Cemetery. The Chileans' sense of what is suitable for a former president seems to have won out over Dr. Allende's own socialist principles. Twin marble pillars thrust toward heaven over his remains, located among the luxurious mausoleums of Santiago's moneyed aristocracy.

His funeral was held seventeen years after he died of bullet wounds, now believed to have been self-inflicted during the coup, twenty years to the day after he was officially elected president of Chile. His remains were removed from the family crypt where they had been anonymously buried after the coup, convoyed to Santiago for a full funeral mass in the Cathedral, and rushed past thousands of onlookers, many of whom wept openly, to his monumental resting place in the General Cemetery. When the Carabineros finally reopened the cemetery gates to the public, thousands of mourners filed by, puzzled by and resenting the police presence, but determined to lay their red carnations on Allende's grave.

Just a few blocks away squats a boxy, marble-pillared monument with the names Pinochet-Hiriart engraved upon it. A guard seldom takes his eyes off the tomb, which has been vandalized more than once.

I've been avoiding the General Cemetery lately. I have come to hate the sense of homecoming it started to produce.

But there are still memorial marches, called *romerías*. For Neruda, for Victor Jara, for the names without bodies and the bodies without names. And there are still funerals. For Jecar Neghme, a leader of the moderate faction of the Left Revolutionary Movement, shot down by the unidentified armed civilians *de siempre*, one rainy night in September 1989. For Jaime Guzmán. For police officers and "terrorists" and delinquents, for the ordinary and the extraordinary.

In the years following the regime's demise, Chile has sometimes seemed like one enormous cemetery, riddled with secret graves, fragments of people's skulls and hopes. Widows carry on their search for bodies, sometimes finding scraps of familiar clothing in ravaged graves, hurriedly emptied of their more significant contents. Pathologists, anthropologists and other experts spend weeks piecing bones together for identification.

Children have grown up and led the *romerías,* learned to make speeches and rebuilt their lives. Some carried weapons for a while, seeking justice or revenge, others studied forgetfulness, all are trying to graduate.

Amidst the clamour of reborn political debate, scandal and controversy, rhetorical swords crossed and clanging, the everyday clatter of bills and red tape and the ongoing struggle against the bureaucracy and the trying to survive, the dead beget silence among us. Their photographs in newspapers mark the anniversaries that have passed, that continue to pass, uncelebrated birthdays. Nameless hosts of children and women and men, orchestra conductors, jacks-of-all-trades, union leaders, students and housewives. Murdered, every one. And waiting for justice. That much hasn't changed.

Chapter two

GOING TO
ISLA NEGRA

THE CENTRAL VALLEY 1979

Too long a sacrifice can make a stone of the heart.

YEATS

There's a small square at the foot of Santa Lucía Hill, part fortress, part natural park, breathing green air into Santiago's smoggy heart. From its heights, on December 14, 1540, Pedro de Valdivia and a hundred and fifty men surveyed the lush central valley and decided to found a city, Santiago. They baptized the hill for the Catholic saint whose day they were celebrating. There's no record of when or if they realized it already had a name, Huelén, a Mapuche word for "presentiment".

In my mind's eye, a small boy plays forever in that square on an overcast day, under trees that look rickety and sad. It's a rare day out with his father, a small man with pale, freckled skin, a thick black beard and curly hair that has been slicked down to one side, but is already asserting its right to stand on end. He has oval brown eyes of a peculiar honey colour and his long nose curves protectively out and down, as if determined to sniff out any problems before the full sensual mouth gets his whole body into trouble. Or perhaps the nose is really an advance scout.

Today the man's nose – and his attention – focus on the boy, a stocky three-year-old with thick sandy hair matted with sweat, his luminous green eyes caught on the purple throat and pearly wings of a pigeon who struts around the square, pecking at crumbs of sugared popcorn. It's

9

the ubiquitous city pigeon, *paloma* in Spanish, meaning both pigeon and dove and sailing gracefully off the tongue.

The *paloma* bobs so close, the child sallies out to catch her, his small stubby fingers open with hope — that evaporates as the scuffed shoes crunch the rough ground and the pigeon takes off. The boy stares after the bird, considering his options, but his father calls him and he runs across the square, leaping into the treehouse of his father's arms. Laughter bubbles out of him like an underground spring, bursting free and fresh from the earth's granite.

A decade later I watch my own son Camilo in bed beside me, a hope-filled letter slipping into sleep's envelope, posted to the future. My throat tightens, aware that with each day he's writing more of his life himself, with only the vaguest reference to us. As the day's puzzles and discoveries, rages and bruises, vanish from his cheeks, I feel also a pang of loss, an opportunity I have lost. Day in, day out, he is here, interrupting the nightly newscasts with his questions, begging for a game of chess, pushing for permission to play football, tugging at an elbow, complaining about his homework, adding to the din of baby's screams and the whistling kettle, refusing to go to bed, lurking in the stairway, listening unobtrusively.

Childhood is fraught with dangers which only the most magical measures can prevent: not stepping on cracks, whispered charms that give us the courage to carry on, regardless. Camilo invites me back to the irrational, instinctive world of childhood, where the rules change according to the game and the game is constantly shifting. He's an open door, a cave-mouth beckoning, the long fall into Wonderland, the nervous shiver at the thought of maybe not returning. Alice sleeps in his eyes, or tastes a potion, stretching to bump her head on the ceiling, shrinking to tear-drop size. Some nights a Chilean boy of paper-words nudges her offstage: Papelucho lost on a south-bound train, Camilo bumping along in the next seat on the aisle.

He'd like to take me with him, but I am always saying, no, not yet, I'm busy, wait ... Is there anything more important than being an adult? With appointments to keep, a watch to consult, taxes to pay?

So easy to turn my back and forge ahead. But then I realize how downright crazy adult behaviour is, a compass with nothing but norths marked all around its circle. I must turn back to childhood for the south. It's dangerous, Camilo and his friends remind me, to take yourself too seriously. Diapers have to be changed, dishes washed. On the way to that crucial meeting, a bird could shit on your head.

All this subverts my grand old view as I gaze down from the Mount Olympus of middle age. Suddenly, pigeon chasing looks like an important rite, on a par with losing your virginity. The toddler's declaration of independence, the first threat/promise/statement of intentions: to chase those flighty *palomas*, fall on your face, take the great leap without necessarily knowing where you'll land.

In the arbitrary years when the Red Queen ruled, condemning prisoners before they'd time to contemplate a crime, chasing *palomas* became a life-saving skill. I don't know if it was the momentum of their flight or the windy rush of escaping wings that picked us up and pushed us along when everything seemed as grim as Santa Lucía square on an endless wintry day and the bandy branches of trees looked as though they were dying. The Agrupación Cultural Universitaria, a university-based cultural association known affectionately by its acronym, ACU (pronounced A-Coo), came to embody this life-giving lunacy, for me and many others.

They called it "The Plum", *La Ciruela*, because according to Pablo Neruda, "the plum tree always blooms before the spring." The main character was a plump, plummy fellow, backed up by a chorus of mice demanding cheese, and a host of bearded, bespectacled or braided characters, the typical assortment of unwashed university types, rubbing elbows with the over-elegant, sprucely dressed aspiring yuppies.

The ACU published it between 1979 and 1982, whenever they could pull together enough money and material to make it as full and fruity as home-made wine. And they hawked it on the sidewalks outside city campuses, in hallways and cafeterias, passing it from hand to hand until it grew wrinkled and stained. The inside front cover always contained a fragment of Neruda's poem, along with the credits for each edition:

> Yes,
> in that hour,
> whenever
> it may be, full
> as bread or a *paloma*
> or bitter
> as
> a friend's betrayal,

I will raise a plum tree for you
and in it, in its small
cup
of purple amber and fragrant thickness
I drink and toast your life
your honour,
whoever you may be, wherever you may go:
I don't know who you are, but
I leave in your heart
a plum.

"Don't bother to subscribe it's not worth it," is printed below. "Anyway, you'll always find someone to lend you a copy." The first editorial declares that "Expression and dialogue are the foundations which sustain, along with transforming creativity, the cultural and intellectual development of a people and allow the cultural agent to soak up the times and seek historic syntheses that can then be made universal.

"Without free expression and dialogue, art and other cultural manifestations tend to become intimate, ethereal and unilateral, reflecting only partial realities and losing their ability to transform, as powerful vehicles of communication and consensus among men. Censorship is the ally of darkness; prohibition is the threshold of backwardness.

"We think students, because of the privilege that society has bestowed upon them of having access to science and the arts, are called upon to become agents of social and cultural development. For this, a real connection with the problems of their society and times is essential. Participation, dialogue, criticism aren't isolated concepts ... They are a coherent unity, indispensable to the formation of an active, transforming student ..."

On the cover, cartoon students and bulbous-nosed gnomes labelled "Editorial staff" sit around a table staring intensely at a small plum. In the background a frazzled-looking bird asks: "Can you eat it?" And another replies, "Not this one." Two mice chase each other past the watchful eyes of a famished cat, while another pair angrily saw away at a stool with a miniature swede saw.

The editor explains their irreverences: "Neruda can't appear with a skeletal cat? A cultural magazine has to have a serious cover? We ask you: who decided those rules? Who says that everything's been done. Aaaaaaah! to open brains is our watchword ... 'Poetry, without a few drops of madness, dies of pure logic,' Neruda said. And we're applying this to everything."

What kind of university gave birth to this Plum, *La Ciruela*, this "quasi-magazine attempt at journalistic-cultural assassination published by the ACU"? Like mushrooms in damp hollows hidden from the harsh light of the censors, literary, musical, theatrical and artistic workshops sprouted and grew on university campuses scattered through Chile. And students, faculty and staff harvested them, first in 1977, when folk music workshops joined together to form the University Folkloric Association. The next year, they officially formed the University Cultural Association, ACU.

By the second edition of *La Ciruela*, in October 1979, the cover cartoon is the pandemonium of a theatre packed with students waving ACU banners, while backstage a puzzled director tells a zoo-keeper, "There must be some mistake, we didn't request an elephant acrobat ...", Cyrano de Bergerac is horrified to hear he's arrived late, and an "allergic cartoonist" stares with horror and a red nose at three flowers he's just sketched onto the page ...

The editorial describes the opening day of ACU's first Theatre Festival, being held at the Manuel de Salas high school: "We found Carabineros, following higher orders, had cordoned off the entire sector and were forcing students to leave." Only by alerting the entire university community was the ACU able to overcome the prohibition and carry on with its festival as planned.

The festival's structure is competitive: workshops present their plays on different university campuses and other venues, wherever the students can get permission to perform, and a jury selects the best for a final performance at a large theatre. The festival has been boycotted by the generals currently heading Chilean universities and those who follow their orders. In the Faculty of Medicine, for example, the dean runs onto the stage and threatens to arrest the audience. "The Auditorium is struck dumb; then conspiratorial looks; finally the audience bursts into applause." An embarrassed dean splutters with rage, word arrives that the campus is surrounded by police, organizers ask students to withdraw so they can negotiate. They finally reach agreement: by signing a paper promising that the activity isn't "political" and is not the responsibility of campus authorities, the day's presentations go ahead.

La Ciruela describes more problems at the Education campus. Students from other campuses and the jury of theatre's *éminence grise*, including the portly, elderly, bearded and balding actor Roberto Parada, manage to hoist themselves over the railings built around campuses after September 11, 1973 and carry on their festival. When the campus's electrical current is turned off, an extension cord snakes its way through grass, fences, along asphalt streets, to plunge its 220-volt snout into the socket of a private house. The lights go up, the show goes on.

La Ciruela's plummy hero, Ciro, also appears shaking hands with Asterix and Obelix, from the famous French cartoon series: "Avec amour," he says, as an article announces that a band, Ortiga, will be taking its human rights Cantata on tour in Europe. A noted scientist, unsung by the pro-military press, has returned to Chile; a forum's been held in Engineering to discuss the military's plan for restructuring universities; ACU's third music festival is on its way.

La Ciruela No. 3, November 1979: the cover cartoon is a typical line-up at a university cafeteria. "A bean or a lentil?" the man serving offers the students, whose conversation bubbles have black squares erasing the three letters A, C, U, wherever they occur. "Test" we're told in one corner. "What's the tell-tale word? (*La Ciruela* rides the wave of self-censorship.) Far out!" And Ciro whispers frowning, "I know what the word is ..." The price is ten pesos "with gift staple included!"

The ACU has come under the first of many attacks, from the university authorities, the appointed student council president, Santiago's main daily newspaper, *El Mercurio*, and others. "This has been the fundamental feature of this Festival. The forbidden word, that we can't pronounce in public or put on posters, or say, or sing: the name of our own organization: ACU. Oddly enough, [it means] love in the language of Easter Island."

It had been a long flight and I was tense as I got off the plane, wondering what I should expect from Pinochet's Chile, only six years after the military coup. I also wondered if anyone would be there to meet me. As I wheeled my bags down the gauntlet of excited Chileans, my eyes caught on a placard reading "Lake" and I looked up to meet the brooding eyes of a short, dark-haired man, with a quiet, slightly brusque manner. Jorge Rozas, ACU president and director of a folk dancing and singing group, waved at two more students and we piled into a Citroneta and rattled our way into Santiago.

In a small apartment overlooking the city's grandiose Municipal Theatre, Jorge introduced me to Nicolás Eyzaguirre, stern-faced member of the musical group Aquelarre (witches' meeting place), and Juancho Pérez, tall and thin with a cadaverous face, flowing gestures and comprehensible English. Nicolás was stern and disapproving, with clear and rather limited ideas about what was proper behaviour in a young foreign woman. I found Juancho puzzling but endearing: early on he admitted everyone was calling me "yoghurt face", because I was so pale.

"So who do you think studies what?" someone asked me, as we stood around the table in Juancho's apartment. Juancho was already a practising doctor; Jorge was well on his way to becoming a computer engineer, and Nicolás was studying economics – he later became Director of Research at the Central Bank. It was my first taste of a culture where music and economics or engineering and poetry were as compatible as wine and cheese.

"Can you sing?" Juancho asked me. I contemplated how my answer might affect the success of my "fact-finding" mission, on behalf of Canada's National Union of Students. Groping through memories, I remembered an old folksong I'd learned from a room-mate. Fortunately, though, I opted for an honest answer: "Not really."

I discovered later that since they were in the midst of organizing the music festival and already had (singing) guests from Germany and elsewhere, they'd assumed I'd come to do the same. I narrowly escaped performing my rather tuneless, a cappella version of "Everybody thinks my head's full of nothing", centre-stage before seven thousand people.

I met Patricio Lanfranco, the man responsible for the music festival, a few days later. He showed me Valparaíso, introducing me to the reality of students outside the capital city, and filled me in on student organizations in Chile. As the day and the official reasons for our outing faded, I learned about how the regime had affected Chilean families. In 1973, he was a student at the University of Concepción on the coast, about six hours' drive south of Santiago, and he remembers the coup as a leap out the window of the university residence and a run for refuge in a distant poor community, a *población*. He remembers hunger and the joy of an occasional meal, lost books and a young girlfriend he never saw again. Far to the south in Punta Arenas, the coup had meant the imprisonment of his father and two brothers on inhospitable Dawson Island. Their arrests, followed by the exile of the brother closest to him, shrunk his options: he dedicated himself full time to opposing the military regime.

On his own, on the run, he spent eighteen months cut off from normal life until he finally moved to Santiago, where he applied to the university as a new student and was accepted. Like many young people of his generation, the need for uncensored communication with at least one other human being led to a hasty marriage, followed by a son and a bitter separation. When I met him, his political commitment battled with his need to father his son. Speaking publicly, he was always serious, tension vibrating in the taut lines of his brow. Even when he sang, while his vibrant tenor voice mourned the life of a child prostitute or celebrated the varied work of women's hands, he kept his eyes closed, head thrown back, looking pained.

The preparatory events for the ACU music festival didn't seem particularly special: forty students crammed into an ordinary university classroom, organizers putting up microphones, trying to make faulty sound systems resound with the guitars, *charangos*, the Latin American stringed instrument made with an armadillo hide, along with the voices of students, faculty and staff from all over Chile, who wanted to participate. The grand finale coincided with my visit and I was hardly prepared when Juancho picked me up, took me across town and set me down in an orchestra seat in Santiago's huge, circular Caupolican Theatre, which can seat about eight thousand people.

I had expected to see Patricio again, but I barely caught sight of him in the distance. He was busy organizing the steady stream of surprises that poured across the stage.

As the lights dimmed, the enormous amphitheatre, used for circuses, boxing, rock concerts and other events, held only a scattering of people. But I forgot about the meagre audience as soon as the festival began. A huge banner, with a *paloma* escaping from the sound box of a hill-sized guitar, announced that "The university sings for life and peace." The show began with a skit featuring the Four Horsemen of the Apocalypse (a veiled parallel to the four-man military Junta), trotting on broom handles toward the stage. With scripts written by Isadora Aguirre, one of Chile's foremost playwrights, performances by Roberto Parada and three of Chile's most eminent actors and actresses, skits by the ACU's semi-professional theatre workshops and music by ten bands of budding musicians, I was alternately surprised, moved, delighted.

Among the winning songs was one with a rapid, dance-worthy beat, by Javier García de Cortázar of the Branches and Leaves Workshop. I caught a glimpse of Patricio, strumming energetically and singing back-up harmonies. "I'm no lord of the land/ and I know this isn't my war,/ so don't give me any weapons,/ because I have no reason to fight/ and you know that you're my brother/ don't let them force our hands/ they want to make us enemies/ and extinguish our awakening." And heard the chorus: "Even if you're on the other side/ I think we could still get together,/ because I'm no lord of the land/ and this isn't my war ..."

When the lights went up at intermission more than seven thousand shouting, laughing, banner-waving students had packed into the theatre. It was humbling to think that in Canada, even our largest student unions, with multi-million-dollar annual budgets, couldn't have pulled together that much talent for a festival. In Chile, on a shoestring budget (they ended up hugely in the hole), with permission withheld until the last possible moment, surrounded by riot police, they had managed an artistic phenomenon full of grace, laughter and serene courage. Who were these people? What invisible springs made this possible?

Dr. Juan Manuel Pérez, the man I still think of as Juancho Pérez, psychiatrist, professor at the University of Chile, walking skeleton, calls himself a sewer rat. Born and bred in Santiago, he's barely set foot outside the city's limits. The noise bothers him more than the smog and these days he usually walks around with plugs in his ears. From the moment I met him, he always left me slightly off balance. For years I used to drop in at his apartment, for *Ciruela* meetings, medical advice, company. I invariably found him doing something completely unexpected: hunched in the pool of light showering a drawing table, putting the finishing touches on a cartoon sequence for *La Ciruela*. Or playing impeccable flamenco guitar, his long fingers with their even longer fingernails, vibrating on the strings. Composing a Brazilian samba with polished lyrics and irresistible rhythm. Or developing black-and-white photographs in his bathroom. Preparing a sharp, cheesy omelette, spiced with nutmeg. Or designing a poster for a theatre festival.

He graduated from high school, a precocious fifteen-year-old with ultra-left views and a great thirst for action. He was eighteen, finishing his third year of medicine, when the military coup knocked the shape out of his life. But before that there were years of struggling with the seriousness of medical school, at an irreverent, hungering age.

"I remember in Anatomy class, a friend and I used to make television programs during the dissection. It was a game." He re-enacts, pretending to film as he talks in a brittle, TV announcer's voice, "We want to interview this little lady who's just a step away from me, please, tell me your impressions of death ..." He never really got along with surgeons.

"The Medical School weeks were a flood of imagination, entertainment. I was in school with Pepe Venturelli, son of the painter Venturelli and there was a tiny party called the Revolutionary Communist Party which must have been about fifteen people; I was number sixteen," he laughs. "It was a time of tremendous excitement, the first year of the Popular Unity government. Everyone went around wearing shirts with their party colours. My position was pretty much that of a little boy because I was just sixteen. The university was an explosion of so many things, you didn't know what to grab onto, I lived in a such a whirl I could hardly settle down. There were shows, plays, marches, trips to the Moneda, the presidential palace. Around 1972 I joined the MIR, a left-wing political party, critical of the Popular Unity government.

"I felt then, and after twenty years I'm much clearer about this, that there was a tremendous polarization and nobody listened to anyone else. People had a huge hate for anyone different. It was horrible. The MIR hated the Communist Party, and vice-versa, and everyone spoke of 'enemies' – who were the enemy? It was never very clear: the right, the left, it was very strange. I lived that polarization very strongly and couldn't even talk to some classmates.

"The disqualification was absolute. Each one had right on his side and was prepared to die for it. If it was necessary to train with arms or bombs so be it. But there was a huge distance between rhetoric and reality: there were no weapons anywhere. My experience was slightly different. I did hold a weapon in my hands and receive minimal military training. Now I think: what madness! My mom had a little Renault and we used it for everything, from moving an underground printing press to carrying things which I never knew what they were, but supposed they were machine guns. A series of signs, codes, of entering with your eyes on the floor so you never knew where you were, security measures, which in the end were just starch. Because it was child's play: entertaining and frankly romantic.

"I moved into politics almost as a moral or ethical imposition. I don't know that I was very conscious of it. I dropped theatre, music and so on. It was a great loss. I used to do guard duty at the MIR radio station, wrapped up in a scarf, frozen stiff, and with a pistol, waiting for someone to appear over the wall, thinking I'd have to shoot and wondering if I'd really be capable of it."

The coup found him in the University of Chile's teaching hospital, near the Buin regimental base. "You could hear bombs, shooting. The order was to close the hospital and not let anyone leave, because we expected the wounded to arrive and needed doctors to attend them. I remember people from the School of Theatre arrived ..." and he set out at the head of a straggling column, walking by ones and twos toward a small community in Santiago's north end called Renca.

"We walked all afternoon until we reached Renca. And they really didn't know what to do with us. There was gunfire all night and we discovered that the soldiers had come and taken all our leaders. So there we were, waiting for arms all day. And I'll tell you something, if they'd handed me a machine gun I was capable of using it. I was so convinced. And the weapons never arrived. Of course. And on the 14th, we were told to dissolve and go home, *calabaza, calabaza, cada uno a su casa,*" he says, using a typical children's rhyme.

In a matter-of-fact tone Juancho describes how, in December 1974, a man took his arm as he crossed the street. A glimpse of an army ID card, then he was thrown into a pickup truck, with others, face down, tied up, their eyes covered. "I thought I would die on the spot.

"Many years later I heard they had investigated all the leaders in the university and everyone [was arrested]. Amongst them was *el gato Sepúlveda*, who was in second year. I never knew his real name. He complained a lot and they let me examine him. He's one of those who disappeared."

They took Juancho and his companions to "La Venda Sexy", a house on the corner of Iran Street and Los Plátanos, near where his mother lives today. "There's a playground there where I often go with my daughters. I always look at the house and think, that's the place ..."

"What kind of treatment did you receive?"

"First class," he laughs. "I was only there a week. Well, they hit me, used electrical current, interrogated us. They did a lot of things. They put a staple in my ear. I'll never forget that," he says with wonder. "It was really so surprising. And they let me go after I signed a declaration saying I'd been treated wonderfully."

He remembers being herded into a truck with friends. One nudged him and asked under his breath, "Hey, skinny, have you got Scotch tape [on your eyes]?" "When I heard that I realized that he didn't and I asked him, 'and you?' 'No, I've got a blindfold,' he said. And we said goodbye to each other. He spent two years in a concentration camp, but they threw me out on the street.

"It was like a birth. During my arrest, I think I was psychotic: I was always trying to maintain my sense of reality but constantly lost it. One of the most critical moments for me was in the bathroom with the door closed, when they'd let us take off the blindfold. I stood there with my hair on end and looked in the mirror and knew I was there and at the same time thought, maybe I'm not here, it's not true, and maybe it was a nightmare. I was half-crazy, just nineteen years old, although there were other kids, sixteen or so. They hit them a lot; I could hear them shout."

He was jumpy for a long time, but kept on studying. By fifth year he organized a choir and the first musical group in the University of Chile's Medical School, which used the name of a local bus line, the Carrascal-Santa Julia. He went back to his first love, theatre.

"At that time, anything you did had political content, ANYTHING. Because people wanted to say things. I remember those first meetings, theatre events with miserable light bulbs in the roof. Half-depressed and everyone scared. We'd organize a sort of happening, put up a swing and a guy would hang upside down from it, declaiming some kind of nihilist poem like 'I'm nothing, nothing.' I remember once we formed a circle of men facing toward the audience and suddenly we opened our flies and pulled out a carnation and threw it at the audience. We did really strange stuff."

Another time they collected small change throughout the campus, until they had enough to pay for a large bill, which they then tore to pieces. "It generated an incredible debate because people began to argue that the money could be used for the poor, for a lot of different things. We were happy because that's what we wanted."

They had gone back to the language of dreams, metaphor, a child's juxtaposition of images to pull them through and past the barbed wire of forbidden terms, proscribed ideas, taboos. Through mime, theatre, "gratuitous things which sometimes had no meaning", they were provoking encounters, confronting paralysis, breaking the mirror of silence with mere noise.

It was no mean feat. The military authorities did not look kindly on cultural or artistic activities. Two days after the coup, three small tanks surrounded the Fine Arts Museum and bombarded the almost empty building, damaging many of the paintings inside. Sculptures that had just arrived at the airport were thrown in the garbage. Paintings that didn't meet the taste of the new military authorities were abandoned on the streets.

By February 1974, half of Santiago's journalists were unemployed, thanks to the closing of the media. Of eleven newspapers, four remained; five radio stations had been bombed and expropriated; censorship mutilated the pages of those few magazines still allowed to publish. *La Segunda*, *El Mercurio*'s afternoon tabloid branded a play based on work by a prominent poet Nicanor Parra, an "Infamous Attack on the Government", and the secret police doused the tent which housed its performances with gasoline and burned it to the ground.

The military government also banned a long list of books, including poems by Pablo Neruda, a children's story called "Monkey See, Monkey Do", a book on cubism, because a military officer thought it was about Cuba. The author of a detective novel, published six months before the coup, was arrested because the title, *The Suicide's Killers*, cast aspersions on the official version of Allende's death. Censors ordered the destruction of history texts, poetry anthologies, novels, biographies of prominent Chilean religious thinkers. They banned novels by Jerzy Kozinski, Manuel Puig, Mario Vargas Llosa, Gabriel García Márquez and Julio Cortázar.

Naval officers sank in Valparaíso Bay all copies of *How To Read Donald Duck*, by Ariel Dorfman, a prominent left-wing writer. Air Force General Diego Barros Ortiz took over the government publishing house, Quimantú, which had been producing 25 books a month, some with a print run of 80,000. Between 1974 and 1977, 121 movies were banned, among them *Fiddler on the Roof* and *Nicholas and Alexandra*.

These attacks eliminated an entire generation of artists and intellectuals from Chilean society, along with their works, creating a vacuum which the military government filled with a censor-approved, official culture. Perhaps, from the regime's point of view, the most serious crime of the University Cultural Association, ACU, was its success at bridging the chasm between new generations and older creators. Patiently, painstakingly, ACU reassembled art expositions, often with work lent or donated by prestigious Chilean artists living abroad; its literary contests were judged and supported by many of Neruda's contemporaries, Diego Muñoz, Sr., Juvencio Valle, Enrique Lihn. ACU provided a stage for young musi-

cians eager to carry on the New Song movement, founded by Violeta
Parra in the mid-sixties and flourishing under the Popular Unity government, which most of its members supported. Contraband tapes of exiled
musicians, Inti Illimani, Quilapayún, Isabel and Angel Parra and others,
circulated, while young singers interpreted their music on university stages.

I don't know when I first noticed Diego Muñoz, a solid, quiet engineering
student with a mop of blue-black hair and small intelligent brown eyes
that panned gently across every problem, observing details. Perhaps it
was while sitting in on meetings of the ACU's *directiva*, representatives
from each faculty and each area of artistic activity, who met regularly.

He starts to appear in some of the photographs I took: on the beach
in Cartagena, demanding the release of an ACU photographer in the San
Antonio police station, sitting comfortably on a curb somewhere waiting
for an impromptu meeting to start. "His father's a well-known writer,"
someone told me. "Pablo Neruda used to bounce him on his knee,"
someone else.

An unquiet sixteen-year-old, he had joined but later quit the Communist youth organization, becoming a political outsider and a reluctant
Cassandra, no one believing his predictions that a coup was coming.
After the coup, he felt a responsibility to act collectively, looked around
and decided that, compared to others, "where he'd come from wasn't so
bad." His first novel, *Todo el amor en sus ojos* (All the Love in His Eyes),
tells of high-school exploits broken and reorganized after the coup. And
it reveals the inner workings of party membership and underground
organizing against the military regime during the fierce repression in
1976 and 1977.

"Most of the people I knew in 1976 are not alive now. I have the
sense that I'm a survivor, at least of that period. The slightest error meant
something unspeakable. In the university there was such a climate of
distrust that I often kept a distance from people who could have been
friends. I feel guilty – in 1976, two of them disappeared. One was from
the north, I thought, he's probably gone home. The other just stopped
attending. And I remember that some time later I found one going
through the red tape to re-enter the university and he told me he was just
getting out of *Cuatro Alamos* [the secret detention centre within a concentration camp]."

In the University of Chile's Faculty of Engineering, students began looking for spaces "to communicate, to break through the impossibility of conversation". Diego and his friends tried to ignore the fear. "It exists, but you try to know as little as possible because if you remember, you're paralysed. But there are moments when you're really afraid, when you have to show your face, enter a room where there are two hundred people waiting and stand up and say something."

In 1977, with the help of Nicanor Parra and Enrique Lihn, two poets who were professors in their department, the engineering students started up a literary workshop.

"Among the better trained engineers, there's a tradition of integral education in the University of Chile and that's what we cultivated. In the school we used to sell four hundred or so of our magazines. *La Ciruela* sold even more. That was about 10 per cent of the school and was a lot, because each magazine was read by several. Many professors supported us with money, in spite of remaining silent."

Diego described how many of those who struggled to change the military regime began to postpone their own lives, feelings, children. This was easy to do. Like laughter at a funeral, an afternoon spent playing in the park, reading a good novel or setting a poem to music often seemed frivolous beside the drama of arrests, torture, disappearances, the overwhelming need to shake off the limitations imposed by the regime in order to move ahead.

Diego's literary workshop organized a forum on the future of the university in 1978, with major scientists. For the first time, six years after the coup, prominent engineers, scientists and students publicly referred to the military's control of the university. Several of the organizers, Diego among them, were investigated. "But the dean stuck his neck out to defend us from expulsion," Diego says. The students had staked out a patch, a few square feet of freedom.

There were other problems though. Diego's house was searched. Someone tried to run him over. He was watched constantly for almost a year. Late one night he rounded the corner and had started down the quiet cul-de-sac where he lived when he saw a car and two trucks in front of his house.

His calm, low voice tenses. "I thought, if I run, they'll kill me, I don't have any choice but to keep walking — toward what? They're going to kidnap me, kill me. As I crossed the street one started its motor and I thought they're going to run me over, but I kept walking like a robot, and, when I got to the gate, I realized the house was open, there was an effigy hanging from the bell cord. I saw them in their cars, with dark glasses. Typical. In the house I thought what to do, who to phone, I didn't want to get anyone in trouble. Finally I called a friend who had nothing to do with politics, just in case: to let him know that I'd arrived home, that I was there and then not there.

"After that I sat for hours, until first one car, then the other left. I went to bed absolutely exhausted and started to shiver from nervous tension. The next day it was as if nothing had happened. Well, you get used to living like that."

Besides the harassment and the threats, ACU suffered arrests and internal exiles. I moved to Chile, to live with Patricio Lanfranco, at the beginning of 1981. On May 1st of that year, Patricio, who by then was ACU's president, went to a police station to protest the arrest of several ACU members during May Day demonstrations. On his way out, he was kidnapped. For five days, we had no idea where he was or what was being done to him. We did not know when or where or even if he would reappear again. I did not know who I might find at the end of our search. I was haunted by a report in the Catholic church magazine, *Solidaridad*, of a wife recognizing her husband in a man, broken and begging in the streets of a small town, years after he had been arrested and disappeared.

It was Diego who brought the news that Patricio had been kidnapped and I spent long hours in the warmth of his parents' house, while Diego and others mapped out a campaign to get Patricio released. They succeeded, thanks to their efforts and a flood of telegrams from Canadian student organizations and European human rights groups and political bodies.

Secret-police agents bundled Patricio into a closed van and dumped him at his mother's apartment on the fifth day. He was bruised, shaven and shorn. His mother had to tell me who he was. I did not recognize him. After a brief reunion with his family, his first priority was to thank the ACU members who'd campaigned for his release. Later, he took time out for a picnic. He went for a walk with his son, and the two returned transformed, crowned with garlands of willow leaves, giggling like delighted followers of Dionysus. For Patricio, as for many, brushes with death, the drama and the tragedy which touched his life during the military government, sharpened his need for humour and play.

After the regime ended, "a few went on to more lasting artistic activities," Diego says, "but others continued with our initial idea for a more integral education, to be more human. ACU was a school of sorts. It gave us something the university didn't have. It taught fraternity, interest in culture. It forced you to reason, to criticize more deeply."

Women enjoyed an unusual level of participation and leadership within the ACU. Pati Hofer, organizing on the North Medicine campus until she graduated as a physician; Isabel Sanchez and her sisters pulling off the arts exhibition in spite of its prohibition by university authorities; Catalina Ruiz, working hard to make literary activities a success. But there were others who didn't participate in the leadership of the ACU, but nevertheless, thanks to its existence, recovered something important.

Cecilia grew up in a large house with a grand piano in the middle-class neighbourhood of Nuñoa, riding her bicycle along tree-lined streets under the protection of an autocratic grandfather. Her mother was good-looking, tender and proud. Her father left for the United States when she was five years old and she missed a whole school year waiting for him to send for them. Her grandfather died, her mother moved in with Cecilia's aunts. Small and delicate, the mother was good with her hands, repairing woodwork, wiring, designing record covers. When Cecilia was eleven, her father staged a glorious return, bringing with him a production of the opera *Othello* and lead singer Ramón Binet, a man who would sing on stages around the world. Binet practised, standing by the grand piano in their living room. She learned every song. Music carried her into a world of blazing love that warmed and shielded her when her father left again.

At thirteen, Cecilia's mother's quiet suffering sank into full-blown depression. Cecilia walked alone through adolescence, watching her sister fall through love, land with bruises on the hard ground of solitude. Desperate to prove that she could be loved, she sought a partner but found herself forever cast in roles: Lolita, little mother, long-suffering.

Her mother died the same year she started working and Cecilia annulled a difficult marriage. "Suddenly, of bronchitis, she just didn't want to go on living. It helped me for what came later ... I cried because she'd been a good woman and she'd had so few satisfactions in life. But it was also a relief because she had nothing. I felt she wanted to die.

"I cried and lived through that grief. For me it was important to find love, to prove it was possible."

Alone, Cecilia compensated by studying music, but day-classes soon conflicted with her full-time job and she quit. "But I had the satisfaction of being in the [university] choir."

"I was alone but with a different attitude. Finally I could tell myself that I might not have a good partner but I could at least have a good life. So I was in high spirits. And around then the Temu musical workshop, made up mostly of economics students, began and they invited me to a festival in 1977. After that I went on one of their outings and that was when I met Ignacio.

"The first time I really noticed him was during an activity for Pablo Neruda in the cafeteria. I saw him looking at me, noticing me as a woman. I noticed his green eyes, very tender, pretty, but he had a baby face, a little beard. Later I thought to myself, what a shame that he's so young – and so good looking."

They began the delicate dance of courtship, intricate as the *cueca* that ACU's members liked to perform, with slim young women waving their white handkerchiefs gaily over their heads as they stomped their feet in the one-two, heartbeat rhythm of Chile's national dance, while their partners whirled around them, alternately ducking and stretching to full height, trying to both dominate and offer humble admiration.

They started to see each other. "I realized that I felt really good with him. But afterward I decided no, he's too young – I was thirty already. I was afraid." She broke through the fear long enough to return a phone-call and go out with him again. "I realized I really liked him. This made me panic and I told him I was only twenty-seven. And he said, 'Cecilia, I want us to keep seeing each other. Why don't we try – I like you a lot.' And that's where it all began."

Between choir practices, movies, and attempts to reach Isla Negra, Cecilia and Ignacio fell decidedly in love. She confessed her real age and they moved into a small apartment. Their son came along quickly because she was all too conscious of her age. His birth almost cost them their life together: Ignacio was ever impatient, quick to move and change, and Cecilia was slow, frightened of giving too much of herself away, but they patched a bridge between them and walked across it.

"I always wanted to be honest and open, without having to hide things. And I felt with Ignacio that things were clear. He was very mature, with an experience, an internal world, an intensity of life unusual in a man of twenty-seven. I felt that he liked how I talked, how I gestured and it made me more secure. I was very affectionate with him and he needed that."

There was one conversation that she never forgot. "Cecilia," he said, "there's something I want you to reflect on, because there's still time. You must have realized by now—"

Little by little, he had told her things, that he was a member of the Communist Party, that he opposed the regime. "I love you and I want to stay with you always. But my first priority, before being an economist, before being your companion, is my political commitment. That's why I'm telling you that I'm going to do whatever's necessary. I'm really scared and I want you to reflect and that we not see each other for a couple of days, please, so that you'll understand the weight of this. I don't want to force you to take risks; it's complicated, terrible. But we're in time, if we separate and each goes a separate way, then maybe we can still be happy."

"We cried a lot," she remembers. "I trusted his seriousness and the way he did things. It was a decision that I'm happy I could make with such clarity. I said, I don't know how I'm going to do it, but I will. His commitment came first, but he was a man of flesh and blood. He needed a companion. If it hadn't been politics, anything he got involved in, he would have given himself 100 per cent. He lived so quickly ..."

It was a decision that she would question for the rest of her life. She has always reached the same conclusion.

Every July, the ACU joined with other cultural workshops in Santiago, Valparaíso and San Antonio to organize a pilgrimage to Pablo Neruda's house in Isla Negra. Closed after the coup, the house was the object of a quiet struggle between the Navy and Neruda's widow, Mathilde Urrutia, backed by a foundation of prestigious Chileans determined to win back the old stone building, with its rambling additions, secret passageways and eloquent collections of shells and bottles, bowsprits and books which Neruda had lovingly culled from his world travels. Year after year, the bus-loads of singing students, university staff and people from the poor communities that ring every major city, *pobladores*, would journey out from Santiago toward the coast; and every year armed policemen blocked the route and forced a detour.

One year, it was Cartagena. I remember how the massive rocks that broke through the white sand suddenly sprouted poets. On every outcropping, they stared dreamily out to sea, then scrawled their impressions in university notebooks. The choir gathered on the sand to sing, while theatre students acted out skits, young parents played with their children and everyone munched on sandwiches, sipped hot tea from thermoses and joined the enormous *rondas*, holding hands and wheeling around the beach in a gigantic version of Ring around the Rosie. Patricio gave the keynote speech, compact and fierce on the windy beach, then went for a long wander over rocks and around ocean pools with his young son.

Another year, we were turned off so far from the beach that we ended up begging a scrap of land from an old farmer. Medical students lined up and mimed the propellers, wings and fuselage of an old plane, and proceeded to soar and dart and divebomb the small clearing beside a stream that formed the stage. Irma sang some of Neruda's poems, musicalized by a Greek musician, in a fine, high voice, the melodies at once melancholy but exuding a subtle strength.

On a ridge above us, we could see the silhouettes of silent watchers, large men in dark glasses, even though the day was overcast, using binoculars to follow our movements. Tension rippled through the crowd and then dissolved as we returned our eyes to the performers and turned our backs on fear.

In those years, as I got to know Chile through the young people who formed the ACU, university students who were rescuing their right to criticize and create, to cuddle and couple like young people anywhere, we were always travelling to Isla Negra. Although we never physically arrived at the boarded-up stone house with its long, weatherworn clapboard fence covered with loving graffiti, we celebrated creation wherever we finally stopped. We conjured up a living, laughing Neruda. We rescued normalcy, or at least its image, making it last for the span of a child's game and we drew nourishment and strength from that illusion.

Wherever we were, we created Isla Negra, a place where "everything flowers. Small yellow buds pull themselves through winter, then turn blue and later, in spring, the colour of burgundy. The sea flowers all year round. Its rose is white. Its petals are stars of salt."

The students sang with the band, Santiago del Nuevo Extremo ...

In my city one day
the spring sun died

they came to my window
to let me know
come, take your guitar
your voice will belong to all
who once had a story to tell ...

Santiago, I want to see you in love
and your inhabitants
show you without fear
on your streets you'll feel
my firm steps
and I'll know who breathes
at my side ...

They meditated ...

We were in the middle of a great party, with so much noise, that the police came along and the whole thing went to pieces. They cut off the electricity, the stage went dark.

There was a change in the lighting system, the microphone amplified fears, this story's sound became deafening, dry, painful. The audience faded off into darkness. We had to do something to put together another party. The musicians, in the midst of desperation stopped to reflect and seek another sound, another voice, another verb for another stage and for an audience that had learned to read in a different language. Faced with the cultural blackout, light bulbs began to go on.

They poured moments into poems, like this one by Eduardo Llanos ...

Goodbye

... It tattooed my heart, the image of your face pressed against
the window
distant from setting stars and nurses.
I know that in the long nights of silence
echoes pained you of those children and grandchildren
that exile had torn away;
I know the country's misery laid you low,

the absurd struggle which in the end was only filming mist,
tilling the ocean, sweeping in the storm.

María Elisa, María Elisa,
this memory is almost morbid
now that worms devour your cadaver.
Better to contemplate the wreathes
and believe in good faith that while they shrivel
other flowers will open, new children will be born
and everything will change
little by little.

"There was something basic there, not very translatable to words," Juancho Pérez says. "It was the need to show we were alive. I think that when you're faced with extreme situations, reason, more elaborate elements don't work much, but rather you rely on the primary, the emotive, the most symbolic, and all that is related to art. Poetry, theatre, mime have no words and in that context poetry itself is wordless.

"Each generates a world, is interpretable, and I think that's what ACU channelled, a sensation of being alive, nothing more. Many of us thought it would be forever, but as there was more space for real participation and other kinds of work, the space for this creative expression started to get lost.

"Nineteen seventy-three was an explosion of disunity, of mutual disqualification, of rancour, of having right on one's side. And one of the great uses of the ACU was to build a moment of great unity. I never joined another party. But I was clear that wasn't important. No one asked who was who, but rather everyone worked."

In its six years of life, ACU brought together students, faculty and staff, organized four massive music festivals, three major theatre festivals that were celebrated as important renewals by professional theatre groups, two national literary competitions judged by important writers, and a festival of visual arts. Faced with yet another prohibition against using university premises, ACU members donned the paintings, prints and sketches and walked them along corridors, out into busy streets, through classrooms and cafeterias, before people's eyes.

Many fine actors and actresses, musicians and writers found their

first audience through ACU events and brought to life the works of a
generation whose culture and communication were otherwise forbidden.
They went on to emcee political rallies, to animate crowds of protestors
with their music, poems and skits. But few survived the seventeen years
of official censorship, coupled with physical punishment and permanent
tension. Everyone expected artists to perform free and they gladly did
so, until they could survive no longer. I remember Capri, whose powerful
voice represented Chile in a major Spanish-language song festival, and
who went on to success in Chile's International Music Festival in 1981.
When I met her that same year, she and her small son were moving
from one dilapidated apartment to another. The gas company removed
her meter for lack of payment. She finally took refuge abroad, in Sweden.
Illapu, a band of shiny, satin-shirted folk musicians who specialized in
the Andean instruments of northern Chile, set out to tour Europe and
was never allowed to return. I remember the habeas corpus filed on their
behalf – written in elegant folk verse, it was nevertheless ignored.
Oswaldo Torres, the author of that habeas corpus and a musician himself,
unable to support his wife and newborn son, left for France. Santiago
del Nuevo Extremo, whose songs connected forbidden feelings by saying
them out loud; Abril, also selected for the Viña festival; Ortiga, Amauta
and numerous others gave until they could give no longer. The opposition
political parties did nothing to care for their artists. I learned the expression *"el pago de Chile"* in those years, meaning, Chile pays off those
who do it a good deed, with envy, indifference, neglect.

"The atmosphere was too hostile. In the face of that there was no
point in maintaining silly differences. ACU was a school of sorts. When
ACU formed with the sense that anyone in the university could join, that
contributed to maintaining hope, rescuing the social fabric," says Juancho Pérez.

It was also a school for democracy, at a time when there were few
opportunities to discuss, debate, make decisions collectively.

"I think at least for those of us who were inside it, we learned to look
at the other side as having a right to its opinion and being worthy of
respect. Now if that exists in other parts of society it's not necessarily
because people remember ACU, but something has transcended. Especially if you think that at its best ACU had hundreds of people involved, a
thousand or two in the different workshops. I believe the people who went
to our events have scattered and those teachings have reached many

places. I have some influence in my environment and I draw a lot on my reminiscences from the time I was in the ACU."

Oddly enough, although university authorities' main accusation against the ACU was that it was "political", few, if any of its members have gone into politics. Many early organizers became leaders elsewhere, though: Miguel Angel Larrea, who photographed most major moments in the life of the ACU, went on to head the photography department of the opposition newspaper, *La Epoca;* Paula Edwards, a gifted journalist, became a communications specialist; Gregory Cohen, with his quick wit and sharp tongue, catalyzed interesting renewals in Chilean theatre and became a respected young novelist; a psychiatrist, Marco Antonio de la Parra, led the same movement for renewal of Chilean theatre and later became a prominent columnist and author. Eduardo Llanos, Esteban Navarro, Pía Barros, Ramón Díaz Eterovic, Jorge Montealegre, Heddy Navarro, Bruno Serrano, Carmen Berenguer and other writers who first distinguished themselves in ACU's literary competitions have gone on to win other prizes.

In the early eighties, as student organizations began to form and more and more people were caught up in the movement to defeat the military regime, ACU's importance faded and the organization disappeared. A decade later, however, its more active members still hold reunions, where they celebrate a unique experience, almost inconceivable given the political and social conditions in which the organization was born and, in its own haphazard, gleeful and defiant way, thrived. Some have become professional artists and writers.

I spoke to my old friend, Diego Muñoz, in the Society of Writers of Chile building in 1992: he was the vice-president of Chile's national writers' organization, as well as a practising engineer. Diego continues to explore Chile's experience with the military government in his work. "We're all linked to these kinds of events, so we must understand why they happen. I don't know how much real justice is possible, but at least the leaders should be punished and, if that's not possible, then people should at least remember that the criminals, the torturers, exist, that we're all capable of doing these things."

For Juancho, the lessons of that period are inseparable from the organization that allowed him to grow up in a relatively "normal" fashion, at a time when nothing was normal. "It's impossible to understand the dictatorship without understanding the history of Chile before the dictatorship," he says. "I'm as responsible for the dictatorship as anyone else, even the soldiers. Because I participated in this madness of disqualifying others, of saying 'I'm right and when I have a weapon in my hand I'll kill you because you're not right.'"

For those who built the ACU, who sang and wrote and painted and mimed and laughed thanks to the ACU, those difficult years were not a waste. By rescuing the child in themselves, young men and women were able to grow up, relatively whole, relatively unharmed. They lived the long sacrifice, survived, with *palomas* instead of stones in their hearts.

Chapter three

ESCAPES
FROM PARADISE

LINARES 1966, 1994

I always remember the horses of Linares, a small farming community about a four-hour drive south of Santiago. Fragile living craft, they graze and gallop the green pastures which roll outward from the Panamerican Highway like ocean waves, creating a landscape that is at once peaceful and strange, nostalgic for a golden age or foreshadowing a new era. Dotted about the fields, men lean into wooden ploughs, leaving trails of dark loam open to the sky behind them. There are no tractors at work, although somewhere there must be, because every so often a fenced yard full of farm equipment and a crudely painted sign announce sales of agricultural machinery.

I've never been able to separate Linares from its horses. But in spite of their beauty, the place makes me shiver. Linares is the capital of a region which uneasily shares its fields of juicy melons, its modest, modern brick cathedral, its sky, with a controversial German settlement known as "Colonia Dignidad".

A photograph of two women dominates the front page of the April 6, 1966 edition of the Chilean magazine *Ercilla*. Ursula Schmidt stares boldly at the camera, her dark hair swept away from a round and rigid jaw. Her humourless eyes appraise the camera's capacity for damage and how best to confront it. Most of Wilhelmine Lindemann's slim figure in a dark coat is hidden behind Schmidt's solid bulk. Lindemann is the reason for the photograph, but she shows no interest in it. Wisps of blonde hair have escaped from a severe bun and shine in the soft, southern sun. Under translucent eyebrows full of light, her eyes are dark shafts of worry, her thin cheeks, nose and mouth strain down toward an abyss opening before her. She is walking into it with her eyes downcast, but open, perhaps convinced there is no other road.

This is the image of a prison warden and her prisoner: a woman with no right to appeal, no way out of the sticky web which brought her to this moment, a web woven of her own mistakes.

The photograph haunts me as I search through congressional files, old newspapers and magazines, a recently published book, a journey through springtime bursting into yellow flower and fragrance along the Panamerican Highway, interviews with the Bishop of Linares and a former regional governor Hector Taricco, looking for clues to the survival of Colonia Dignidad.

It becomes particularly acute when Taricco invites me to lunch and introduces me to his wife, Kika Sanino. He urges her to give opinions. "Women's intuition," he says, enthusiastically. "Even when I believed the Colony was a maligned charity, she was warning me there was something strange going on."

Kika's story begins with Juan Müller, a German sailor whose ship was moored off Valparaíso when World War II broke out. He had no way of returning home and by the time the war ended, that home no longer existed. He married a Chilean and had several children, living as the Tariccos' employee until he died suddenly of cancer. Her concern for his children led Kika first to German schools in Santiago, but they were too expensive for Müller's widow. Finally she decided to visit a community rumoured to exist in the Andean foothills, near Parral, a small town south of Linares.

On a rainy afternoon in 1960, Kika, her husband, Hector, her oldest daughter and her fiancé struggled along a deserted stretch of country road, trying to reach the mysterious German colony that could, perhaps, take in Juan Müller's children and give them the upbringing that was now impossible for his widow. Several times the harsh weather and rough driving tempted them to turn back. Instead, they boosted the heat in their car and carried on.

When at last they reached a wooden gate in a high fence, a young girl with long blonde braids and the traditional skirt and apron of a German peasant received them. Their combined efforts in French, Spanish and English did not bring communication. Sadly they returned to the car and made their way back down the rocky road.

"It was clear they only spoke German, not even sign-language could help us," Kika later wrote in her memoirs. "And between us the only words we knew were *Guten Tag* and *Ich liebe dich*." Two years later, new contacts with the Colony added another word to her German vocabulary: *verboten*.

Of all her experiences with the controversial colony, Kika Sanino remembers – and regrets most – what happened to Wilhelmine Lindemann.

German settlers have been a feature of life in southern Chile, especially around the cities of Temuco, Valdivia and Puerto Montt, since the early 1800s, when successive Chilean governments encouraged immigration to the region in order to establish its control over lands occupied by the Mapuche, the largest native group, and to extend the national government's influence from the relatively small, agricultural central valley area where population had concentrated since the conquest.

The Chileans have never hesitated to peg people according to nationality and race. The writings of nineteenth-century historian Benjamin Vicuña Mackenna are a good example. Vicuña Mackenna saw southern Chile as an untouched Eden, ripe for foreign colonization, but which foreigners?

He thought the honest, hardworking Swiss, for example, were problematic because they insisted on returning home once they'd made their fortunes; the only acceptable Italian group were the Piedmontese; the Irish were too rowdy; the Spanish were incapable of forgetting they once owned America; and the French were "passing birds lacking in religious spirit who waste their best strength on wordiness". As for the Anglo-Saxons, their sense of justice and tolerance was admirable, Vicuña wrote, but they tended to look down upon any non-Anglo country of settlement. According to Vicuña and other like-minded Chileans, the Germans were ideal: hardworking, educated and "less dangerous" for Chile, because they came from a divided country.

The German settlers who arrived in Chile were hardly the penniless or persecuted masses that the North American imagination tends to invent. In fact, they brought money, training and ideas. As Jean-Pierre Blancpain put it in his book on the Germans in Chile, *Los Alemanes en Chile (1816-1945),* German settlers, Karl Anwandter among them, "didn't come to Valdivia in search of a fortune: he brought it with him and in three years he would loan 27 other immigrants more than 10,000 pesos." City records indicated other prominent German settlers bequeathed 30,000 pesos to their descendants and their voluntary contributions to the Prussian war (1870) added up to more than 70,000 pesos.

Further south, in the Osorno and Llanquihue regions, the arrival of moneyed and educated German immigrants contrasted with illiterate, untrained Chilean settlers, creating "a psychological frontier rather than genuine segregation", between well-off foreigners who became major land-holders, *latifundistas*, and their semi-skilled, illiterate Chilean workers.

Although Anwandter himself was liberally inclined, the German com-munity was generally conservative. During World War II, Chile officially supported the allies because of the impact of American ownership of the wealthy saltpetre mines in northern Chile, but many Chileans' sympa-thies lay with the Berlin-Rome axis.

The German influence became a powerful one throughout Chile. In the 1800s, German artisans developed the southern city of Valdivia into a thriving metropolis famous for beer, liquor and leather goods. Later, at the turn of the century, German officers reformed and retrained the Chilean army, turning it into what has become known in military and interested circles as the last Prussian army in the world. German teachers and Chileans educated in a liberal German tradition built up a network of German schools which continues to train countless Chileans today. The Bavarian Capuchins opened up important missions dotted throughout the lands which, until 1881, were solely controlled by the Mapuche.

Even a cursory look at the surnames of major figures in Chilean poli-tics shows how the descendants of Chile's German settlers play key roles in national life: Fernando Matthei, until 1991, commander-in-chief of the Chilean airforce; Rodolfo Stange, head of the Carabineros, Chile's uniformed police force; Enrique Krauss, Patricio Aylwin's first Interior Minister; Edgardo Boeninger, President Aylwin's general secretary.

Among the first army recruits to form the DINA, Pinochet's secret police, were Guy Eduardo Neckelmann Schutz, nicknamed the "Gringo" for his blue eyes, Rolf Wenderoth Pozo and Augusto Deitchler Guzmán.

The Chilean ambassador to Germany in the early sixties, Arturo Maschke, played a key role in convincing the leadership of what would become Colonia Dignidad that Chile would be a fine place for them to settle.

Long after the original German settlers had staked out their territory and
put down roots in southern Chile, a new group began to test the possibilities of transplanting their small community to the region of Linares.
In the late fifties this group purchased a large farm in the Andean foothills
close to Linares and Parral, and by 1961 several of their leaders and a
contingent of young boys had set up tents and begun to clear and build
their new settlement.

The foreign colony's presence began as rumour and grew rapidly into
admiration and praise, as it successfully defeated the rigours of the Andean
mountains, planting fields of grain, raising animals, starting small cot-
tage industries, installing a generator, workshop, garage, bakery and
other services. Financed by admirers in Germany and supplied with tax
and customs benefits which rendered their growing business interests
extraordinarily profitable, the new colony flourished.

Chilean visitors toured the green fields in the community's well-kept
Mercedes Benz buses, oohing and aahing with a kind of reverse racism
at the lovely blue-eyed, blond-haired Germans and their wonderful,
clean, orderly settlement. When the first conflicts and criticisms began
to emerge, many defended the Colony on the basis of these images and
the tasty flavours of its juices and *kuchens* alone.

In 1964, Eduardo Frei, the Christian Democratic party's candidate, was
elected president of Chile. He appointed Hector Taricco governor of
Linares and both Taricco and his wife, Kika, assumed new responsibilities.
As local dignitaries they were invited to visit the Colony, regaled with its
fine cooking and delicate pastries. Taricco was impressed by the Colony's
success in building a thriving agricultural community on a large and
isolated farm in the lap of the Andes: the powerful generators, machine
shops, farming equipment, mechanics; a children's orchestra and choir
which sang like angels; a neat, orderly, disciplined approach to life, so
different from — and admired by — the Chileans. The Colony's achievements were particularly remarkable given the failure of a previous settlement attempt by a group of Italians. In retrospect, Taricco believes the
Italians' failure was simply because they were poor and undercapitalized,
but at the time all served to underline the Germans' efficiency at bringing
modern, prosperous farming techniques to Chile.

There was something about the German leadership's cold disregard,
even contempt, for their Chilean guests which bothered Kika Sanino

though. The beauty of the choral music moved her, but she found the children's rigid, inexpressive faces and their lack of spontaneity disturbing. On a bus tour of the farm's properties she'd noticed a lovely girl with long blonde braids staring out the window, huge tears rolling endlessly down the ruddy German cheeks.

Wilhelmine Lindemann and her three children were among the first settlers to reach Colonia Dignidad in 1961. Her husband had promised to follow within days, but never came. Five years later, local farmworkers complained about the Colony. Regional authorities, among them Hector Taricco, began an investigation.

Taricco and a committee visited the Colony and interviewed twenty-five people at random, who all declared their satisfaction with life there. To everyone he met, he repeated they were living in a free country and could do as they pleased; that if they wished to leave the colony, they would be protected by Chilean authorities. What followed indicates that Taricco was sincere in his offer. But he was also very, very wrong.

Within days, a group of three or four women escaped but were recaptured by the Colony's security squad. Wilhelmine Lindemann managed to get as far as the home of a school teacher in the rural community of Catillo.

Of Lindemann's first attempted escape, Kika Sanino writes in her memoirs "without knowing her, I felt that we were close; something told me she needed me. In a matter of seconds the mind travels the universe; with faith in a prayer's strength it was easy to place myself at her side; I tried to tell her to be patient and brave, that we would do something to free her from her tragedy. No one exposed herself to run away, without having powerful motives."

Kika found herself receiving the Colony's leadership in her home. "They said that these escapes were the collective psychoses of nervous women and above all Lindemann, who had a very bad temper." When they insisted that Lindemann, like all the colonists, could go where she pleased, Kika invited her to tea the next week. She wasn't surprised when in her place the Colony's directors arrived, explaining she was sick. When Kika insisted on seeing Lindemann, the men expressed wonder that a respectable woman like herself would be interested in "such a repugnant woman".

They then produced a typewritten letter, with no logo or signature.

"Not being a puritan and even though I was a mature woman, a shudder ran through me as I read so much filth. The least that they said of the poor woman (and with a wealth of details) was that she was a prostitute well known in Germany as 'Sunbeam', because of her blonde hair, famous for her deals with soldiers from World War II."

They accused her of being "born from incest and that within the Colony her behaviour with other women was aberrant. All these accusations were written in an explicit way, inconceivable except as the product of unbalanced minds.

"My husband asked them how many more crazy, mentally sick, prostitutes were still inside the Colony, since up until then, all 'escapees' had turned out to belong to these categories."

Concerned about Lindemann's illness, Hector Taricco, Kika and others returned to the Colony unannounced and demanded to see her. They attribute their success to the absence of the Colony's main leaders, away in Santiago. Nevertheless, it was a frightening visit.

Not only did the Colony's security people "run about, as if preparing for combat" but when Kika Sanino and others tried to return to Linares for help, they found themselves shut in by armed guards. Finally the expedition succeeded in having Lindemann returned to Linares, where she was immediately hospitalized. There was no sign of the gastro-intestinal infection the Germans had spoken of, but she was starved and covered with marks left from injections.

Her children were welcomed by the Taricco household. Surprisingly, from Kika Sanino's point of view, they showed no interest in their mother. When she took them to the hospital for a visit, they rejected her coldly. Apparently the lengthy separation and whatever the Colony's leaders had told them about Wilhelmine Lindemann had destroyed their feelings for her.

"Her ruddy face took on a deadly whitish hue. Her lips formed a terribly bitter smile. Her blue eyes silently questioned her children, but remained without response from the children's tight mouths, held in a grimace of anger and disgust," says Kika of that visit. Finally one of them accused her of being an evil woman, a deserter. Kika ushered the children out of the hospital and back to her house.

All was quiet for a few days and then Lindemann's husband arrived from Germany, accompanied by Colony members.

"He was a Nordic type, tall with a wrinkled face and reddened skin.

He tried to smile, but managed only grimaces, which were neither spontaneous nor sincere. There was something about him which communicated deception and a disagreeable cynicism," writes Kika. The father, his Colony friend and the children met together at the Taricco home, alone. Afterward, the children's behaviour changed radically. When one of the boys tried to burn down her home, Kika called the hospital for help. Within hours, Lindemann and her children had returned to the Colony.

"I felt that I'd failed a woman who had risked everything for her freedom," Kika meditates. "We did what we could to help her recover her children and return to her distant country." But she has never forgotten the last words of a German-speaking nun who had cared for Lindemann in the hospital: "Don't feel so badly; these are not human beings."

My photograph from the cover of *Ercilla* was taken as Wilhelmine Lindemann was on her way back to the Colony the first time, frightened by what she had done, but hopeful that she would now be allowed to see her children. Beside her photograph, in a second shot a vigorous youth gazes confidently off at something to his right, seated safely in a flowering garden. He is Wolfgang Müller, one of four Colony boys with that name, and he had just completed his third escape when the picture was taken. Unlike Lindemann, he would succeed.

Müller's first escape had taken him to Chillán, where he had lived in peace with a family, the Echeverrías, for several days. Then the Colony security squad found him. The house was raided and, when the squad failed to find Müller, so was a neighbour's. The owner expelled them after a loud argument, but the Germans kept both houses under surveillance. Friends of the family successfully captured one of the Germans, whom they dragged to the local headquarters of Investigaciones, Chile's plainclothes detective force. Colony security attacked. With the aid of Carabineros, the five Germans were arrested, accused of assault, aggression and violation of private property.

Müller's flight ended abruptly the next day, when a police sergeant and a Chilean of German origin, Ernesto Thun, arrived at the home of Udo Schweitzer where Müller had taken refuge, demanding Müller accompany them. He did. According to Schweitzer's testimony in court, the police officer, Müller and Thun entered a white van waiting outside his door. No one outside the Colony saw Müller again until three days later when he arrived at the courthouse to testify. Mrs. Echeverría told *Ercilla* reporters that Müller didn't recognize her, treated her coldly and "seemed drugged". Two months later, the judge dismissed the case against the colonists who had raided private homes and the local police headquarters.

In what became a constant in trials involving the Colony, *Ercilla's* journalists noted: "Although all the Germans arrested denied having been in the Echeverría family house, there were many Chilean witnesses who certified or could have certified the contrary, but they were never called upon or the trial didn't pay them any attention. All the Germans declared that Hermann Schmidt (the Colony's official spokesman) had custody of Wolfgang Müller, but there's no record that the judge saw or even requested a legal document to that effect."

In September 1963, Müller appeared at the Echeverría family house again. He explained that he had been beaten and forced to deny that he knew Mrs. Echeverría that day in court. She tried to get protection for him but both police and the local judge refused. Colony security recaptured him at the home of the German consul in Temuco (ten hours south of Santiago) and he returned again to the Colony, to drugs and punishment.

Then, in March 1966, Müller took advantage of the arrival of an important visitor. "I escaped along the bank of the Perquilauquén River. I heard a siren, the dogs barking and the cries of the guards in charge of the sect. From a distance I could see flashlights being lit. After running or walking quickly about seven or eight kilometres to get out of the Colony's centre, I spent the night in the woods, crossed a bridge escaping from some guards, something which I can't explain to this day: I recognized them and they must have recognized me, but they let me pass.

"Afterward I hid in a cave and the next night reached the Catillo Hot Springs, where I made contact with people and for the first time in several years I felt affection and love from my fellows." Müller was helped to nearby Parral and took a train to Santiago, where he managed to get the protection of the German Embassy. A Colony squad, fifty-men strong, tried several times to recapture him, fighting several battles with Santiago police.

In what would become another constant of court cases involving the Colony, Wolfgang Müller passed abruptly from being victim to being on trial. He had accused Colony leader Paul Schäfer of homosexually abusing him: the case which came to court featured Wolfgang Müller, on trial for sodomy. Eventually his struggle for freedom ended with his reunion with his mother, who had also been victimized by the Colony, and for them both a painful, poverty-ridden return to Germany.

Lindemann's and Müller's testimony revealed that men and women were kept separately in the colony; that sect leader Paul Schäfer routinely sexually abused the colony's young boys; that colony members worked seven days a week, without pay and, in the case of the children, without the schooling promised to their parents before leaving Germany. Nor had the Colony received the Chilean orphans created by the Chillán earthquake (there weren't any) – the main justification in its charter for its existence and its exemption from customs and all other taxes. Electric shock treatment was commonly used by the Colony doctor, Gisela Seewald. Adults and children, particularly females, were frequently and brutally beaten, in some cases to the point where they lost control of their mental and physical functions.

A later escapee, Hugo Baar, described how his 28-year-old daughter, Dorothea, was beaten one day. "Mr. Schäfer began to scold her in a very loud voice and then to punch her. She flew from one wall to another and when she fell he kicked her until he shouted at her to leave ... My wife – whom I told of this in the evening –and I could say nothing. If we'd protested or intervened, this would have brought consequences for me, eventually more isolation or other punishment."

As far as is known, Dorothea remains in the Colony, as does Peter, another Colony member who fell foul of Paul Schäfer. After receiving three years of shock treatment from Dr. Seewald and being drugged daily and beaten on a regular basis, Peter was permanently hospitalized. Baar, who was sent to bathe him, said: "I can't forget how Peter looked. A thick liquid ran permanently from his mouth, his whole body shook, he could hardly walk, he couldn't wash or shave himself ... I found out later that the reason for this treatment was that he'd been courting a childhood friend to whom he'd spoken or written a note."

In the years since Wolfgang Müller successfully escaped and Wilhemine Lindemann failed, other members of the Colony have followed their example. Their testimony has provided a relatively complete, if frightening, picture of life behind the barbed wire fences that enclose the sect's members and its secrets.

In 1989, after helping Hugo Baar and Georg and Lotti Packmor escape from the Colony, Heinz Kuhn, a Colony founder and the only escapee known to have remained in Chile, finally revealed his experiences. Kuhn's problems began after Müller's escape, when he and a Colony nurse were put in charge of public relations.

"We spoke with parliamentarians from different parties, visited their houses," he said. "We spoke about the Colony's children, of how they're freely educated, with respect for morals, work and good habits. We did a very good job defending the Colony ... how I regret that now!"

Kuhn and his assistant fell in love and she was three months pregnant before they realized it. They were afraid of Schäfer's reaction, especially after seeing what had happened to Wolfgang Müller after his earlier escapes.

"I was in charge of defaming Wolfgang Müller and one night Schäfer sent me to sleep in the hospital. I saw Müller half-dressed, inside a wooden cage; his body was impossible, full of torture marks." The next day Kuhn and Ursula fled the Colony, but were followed and picked up by a Colony bus. They were returned to the Colony and separated: "I was taken to the Kinderhaus, where Schäfer lived with the children. I entered a room, saw a bottle of medicine and remember nothing more until I woke up in the hospital several days later."

Kuhn knew nothing of his wife until he was released from the hospital. Eventually he discovered that hardly had they been returned to the Colony then they'd forced her to have an abortion. In 1968, Kuhn sucessfully escaped the Colony and was later joined by his wife, but in 1975 they separated and she and their two children returned to Germany.

After Kuhn, Franz and Teresa Wohri escaped, leaving one of their four children in the Colony and, in 1970, Peter Packmor (now dead) escaped. Fourteen years later in December 1984, Hugo Baar fled, leaving wife and children behind (he was later able to have his wife rejoin him) and then in March 1985, Georg and Lotty Packmor, who had worked closely with the Colony's leader, Paul Schäfer, successfully escaped, leaving their adopted son behind.

The Colony reacted by accusing the escapees of sexual deviation, insanity, robbery, alcoholism and drug addiction. During a visit to the Colony gates in 1987, I was handed typed, unsigned sheets, ostensibly written by Baar and Packmor family members who had remained inside.

The last known case of a youth escaping from the Colony occurred in April 1988. But no one had to discredit Jürgen Szurgelies's testimony: Colony security recaptured him before he had a chance to talk.

The experience of Lotti Packmor, who worked within the Colony's security system, suggests there may be few escapes in the future: "Schäfer surrounded the farm with a barbed wire fence and a very fine wire of metallic threads like a spider web which encloses the whole place, along with certain roads within. If a person on foot or in a vehicle goes through one of these wires an alarm goes off ... and immediately German shepherd dogs and men in fast vehicles appear ...

"For Schäfer there are three kinds of people: those who live on the farm and do what he orders without conditions. These are true Christians, the men of God. Then there are the renegades, who no longer respond to his demands. Those who run away, are incurably sick. He proves this using medical certificates [signed] by Dr. Seewald ... The third kind are communists."

The Müller and Lindemann escapes from Colonia Dignidad sparked judicial and parliamentary investigations throughout 1966-1968. In spite of abundant evidence to the contrary, including the testimony of the escapees themselves, the investigations almost invariably ended with the Colony being praised for its technological progress, hygiene and hard work.

Chilean law grants authorities, like members of Congress and regional governors, immunity from prosecution. Nevertheless, the Colony challenged Hector Taricco's immunity from prosecution and, in 1968, a senate committee examined charges that he was persecuting an innocent group of settlers and listened to
his defence. The Committee found in favour of Hector Taricco, but its recommendation failed in the Senate for lack of a quorum. For the next few years he was trapped in an endless labyrinth of court cases and legal suits. Eventually he was absolved.

The scandals around the Colony continued to excite attention from governments around the world, as German and Austrian authorities and private citizens attempted to rescue people who had disappeared inside it. In 1968, a Chilean parliamentary investigation found serious irregularities, but ended up excusing them, recommending a few changes and finding in favour of the Colony and its leaders. It was a most peculiar investigation indeed. No sooner was the final report presented to Congress, then several of the commission's members stood up to express their total disagreement with the conclusions.

Pressure from respected governments abroad, congressional debates and investigations, research by concerned individuals: it all bounced off the colony's well-padded back. In spite of its isolation, the sect had successfully built up a network of powerful friends in Chile's courts and police stations, in congress and beyond it.

Osvaldo Muray, the journalist who first broke the story of Müller's escape, recalls waiting outside an investigating judge's home for a comment. The judge refused to receive him but a Colony delegation, complete with a beautifully prepared and roasted pig, waltzed through the judge's doorway to a warm welcome. On another occasion, he watched Colony residents delivering tanks of propane to a judge's home. Neighbours accused a police inspector of receiving a gift of fine blue ceramic tiles for his driveway from the Colony – when Muray asked him where the tiles had come from, the man went red and refused to answer.

"There wasn't a grand plot to protect the Colony but rather the little things – the gift to a public functionary, the tiles to the police officer, the propane for a judge, a roast pig for a minister. All these things I saw myself," says Osvaldo Muray. "That's why I don't have the least confidence."

Jorge Ovalle, a Chilean lawyer who represented the post-regime government in its cases involving the Colony, believes it owes most of its influence to Chileans who supported Hitler and Mussolini during the Second World War. "In Chile we also have a great admiration for the Germans, for their work, especially those who came [to Chile] in the last century.

"The Colony's image was one of being very effective, of great effort, great dedication. This awakened a lot of sympathy in the area."

Magazine and newspaper reports revealed that for years the German Embassy enjoyed close relations with the Colony, whose representatives regularly sold their wares to Embassy employees. Between 1976 and 1979, while Erich Strätling was Germany's ambassador in Santiago, Colony workers remodelled his residence, repainted his Mercedes and repaired the roof, according to German journalist Gero Gemballa, who wrote a book about Dignidad and testified before the Bundestag in the 1988 hearings.

"If you could read the visitors' book you'd be very surprised, because a lot of people were invited to spend a week in the Colony," says Muray, who saw the book during a 1966 visit to the Colony. "Names and signatures: almost all the important government authorities. I think Frei was there but I don't remember. We never involved Frei."

Its uncanny ability to survive questioning and controversy, throughout the presidency of Eduardo Frei, Sr. (1964-1970), the Allende government (1970-1973), the military regime (1973-1990) and the Aylwin government (1990-1994) reveals a remarkable tolerance on the part of Chilean authorities.

Jorge Ovalle goes one step further. "If at one time they assaulted the detectives' headquarters in Parral and then in Chillán — it was thanks to their influence," he says. "Nothing was done [against them] because there was complicity on the part of the Alessandri government, complicity in Frei's time and in Pinochet's. I don't know what happened under Allende but he didn't take any measures with respect to the Colony either."

The Colony's many ties with Chilean authorities peaked during the military regime. General Pinochet's wife, Lucía Hiriart, frequently holidayed there, as did General Manuel Contreras, the founder of the DINA, Pinochet's dreaded secret police. Carabineros General and Junta member, Cesar Mendoza, gave the Colony a radio frequency that linked it directly to the police. Generals Stange and Matthei were among the guests at a Colony bash in Santiago, according to Hugo Baar, the former Colony administrator who escaped. Guests later received a souvenir photo album. Monica Madariaga visited the Colony in its own Mercedes Benz several times while she was Pinochet's Justice Minister and responsible for judicial procedures related to the Colony. Jaime del Valle, Pinochet's former Foreign Affairs Minister also served as the Colony's lawyer.

Under the Chilean military regime the Colony's unique skills and experiences spilled out of its cloisters, taking on a larger meaning, revealing and amplifying the ruthless streak in Chilean society which had lain dormant for decades.

"My body was full of cuts and bruises. I was rotting everywhere. I had pus in my eyes, my nose. My mouth was completely numb. I could feel nothing in my penis and I couldn't feel my limbs. My body was full of cigarette burns."

In February 1975 a young medical student named Luis Peebles spent nine days in Colonia Dignidad. He was not wined and dined, nor was his blindfold removed long enough for him to admire the Germans' technological advances. His testimony, along with that of other survivors and a former agent of the Chilean secret police, formed the basis of reports by Amnesty International, the United Nations and other human rights organizations that accused Colonia Dignidad of functioning as a prison camp and centre for training and experimentation with torture techniques, after the 1973 military coup.

"They tied me to a metal cot, but this time they put a helmet on my head. It had movable earflaps which allowed them to apply electrical current to my ears and rubber bands for around the jaw. This was so that when they kicked or punched me, my jaw wouldn't get thrust out of joint. They taped little wires to my wrists, thighs, glans, chest, neck and applied current in different parts.

"There was also an agent who used a little rubber object which gave off shocks when he hit me with it. They had something they used on my eyes, mouth, teeth, under my tongue and sometimes, when I was shouting, they'd put it right at the back of the palate. I had another one in my anus, at the base of the urethra and another under my nails ... This went on for hours and hours. ... The pain was so great that I twisted and several times lifted up the bed. I even bent the cot which was of iron and broke the straps with the strength of desperation.

"The brutality of the treatment made me think I was the subject of an experiment to find out how much I could resist both physically and mentally. I was the guinea pig and they were there to learn."

Adriana Bórquez of Talca was taken from her home on April 23, 1975, thrown onto a bus "full of people" and taken across the Maule River and past Linares, whose lights she saw shortly before the bus turned off the highway onto a gravel road.

"They took me into interrogation, the shouting grew louder and there was music, I remember having heard Capriccio italien by Tchaikovsky. A man they called the prosecutor (*fiscal*) or 'Doctor' did the questioning. They applied current; when they finished I could still hear the cries of others being tortured. It gave me diarrhoea. ... I had electrodes everywhere and something gave me shocks that passed right through my body. I felt torn apart; just as I felt I was being emptied by mouth and anus, I lost consciousness."

Men speaking with both Chilean and foreign accents shut six-foot-tall Sergio González into a small box measuring no more than a metre, applying electrical current through holes. They also wrapped his head in a plastic bag and then applied current, until the oxygen was used up; almost drowned him repeatedly in special tubs, which were at times electrified; and tied him to a sort of electric grill where they applied current generally and to specific parts of his body.

"Right after the coup, torture by the intelligence services and ordinary police wasn't very sophisticated and a lot of people died," González said. "But in the Colony they produced the maximum of pain, without necessarily killing. They even put me in their hospital for a while, because of the torture."

In March 1991, in its final report on human rights violations during the military regime, the National Commission for Truth and Reconciliation concluded that "a certain number of people arrested by the DINA were effectively taken to Colonia Dignidad, held captive there, where some were submitted to torture, with the participation in these events not only of DINA agents but also of persons living on the farm" and affirmed that at least one of Chile's disappeared political prisoners, Alvaro Vallejos Villagrán, disappeared after being taken to the Colony.

Samuel Fuenzalida, the Chilean agent who took him there, later testified on several occasions to having been greeted by a man with a glass eye who answered to the titles of "Doctor" or "Professor".

"Colonia Dignidad doesn't exist. It's a ghost," Paul Schäfer, leader of the Colony, told a Chilean judge in August 1985 during his first interrogation in twenty-five years. About seventy years old (not even his lawyers know for sure), Schäfer was questioned lying comfortably in a bed in the Colony hospital, since Dr. Hopp had certified that he was suffering from a heart problem complicated by a viral lung infection.

In many ways he was telling the truth. The properties belonging to the Colony, for example, were never transferred to the charitable foundation bearing its name. Rather, they legally belong to some of the Colony's best-known leaders, all close collaborators of Schäfer. The orphans (first from the Second World War, later from a Chilean earthquake in the early sixties) for whom the Colony was supposedly created, were never accommodated. And the school that was supposed to serve them wasn't created until after Wolfgang Müller's escapes and the scandals surrounding the Chilean congressional and other investigations. In spite of the recommendations of the House of Deputies' report, the Colony didn't apply Chilean laws to its labour relations or to the school itself. The hospital, the one, undisputable social service that the Colony provides, is largely funded by the Chilean Health Ministry which until mid-1995 provided its medical supplies.

But Schäfer himself is perhaps the Colony's biggest mystery: a man whose history can be traced back as far as the mid-fifties, when he emerged from the chaos of the Second World War as an itinerant

Lutheran preacher with verve and charisma.

In 1954, Schäfer joined forces with the Baptist preacher Hugo Baar, and together they established their church, first in the city of Salz Gitter and later in Gronau and Siegburg. They started by asking for 10 per cent of their followers' incomes; later, they asked for everything they owned and earned. Often, it was given willingly.

"I think what Schäfer did with us was a process of spiritual domination," Heinz Kuhn said in 1989, after he had left the Colony. "I didn't have the will to refuse any of his requests. It took him about three years to completely control our wills through his preaching and evangelizing."

Already in 1966, the coverage in the magazine *Ercilla* revealed a lot about how the dynamic preacher with a glass eye achieved his ends. The magazine tells the story of Wilhelm Wagner who, when he was convinced of the community's religious integrity, had confessed to Schäfer that he had had incestuous relations with two of his daughters. When Wagner, on the point of immigrating to Chile, changed his mind and refused to go, the sect denounced him in German courts and he was condemned to three years in prison. The Colony took his four children.

Detailed confessions were an ongoing part of the religious cult and often provided the reins by which rebellious members were controlled or broken. Hugo Baar's testimony reveals how effective this was, especially when transferred to the silence and solitudes of the Chilean cordillera.

"Another of Mr. Schäfer's principles introduced by hammer-blows into the conscience of each one is the following: 'No one must keep secrets.' Everything must come out into the light, Jesus is the light. Jesus is also the truth. All that is secret and lies come from the devil.

"If someone tells someone else something, they feel so much weight on their conscience that sooner or later they end up telling Mr. Schäfer or confessing publicly ...

"Another of his principles is that 'He who listens is guilty.' ... To prevent conversations Mr. Schäfer started to condemn the person who'd listened to another with as much force, even more ... This had the effect that as soon as someone wants to tell someone else something, the listener interrupts and says 'I'm not going to listen to you ...'"

Schäfer fled Germany in the early sixties, when the parents of two boys in the sect brought charges against him for homosexual abuse of their sons.

"I was a close witness of the testimonies of his immorality with the boys of our community," Kuhn said in 1989. "By then our church had already become a sect. The sons of the faithful lived in a special house that the state had granted us for war orphans, but there weren't any. This was 1955-56, the war had ended ten years earlier and none of these vestiges remained. We had twenty to thirty children, all boys, because Schäfer wouldn't accept girls."

After he escaped, Wolfgang Müller revealed that Schäfer had continued his practices in Chile. Müller's mother had put him into the Heide Home in Siegburg after her divorce in 1957. "I was twelve and within six hours of meeting him [Schäfer] took me to bed and abused me," Müller told Osvaldo Muray in 1966. "In the Colony there are a lot of boys and his homosexual activities continue with them. Every day a boy does his shift as Schäfer's 'helper' and that includes sleeping with him.

"Schäfer is an energetic man, who speaks with a high voice ... He knows how to joke and be charming. He knows every one in Dignidad inside out. They take their problems to him and he counsels them. Before, he preached about the Bible and they accepted his interpretation. He's an artist in the art of influencing people and venerated by them like a God. ... One day he stopped preaching. He told us: 'I've preached to you enough. You know the Bible. Act accordingly.'

"All the young people must keep a notebook for special events. There they must note what they've done wrong, the faults in obedience, when something's broken, etc. I was the only one who resisted openly. At night, the older boys would come to see me, ask for the notebook and when they saw that the pages were blank they'd take me outside and beat me without compassion."

Heinz Kuhn noted that "No adult received propositions or insinuations from Schäfer. He only liked boys up to twelve years. He'd discriminate with his favours and preferences. When he got bored with them, he'd exclude them from his preferred group and have them punished by their own companions. When he changes lovers, the former lover falls from favour and is punished at any time. In their worst moments, these children had no help from father or mother. Only Schäfer. That's how he fabricated an army of unconditional supporters ...

"Only if you know that we were a sect is it possible to understand that Schäfer didn't hide his torture of members of Dignidad. Children were beaten in their parents' presence, when these lived in Chile. Normally, the father was in Germany and the mother on the farm, working hard all day."

Lotti Packmor, who was a day-care worker by training, found her responsibilities with the children of Dignidad unbearable.

"The children were always under heavy doses of medication. ... At night, completely nude, they were brought together in a large room organized for this purpose. The beds were put in a circle and we in the middle had to observe the twelve-year-olds. At the first symptom of sexual desire the child was taken from the bed and beaten ... after the blows they were put in a cold shower and then taken back to bed. They also used electric *picanas* to work them over. I've been present when Dr. Gisela Seewald applied injections to their testicles."

Paul Schäfer's presence in Chile has undergone transformations worthy of a ghost or at least a magician. According to the Foreign Department of Chile's Investigaciones Police Force, Paul Schäfer Schneider arrived in Chile on July 27, 1961 and left on November 8th of the same year. But in February of 1963, he was admitted to Santiago's Hospital del Tórax for surgery to extract a bullet from his lung. He was released on July 3rd of the same year – long after he was officially supposed to have left Chile.

In 1966, when Müller's escape sounded the first public alarms about the Colony and investigators knocked on the gates with the full force of the law behind them, their requests to interrogate Schäfer met with the curious reply that Schäfer had headed off to the hills with a loaded gun. The implication was that the persecution had driven him to suicide. Hector Taricco was blamed.

Since then, the Colony's visitors have regularly reported seeing the man with the unmistakeable glass eye. Although he holds no official position within the Colony hierarchy, he continues to direct the choir which produces its musical show for distinguished guests the Colony is wooing.

The children of the sixties are now adults and Kuhn calls them a small, unconditional army of Schäfer supporters. "That's what the last escapees have told me. They have military training, use combat uniforms and everyone has a number and weapon."

He compares Schäfer to a successful businessman, with "three hundred people who work like slaves, without timetable, Sundays, salary, taxes, insurance, for nothing more than the food and poor clothes ... In any country in the world that businessman has an important influence."

On Schäfer's influence over Chilean courts, he says "Schäfer always says that everyone can be bought. The range doesn't matter, everyone has a different price" and Kuhn tells of the hasty invention of a classroom for a visit from an investigating Minister of the Court in the 1960s.

"Anyone would have realized that school was a lie," Kuhn said. "Not a scratch on the floor nor the desks. But they didn't want to investigate ... They were satisfied with the façade of a school, that looked clean and perfect.

"It's the typical reaction of the Chilean faced with a blue-eyed foreigner. Anything that we do, Chileans put on an altar. They don't even have a teacher with a degree."

Schäfer undoubtedly wielded – and wields – tremendous power over his followers. Walter Rovekamp, an Amnesty International official in Bonn who has been in charge of the Colonia Dignidad case for more than ten years, told a Chilean reporter: "Herr Schäfer has taught them that he's number one, the leader, the little god. For them he's been the sun and they follow him blindly. If Schäfer dies there's no future for Colonia Dignidad. And that worries me. It's dangerous."

Others, including Hector Taricco, have compared the Colony's inner workings – and possible future if something disturbed its delicate balance – with the Jonestown community in Guyana, which ended in mass suicide.

In 1966, *Ercilla* broke the story of Müller's and later Lindemann's escapes, forcing local authorities to look more critically at the German colony's existence in their midst. In the eighties, small-circulation, opposition magazines became increasingly daring in their challenges to the military regime and began to publish testimonies on the torture and other irregular activities of Colonia Dignidad.

On several occasions, the pro-military media of the seventies and eighties undertook its defence, as did leaders of Chile's traditional right-wing parties. At the end of 1987, when the regime's hold on the country began to weaken and the German government began to push investigation of the colony, *El Mercurio* and the Catholic University's Channel 13 both produced eloquent defences of the embattled Colony.

Even their commitment to defending what they presented as a religiously inspired, charitable institution making an invaluable contribution to Chilean development could not prevent reporters from revealing some curious facts about the place.

The *Mercurio's* enthused reporter expressed some concern at the blank looks on the male choir's faces as they sang and she was also dubious about the reason their voices were still so high, even when most members were obviously passed puberty.

In the Channel 13 report, Colony leaders Hermann Schmidt (who served as a Luftwaffe pilot during World War II) and Dr. Hartmut Hopp guided the crew through lush fields of grains, a modern butcher shop and fully mechanized dairy, bakery, clothes and furniture factory, all serviced by the Colony's powerful generating station.

Miguel Becerra, the son of a Chilean police agent who died mysteriously after telling his brother he wanted to retire from Colony work and whose mother has been unable to regain custody, appeared on screen, repeating in monotonous Spanish with a German accent that "I'm always free here. I feel very happy. I have everything. I'm very happy."

The Colony's official spokesman, Dr. Hartmut Hopp, denied that the Colony is a haven for Nazi ideas or religious fanaticism but highly praised the conservative German politician Franz-Josef Strauss, whom he compared to General Pinochet for his "truth and valour".

I come from a country with a history of small, religious settlements which at least superficially resemble Colonia Dignidad. I can still see the large, square farmhouses of British Columbia's Doukhobors, empty windows gazing sadly at a past where extended families lived in one dwelling, working and producing and praying together in vegetarian communities opposed to violence. And I remember the stories of their persecution during World War II, their children being wrested from them and carried off to residential schools (as happened with many native people), the sensational coverage of their often logical and sometimes dramatic opposition to Canadian intervention in their customs.

From a six-month stay in Kitchener, Ontario, I remember the Mennonites in their horsedrawn buggies, arriving at the central market where they sold butter, cheese and vegetables to the townspeople and the New Age types whose opposition to chemical additives happily coincided with the Mennonites' resistance to most aspects of modern life.

Recently on Chilean television I saw a movie based on a short story by a Canadian, W.D. Valgardson, about an adolescent boy's determined escape from the religious straitjacket that his strict, sect-like upbringing had imposed on him. I've often read and reread Mark Abley's account of his visit to a Hutterite community in Manitoba, wondering if by some stretch of the imagination this could be what Colonia Dignidad is really about.

But the doubts don't stand for long, not only because of the strength and the variety of sources of testimony of the Colony's inner aberrations, not only because of the Chileans' overwhelmingly positive bias toward German settlers and traditions, not only because of the obvious discrepancies between the Colony's alleged charitable goals and its legal and economic activities, but also because of reports, again from several sources, indicating that the Colony is heavily armed and may have been involved in international arms dealing, a most peculiar activity for a small, agricultural community of religious inspiration and charitable goals.

In February 1988, the German magazine *Stern* published the testimony of Peter Pruefer of Dusseldorf who, from 1962 to 1987, was responsible for shipping a container per month from Germany to the Colony in Chile. Normally, these passed automatically through Chilean customs, but in April 1987 customs officers in the northern port of Antofagasta examined a container destined for the Colony and discovered more than a thousand kilos of ammunition.

Hugo Baar told the Bundestag in 1988 that: "I can't inform exactly about the quantity of weapons. Those that I bought were purchased in different periods and sent to Chile in different shipments. There are also some in the Colony which I didn't acquire. What I am well-informed about is that in the Colony machine guns and hand grenades were built."

In his testimony the same day, Georg Packmor said machine guns were manufactured in the Colony under Israeli licences and that 50 people were trained and in possession of these weapons.

Gemballa's book catalogues the Colony's sophisticated security and communications devices, including a transmitting antenna fifty-four metres high, attached to scrambling equipment for electronically ciphering communication, whose installation was examined and authorized by the Chilean Navy.

He also mentions the Colony's relationship with an international weapons dealer, Gerhard Mertins, and his son, who studied medicine with the Colony's doctor, Hartmut Hopp, in the United States. Mertins was one of the founders of the Circle of Friends of Dignidad in Germany and on several occasions spearheaded support campaigns in the German media. According to Gemballa, in the winter of 1975-76, Gerhard Mertins received Manuel Contreras, head of the Chilean secret police (DINA), who was travelling under a false name. Together they went to Iran.

The spectre of old Nazi leaders hiding out in Latin America to plan their own counter-revolution or the re-creation of their new society has haunted the Colony as it has haunted Latin America for the past forty years. From the first reports in *Ercilla,* speculation has linked it to members of the Nazi hierarchy rumoured or known to have found refuge, often with new identities, in Latin America and students of the subject have compared the Colony's symbol of a nurse with a child clinging to each hand to the Nazi's *lebensborn* (lifesource) symbol for its Aryan race reproduction program. They've also found the Colony's set-up similar to German Utopians' proposals for creating autonomous, self-sustaining German colonies around the world. But the relationship between the German Colony, the Nazi legacy from the Second World War and home-grown Chilean conservatism, including Nazism, is more subtle and complex than these links might indicate.

In his first report on Müller's escape, Muray quoted sources identifying Müller as a messenger "between the German commandos in South America", who possessed "many disquieting secrets for the security of former Nazi leaders".

Later Müller himself said, "I don't think this is really a Nazi camp, but the methods used, the discipline and the cult to a superior being (Schäfer) is what they did for Adolf Hitler in Germany ... I know that there are two ex-members of the SS in Dignidad, but I don't think there's anything political or Nazi. In the discussions which we had in the dining room on the basis of some movies, the consensus was anti-Nazi and the persecution of the Jews was criticized."

The Colony does share similar moral values with the Nazis, including a powerful nostalgia for a past perceived to be more morally correct than the modern world, where people are apt to pick and choose their own morality from a number of possible models. Visitors to both the Colony or its restaurant near the small town of Bulnes exclaim at their old world atmosphere: the traditional German costumes, the boys in lederhosen, the women and girls with long braided hair, wearing long dresses and aprons.

"I think originally it was founded as a re-creation of some German city," says Osvaldo Muray. "If you take pictures from Hitler's time, you'll see the women are dressed exactly the way they dressed in the Colony in 1960 or 1970. It's impossible to know which is which.

"I think at first Colonia Dignidad was a city where these old Germans

who were important and influential in Hitler's Germany could live out
their last days in peace, in a Germany made in Chile.

"By now, the old Nazis are dead, but Schäfer and the others carry on
enjoying the Colony's organization. Here they don't have to work, they
have three hundred slaves, they live like princes and earn a lot of money."

After twenty-five years, Muray believes that perhaps the Colony's
power is waning, but he's not sure.

"The right and Nazism are synonyms in Chile," he says. "Nazism
defends the established order, a series of values that aren't very defined,
you never know exactly what they are. On the other hand, the left attacks
blindly too. There's never been an in-depth study of why the colony
exists, what it's for. The initial reason they gave (the non-existent orphans)
is absurd. There are few Chilean children, they don't speak Spanish.

"Then they started using the hospital. But why a hospital whose spe-
cialties are plastic surgery and geriatrics? Why Dr. Seewald, an expert in
illnesses of the elderly, if it's a society that's supposed to raise children?
Hopp studied medicine, specializing in mental sicknesses. [When we did
our reports we found that] the Colony consumed more tranquillizers
than the rest of the province of Linares."

At the time of Müller's first escape, former Nazi Walter Rauff lived
comfortably in Santiago. He is now buried in the General Cemetery, which
also houses a large mausoleum covered with swastikas, where Chilean
Nazis are buried. Every year on September 5th, Chilean Nazis gather to
"Heil Hitler" and listen to speeches celebrating Hitler's rule and commem-
orating the massacre of Chilean Nazis in 1938.

The same issues of *Ercilla* which carried Müller's and Lindemann's
disturbing revelations about Colony life also hold interviews with distinguished Chileans who had participated in the Nazi party during the
twenties and thirties. Elderly men chuckle over the time they set off a
charge of dynamite at the Congress's door just as the president walked
through it and reminisce about what a cheerful, talented, fun bunch of
people the young Nazis were. They regret the passing of a charismatic
leader (of Chilean-German origin) who won the Nazi party thousands of
members and parliamentary representation.

Twenty years later, in 1987, Chilean Nazis held a rousing tribute to
Rudolph Hess in the General Cemetery, attended by about two hundred
people. The organizers admitted that their numbers were small, but insisted that didn't matter. Like their predecessors in the 1930s, they continue

to believe that "National socialism, fascism, [is a movement of] lucid minorities, who see themselves as vanguards of national traditions," as their spokesman, Erwin Robertson, explained.

Racism is an important part of Chilean Nazism. Miguel Serrano, the official leader of Chilean Nazis, once told an audience containing numerous admirals and generals that: "We've been made to believe that racism is something which goes against the people of South America, because they are *mestizos*. On the contrary, this is about keeping our peoples healthy and superior, through an appropriate racial policy, trying to improve rather than deteriorate the mix and particularly to protect the best, not only from the crippled, mongols and imbeciles, just as the members of the presidential guard are selected for height and presence."

"In Chile there's always been classist racism," Gaston Soublette, a Catholic University professor told a reporter in 1987, "the social differences in this country are racist: the upper class, white, and the rest, many would say, a troop of Indians. But this racism hasn't developed its own mystique and ideology in the Chilean mentality."

Not all German-Chileans are nostalgic for fascism, although the well-organized German-Chilean Colony is. A German friend who was invited to several of their social events spoke with horror of the sensation that for these people time had stopped: they sang old Nazi hymns and spoke longingly of Hitler. Independent German-Chileans and a high-ranking (and frustrated) member of the German Embassy in Santiago told me they're "cultural fossils" and out and out "fascists".

But not all ultra-conservative Chileans are of German origin. Rather, over almost two centuries of co-habitation the two tendencies have interbred, creating a strong component of often prosperous, upper-class Chileans who are convinced that they form a superior moral minority whose goals justify their means, any means, including sabotage, kidnapping, torture and murder.

For almost thirty years, this stratum of Chilean society has persistently protected Colonia Dignidad. It encouraged the Colony's close relations with ultra-right, paramilitary organizations before the 1973 military coup. And it made the Colony's contributions to the repression unleashed after the military seized power inevitable.

Gero Gemballa's book, *Colonia Dignidad,* summarizes the testimony, the evidence, the letters, the pleas, the history and the speculation that have surrounded the Colony for almost three decades. It's a brave book, given the number of unexplained deaths and survivors' lives which have become entangled in Colony lawsuits and investigations, virtually forever. In it, relatives plead with German and Chilean authorities for help in contacting their sons, parents, daughters who have disappeared into the Colony without a trace. Colony members themselves send messages to the outer world, messages which are often intercepted or, when they get through, abruptly contradicted by a standard, typewritten statement.

What is perhaps most shocking about the stories of those who survived torture and imprisonment there, the comments of lawyers who have represented Amnesty International, the Chilean and German governments and other interested parties and the experience of people like Osvaldo Muray, Hector Taricco and Kika Sanino is how stubbornly the Colony has managed not only to survive, but to attack and often destroy the lives of those who criticize it.

In a country which prides itself on its legal system and fairmindedness, Colonia Dignidad has demonstrated in times of democracy and unrest, dictatorship and violence, and now, in transition, that the Chilean legal system best protects the rights to privacy and property, rather than those of the adults and children who have been willing or unwilling guests inside its barb-wired fences.

"In Chile a charitable society could never do what the Colony has done without the complicity of the political and administrative authorities," government lawyer Jorge Ovalle freely admits.

Patricio Aylwin, Chile's first elected president after the military dictatorship, was one of the senators representing the Linares region when the first scandals exploded. He supported Taricco and, in a lengthy speech, criticized conservatives who defended the Colony. In that same speech to the Congress in 1968, he outlined the strategy which, after 1990, the Chilean government used to try and clip the Colony's wings. Tax and customs exemptions have been eliminated and Internal Revenue is going through the lengthy and difficult process of charging the Colony for tax fraud worth more than 250 million pesos; the Ministry of Labour investigated the Colony for violating Chilean labour laws; and the Ministry of Education and Ministry of Health (which continued to financially support the Colony-run hospital until 1994) also carried out investigations.

Early in 1991, President Aylwin suspended the Colony's legal status as a charity, but since its properties and other holdings are all in the names of individual Colony leaders this change would have little permanent effect.

"The government wants to dissolve Colonia Dignidad. If the commercial companies formed by the colonists wish to continue they may but according to our country's laws," said Ovalle. "I don't think the government will go beyond that."

Throughout the nineties, in true Dignidad style, the legal battles have continued. Fifteen ultra-conservative senators filed a plea of unconstitutionality with Chile's national Constitutional Tribunal to try to stop the suspension of the Colony's charitable status. When that was rejected unanimously, the fight went on in the Supreme Court and the Court of Appeals. And went on until the end of 1994, when the government's suspension was finally upheld, in spite of a hunger strike and other pressures from the Colony's supporters.

In the early nineties, frustrated officials of the German Embassy in Santiago demanded personal interviews with Colony members wishing to renew their passports and they insisted on documentation from those receiving German pensions. But what would be an administrative problem in most European countries, dealt with by social workers, psychologists and other government officials, has become an eternal, Kafkaesque legal tangle in Chile. There are few signs that anyone in either country will be able to do much for the estimated three hundred German citizens and fifty Chileans now resident there.

On a clear spring day I finished my interviews and left Linares, feeling as if a throng of ghosts had squeezed itself into the backseat of my car, their soft persistent voices murmuring in my ears, their gestures stirring the air with arguments and pleas. Looking out the window I saw fewer horses grazing the pastures south of Linares, but I passed a truck which had obviously run into one, parked and waiting for assistance. I caught a glimpse of the horse's cadaver, a huge hole in its chest where one leg had been completely ripped away: all that vitality, incessant motion, reduced to raw meat.

I thought of Wolfgang Müller who had made good his first escape from Dignidad on a horse, which he'd left tied by a gas station with a note neatly pinned to the bridle, requesting that the finder return the animal. The Colony later included horse-theft among his list of crimes.

Hector Taricco's and Kika Sanino's voices echoed around me, telling me that Wilhelmine Lindemann is long dead and buried in the Colony's private cemetery. They worry about her children sometimes, although the nun's caustic remark about the worthlessness of the Colony's members still rings in their ears — and mine. The ghosts of the zealot Paul Schäfer, of Latin America's dead Nazis, of that ordinary man Juan Müller muttered behind me too. I ticked off all the uses that have been made of the Colony since its founding — sect, resource, scam, prison camp, moral bastion, hideaway, torture school, weapons centre, model farm.

For all its faults, liberal democracy and, particularly, the separation of church and state have made it difficult for the Paul Schäfers of the world to put their vision of a moral society into practice. There just hasn't been enough consensus to support them. In Colonia Dignidad they got around this by creating a state within the state, where a minority could forcefully impose its views with at least the passive acquiescence of the group.

In spite of the efforts of some media and a handful of brave people from both Chile and Germany, Chile's liberal democracy failed to confront this aberration long before intense social conflict provided the excuse for the Chilean military to seize power.

Their failure to stop the Colony when they first learned of its vices cost Chileans dearly. For seventeen years they became the victims of an authoritarian experiment which made the whole of Chile one long, slender, tragic version of Colonia Dignidad. A minority rallied all the resources of a modern state to impose its version of reality, of morality, of economic and political correctness on a large majority of people whose voices were silenced unless they agreed with official history.

There are still many Chileans today, perhaps as many as a third, who believe this was the right thing to do, will be the right thing to do again, if they feel the pendulum of political power swinging too far out of their reach.

What happens to Colonia Dignidad under Chile's fragile, flawed democracy will be as significant to Chile's future today as it was in 1966, when Wilhelmine Lindemann's troubled eyes first appeared on Chilean newsstands, looking away from the camera, toward an abyss gaping at her feet.

Chapter four

PRONOUNCEMENTS

SANTIAGO, THE LAKE DISTRICT 1973

Pronouncement. My Webster's dictionary tells me, "A formal expression of opinion. A judgement. An authoritative statement." For those who planned it in the secretive cloisters of military institutions, September 11, 1973 was not a *coup d'état*, nor a *putsch*, (and why is it English has no word for this?). Alejandro Medina Lois, retired Army general, Black Beret, artillery commander, professor in the National Academy for Political and Strategic Studies, led his soldiers into battle on September 11, 1973 and he clearly enjoyed his moment of glory. "I was shot at many times," he tells me often during one of our two lengthy interviews at the National Academy for Political and Strategic Studies in the spring of 1992. "I'm lucky to be alive."

He arrives a few minutes late, wearing a pin-stripe suit with a tight vest visible under the jacket, a silver-stemmed pipe in one hand. He suffers from the thick, mucous-laden cough of the heavy smoker and confesses that only once did he quit smoking — for a month, while he trained as an élite commando. The son and grandson of generals in the Chilean Army, one of his own sons is now a major working his way upward. Alejandro Medina speaks of the pressures this brings: with pride.

General Medina clearly sees himself as the essence of a traditional Army officer, valuing honour, loyalty, flag and country above all. He is gentlemanly in the extreme, neatly dressed, formal and considerate, offering coffee and speaking a slightly stilted but clearly understandable English.

And he makes an effort to be gracious, urbane, even witty. When a long, earth tremor sends shocks of movement through the city and our conversation, he jokes about what a shocking interview we are having. Laughter momentarily rounds his tanned face, which is long and lean; and when he smiles boyish dimples topple the deep, vertical parentheses around his mouth. But the habitual lines of his face are straight and harsh, his boyish grin administered with parsimony.

"I come from an Army family, was born in Santiago. My father came to be a general and my grandfather also was. But on my mother's side I come from a family of law and my grandfather was a minister of the Supreme Court, so in a way I feel I have both sides of the Chilean coat of arms: By Reason or Might. And that is how many people feel and think of Chile," he tells me.

Alejandro Medina's education began in a Santiago school, run by German nuns and priests, many of whom had fought during the First World War. He chuckles remembering how he organized pro-Ally demonstrations during the Second World War, "hailing the Allies and [shouting] down with Hitler. I don't know how those German priests didn't kick me out."

In 1944, his father became military attaché in Chile's Washington Embassy and the whole family moved to the United States where he began high school "with girls sitting alongside for the first time. That gave me quite an impulse to be able to communicate". He learned English quickly. "I was in a sort of reserve officer training corps," he adds. "I won a medal for the best soldier in the regiment and was very proud."

He fell in love with a classmate and for a while couldn't decide between eloping or returning to Chile, but "I believe I was born thinking about the military." At sixteen, he returned to Chile and entered the Army's Bernardo O'Higgins Military Academy. A typical day began with a cold shower at six, followed by fitness training in the gym, a brisk run, breakfast and the daily drudgery of minor housework before classes and a lecture from the company captain.

"The Military Academy was and still is a school for a man." By the time he graduated he was in such good shape that he could "run, jump on a trampoline and make a somersault over a car and get about four metres farther," he remembers. But what he enjoyed most were the social sciences, where he got his best marks. "Our teachers were very good, civilians, dedicated people. The Army instructors were young lieutenants, although they looked very old to us!"

He moved quickly, surely through four years of military training. At eighteen, he was a full officer, in the same Artillery Regiment in Talca, near Linares, which his father once commanded.

"All the non-commissioned officers knew me as a boy, so they were very good about trying to help, but it was very difficult for me to use my authority as an officer. For instance, if I had to reprimand one of them, he might look at me, maybe with tears and say, to think that I knew you when you were a small boy ... That tied my hands."

As in Washington, in Talca he fell in love, and, like a monk of sorts, he once again renounced the love for his military career, forsaking the pleasures of life in the provinces for a regiment in Santiago, where he continued to ride, fence and study radio communications. He also read philosophy and faced a religious crisis that laid the foundations for the values he has held for most of his life. At sixty-one, he looks back on his nineteen-year-old self and his discovery that "you are just a small part of the universe, a part of something that begins with your family, followed by the institution to which you belong, the Army, which is like a larger family, and your country. My life has been dedicated to those three things that probably are in the minds of most people in Chile." But his faith, in his fellows at least, has been shaken in recent years. "I'm not sure about [the value of] country right now, because for some reason, maybe faults in education, some international views have made [people] lose their view of patriotism."

For Alejandro Medina, the Army was always a vocation, not a mere profession. To him it meant that, as with the priesthood, he would have "a very hard life with many activities that are going to exact the most from you." Although he did, eventually, marry, the Army remained his first priority. "Sometimes you will have problems, illness in the family, whatever, but you will have to do your duty first. We used to say that you get married first to the Army, then to your wife. Of course, wives don't like that very much, but that's what we try to foster in our officers. If you're going to be an Army officer, you know you're never going to be rich."

He feels he's successfully passed these values on to his family. Of his two sons, one is an Army major, "an artillery man of course, the fourth generation". His oldest son tried the Military Academy but didn't like the system and went on to become a television director. Both daughters married Army officers, who are in turn sons of Army officers. His son's wife is also a general's daughter. This kind of intense intermarrying is so typical of the Chilean Army that it has been studied by political scientists.

For the next twenty years, Alejandro Medina continued his climb up the ladder of Army hierarchy, studying in Panama, working in the northern city of Iquique, teaching at the Military Academy. There he assisted the school's deputy director, Lieutenant Colonel Augusto Pinochet, for two years, then went on to study in Oklahoma and Washington, before returning again to Santiago.

"Every year there's a very severe review of each officer's situation and if you are selected as the best you go on to higher ranks. You have to be good and not have any faults. If you are successful you advance. If not, you know you're going to have a limited career."

At the Parachutists School, outside of Santiago, he overcame bruises, aches and a fractured arm to become a Black Beret. While his family lived in the city, he juggled paper work, commando training and leaps from airplanes into the night sky. Often, he slept in his office.

With the government of Eduardo Frei in full swing in the late sixties, General Medina says, "There were a lot of things that we did not like as military men, because we felt that the government didn't have the proper attitude of authority to prevent those left extremist people who were starting to raise hell everywhere."

Officially, the Chilean armed forces don't think about politics and the Schneider doctrine (named for a former commander-in-chief) spelled out their duty to respect the constitution and the elected government of the day, no matter what. In fact, while the Chilean Army has shown considerably more restraint than their counterparts in other Latin American countries, Bolivia or Brazil for example, they've seldom fully realized this ideal.

By the early seventies, after Salvador Allende had assumed the presidency of Chile, "everything was horrible. In 1973 especially there was nothing to eat. It was horrible how the ladies had to line up to get a chicken. They created these JAP [Popular Supply Boards: see Glossary] to administer all the food and they were ruled by the Communist Party. Those who belonged to the Party and belonged to the JAP received their food; the rest, nothing. It was absolutely the worst of these Marxist-style ways of getting hold of people."

Worse still, in his view, left-wing organizations, particularly the MIR, the Left Revolutionary Movement, a party that did not support the

Allende government, were making inroads into the Armed Forces, seeking the military's support for their political projects. The pressures on
officers like Alejandro Medina began to mount, as the political stakes
rose ever higher.

"It was a very difficult time to have the Army stick together because
they were resentful about everything that was happening in the country.
As a commander of troops, [I had to convince people] that they should
not be pressured by anything, that if it became necessary to act, the
Armed Forces must act together as a body. Any separation would not be
good for the country."

Alejandro Medina always knew there was an enemy and the enemy's
name was Communism. Analyzing the phenomenon "as an academic,
you can see very clearly that [communism is] a mistaken theory, never
fulfilled." He also notes that "this trend appears in Chile even before the
Russian revolution and it was the reaction of people at that time ... to
the horrible conditions" in Chile's nitrate fields. It succeeded because
Chilean workers "had nothing to lose" and "were very uneducated".

Alejandro Medina especially values education. During our first interview he spent hours detailing his own studies, diplomas and degrees and
his work as a teacher within the Army's educational framework. He also
emphasized his non-credit course work at the University of Chile where,
during the early eighties, as General Pinochet's appointee in the University presidency, he created the Political Science Institute.

Medina speaks of General Pinochet's government as if it were a stern,
bushy-browed teacher with a deeply furrowed forehead, judging and
meting out harsh but necessary punishment to those who have failed to
live by a strict, moral code. I remember my friend Chabela's stories of
her father teaching her to read by striking her on the head every time
she made a mistake. My father-in-law routinely beat his three sons until
they left home. Neither was considered particularly cruel, in fact, both
were probably milder than others of their generation.

Education through corporal punishment was long an accepted tenet
of the Catholic Church, in fact, was one of the main principles supporting the brutality of the Holy Inquisition. It remains an accepted principle
of military education today. Small wonder then, that General Medina
should emphasize the *educational* value of the authoritarian government
which he served so loyally. With a hearty chuckle, he mentions Chile's
"Renewed Socialists" who now recognize the role of the market in the

economy, as if all that followed the military's "pronouncement" on September 11, 1973 could be justified by its educational value.

As we sat on the plush couch in the carpeted salon of the Academy, Medina grappled with English and his search for the neat, neutral words that would faithfully portray his surgical view of procedures, rather than the bloody horror they touched off, while I struggled to listen with an open mind. I realized that so intent was he on proving what an educated man he was that he'd passed over September 11, 1973 in one breath, just another non-credit course of sorts. He was well launched into 1975 before I realized we'd skipped something essential and made him go back to the day of the coup.

With the pleasure of a true professional who, after years of training, finally has the chance to put his knowledge and experience to work, he remembers how the military seized power on September 11, 1973.

"I was a commanding officer so I knew the day before. I was happy in a way because steps were being taken to change the things that were horrible for Chile and I was worried because it was a difficult decision, I didn't know how much bloodshed would happen.

"My instructions were to move my unit – battalion size, five or six hundred men – to General Pinochet's command base in Peñalolén the next day in the morning. They were very specialized, the best soldiers in the Army. I'm very proud to have been commanding them. [The night before] I had to tell my wife I had something to do the next morning. It was very special, because my father, who was alive at the time, called me on the telephone and asked me to get him some gas because he had run out. And I told him, I'm sorry Dad, I cannot do it tomorrow and he was very angry with me." He laughs merrily. "Later on, after the 11th, I was able to pass by his house and tell him, you see: this is why I couldn't get you the gas!"

That morning General Medina led his troops in the occupation of Santiago's city centre. "Our first mission was to ensure the safety of the area; later on, the problem was at the presidential palace, the Moneda. The General ordered me to land with my unit from helicopters on top of the high buildings in the city centre. But as the shooting from the Moneda was stopping the troops and injuring and killing too many, the pilots said they couldn't land.

"Finally, I came with my unit by truck along Alameda," dodging up the normally busy main street on foot, sheltering in the big steel pipes that would later line the walls of the Santiago subway. "There was a lot of shooting. In one building they had a .50-mm machine gun."

How did he feel, as he led his unit charging into battle? "I believe there are no emotional reactions for a well-trained officer. I knew I had a mission. I knew it was important. I worried that my people not get injured. And then we came to the State Bank building with its door closed."

They blew the door down ("fortunately," he laughs, "there were no complaints about the damage") and entered the bank. "There were workers, bank employees, clients who had got caught. There were babies in the nursery; there was a lot of money. It was quite a problem."

Sharpshooters defending the government fired at random across the Alameda. "Any movement and they fired, so it was not easy to round up all the people to bring them underground to be safe; then to begin cleaning up floor by floor. We captured some people, then went on to the Public Works Building. The corridors were just like the movies. Who shoots first? Them or me? Not very pleasant.

"[After that] we had to act in other parts of Santiago and give safe conduct passes to people who were caught in the city centre. And those people under suspicion were sent to places located as prisons, not prisoner camps, just places to get them together. There was a lot of shooting in many places. I believe that it was getting dark when I got back to Peñalolén and reported to General Pinochet, ready for my next mission.

"I had a lot of combat activity that day and the next. I was shot at many times. I think [the enemy] didn't have very good marksmanship training. Thank God. I was very proud that [between September 10th and November 30th] I had no combat casualties in my unit. First I believe there was a lot of protection from the Virgin del Carmen, second, because they were well-trained people, and third the commanding officers at all levels made no mistakes."

General Alejandro Medina believes the military had Santiago under complete control by the fourth or fifth day, "because the sharpshooters came out at night and shot a couple into the air. It's good to remember there were about 100,000 different types of weapons captured during the first days and months. There were many more weapons than the people in all the armed forces.

"Of course, the general control of the country was from the first day," he says. Nevertheless, the military took no chances. Once they'd dealt with Santiago's sharpshooters, they headed south.

Not all of Chile's military officers were cast in the same mould as Alejandro Medina. A small, but significant minority had supported the
Allende government, some, simply because it was the elected government and therefore they were sworn to defend it. But others, because
they were convinced that what it was doing was vital. Among them, Air
Force Captain Raúl Vergara.

Captain Vergara retired on September 12, 1973, even though he was
only thirty-one years old and, up until the day before, had looked forward to a promising career in the Chilean Air Force. As Alejandro Medina was sweeping through southern Chile from the Pacific Ocean to the
high Andean passes that connect Chile with Argentina, Raúl Vergara was
sitting blindfolded, with his hands tied behind his back in the basement
of the Air Force's new War Academy on Santiago's eastern edge. This
was on the good days.

He had grown up in a modest middle-class family, headed by his
father, a non-commissioned officer in the Chilean Army. He attended a
school run by the Salesian religious order, which placed a high value on
social awareness, justice, charity and change. For a while the priesthood
tempted him, but full adolescence and his first love closed that door. It
was then, almost by chance, that an Air Force officer visited the school
and he knew that flying was for him. At sixteen he entered the Air
Force's officer training school. He had never flown, not even in a passenger plane, but to this day his mother treasures a certificate from his
first day-care, confirming his sworn determination to become a pilot.

"My parents kept a lot of magazines from World War II and I was
fascinated by the stories of war aviation," he remembers. Of medium
height, with dark curls rolling away from a high forehead, Raúl Vergara's ready smile and exuberant voice vibrate with energy and a joy of
living roused to new heights by repeated brushes with death.

Trying to recall the values which accompanied him into the Air Force
academy he considers his traditional family and his father's rigid discipline, coupled with his own religious faith, accentuated by his school.
He wasn't particularly stirred by the flag or the fatherland, "but that's
why the armed forces recruit very young people to be officers, because
those things are taught, incorporated into military training. I remember
very well the emotion that I began to feel, the first time that I carried a

69

rifle, or had to give honours to the flag.

"Our whole education is very oriented to symbols and from the time we're small we learn the history of our homeland, which is practically a military history ... For a soldier, it's a functional necessity to create symbols of attachment which help generate an *esprit de corps* and a much deeper and more radical commitment than civilians.

"You could see this in the military parade during Independence celebrations where everybody felt like a soldier and you marched through streets overflowing with crowds vibrating with the military bands, the uniforms and so on."

For the individual soldier, says Vergara, the flag becomes the visual trigger for a reaction in the practice yard, on parade, or ultimately in battle, that helps him to "face a borderline situation, where his life is at risk, in such a way that he can still obey, feel the profound motivation that helps him to overcome his fear, hone his instinct for self-preservation and carry out the orders he receives."

While armies depend on troops and a strict chain of command, Air Force officers must cultivate independence and a capacity for quick decision-making, since they often fly alone or at most in small groups. Their subordinates are the support staff who keep their planes running and provide general services. Recent recruits to any branch suffer the typical abuses of their seniors, in a system deliberately designed to reinforce hierarchy and authority and break emotional ties with the civilian world.

"On November 23, 1960 I flew alone for the first time. It's really moving," his voice softens, "but like many things in life the emotions are stronger beforehand, because while you're flying you're completely absorbed by all it takes to control the machine. All of a sudden you look behind and see an empty cabin, where there's usually an instructor, and that gives a very special feeling."

Years later, flying combat missions in Central America, he had the same experience: excited anticipation as he prepared to fly, then stillness. "All the feeling, the fear, the tension, is conscious until the moment you set the plane in motion and the whole system starts to function. And after it's over you feel the emotion too, especially when you've faced great risks. I had some very serious accidents. Afterward, when everything calms down, it hits you, my gosh, how could that happen? I was so close to death ..." His voice fills with genuine wonder.

Air forces tend to be atypical as far as military institutions go, and within the Chilean Air Force Raúl Vergara, with his thirst for study, his openness to new ideas, his lively interest in the processes that were stirring the foundations of Chilean society during the late sixties and early seventies, became increasingly unusual. He finished high school and six more years at the Air Force Officers' School. A brilliant student, he became the first graduate to be appointed an instructor, fresh out of school. He took advanced courses in the United States, before returning to the School of Aviation in the mid-sixties.

But Vergara was avid for more. He requested permission to go on studying and entered the University of Chile's Faculty of Economics in 1968. Inspired by similar movements in Paris and the United States, Chilean students were leading their own broadly based movement for major social and curricular changes in Chile's largest university, the intellectual and cultural backbone of a country anxious for development and progress.

"In that flood of ideas, all my own frameworks soon looked too small. During the first semester of sociology I clarified the whole framework and all my values assumed an absolute harmony with what I was learning," Vergara says. "To this day I have no doubts about the values which I assumed then, consciously and rationally, all centring on social justice, not only as something of charity but also as change in the structure of our society."

Vergara became convinced that the State had a role in ensuring social justice and change. He brought his ideas back to the base, where he debated them with his peers. "Some treated me as 'that intellectual' but a lot of people discussed things in a very serious way."

He has never belonged to a political party, but the left-wing parties of the time, the Communists, the Socialists and the MIR, courted him, inviting him to meetings. "Opinions were natural then. There was discussion everywhere," he remembers. But "with their differences, they were taking away strength from their central objectives. I thought that building unity was first. One thing that couldn't be done was to take their [party divisions] into the armed forces. The parties didn't think the same way, each one wanted people on their side, which was a tremendous error."

In 1970, Salvador Allende was elected president of Chile, with the support of a coalition of left-wing political parties, the Popular Unity. The heart of Santiago's city centre is called the "Civic Neighbourhood", a central core of small plazas surrounded by long, grey ten-storey buildings filled with government offices and the bureaucrats necessary to make them run. In the middle sits the Moneda, a gracious building originally designed by Toesca in the nineteenth century to serve as the Mint.

Raúl Vergara moved to the Ministry of Defence's Direction of Instruction, in the heart of the Civic Neighbourhood. There, he watched as the Armed Forces developed anti-subversive training programs and specialized units. Worried, he began to argue "about procedures, I didn't agree with them, because I could see that ultimately the military force/might was in the Armed Forces. The civilian population had a military potential, but the great military might was in the Armed Forces and that was what had to be won over.

"I wasn't thinking about a civil war, because that would be a terrible disgrace. But the only way to avoid one was to have the might, not balanced, but tremendously unbalanced, that is, if the military power supported the social project there was no possibility for confrontation because it was a force with no counterweight."

He firmly believed that the new government should put military officers in charge of some of the interventions in enterprises, "first, because soldiers are good executives, they get things done; secondly, there was no question of their representing or favouring a particular party; thirdly, officers tend to commit themselves fully to whatever they're doing; and fourthly, they would see the process from the inside and see that the surface image of disruption was the product of important and positive changes."

This would also have brought the cloistered military world into more profound contact with civilian organizations, he says. The government eventually did appoint military officers to key positions, including posts in the Allende cabinet, but Vergara believes it left it too late. "In 1971 the government had great prestige, was growing in popularity, with fantastic economic results. By the end of 1972, 1973, it was a call to put out a fire."

Vergara worked on within the Armed Forces, trying to win them over to the process going on in Chilean society. At that time, democracy was not considered a value in itself, "it was something given, we didn't perceive it as threatened. And we had no memory of an undemocratic experience. The experience of the Ibáñez period [of authoritarian rule] was in the thirties; older generations remembered it, but the later development of our society had been marked by a growing democracy. We never perceived the danger of losing it."

By 1973, Raúl Vergara was working as adviser and second-in-command to General Alberto Bachelet, in the National Secretariat for Distribution, the central organization responsible for the JAPs, the same neighbourhood distribution centres that so enraged General Medina.

On the night of September 10, 1973, friends phoned to tell him of troops moving through city streets during the dark spring night. On September 11th, he heard the roar of the planes he so loved to fly, diving toward the city, bombing the president's stronghold in the Moneda. The next day he lunched with some fellow officers. On his way out the door, a sentry barred the way. He was under arrest.

His reaction is telling. Even a man who had spent his entire adult life within the military had no sense of the horror to come.

"I was very expectant. I had the feeling I was living through something extraordinary, interesting, novel even, exciting from the political point of view. What was happening was foreseeable and it was normal, but I was a little afraid."

While General Medina completed missions, "cleaning up" Santiago, a military force occupied the six-storey building where Raúl Vergara rented an apartment and stripped him of everything connecting him to the Air Force. Then, as a courtesy because they also took away his identification papers, they dropped him off at his parents.

By the time the curfew lifted the following Saturday, he knew that General Bachelet and many of his companions had been arrested. At peace with himself, convinced he had done nothing wrong, he awaited the inevitable, a small suitcase packed with the bare essentials at his feet. Early on September 16, 1973, they came for him too.

At first they took me to the basement of the Ministry of Defence, where they'd started an investigation of me and the other prisoners: a general, two colonels and me, a captain. They accused us of holding a meeting with Cubans in the State Bank. We were held incommunicado and taken to the Air Force regiment in Colina, where we were each put in an officer's room and interrogated again. Everything was predictable, normal, until Wednesday ... That day they take us out in the morning, with lots of guards, lots of aggression toward us. They put us on a bus. I sit down beside the General [Bachelet] and he says, "they're going to shoot us."

"No," I said. "I don't believe it."

We headed off in a bus in a line of military vehicles. Suddenly, a helicopter appeared with motor running and I thought they're going to

take us to Dawson [Island — used as a prison camp after the coup].
Because the officers had radios on all day long and we used to listen.

One by one they took us off the bus, tied us up and put us on the
helicopter. It was something new. The helicopter set out toward the east.
"Aha," I said, "the Military Academy," because I'd heard that was where
they had people they were sending to Dawson. The General was worried.
"We're going to the Military Academy," I told him, but all of a sudden
we went right past. I thought they were going to throw us out. That's
what occurred to me. Then it turned around.

"Ah," I told myself, "The Air Force hospital." Then suddenly we were
arriving at the Air Force's new War Academy. We landed. It was full of
sacks of sand, machine guns. They took the general out first and we saw
them use a rifle, with much violence. I was last.

"Look to the side and we'll kill you, so walk straight," someone tells
me. And we descend into a basement. There's a long hallway with rooms
on both sides, guards. People with blindfolds, tied up. We get to the end
and we're lined up against a wall and they call us one by one. Then they
take everything I have in my pockets, tie me up and put on a blindfold
and a hood.

The bad treatment starts. "I'm going to kill you, I'm going to send
you a bullet," and blows with their weapons and all those provocations.
A colonel has an attack and they leave him alone on the floor.

I begin to realize how serious this is, but I still feel privileged to be in
that situation.

We're left standing for two days. Then they separate us and I'm
alone. I can hear shouts in the night from people who are beaten and
then they come for me too. They hit me a couple of times. I can't breathe
because of the blindfold. And having your hands tied behind your back is
terribly painful in the shoulders. After a long time it's unbearable.

We reach a place and they push us inside and begin to hit me without asking or saying anything until they tire. When they come back — I
knew who they were, Commander Ceballos and Commander Cáceres —
these guys say there was an organization and I was the head.

Back in the Academy they let me rest and then the good guy says
"How can this be? My best student, involved in something like this. Look
what they've got you into. Everyone else has fled and you here in jail.
I'll try to help." I don't remember feeling anything then, but I made a
resolution to endure. They incorporate electricity, the parrilla and that

whole system, simulated shootings, of firing over your head, and after this the torture begins to become routine.

The most terrible moment of torture is just before it begins, when they're taking off your clothes and connecting the little cables. That part is terrifying because you know what's coming. In the midst of torture there's the physical pain and trying to build up your resistance — because a lot is to force you to admit to things that aren't real and are very grave, so it's no, no, no, no.

And they put you on the parrilla *which is a sort of bedspring, naked, tied above and below, with a sort of small pipe to protect you from the parachute cords, which are rough, but with all the coming and going it's raw flesh that's tied down, you move from the blows and the electricity that's making you jump without control.*

I don't know how many sessions. I lost count. We were in this morning, noon and night, without much notion of time. I felt so powerless: it's feeling you're an ant and if they want to they'll crush you. I was in the hands of people with a lot of hate, because they were really afraid this was a powderkeg, that we were involved in something important. And there was an extreme polarization. They felt we were traitors.

In December we passed on to the public jail. Reaching the jail was like coming home because we were out of the military's hands. We were all together, we could talk, share cells and there was relief. We could spend time in the sun.

There were twelve people in very small cells, but they were very high so like birds we piled ourselves higher and higher, building the beds. And we got organized for living in jail, we made food, cleaned up and everything.

They had told his family he'd faced a firing squad, it seemed because they had actually intended to execute him, but then they thought he had valuable information so his death was postponed. Barely a month after reaching the jail they took him back to the War Academy. The first day they hung him naked and beat him almost to death.

"In the first session, it lasted three or four hours, I almost passed out. They broke my ribs because they were hitting me with brass knuckles. They had a list of things: that I was going to occupy the school and kill all the officers, that I was going to blow up one of our bases, Group 7. When I heard these things, I thought, with this I sign my death sentence. No, no, no, no.

"But suddenly I realized that if I didn't sign I would die there and then. I felt that with each blow they were taking a part of my body. A blow to the face, everywhere, the brass knuckles in the hands of several people. I felt they were killing me and I said, all right, write it down and I'll sign anything. 'No,' they said. 'It's not like that.' They took me down and I could breathe. There was a moment when I was sitting at the table and the guy who broke my ribs — I knew him because we'd been companions at school — went to see how I was and I told him I couldn't breathe."

A doctor examined him and left a prescription of sorts: "When it hurts, remember everyone you were going to kill in the Aviation School." That was all the medical attention he received. "And they take me, stand me up and walk me back to the chapel, because that's where they tortured."

They prepare him again and the same men return to carry out their work.

"Look, he's unrecognizable."

"You're a fool who's been used."

"And you were such a good student ..."

"Now you could be Minister of the Economy in this government ..."

They started to argue and finally, instead of torturing him they spent the session arguing about his ideas on distribution, Chile's national economy, development. The next day, they threw Vergara into a truck with another man and, peering through the hood, bitter with the sweat and vomit of prisoners before him, he saw they'd returned to the public jail. "What a relief!"

Guards take his fellow out of the truck, but restrain him when he moves to leave, "You, no."

"Then I told myself, with all that I've confessed now, I've had it. And the trip continues down the highway. They're taking me to the Aviation School for the War Council [military trial], they'll condemn me and this afternoon I'll be shot.

"I felt an emotion, I don't know if it's fear, because it's controllable, that now everything's lost, I have to face all those people with dignity and figure out how I'm going to defend myself. And in jail I'd been reading Plato's dialogues, the death of Socrates, so I tried to prepare something similar."

All this raced through his mind as they passed the Aviation School and continued on to the Military Polytechnic Institute and he was handed over to the sergeant in charge who signed a receipt for him. After his guards had left, the sergeant helped him to a bathroom. Propping himself up, Raúl Vergara looked in the mirror. He saw nothing familiar. A swollen face distorted by blows, now every shade of brown, violet, green, beige.

"It all looked like a surreal painting. And I'd never been so thin, just skin and bones."

"Did you cry?" I asked.

"I don't remember. I must have cried a few times but it was from powerlessness. I just remember the sense of looking in the mirror and not seeing myself."

Once they'd fattened him up and the bruises had faded a bit, they took him back to jail.

For Mario Morales Mondaca, the events of September 11, 1973, meant little more than a change in his routine and some anxiety about his wife and family. He kept his head down, his opinions, when he had them, to himself and his career steadily on track. Of the three officers I spoke to, Morales Mondaca's approach to the "pronouncement" and what followed is probably most typical of the attitude of the majority of officers in the four branches of the armed forces, the Army, the Navy, the Air Force and the Carabineros, Chile's uniformed police force.

In 1973, Mario Morales Mondaca was a Captain in the Carabineros, assigned to the Minors Division, supervising the mostly female personnel who work with children and family-related problems.

The oldest of nine children in a *campesino* family, he grew up in the area of Molina, near the southern city of Talca, where he boarded while he was attending high school. He would have liked to have gone to university, but the family's resources made that impossible. Several of his high-school companions applied to the Carabineros. When he turned eighteen, he did too.

He did well and after four years as an officer in the coastal town of Quillota he was moved to the Carabineros' school in Santiago, where he worked as an instructor. The school had university-level courses on constitutional, civil and penal law, along with technical studies, including laboratory work and computing. Many students went on to get law degrees, but Mario Morales Mondaca was looking for something closer to his earlier ideal of engineering: he found it in the University of

Chile's Economics faculty, studying accounting at night school.

By the end of 1969, he was hired as a professor in the faculty. Later he would become its head. In 1990, his fellow professors elected him to the faculty council. In August 1992, he tells me proudly, "I've been a university professor for more than twenty-five years."

When I interviewed him, in July 1992, he had a comfortable, if rather threadbare office on the fifth floor of the Carabineros' national head-quarters in Santiago, across from the Moneda, connected to the Army's main building, looking out over "Liberation" square where General Pinochet's "liberty flame" had been burning for almost twenty years.

He wore the Carabineros' olive green wool uniform, with the full insignia of a general. His short brown hair, peppered with grey, framed a pale still fresh-looking face, with oval brown eyes and an earnest, slightly anxious expression that enhanced the youthful effect, although he was over fifty. A former aide to the head of the Carabineros, by then he was Director of Order and Security, one of the highest positions in the pyramid which organizes Chile's national police force.

It's probable that he and Raúl Vergara never met, even though they were attending the same faculty during the same period; day and evening students seldom mixed. While Raúl Vergara debated and eventually joined the process of transformation then spilling out of the universities and spreading through Chilean society, Mario Morales Mondaca quietly observed it, and was somewhat relieved that he never had to participate in the riot control squads that regularly repressed his fellow students.

"Here in Chile, those who wear uniforms, Carabineros, close ourselves into our bases, relating only to other Carabineros or, at the most, other officers in the Armed Forces. Our circle is very restricted. For me, relationships with the variety of people who go to university, academics, people with different ideas was always very important and very valuable.

"Inside the University I didn't have many problems. They asked me to develop a flexible curriculum, because at that time it was fixed. My main problem was that as a lieutenant I was the head of the groups that act on the streets and for a while I was even in the Special Forces, so I had to work in crowd control, re-establishing public order. Fortunately I was never in a situation where I had to [hit my fellow students], but I was in some situations where there were possibilities for confrontation."

He remembers the early seventies as a period when there were occasional outbreaks of violence during student mobilizations, but "it never reached the levels that it did later or now. The sole presence of the police was enough for students to withdraw. There was more respect for authority."

His eyes rerun the almost forty years of Chilean history that he's observed since entering the Carabineros in 1957. "In general, in Chile there were never really violent demonstrations, like those of other countries. The situation is never that extreme, except for the Popular Unity period when the ideologisms become extreme and there's a spiral of violence. Little by little, this generated a climate of violence that ended in crisis, a sort of civil war in 1973 that led to the military pronouncement.

"I'd say there wasn't really a war but everyone who lived through that period is conscious that Chile was on the verge of civil war."

"What were the causes?" I ask, but he's reluctant to comment further on what is essentially a political question.

"The truth is, I've never got involved in political opinions, not during the military government, not before, not after, not inside the university. I've always tried to stay within the concepts of academic dialogue and as a professional Carabinero."

On September 11, 1973, Mario Morales Mondaca left his apartment with his two sons as usual, planning to drop them off at their school on his way to work. But a police chauffeur arrived with the news that there were tanks all over Santiago. He returned his sons to the apartment, told their mother they wouldn't be going to school that day, and set out for his office in the Department of Minors.

"I reached the office, [where we were] under the command of a lieutenant-colonel. The radio news, the broadcasts of music began. We were pretty well ignored all that day and the following. We had absolutely no participation in what was happening, except that around eleven o'clock that night [September 11th] there was a women's police station nearby that was attacked and a few of the men went over afterward to provide some protection.

"Uncertainty is complicated, not knowing exactly what was going to happen. I phoned home to tell my wife not to go out. I wouldn't say I felt afraid, but I did feel a lot of uncertainty. Even though the situation in the days before was pretty conflictive, this new situation was a surprise for me. Honestly, I couldn't say I felt grief, nor happiness, nor relief. Just uncertainty and worry about my family, which I didn't see for five or six days.

"I didn't [lose any friends]. Of the people who died there were two or

three that I'd seen and an officer who'd been on a course with me."
Afterward, he continued to teach at the university, completing his masters degree in 1980. In the Carabineros, he went on to design better accounting and supply systems, and, eventually, a code of ethics.

There are a couple of lines in Tom Wayman's "Chilean Elegies", written shortly after September 11, 1973, that travelled to Chile with me and echoed in my thoughts throughout the military years. "In Chile, in Canada, the Army/ day after day is patiently training to kill./It cannot so much as make its own rifles/or run a railroad for very long. And it has no one to shoot/but its brothers ..."

Alejandro Medina says:

We came sweeping from the sea to the border in the Andes mountains and practically from the Maule River as far as Puerto Montt. Many kilometres, many days with very little sleep.

All the troops were under a special joint command. There were batallion-size units in each of the mountain passes to Argentina, from Chillán to south of Temuco, and together there were actions in the Central Valley, so everything had to be covered. I was the second-in-command. We did a lot of reconnoitring, talking with people, because in this type of thing no one has a sign saying "I am your enemy." You have to find them first. If they shoot at you, you suppose they're an enemy. We were Chileans with Chileans and that was very important, our brothers. Unless they did something stupid you must have the best treatment with them. That was part of our training as the special forces.

In a way it was not just fighting, but trying to return everything to normal in the shortest time.

We had one corporal caught stealing. We put him in a mobile jail, a trailer. He had a proper trial and went to jail. Most [of our prisoners] were processed by civilian courts, because they had a lot of dollars or weapons or whatever. So there were proper procedures.

Usually, we were with people from every service, even had police dogs to follow people, people from the Navy for the lakes, planes or helicopters for hard-to-reach places.

The main objective was to make a country which had been stopped and destroyed work again; to make it clear to people that there was an authority that could handle things, meet their needs, and that anybody who did not obey should be put into the proper courts; and also to

*ensure that nobody would have the nightmare that there were guerrillas
and armed people everywhere.*

*Chile has a very difficult geography. It's not easy to get around. But
generally speaking, I'd say we had control of everything in about twenty-
four hours and then maybe one or two weeks for special areas which
were worse.*

*It wasn't an open war, not like what's happening in Sarajevo, for
instance. That happens if the Army or the Armed Forces split. This was
the type where you're maybe patrolling in a jeep and they fire at you
from behind. Or the terrorists put a charge of dynamite in your house.
Or they sabotage the electrical supplies. It's like we had a cold war, with
no firing, but absolutely a war, between the eastern and western parts of
the world. It was a war with terrorists, economic sabotage, covert activities of the opposition, intelligence and so on.*

*I went by helicopter to look over the civic actions we had done, for
instance in Panguipulli with the students of the high school and community leaders. I was part of the psychological operation, of help to the
communities. We brought them doctors and dentists and veterinarians
and lawyers and chaplains: everything in order to understand the most
urgent problems and give them support.*

*Most places were absolutely calm, but in others, like Panguipulli
where there had been an attack on the police headquarters, they'd been
training workers as guerrillas and there were a lot of problems. There
was actually a guerrilla base. It was not easy. There were many things
about people captured or not, going to military courses and so on.*

*One small story: when I went back to Panguipulli, the kids in the
school were singing the hymn of my unit. That's a beautiful type of
music that boys and girls catch very fast. That was part of how to have
a good understanding.*

Panguipulli. In the heart of the Lake District, about a twelve-hour drive
south of Santiago. The gravel roads are lined with roses, the horizon
dwarfed by the massive, snow-capped shoulders of volcanos. I remember
the drive, winding upward on corkscrew roads through high mountain
passes, the multi-coloured cubes of beehives dotting green fields and
family-sized orchards, the occasional team of oxen or a small herd suddenly flooding the narrow roads with their brown-and-black patched
bodies. I remember bumping up the dirt road to the Liquiñe hotsprings

in 1989. We camped, waking to sun-shot mists and steaming wooden tubs, fed by fiery water streaming out of the earth.

General Medina talks about his missions in the area around Panguipulli as if the Armed Forces were involved in some sort of social work. But eighteen years later, in March 1991, a special report prepared by the commission for Truth and Reconciliation described something quite different. Upon taking office, President Patricio Aylwin had appointed the eight-person commission, headed by Raul Rettig. The commission, known as the Rettig Commission for short, was a mixed panel of respected lawyers, historians, individuals. Some had supported the military government, others had defended its victims, while others worked quietly for democracy.

For twelve months, the Commission and its staff sifted through thousands of pages of testimony, listened to witnesses, deciphered old autopsy reports and death certificates, heard military officers, deserters, and relatives of the dead and disappeared. Finally, they presented their report, a two-volume document that comes as close to representing a consensus on what really happened after the military's "pronouncement" as Chile will probably ever get.

The Rettig Commission described those who died in military operations around Liquiñe and Panguipulli as *campesinos*, farm workers who owned their own land or worked a small tract lent to them by the big landowners, the *latifundistas*. Some belonged to local parliaments, or headed high-school student councils; one was an educational director for the region. In the small southern city of Puerto Montt, people with no political involvement died for "criminal activity or vengeance". Andrés Silva, thirty-three years old, was the first man to die near Panguipulli.

"The 7th day of October, 1973, Andrés SILVA SILVA, 33 years old, logger, was executed by army personnel in the Panguipulli Forestry Complex. He was arrested in his parents' home on October 6, 1973, by a military contingent which took him to a farm in the Nilahue Sector. The next day, the same soldiers took him to his home which they searched. Later he was executed in the area called Sichahue and his lifeless body abandoned in a small wood in that place. Carabineros of Llifén prohibited his burial and the family, after two months, decided to inter [his remains] regardless, because dogs had already completely destroyed the body. ... The multiple declarations by witnesses and personal inspections and investigations included in the case currently under investigation by the visiting judge lead this Commission to form the conviction that Andrés Silva was executed by state agents who violated his right to live."

On October 9, 1973, a military patrol arrested seventeen union leaders and loggers, executing them at a large farm belonging to a civilian near the Chihuío baths. "The day after ... a witness recognized several of the victims and could see that most of the bodies had cuts on their hands, fingers, stomachs and some had had their throats cut and their testicles amputated, with no signs of bullet wounds ... About fifteen days after the execution, they were buried by soldiers in different sized graves."

(On New Year's Eve, five years later, long after the military were firmly in control, civilians arrived at the Chihuío farm and demanded to know where the graves were. "These civilians, accompanied by others, dug all night in the place of the graves, moving the remains to a place which has been impossible to determine.")

During the night of October 10, 1973, soldiers in combat gear went to the Panguipulli Forestry Complex in the Liquiñe sector and took from their homes fifteen men and a woman, aged eighteen to sixty-eight, union leaders, most of them members of the Socialist Party or the Left Revolutionary Movement's (MIR) Campesino organization. Soldiers promised the prisoners would be released once they'd made a statement.

"Testimony received by this Commission allows us to presume that the soldiers belonged to Group 3 Maquehua Helicopters of Temuco, belonging to the Air Force." Carabineros also participated. They were using a list provided by helpful civilians. After the arrests, the patrols met "at the Coñaripe crossroads, close to almost all the detention places. There, they took the road to Villarrica and, on the bridge over the Toltén River located at the city's entrance, they killed [the civilians] and threw their bodies into the waters. Two were recognized by local people, before they sank definitively into the river. The Commission formed the conviction that these sixteen people were executed with no trial, by State agents who violated their right to life and then hid their bodies, preventing a suitable burial by families."

The Commission adds that their efforts to obtain official information from the military authorities bore no fruit. The report goes on enumerating cases, the pattern of detention and disappearance repeating itself in fine print for another twenty pages.

What about the claims of war, civil war or guerrilla warfare? There were victims among the military and the Rettig Commission examined their cases too.

"These victims are remembered by the institutions which they served," the Commission reminds us. "We hope that society as a whole will remember them among the victims of a painful situation whose repetition it is our duty to avoid."

The report goes on: "An important number of the causes of these deaths are attributable to shots fired by unknowns against [military or policemen] who were carrying out orders to guard or protect public property; some died from shots fired by other [military or police] agents as the result of the commotion provoked by the climate of confrontation ... and the rest were the product of confrontations with armed civilians."

There was a genuine armed confrontation between the Carabineros and a small party of supporters of the Allende government trying to escape to Argentina. The civilians took the weapons away from several Carabineros, kidnapping them and carrying on their flight until they reached the La Mina sector in the foothills. There, a party of Carabineros and military officers stopped them. A Carabinero, thirty-two-year-old Orlando Espinoza, died in the ensuing gunbattle. "This Commission reached the conviction that the Carabinero Orlando Espinoza was a fatal victim of the situation of political violence."

Elsewhere in the region, two soldiers died of bullet wounds received during confrontations. A recruit accidentally shot and killed a detective. The remaining 128 people who died were all civilians, executed or disappeared.

"At home" again in Santiago's public jail in 1974, Raúl Vergara began what he unconsciously calls a "normal" life, "that thing about torture that had been driving me crazy began to recede, that part was over. I was still afraid, but not so much. Even so, every time they banged on our door at night, our hearts all stopped."

In March, he and about a hundred others faced a military court martial whose members, "all sensible people" guaranteed, the accused believed, that none would receive death sentences. "The lawyers had to present their arguments in writing the day before, for censorship, and during the public trial they had to read them aloud.

"I was the last to face the Court Martial. They accused me of two things: high treason, based on the concept that during the Popular Unity government all ministers, the president, etc. were all enemies of the

84

fatherland; and sedition, based on the concept that I'd tried to seduce a group of companions and organize a *coup d'état.*"

The Court Martials, called Councils of War, took fifteen days to reach their verdicts. Because the military had declared a state of war, no appeals were possible. "The judges went to the prison, with much pomp and ceremony. We gathered in the yard, entering from one side and leaving by another, so we didn't know what had happened to the other people.

"I was the last to enter. I left with a death sentence, by firing squad, on my head." He and three companions were moved to yet another chapel, in the jail, to await the court's setting a date for their firing squad. A major, international campaign, organized by human rights and concerned citizen groups and Chileans in exile, managed to stay the execution. Their sentences were commuted to thirty years and a day in prison.

In 1975, he spent a year with the common prisoners, an experience he describes, rather tightly, as "very interesting. I got out of there with a hunger strike in which the common prisoners supported me, because I had supported them, teaching them to read and write. I'd also organized a campaign to get them clothes and blankets, because many had nothing."

In 1978, his sentence was converted to exile. He tasted freedom again on a commercial airliner, flying to England. During his year there he completed a Masters degree in Economic Development at the University of Sussex. Then he went to Nicaragua, where he helped form the Sandinista's Air Force. In 1985, he returned to civilian life, working with international developmental organizations, studying and writing papers about military sociology, participating in conferences. Shy of political parties as ever, he never joined the armed resistance to Chile's military government and he's reluctant to comment on its evolution. In March 1990, he and his Nicaraguan wife returned to Chile when she was accepted for post-graduate work in environmental studies at a Chilean university. When I spoke to him in 1991, he was working as an economist in the Ministry of Planning, co-ordinating efforts by non-governmental organizations from Japan, Korea and Scandinavia.

General Medina and the rest of the Army's Corps of Generals dismissed the Commission for Truth and Reconciliation's report as one-sided as soon as it was released in March 1991. General Medina lends no credence to the Commission's conclusions about what happened in Panguipulli or anywhere else. I ask him why, if there had been a war, there were so few casualties among the Armed Forces.

"That's natural," he says, "because [to calculate properly you have to ask] what is the percentage of the military and police in the general population ... The first rate is not right. You always think how many were killed on one side, but not the other. If you go for that sort of solution [a military pronouncement], you must accept all that comes afterward. You cannot make an omelette without breaking eggs." As we speak, he grows increasingly agitated. "Now I must ask, what is your real interest about this interview?"

"Your opinion," I answer, knowing that any suggestion that his version is not the one absolute and exclusive truth is entirely unacceptable. I worry about my tape recorder, clutched near his mouth, so that I'd get the best quality sound from the built-in microphone.

"Well, I've told you my opinion." Angrily he refers to a prestigious Chilean interviewer who asked him how many people he had killed. "When you are fighting, you don't count how many people you are killing." Chile faced civil war, he repeats, "and it was necessary to take action to stop this war because millions of Chileans were at risk. Of course, to take this action, realities have to be faced. First you have to make the coup, second to have certain security."

He argues that what happened on September 11, 1973 was not a coup, but rather a "military pronouncement", because the military acted on behalf of two-thirds of the Chilean population, those disaffected with the Popular Unity's government.

"Why not wait for an election, then, if it's a democratic system?"

"Because the democratic system was in crisis and the president was lying and in conflict with the constitution, the Congress, the Supreme Court. Everyone was saying [the government] was outside the constitution. Usually a military coup is organized by a small group of military people who are just in pursuit of power, in many places it's just like a change of guard. So it's good to know that the military acted first as a shield to protect those two-thirds and then after to prevent a civil war; but second, they acted as an arbitrator trying to put all the people in the same boat."

"But they put some people right out of the boat ..."

"No. Those people were out of the boat, those who did not accept our government. They were in opposition, taking up weapons and fighting. The war was like a Cold War that didn't have any military action. And many of those actions were continued by people who left Chile, in order to obtain money from governments and other organizations.

"So what is the solution: you kill people? You put them into prisons? You send them to another country? Probably the solution at that time was not very good, because instead of putting them inside jails or concentration camps, they sent them out of the country. And that way they have a lot of propaganda against the country.

"Of course there have been many things that are not nice to remember. Probably there were faults, maybe on both sides. When they finally captured someone, they had to fight against him, and probably he's wounded or killed one of their fellows. The reaction is a very hard one. It's good to remember that many hundred of military and police were killed."

"Every government has an opposition. Are you saying that the military's opposition was only military?" I ask. Medina is becoming increasingly excited and so tense that soon he'll begin to squeeze my tape recorder so tightly that he starts to pressure the fast forward button, making the latter part of the interview oscillate between a bottomless howl and a high-pitched squeal.

"There is a war when there are 100,000 weapons collected after September 11th and when there were many types of guerrilla action. We have many, many Cuban [guerillas] who were against those who fought for freedom."

If there were so many Cubans invading Chile at the time, I ask him, "Why were there so few arrests of Cubans and so few killed?"

"Many escaped ..."

"But there were people who opposed the regime, who didn't use weapons, the doctors, lawyers, students and others arrested in 1986, for example?"

"They weren't respecting the laws and the institutions of the country, so they were put in jail. If you are in a society, that society defines the terms, the laws, the institutions that will work."

"Aren't they part of society?"

"Who?"

"The doctors, lawyers, etc."

"Of course, but they think they can go on being rebels against the system they don't like."

"But how were they to express disagreement?"

"If a government prohibits certain things, well, they should accept the punishment they will receive and that is in any country around the world."

"But most countries don't consider holding an opinion a crime."

"You just cannot divide what is your opinion and what you do. If you give an opinion, if you go to the media, that is your opinion. But not when you move to a meeting that under certain conditions is illegal, then you must accept that you're going to receive punishment."

"Don't you think society obeys the rules because society makes them?"

"At certain times, certain priorities were necessary." General Medina likes to use analogies to make his point. "It's the same when you're sick − if you want to recover your health then you cannot be free [he starts to cough] to do what you want. It's the same with a country. Chile was −"

"But you still smoke? You're coughing and you still smoke?"

"Yes! and that's my right to do it and I reject that by law somebody will forbid me to do it!"

His voice vibrates between passion and anguish, trying to convince only me? or himself as well? or an anonymous jury that will deliberate somewhere in future history? I sense that he is locked inside the carapace of his military personality like an armour or, to modernize the image, like a robot, which, once activated moves swiftly and efficiently to its inevitable conclusion: the elimination of the enemy's leaders, the neutralization of its troops, the occupation of its territory, in this case, the public space where political conflicts are battled out by contending factions.

He wants everyone to know he has done his duty − efficiently − with courage and dedication. His version is completely coherent and for many years was the only version publicly allowed. But now, many of those he expected to applaud him have turned their backs. Worse, they have condemned what he has done and another history has replaced the mathematical precision of his political sums and subtractions. He rejects that history, but no longer holds the power to suppress it.

He can't forgive then-President Patricio Aylwin for attending the funeral for Salvador Allende, held at last in 1990, seventeen years after his death. "Hypocrisy!" he shouted, when he saw what happened. "Can't people change their minds?" I asked. "Hypocrisy," he repeated and told me at length about then-senator and president of the Christian Democratic party Patricio Aylwin's support for the military's actions in 1973.

"The Christian Democrats thought we'd hand power over to them," he says, bitterly. "But if we had done that it would not have been fair to the other parties." So they declared them all "in recess", and handpicked a select group of ex-politicians, lawyers and advisers to assist the military in putting Chile back on its feet. Absurdly, I am reminded of Humpty-Dumpty. The rhyme doesn't mention how the politicians confronted his fall, but the soldiers' failure to put him back together is lucidly described.

This is not General Medina's insight, however. He recognizes no successful pressuring from outside the military government. And he certainly doesn't acknowledge any failure on the part of the military in achieving its goals. His version emphasizes that the military said they would rebuild Chile and eventually return it to a civilian government in a "protected democracy" and that's exactly what they did. "Mission accomplished!" he tells me repeatedly as he escorts me to the door. "Mission accomplished!" he nods emphatically, "just like the medals President Pinochet handed out before leaving power."

Conveniently, he skips the defeat of the military's supreme commander in the plebiscite in October 1988. For him, the seventeen years of war, of wrestling with a growing political opposition struggling for a return to civilian, democratic government, represent the treachery of Chile's "political class", the middle-class and upper-class élites which have governed Chile's destinies practically since its birth almost two centuries ago. For General Medina, the "political class" pressured and begged and manipulated the military into rescuing the country from civil war, then deserted them when the going got difficult.

A facet of the truth gleams here. But he would like it to be the whole truth, the only truth.

Chapter five

THE RICH VILLAGE

THE LAKE DISTRICT 1881, 1993

We are leaving Villarrica, literally the "rich village", at the start of a twelve-hour drive home from our cabin in Tinquilco, northward, to Santiago. I have always liked Villarrica's modest cement and clapboard buildings. They remind me of old neighbourhoods in Western Canada. The similarity is no coincidence. Although Villarrica has a stubbornly Spanish name, the town has never lost the slightly wild, abandoned flavour of a frontier town.

It is 1993. Two decades ago, Alejandro Medina swept through this region with his troops, "cleaning" it up and preparing it for the military regime to come. He was not the first to sweep through the Lake District, preparing it for a new era.

The road winds through lush fields and groves of silvery eucalyptus. Unlike the Panamerican Highway and the spiderweb of muddy country lanes branching off it, the road to Villarrica is always in excellent condition: like a discreet butler, the banked curves and smooth pavement guide the car to its destination, no questions asked, or answered.

The fluorescent colours of tourists, who promenade through Villarrica in the summer and during the ski season, muffle the earth colours of hand-dyed, handspun wools, the muted shades of frayed clothes, washed and worn under the bleaching sun, in the pouring rain, by the people who work here all year round, and the Mapuche, who sell their wares not in the stores but on the streets. Mapuche, meaning people of the earth, is

Chile's largest group of native people, at least half a million strong.

Along the lakeshore, signs announce the luxury hotels, condominium developments, motels. They offer exotic names, suggest an ancient nation, an unknown tongue: Ritué, Tatalafquén, Quintú, Millaray, Castañandú, Truyulén, Suyay, Lefun, Rucalemu, Aillarehué, Cuñifal, Calatraco, Liqalma.

That noisy throng drowns out the voices of the people whose names for birds and plants, their own beliefs, also come from Mapudungun, the Mapuche's language, literally *tongue of the earth*.

Panguipulli, the name of the region where so many died in 1973, comes from Mapudungun, meaning *the Puma's Hill*. I can find no interpretation for Coñaripe, but *Coña* is youth, warrior. *Ripe* might be from *Rihue*, place of flowing water. Did Mapuche warriors once pour like water through the high mountain pass called Coñaripe? The Carabineros who would not allow the family to bury Andrés Silva came from a town called Llifén, from *lúf*, which means burning, *wún*, meaning dawn. A *Chihuío* is *a yellow bird*.

But the native people whose language and customs have been borrowed to baptize these, the luxurious summer refuges of Chile's wealthy élite, remain elusive. We see the Mapuche selling handwoven ponchos and mantles or the products of their kitchen gardens, verdant bunches of fresh coriander, handfuls of chives thick as shoelaces, huge heads of lettuce with the slightly bitter taste of Andean frost.

It's hard to capture Villarrica, to sift through the cacophony of clichés and hear again the soft, smothered voices speaking native words, not to trumpet expensive tastes but rather to tell devastating truths. Villarrica's insistent Spanish title, haunted by Mapuche faces, whispers something essential about Chileans, who they think they are, who they want to be, the deadly choices they have made to build their nation.

On the long drive back to "civilization", through shifting landscapes and changing weather, Temuco (*Water of the Temu Tree*) is our first taste of city life. Off Avenida Alemania, an old gabled house has become Temuco's regional museum. Richly coloured squares of fabric glued to dark backgrounds tell the official story. Temuco and Villarrica are the result of what some Chilean historians chose to call the "Pacification of the Araucanía".

In the Temuco museum, a map shows lines of forts cutting their way across Mapuche territory. A drawing shows Colonel Cornelio Saavedra, perched comfortably on the edge of his chair, addressing a crowd of attentive Mapuche, who sit crosslegged on the ground. You could mistake Saavedra for a priest, initiating his followers into modern mysteries.

My guidebook offers:

Until 1881 the Mapuche territory remained a discontinuity within the country ... Just 15 years later, almost at the end of the War of the Pacific and when the railway had already reached Angol, the government decided to unify the country: the Army advanced toward the borders of the Cautín River, where it founded Temuco in 1881 ... The incorporation of Mapuche territory was carried out with extreme rapidity.

Chile's "discoverers" spent three hundred years trying to convince the discovered that civilization was worth the sacrifice. The Mapuche fought for the forests, beaches, rivers and clearings that had fed them and made them prosperous for thousands of years: the earth, inseparable from their flesh, their dignity, their passion.

The earth of man was made and
the man of earth was born.

The rebirth of the stone culture,
the strength of our Ñuke Kütralwe,
revive man's pure song, the
music held by the echoing peaks,
recreates the spirit, makes the soul,
    the body resonate.
Inheritance from our ancestors, treasure
    of the forest, of the earth wounded
    by man's hand.

Conjunto Wetchemapu, 1983

Villarrica was key to that ongoing struggle. After founding Santiago in 1541, Pedro de Valdivia continued southward, claiming the land with flag and fort. But the Mapuche would not tolerate the forts. In 1554, they burned Villarrica and drove the Spanish back toward the coast where Valdivia's former slave, Lautaro, slew him. The Spanish were forced to negotiate agreements with the Mapuche, who, at war as at peace, proved better riders and fighters than those who had brought the horse to America. The lack of a written language didn't prevent the Mapuche from successfully recording their history. On January 14, in 1870, during a meeting with yet another advancing Army, Cacique Calfunao (*Blue*) said:

How do you know that Villarrica has belonged to the Spanish?" The meeting fell silent, until a captain replied: "The history of our people says so and it is written in the archives." And the Cacique replied: "So what if it's written? Paper knows nothing, you can do what you like with it. I don't believe anything, unless you bring me a living witness ... I know what I know from traditions: my father from my grandfather, my grandfather from my great-grandfather ...

Paper can be burned, the meaning of runes lost, but the only way to destroy the Mapuche's history is through the language, the silencing of the eloquent tongues and lips, endlessly trained to re-create their music.

In *Historia del Pueblo Mapuche*, José Bengoa records a voice raised during the same late-nineteenth century round of negotiations that is pictured in the Temuco museum. A Cacique rejected Saavedra's bid for permission to rebuild Villarrica.

Look, colonel. You see that rushing river, the farflung forests, the quiet fields? They have never seen soldiers in these places. Our homes have grown old many times and we have always rebuilt them! The passing of years has rotted our boats and we have worked new ones, and they saw no soldiers: our grandparents never allowed this. How can you ask us to accept it now? No! No! Go away, Colonel, with your soldiers: humiliate us no more, trampling with them our soil.

Chilean independence in 1818 changed the Mapuche's fortunes. The Chileans wanted to forge a nation out of the loose collection of territories surrounding the Central Valley, a thick belt of Bolivia in the north, Mapuche lands in the south and, in the far south, Patagonia and Tierra del Fuego threatened by the Argentines.

For fifty years, Chileans struggled to master the endless procession of volcanoes, the dense rainforest, the rocky fjords and channels, the desert they longed to call theirs, stringing them with telegraph wires, guarding them with battleships, scoring the damp earth with the cold steel of railway lines. In 1883 they won the Pacific War. Bolivia lost access to the sea and Peru a large chunk of land. The Army modernized.

Experiences with putting native peoples in reserves in the United States, Canada and Australia, the Industrial Revolution and Europe's surplus of farm labour inspired Saavedra's proposal to break up the Mapuche's holdings. The Chileans would combine military invasion with state seizure of "empty" lands. In 1869, the Chileans began their conquest of southern Chile, technically a civil war.

From then on the plans for peace became a war of extermination which the ex-Minister Errazuriz didn't hesitate to recommend and even your excellency forgot his ... promises of safety and protection made to the Caciques.

It was vertigo that possessed the government then and it's still vertigo ... Cornelio Saavedra, no matter how you try to hide it, is one of the authors of the current war, since time and time again with no reason whatsoever, he threatened the Indians of Quilapán with war ...
The Meteor, 6 March 1869

The Mapuche seldom faced the Chileans as one united mass. They lived in extended families, consolidated through polygamous alliances, led by a father-leader known as the *Cacique* or *Lonco*. But what had been an advantage became a tragic flaw. They tried different strategies, from peaceful coexistence to open warfare.

They were brilliant, bold fighters. In 1870, an officer wrote:

Their long and abundant hair tied with scarlet or other coloured scarves; their bodies half-naked, back and chest bare; their faces illuminated with different inks, mostly blood-red; the lance held in both hands, they show an insatiable thirst for blood and with amazing courage they resist attack and offer firm resistance to the death, because although the Araucano doesn't accept or declare war except as a last resort, when it's unavoidable, he fights aggressors to defend his territory and his freedom.

One of the Mapuche's successful tactics was to send wave after wave of warriors crashing over the enemy's foot soldiers. When the Chileans changed their Minie carbines for Spencer repeating carbines in the summer of 1871, this tactic became a recipe for massacre. The Mapuche seldom used firearms, possibly for cultural reasons (metal was considered evil; wood good), possibly due to problems of supply. In March 1871, the great Cacique Santos Quilapán wrote a letter to Saavedra's second-in-command:

Friend, I have suffered much; but I am not tired and if I don't make peace I will make war, and when I have no young men and horses left I will go to the other side of the cordillera to plead for more heads to help and to return with more strength ...

Friend, treat my Caciques with great respect and don't take away their land nor their children and live with them as brothers as every decent person should ...

Quilapán died and the situation worsened. In 1880, settlers attacked a Cacique's home, raping and killing the women and their children. The naked bodies were left in a clearing, skewered on wooden stakes.

For the Spanish, Villarrica symbolized bitter defeat. For the Chileans, a challenge. For the Mapuche, Villarrica, whose ruins lay hidden under a tangle of dense rainforest in the heart of their territory, became a powerful cry for unity. By 1881, virtually all the communities, whatever their strategies had been, were tired of atrocities. *Huerquenes,* messengers, travelled from one community to the next, with knotted red cords fastened around their wrists. In each place they said:

This is our signal,
it contains the counted days,
each day one knot must be undone;
the day of the last knot
there will be gatherings everywhere.

War was a ritual, an enactment of memory, a path holding past to present. Bengoa says they knew they would lose the rebellion, but adds, "greatness is often the ability of a people for realizing impossible acts. The Mapuche knew they would lose and that most would die in their general insurrection; nevertheless, it had an undeniable historic, ritual meaning. The Mapuche's independence would die, by dying."

On November 5, 1881, the rebellion began with assaults on forts an Chilean outposts in Lumaco (*Water of the Luma Tree*), Budi (*Salt Water*), Toltén (*Lapping of Waves*), Carahue (*People's Place*), Tirúa (*Place of Recruitment*), Ñielol (*Hill of Caves*), Choll Choll (*Thistle*) and finally in Temuco, on November 10th. In spite of some successes, the Chilean Army quickly beat them back, pursuing and massacring the losers. Many Caciques faced a firing squad; others were imprisoned. General Urrutia charged through Mapuche territories founding new forts, sometimes on the smouldering ruins of Caciques' homes. He appointed Venancio Coñoepán (Son of the Lion), who had remained loyal to the Chileans, "General Cacique of the Pacification of the Araucanía".

Throughout 1882, General Urrutia prepared his expedition to Villarrica. The Army quickly smashed the area's last Cacique. On New Year's Day, 1883, the palisades went up. Sentinels stood guard to keep Villarrica, the symbolic heart of the Mapuche's earth, safe from the Mapuche themselves.

Nothing remains of the original Spanish fort, burned to the ground in 1554. The wealthy Mapuche ranches that once nestled in the volcano's lap have been reduced to small farms, huddled out of sight. But words remain – the names that conjure up local birds, beliefs, shrubs and trees, bestowing upon them healing or wounding properties, life itself.

Mapudungun, the earth's tongue, haunts the Spanish name that proclaimed the fort and the king's rule and the centuries of struggle which have continued to this day: against racism for pride, against poverty for self-determination, against silence for Mapudungun to be heard again and forever in a village whose riches are shared and where all are welcome.

Chapter six

OPERATIONS

CHILE 1973–1990

Statistics show that most of those arrested by the secret police, the CNI,
are innocent. What does this prove?
The CNI's honesty.

GENERAL HUMBERTO GORDON, CNI DIRECTOR

At first you cry, hidden away, so no one notices. Afterward, you feel sorry,
you get a knot in your throat, but you can stand it. And after that, without
really meaning to, you get used to it. Finally you don't feel anything about
what you're doing...

ANDRÉS VALENZUELA

We confuse language with thought itself, forget that language is a sort
of clothing. It may disguise, distort, protect; define, reveal. We never see
the naked thought. Perhaps we simply wouldn't recognize it, would find
it a pale, sickly creature without its magnificent robes and jewels. Words.
They made the Frente Patriótico Manuel Rodríguez either freedom fighters
or delinquents, either inspiring, or merely cruel. They made Chilean soldiers heroes or killers, saviours or cowards. They left people silent. They
forced them to speak.

It's easy to forget what the words mean, especially the most obvious
of words, those we use everyday. "Missions", so close to missionary
some of the mystique tends to rub off, giving an aura of saintly predes-

tination. General Pinochet and his advisers often compared the enemy they were battling to a cancer, arguing that you have to cut out the organ that hides the tumour to save the patient. And they called their actions against their enemies "operations", a clean word that evokes "any surgical procedure, performed with or without the aid of instruments, usually to remedy a physical ailment or defect" or "in mathematics, any process involving a change or transformation in a quantity: as the "operations" of addition, subtraction, etc."

If you don't like the words that exist you can invent new ones starting with relatively innocuous expressions. *National, Intelligence, Centre, Direction* are good foundations on which to build a new word or even a new language.

In Chile, they began with acronyms.

The first acronym was DINA. Decree Law No. 521 officially created the Dirección de Inteligencia Nacional, DINA, on June 18, 1974. Articles 9, 10 and 11 of the law were secret. They gave the governing military Junta the power to involve Army, Navy and Air Force Intelligence departments in DINA or DINA-type activities, including searches and arrests.

Army Colonel Manuel Contreras became the DINA's controversial leader. Long after the DINA, and its successor, the Central Nacional de Informaciones, CNI, had been officially disbanded, he told a journalist: "When one has been director of the DINA and the CNI, logically one leaves numerous networks of informants all over the country who used to send in periodic reports. It's logical that many of these informants keep up their habit of sending me information, which I send to the appropriate [person] in the intelligence field."

Along with the DINA there were other, often competing, organizations: the Joint Command (Comando Conjunto) an attempt at co-ordinating the different intelligence agencies that was skilfully dissected in Monica González's and Héctor Contreras's book, *Los Secretos del Comando Conjunto (The Secrets of the Joint Command)*; the SIFA (of the Air Force) which was later known as the DIFA; SICAR (Carabineros) which became the DICOMCAR; the Navy's SIN. All this on top of the Carabineros' (police) regular departments; and the detective police force, Investigaciones. Sometimes conflicts between forces led to gunbattles and sometimes this led to the rescue of prisoners.

Little by little, investigations by rare and courageous individuals — human rights lawyers, the victims' families, journalists, an occasional judge – reveal pieces of the truth about the security forces. Often, the best information comes from people on the inside who decide to quit. The search for the truth depends largely on the luck of finding an informant; the search for justice is impossible without them.

In March 1991, the Rettig Commission was forced to leave unresolved 642 cases of people who died violent deaths during the military government, thanks to the disappearance of the bodies, witnesses who vanished or died, families scattered around the world, children too young to provide sufficient information, lack of information or co-operation from arresting institutions. For the 2,279 cases it managed to resolve, informants from within police and military forces played a key role.

The first significant deserter from the regime's ranks was Juan Muñoz Alarcón. He had been a member of the Socialist Party and leader of the Central Unica de Trabajadores, Chile's national labour organization. In 1973 he quit the Socialist Party because of disagreements. He said afterward that his former comrades retaliated, burning down his house and forcing him to leave his wife. But his wife says simply he left her for another woman. After the coup in 1973, he went willingly to the National Stadium to denounce his former comrades.

"Security services put a hood over my head and took me through the different sections where the prisoners were. I recognized a lot of people. Many of them died and I'm responsible," he told church human rights workers in a confession in 1977. Throughout 1974, he combed the streets with military patrols, searching for former members of the Popular Unity parties. Juan Muñoz Alarcón's pointed finger, a nod of his head or a poker face were all it took to decide whether someone lived on unidentified, or was imprisoned, perhaps killed. He was freed on the condition he continue to co-operate and he trained for interrogation and intelligence work at the secretive German colony, Colonia Dignidad, in southern Chile. Muñoz Alarcón's wife lived in the Colony for a while, but she quickly tired of it and returned to Santiago.

When he decided to desert the DINA in 1977, Juan Muñoz Alarcón named people in the media, on university campuses, on the street, all employed as secret service agents. He described how prisoners were treated and revealed where most of Chile's disappeared were being held at that time. He also said that all prisoners received false names upon arrest, thus leaving no record of their imprisonment. Sometimes agents would travel abroad using a prisoner's identification. This provided evidence to support the government's allegations that the disappeared had merely deserted their families.

Muñoz Alarcón reported that a sophisticated radio service enabled the DINA to maintain contact with agents and foreign police services around the world. He said that half the Argentine vehicles entering Chile as tourists actually brought secret police agents who operated freely, exchanging prisoners with the DINA.

According to the family of Muñoz Alarcón's common-law wife, he had no regular job. Every night, a car would come by Muñoz Alarcón's new home in Puente Alto, a small town south of Santiago. He usually returned early the next morning. On October 22, 1977, they came for him in an Austin Mini. "I'm in danger," he told his common-law wife. The next day his lifeless body with multiple stab wounds appeared among the refuse in an empty lot in the south side of Santiago.

By November 12, 1973, Manuel Contreras had presented his plan for the DINA to the country's new military authorities and received approval. Each branch of the Armed Forces, along with the Carabineros, sent between four hundred and five hundred men to work in the DINA, which began to identify, interrogate and eliminate the regime's enemies. In 1974, virtually the entire leadership of the MIR (the Left Revolutionary Movement) disappeared, followed by the Socialist Party (1975) and the Communist Party (1976). The DINA's external department also organized the assassinations of Chileans abroad, activities which would, in fact, eventually lead to its downfall — the killing of General Carlos Prats, former Army commander-in-chief, in Argentina in September 1974; the attempted killing of Christian Democratic leader Bernardo Leighton and his wife, Anita Fresno in Italy in 1975, with the co-operation of Italian fascists; the bombing death of Orlando Letelier and an American co-worker, Ronni Moffit, in Washington in September 1976.

The Rettig Commission concluded that the DINA was "secret and above the law; its internal organization, composition, resources, personnel and actions were not only unknown to the general public but also [free of] any effective legal control." The DINA, the Commission's report emphasized, was systematically protected from the Courts, the Executive, high officers of the Armed Forces and even the Junta itself. Although it theoretically reported to the Junta, in fact it responded only to the president, General Augusto Pinochet.

The DINA, which became the CNI in 1976 and whose resources and personnel were passed on to the Army's intelligence department (DINE) in 1990, grew to be a huge bureaucracy, employing administrative, operative, medical and advisory personnel. It enjoyed government financing but also generated its own finances, often by robbing its victims of vehicles, possessions, savings.

But who were the physicians hired to wield the knife, carving up Chile's body politic even as they claimed to save it? Who were the mathematicians who decided which life could be subtracted from the gritty, busy streets of Chile's cities?

1970

Osvaldo Enrique Romo was born on Hitler's 49th birthday, April 20, 1938, son of a driver for the Paper and Cardboard Manufacturing Company and a housewife. When he was eleven, his mother died and the family divided. The aunt he was sent to live with ran into financial problems and he had to drop out of high school. At fourteen he started work in a small liquor store. At eighteen, he went into hiding because he didn't want to enter Chile's compulsory military service. He was fired from his new job in a warehouse when he was caught stealing. In the sixties, he married and had five children in quick succession. He went to work in a textile factory and later received a small house in the La Faena community, on the east side of Santiago. He joined the Socialist Party in 1967 and he split with the more radical "Usopo" faction in 1969. Critical of the Popular Unity for being "reformist", he headed land occupations and violent mobilizations against the Allende government, calling himself "Commander Raúl". He ran his neighbourhood like a king, applying his own laws, putting those who infringed them in an improvised prison.

When Allende visited the Lo Hermida community in August 1972, Romo walked at his side, reproaching him for a shoot-out between police and *pobladores* the day before.

1972

Before the 1973 coup, Michael Townley and Mariana Callejas enjoyed secret meetings, bombings, sabotage as members of Patria y Libertad (Fatherland and Freedom), a right-wing, paramilitary organization opposed to the government's reforms. Afterward, they joined the DINA and began to travel – to Mexico, the United States and Italy. Today Callejas claims she never really worked for the DINA, just accompanied her Chilean-American husband on his trips. "They put me on the pay-list in order to pay Michael a little more. His salary was pretty thin. But no one in Chile can ever get up and say I arrested or tortured anyone." Sometime in the early seventies, the DINA bought them a luxurious house in the Lo Curro neighbourhood of Santiago where she lived until her eviction in July 1995. Then it moved in with them.

The DINA established a laboratory in part of the house, where Michael Townley worked with Francisco Oyarzún to develop a lethal gas, Sarin, that produced heart attacks in its victims and was virtually undetectable. Oyarzún was a University of Chile physics professor, famous for a "BIOS" project whose goal was the "design and construction of living beings". Oyarzún eventually took a leave of absence from the university and went to the United States, where he now lives in California.

Mariana Callejas says she knew little of the Sarin or other projects. What she did notice was that little by little, Townley's commitment to the DINA began to destroy their relationship.

"When I married him, he was a good man, courteous. The perfect husband, the perfect father. Until he joined the DINA. But the Michael Townley I knew doesn't exist any more." She believes the break began during a visit from members of the Italian fascist group Vanguardia Nazionale who are accused of having aided Townley in his bid to assassinate Bernardo Leighton, a prominent Christian Democrat and his wife.

"I'm pro-Jewish and they were always very anti-semite. One night we were eating with them and suddenly one of them began to say horrible things ... I said 'Gigi, keep your comments to yourself in my presence. I don't accept them when we're at my table.' And he answered, 'But we're not at your table or in your house. This house is Michael's.'

"I thought Mike would get up, grab him by the neck and throw him out. But he didn't do anything. So I got up and said, 'All right, if this isn't my house, what am I doing here?' And I went to my room."

Later, she had similar disputes with Cubans from the United States hiding in their house. By 1975, she was trying to convince her husband to leave the DINA. "But he really liked Colonel Contreras and General Pinochet. I think at that time he would have died for him. I'd say, let's go, let's run away. He didn't want to, I don't know if out of fear or loyalty."

She spent as little time at home as she could. Her children, three from previous marriages and two with Townley, left her. He worked day and night; eventually they communicated only through his secretary. Townley was later convicted for the killings of Orlando Letelier and Ronni Moffit in Washington. She saw him for the last time in 1983, when she visited him in jail in the United States. "That's where it all ended. I felt it was my duty as his wife to be there with him. ... I saw him as an orderly man, a little frightened, sad, with a tremendous melancholy for Chile. I know he feels much more Chilean than North American and would like to live out his days here."

Townley made a deal with the American prosecutor who investigated the Letelier case and was released after ten years in jail with a new identity. For years Mariana Callejas lived in virtual isolation in the dilapidated mansion in Lo Curro. The house is the focus of several judicial investigations: of the Letelier bombing, of the DINA's relations with Italian and Cuban fascists, of the death of a former diplomat Carmelo Soria, said to have been murdered there.

"I think we're all architects of our own destiny," Mariana Callejas told an interviewer, Odette Magnet, in 1992. "I've thought about it a lot and I don't know what I could have done. Perhaps it was just bad luck that Pedro Espinoza of the DINA offered us a job just when we needed it so much. He said it was in electronics, which Michael loved. I was fascinated because in the midst of my fantasy I thought it would have something to do with espionage, but never terrorism."

1973

On September 11, 1973, Osvaldo Enrique Romo amazed his neighbours by appearing in his *población* dressed in military uniform and pointing out left-wing party members to police. In 1974 he went to work as a security guard at the Education campus of the University of Chile – a traditional hive of left-wing activity. Shortly thereafter he went to work for the DINA, becoming "the fatman Romo". "Many officers found both [Romo and his companion "the troglodyte"] repellent. Their obscene commentaries, indecent vocabularies and their almost compulsive inclination toward raping women and later verbal amusement at these acts provoked the rejection even of their boss, Miguel Krassnoff Marchenko," reporters wrote in *La Natión*.

For Andrés Valenzuela it began in the same cell-lined corridors of the Air Force War Academy where Captain Raúl Vergara was tortured by his fellow officers. Valenzuela arrived, a fresh-faced young recruit from the countryside, eager to prove himself a good soldier, nervous and insecure.

When he and his companions descended into the Academy's gloomy depths and he set eyes on prisoners for the first time, he was shocked to see women, but even more startled to find uniformed Air Force officers among the prisoners. "How should I address them?" he asked his commanding officer. "Should I call them captain?" "No! You jerk!" his officer shouted back. "They're only wearing uniforms because they have no other clothes."

At first his duties involved nothing more than sitting with his rifle on his knees, "protecting them, that is, preventing them from talking". The first cell he guarded contained an elderly woman sitting on a chair and Carol Flores, who would later become an informant.

At night the shifts were terrifying, for guards as well as prisoners. They had been warned that if an alarm sounded, all the lights would go out and spotlights would go on. The prisoners had to lie down with their hands on the back on their necks. If the officers gave the order, the guards were to fire at them. The first time the alarm sounded he was terrified, but the prisoners acted "automatically. They'd been living with this almost every day and sometimes [the alarm] was a test. That night I saw the officer on shift take a grenade, pull out the security pin and begin to walk the hallways with the grenade. He was watching everything, trying to control us, saying: 'Calm down, boys, if they want to rescue prisoners, they're up shit creek because they'll all die. I'll throw the grenade in the hallway.'" Carol Flores calmed Andrés Valenzuela, explaining that this was a daily occurrence.

After six months in the War Academy, Valenzuela was moved to "safe houses", where he watched prisoners being "punished" and participated in raids. "I never saw anyone die, but we were isolated. They didn't trust us enough – In one confrontation Coño Colina of the MIR (Left Revolutionary Movement) died. An Army officer also died, of bad luck ... I participated in that shoot-out. It was the first time ..."

Little by little, SIFA's (Air Force Intelligence) officers tested Andrés Valenzuela and his companions. He remembers the first time he saw a young woman tortured and a man completely purple from blows. Every time they selected people for the next stage, he was among them. He realized what was happening but "I had to work at something."

1974

Frozen in time, their faces still smile out of photographs, framed by hairstyles and, in the case of the men, the sideburns, beards and mous-

taches of the sixties. On July 15 1974, Irene Peñailillo watched as Osvaldo
Enrique Romo and his men invaded her home, serving themselves a cup
of coffee before carrying off her husband, José Villagra. She never saw
her husband again. That same day, Romo arrested María Cristina Olivares's
son Juan Chacón. He also disappeared. Arrested by Romo in November
1974, Evita Salvadores de Castro and her husband, surrounded by armed
men in a secret prison, traded the whereabouts of their daughter and
son-in-law to save their twenty-two-month-old granddaughter, who was
returned to them after her parents had been kidnapped. Twelve young
members of the MIR (Left Revolutionary Movement) also disappeared in
1974 after being arrested by heavily armed squads directed by the hefty
figure of Osvaldo Enrique Romo.

Among the women brutally tortured by Romo were Marcia Alejandra
Merino, Erika Hennings and Luz Arce.

Luz Arce was neither a resentful ex-member of a political party, nor
an enthused right-winger, nor a young recruit, eager to prove her mettle.
Barely a year before the coup, she had worked in the Socialist Party's
Institute of Social Studies for Latin America, followed by a job with an
internal security team called the Special Support Group (GEA). In March
1974, the DINA arrested and tortured her for almost four months. She'd
barely been out a week, before they arrested her again and took her to
Villa Grimaldi. There a fellow prisoner, who spoke constantly of his
brother who had found asylum in the Mexican Embassy, asked her advice.
Later, in the Tower of Villa Grimaldi her interrogators questioned her on
what he had told her.

"At one point, when they'd taken off the blindfold and I was hanging
naked and they'd burned my stomach, Captain Raúl Carevic said to me
'but he told you about his brother'. Yes, I said, but I hope he told you what
I answered. I heard all the time that they were going to kill him and
they talked about him as a traitor and so on. They often asked me what
he'd said about the institution and they took him away. I never saw him
again." She hung upside down for twelve days, nourished by the occasional sip of water or a piece of apple. Then they moved her to another
house, Londres 38, where she was reunited with her brother. A DINA
agent offered internal exile in exchange for a list of their comrades. Or
more torture. Death. He left them to consider, over coffee and cigarettes.

"My brother explains he thinks we should accept, that we have to
risk all to win all. My brother had been very tortured. So we agreed to

collaborate with the DINA in exchange for living, internal exile and then release. I think my brother believed it. They gave us paper and pen; we wrote up a list, in which we included leaders from the outskirts, those who'd reached asylum, companions we knew were already arrested, and party supporters."

That was just the beginning.

New Year's Eve, 1974/75

As I recall, at about nine o'clock the night of December 31, 1974, they handed out our dinner and a moment later the officer on shift (Pedro) from Investigaciones came to my room [to say] he wanted me to come to his office to discuss some prisoners. I told him I had express orders from Captain Ferrer and Major Wenderoth that all personal activity in the headquarters had to be channelled through them. Nevertheless, about 10:30 p.m. he had guards take me to his office.

... [There] he told me that it was New Year's, a day for partying and he thought we should do something special to celebrate. He had a tray with two glasses and a bottle of whisky ready. At the same time he called a guard named Samuel and told him to hand out bottles of wine or liquor among the personnel on shift.

It was a difficult experience for me since he tried to abuse me at about 3:30 in the morning. At one point, the whisky ran out and he took out a bottle of pisco [strong Chilean liquor]. I told him I didn't like it and kept encouraging him to drink more, saying I knew that good officers, "real machos" drink it all down in one swallow ...

For several hours, from the noise (bursts of machine gun fire, women shouting, guards, etc.) I thought that the staff had taken some women out of their cells. By their cries I realized some were being raped.

In the meantime, I asked permission to go to the bathroom and, upon returning and seeing he had his back to me as he served himself more pisco, I impulsively (this wasn't my intention) grabbed one of the DINA's metallic fists from the desk and hit him on the back of the head. I don't know if the blow was so harsh or he'd drunk so much liquor, but he fell and I took some handcuffs out of the desk and fastened his hands behind his back.

When I realized how serious the situation was – because if a guard entered they could have shot me – I locked the door, took the phone book and dialled a number which I later knew was part of the ministerial network. Fortunately, Captain Ferrer was in his house celebrating New

Year's and he was very surprised when I quickly explained what was happening. I told him my fears and he then passed the phone to an officer who was a friend of his, who kept talking to me until 15 or 20 minutes later, Max, Wenderoth, Moren Brito and Pedro Espinoza arrived, with military personnel, dressed in olive green, who took charge. ...

The next day, when I woke, I was taken to the offices of Colonel Espinoza, who took my declaration in detail and said all those involved would be expelled. He made some reference to the "honour of the men of the Armed Forces" and I discovered that one of the prisoners who had been raped and who had an advanced pregnancy had lost her baby ...

Later, [Pedro, the officer in charge that night] was expelled from the DINA but was accepted in glory and majesty by Investigaciones, his organization.

1975

On May 7, 1975, guards tell Luz Arce and two other women collaborators to dress up "in their best because they were going outside". She's sure they are about to be killed. Instead, Manuel Contreras personally interviews each one and they officially join the DINA. She takes courses, analyzes information captured during different operations and torture, identifies detainees. With the others, she lives in apartments confiscated from detainees. She plays an active role in the intricate relationships between officers and their former prisoners and she hears rumours of the existence of highly explosive memoirs by Manuel Contreras, written while he was "imprisoned" in the Military Hospital after the US requested his extradition in the Letelier case. She knows how interrogators took a military knife *(yatagán)* and cut Claudio Thauby's chest completely open, carving a circle with a cross in the middle. Thauby, a socialist, studied at the military academy and one of his torturers is a former classmate, Fernando Laureani. Laureani promises Thauby a traitor's death. Luz Arce never sees Thauby again. He remains among the disappeared even today.

She watches as detainees are marched through the detention centres, often to their deaths. She too is constantly threatened: "I have the impression that people are killed when they disappear from José Domingo Cañas [a secret detention centre] and their clothes are distributed or when in 1974 they take people out of Cuatro Alamos and give them names from some other part of the country ..." She hears an officer tell Wenderoth that "he'd burned the radio station La Voz de la Costa, because it was too bothersome".

As Luz Arce is being initiated into the intricate world of secret "intelligence" gathering, a DINA officer has transferred Osvaldo Enrique Romo, terrified of reprisals, to the command of a Brazilian general and he has relocated in that country. That same year, Andrés Valenzuela has become a seasoned agent. Carol Flores, the prisoner who calmed him on his early night shifts in the Air Force War Academy, is also working for Valenzuela's unit. In August 1975, he fingers Miguel Rodríguez Gallardo, a Communist Party leader whose nickname is "el Quila Leo".

Valenzuela and his colleagues labour over Rodríguez Gallardo for almost four months, but they can't break him. In a macabre sort of game, he amazes his captors with his ability to figure out where he is. First he guesses they're holding him in a hangar in Cerrillos, a small airport near Santiago.

"He was blindfolded for so long he developed a finer sense of hearing and smell than ours. He was arrested a little before the trees flowered and in "nest 20" there were trees. One day he said: 'I know where I am, on Gran Avenida; I know the siren that goes off ...' He also recognized the whistle of a nearby factory."

"So we became friends with him," says Andrés Valenzuela who doesn't know why Rodríguez Gallardo was killed. "The boss decided." But Valenzuela and his fellow guards could never forget how this man shook their hands, thanked them for the cigarettes, went knowingly to his death.

1976

Seven months later, Andrés Valenzuela will hear Guillermo Bratti, a "colleague of mine, a soldier in the Air Force" being shot, and Valenzuela will throw his body into the turbulent waters of the Maipo River near Santiago. He's known Bratti since they both did duty in the War Academy and they've worked together since. Now he's told that Bratti has betrayed their unit, has given photographs and personal details to the Communist Party and the MIR (the Left Revolutionary Movement).

"They were tried within the institution and the Director of Intelligence expelled them. Two months later, the order came out. We began to look for them to kill them." At the time, Valenzuela and seven other agents live in a house in Bellavista with prisoners, near the street where Luz Arce, in 1979, will eventually take refuge from her past, not far from the office where I work today.

At about nine o'clock one chill fall evening in May, Adolfo Palma

Ramírez comes by and Valenzuela and Ramírez head for the *firma* (company), their headquarters on Dieciocho street. There, they meet officers from the Navy and the Carabineros, all the "heads of the joint operative".

Valenzuela is surprised to see pisco on the table, even more surprised when he's ordered to take a pill. The conversation goes on until the bottle's empty and an officer tells a guard to bring the "package". He sees guards come in with Bratti, handcuffed and blindfolded.

They drive south-east, leaving Santiago behind them, and enter the Maipo canyon. Andrés Valenzuela will later describe how "they stood Bratti up in front of a rock and he insisted they take off his blindfold and loosen the handcuffs. He guessed they were going to kill him. Palma asked him how he wanted to die, if he wanted to run away. They were trying to make a game of it, macabre of course. Bratti said he wanted to die without blindfold or handcuffs. He was very whole. Palma turned to me and ordered me to take off the cuffs." As Valenzuela approached, Bratti said simply, "It's a cold night, Papudo," using Valenzuela's nickname. "'Yes,' I answered, but I was broken in spite of being drugged. I was afraid." As he reaches out to remove Bratti's blindfold and cuffs, Valenzuela thinks that they will probably throw him off the cliff after Bratti. Then he's ordered back to the cars. "I heard the burst of machine-gun fire. When I returned there was rope and he was dead."

Valenzuela binds the body with rope and rocks and Palma helps him drag it to the cliff. As he pushes it over, Valenzuela expects an extra push. His fears prove groundless. When the body is spotted floating in Santiago's San Carlo Canals, he thinks only they should have used something heavier to weigh it down, feels "sorrow, but under that rage" because of Bratti's alleged betrayal. Three years later, while visiting Palma's home, he comes upon tapes of Bratti's interrogation and learns that Bratti's "betrayal" was a plan to switch allegiance from the Joint Command to the DINA.

1977/78/79

Pressure from victims' relatives mounts and from 1976 on, the courts have tried to subpoena Luz Arce as the result of accusations made by the Vicariate of Solidarity (the Church's human rights department). Major Rolf Wenderoth uses his influence to protect her, but in 1978 relatives of the disappeared demonstrate in front of the former Congress building and her name is broadcast over the radio. She tries to resign and is relieved of her responsibilities, but they compromise on a three-year mission to Uruguay, with the promise that she can resign after that. Within a year, the operation falters. She returns to Santiago. They let her quit. That same year, Judge Servando Jordán becomes the first judge appointed to investigate the cases of the disappeared.

1980

My first funeral in Chile belongs to Eduardo Jara from Villarrica, a journalism student. I remember a flower-covered hearse, young men and women in blue jeans, wearing rough, handknit sweaters, colourful scarves around their necks, marching along seemingly endless streets, applauding softly, hushing those who start to chant defiance. We pass a white van, two or three large men in dark glasses piled into its front seats, ostentatiously watching.

I comb the newspapers for information, but their reports read like puzzles and I have yet to master the necessary skills for reading between the lines. The Spanish seems clear as day to me, but the meaning remains a cipher. Through this mist, I watch human rights lawyer Jaime Hales negotiate the delicate, complex web of legal loopholes that allow him to keep the case open in spite of total stonewalling from both the courts and police.

Eduardo Jara was kidnapped, along with his friend Cecilia Alzamora and twelve others, after a commando killed Lieutenant-Colonel Roger Vergara, head of Army Intelligence. By the time Jara was released he was so badly injured he could hardly walk. Cecilia Alzamora took off her blindfold and struggled to remove his with her teeth. Then she dragged him to a streetlight and looked at him closely for the first time in ten days. "He was barefoot," she told human rights workers, later, "with wet socks and deep wounds in both wrists, along with burns on his heels and lips, bruises on his forehead and nose." Together they staggered along dirt roads, pleading for help from passersby, knocking on doors. When she finally reached a phone, it took an ambulance half an hour to reach them. Eduardo Jara died.

1982

Tucapel Jiménez had supported the military regime. As a prominent union leader, he had defended it when international labour organizations began to adopt sanctions against Chile's military regime. But by the early eighties, he had had serious doubts and he was discussing them with his close friend Jorge Ovalle, a lawyer who counselled both the military government and the Aylwin government which followed. Ovalle put him in touch with General Gustavo Leigh, the Air Force commander-in-chief forced out of the governing Junta for opposing Pinochet.

One sunny morning, several vehicles followed his taxi as he left his apartment and headed for a key union meeting. Along the way, three taxis, a private car and a van intercepted him. Someone drove him to an isolated spot, removed the head support from the back of his seat, held a pistol to his head, fired five times. When his heart kept beating, someone took a knife and deftly and deeply sliced three times into his throat. Police found the body that same evening.

In July of the next year, an unemployed carpenter named Juan Alegría died of deep knife wounds in his wrist. He left behind him a note claiming he'd committed suicide out of remorse for killing Tucapel Jiménez during a robbery attempt. The autopsy revealed that the wounds were too deep to be self-inflicted, and now both deaths have become part of the same judicial investigation.

1983

Powerful spotlights focus on a partially burned bungalow on Fuenteovejuna Street, but a police barricade keeps passersby and a small knot of journalists at bay. The motor of a large fire engine parked in front of the house drones loudly. Liliana Martínez of Radio France and I are drilling a policeman with questions. We were having dinner at her house nearby, when we heard the news flash and rushed over.

"What happened here?"

"They cornered some terrorists; there was a shoot-out."

"What terrorists? How did they find them?"

"I can't say any more. Don't worry they'll let you in to see."

"Were they armed?"

"Yes, there's a huge arms cache inside, lots of weapons, really dangerous."

"Let us by," we insist, showing our foreign press credentials, hers Radio France International, mine *The Times* of London, and demanding our right to work.

"Not yet. But don't worry. They'll let you through. There's lots of weapons. Tell the world the truth for a change."

Foreign correspondents, less affected by the self-censorship which governs the Chilean media, use a different language from the local press.

We call the government a military regime or even a dictatorship; we refer to General Pinochet rather than His Excellency. We speak of torture, while local reporters use terms like *apremios ilegítimos* (illegitimate pressures) or omit all mention of physical abuse. We speak of the disappeared, political prisoners, alleged confrontations. Our media publish witnesses' words, even when they contradict officials. We describe the events of September 11, 1973 as a military coup, rather than a "pronouncement", or Chile's liberation day.

We aren't popular with the military authorities, who accuse us of being in league with the Communists, Moscow, the Pope, Ronald Reagan, and a world-plot to discredit the Chilean government. General Pinochet's tirades create a constant pressure that journalists translate into angry extremes, mild self-censorship, or simply extreme caution in checking every fact.

The police and the government's supporters don't like us, but its critics greet us with warmth, even cheers, co-operation and often dangerous revelations. General Pinochet has inveighed against us so often, his opponents believe we are part of their struggle for political change. Perhaps, simply by using the words that seem most accurate to us, we are. In the years to come, I will experience physical danger only in the midst of police charges against demonstrators, an attempt by the CNI, the secret police, to arrest me and during demonstrations by the General's supporters. Nevertheless, every time a regime supporter urges us to tell the truth, I take them seriously.

"How can we tell the truth, if you won't let us in?" we protest. "What happened here?"

"We told them to come out with their hands up, one came running out with a grenade and it blew up. Another set the house on fire and burned to death," he answers. And reassures us, yet again, that there are a lot of weapons in the house and we'll get to see them all.

We wait for about an hour, scanning the overly bright street looking for evidence, questioning the neighbours. When police let us through, I notice the asphalt is an unscarred pale grey. No battle has smeared it with ash or powder. Past the fire truck lies a man's body, surrounded by men in suits. Closer to us, a young woman lies face down on the asphalt, as if she was running and tripped. She wears only underpants. Security agents (yes, we used that term, although I often wondered about it) herd us along. We shuffle toward a gate, as police guide bunches of journalists through the house and yard.

When our turn comes, we step inside that gate and standing under the roof of a car-port strain to see the "huge weapons cache" which has been arranged in neat stacks for us, presumably by the police. We press forward under the intermittent flashes of photographers, resisting the police's attempts to push us along too fast. Crouching, Liliana and I manage to get a closer look. The police miss us as they guide more colleagues past. The "caches" are mostly books, a collection of weapons magazines sold at newsstands, some political tracts from the MIR. Our eyes rake the piles for arms and find a small machine-gun (are all the parts there?), a handgun. A metallic lump that looked like a gun at first glance is actually an old Brownie camera. Where are the arms?

Propelled along, we find a similar pile of books neatly arranged in the back garden. Inside the house, little remains of the roof. Walls have been ripped apart by machine-gun fire; rooms are charred. The police show us something long covered with newspapers in a corner. This, we are told, is the "terrorist" who set the place on fire. Holes riddle the rooms at the front of the house, as if it succumbed to an army of steel termites.

Back in the street, blinking under the bright lights, watching men in suits and ties mill around, we find ourselves alone near the woman's body. We edge closer, both stunned and determined. She was about our age, slim, with firm hips, a small waist, white shoulders. We find it hard to look, harder to look away. Our eyes seek answers, find only the purple shadows of bruises and bullets embedded in flesh.

The men in their formal suits approach and roll her over. We see a huge, square dent over one eye. Only a trickle of blood spots the road. The men accuse us of being morbid and tell us to look away. Again, we're pushed along.

A similar "confrontation" will leave two more dead that same night, but we won't go. The next day, we clip out the news stories quoting official sources who say the trio fired on police agents conducting "routine checks" and were chased to their safe house where there'd been a shoot out. When neighbours speak of evacuation before the shooting began, we'll get a new version. And a year later, Andrés Valenzuela will reveal that earlier that same day, secret police, CNI, agents arrested three MIR (Left Revolutionary Movement) leaders with no shots fired, then called on other security services for help.

"We were about sixty agents," Valenzuela will say. "A jeep with a

.30-mm machine gun arrived. A guy from the CNI, I understand he's a Carabineros officer, called us all together and said: 'okay, not one asshole lives, everyone dies.' There were three of them to our sixty ... They radioed the order for us to take position and then the same officer asked if the fire-base was ready. I had no idea what that meant, but it was the jeep that had been prepared by the CNI, with a machine-gun mounted on a hydraulic mechanism. Out came the machine-gun and started to fire at the house for about a minute. Afterward, by loudspeaker they shouted at them to surrender saying they were surrounded. One came out with his hands up and there was a burst of machine-gun fire. A woman answered our fire from inside the house. The house began to burn ..."

Someone inside the house activated a flare which fell among papers and began the fire. Today there's speculation that the three who died were actually accompanied by agents who had infiltrated their organization.

Across the city, on Janaqueo Street, the police repeated the operation, adding a gun to the hand of a man who died unarmed.

1984

I'm a lousy father. I seldom play with my children. I don't want my children to love me. I know that any day I'll be killed and I don't want them to suffer. That's why I'm like that at home. My children love their uncles more. When their uncles arrive, my children run to meet them, to hug them ... When I arrive, sometimes they run and I don't pay much attention. I'd rather they not love me. I'm the same with my family. I never visit my parents.

As a boy, I did well at school, was affectionate, favoured by my parents in spite of being the middle brother. I was pretty sentimental. Afterward, I lost all those values.

I was eighteen when I arrived at the Air Force War Academy. I'd never been with prisoners before. In the services there are people who entered very young —like me — and who got so involved in the violence that now they can't live without it. I think that afterward it's hard to live within the law. I always thought I was above the law ... The system made us powerful.

On August 27, 1984, a fellow agent dropped Andrés Valenzuela on a busy street corner and Valenzuela walked out of the life that had slotted him into a machine, changing him through harsh, constant use. He wanted to be a civilian again. He wanted to die. Monica Gonzalez, the journalist he confessed to, found herself in the uncomfortable position of trying to convince a man who'd murdered several of her friends to live. He escaped to France. Survived. His confession fuelled several judicial investigations, which ended families' hopes that their lost might one day come home. Officers were indicted, then released by the Supreme Court under the auspices of the Amnesty Law approved by the regime. The investigating judge, Carlos Cerda, was temporarily suspended.

Before leaving Chile, Valenzuela said, "One of the fundamental motives which brought me to the decision to speak was realizing that this system, as well as destroying the victims, destroys those who victimize them. In their personal life, it kills their feelings and turns them into beasts." His comments paraphrase the French writer Albert Camus, referring to torturers during the Algerian war for independence. If there are any laws governing human development and behaviour, this destruction of the victimizer seems to be one.

With the aid of Valenzuela's testimony, Monica González, José Manuel Parada, a human rights worker, and Manuel Guerrero, a former prisoner, worked together through the early eighties, piecing together the story of the Joint Command. But there were more operations to come. In March 1985, the Carabineros intelligence unit, which had inherited the Joint Command's files and main locale, blocked traffic and kidnapped Parada and Guerrero. Their throats cut, they bled to death during curfew hours in an otherwise empty field, along with a third man. In November 1991, a year after the military regime has officially ended, Mónica González and Héctor Contreras, a human rights lawyer, publish *Los Secretos del Comando Conjunto (The Secrets of the Joint Command)*.

In 1991, Luz Arce's declarations to the Rettig Commission are leaked to the press. She hasn't volunteered, but when they call her she goes. "I wish to say that I'm declaring before this commission ... because I believe I have a debt and it seems necessary to me to do this if it in some way contributes to repairing [the consequences of] my actions while I was collaborating with the DINA and the fact that I was a functionary of that organization," she explains. "It's also important to me to contribute to the clarification of the truth and realization of justice, in a context of reconciliation. For some years I have experienced a process of encounter with the Lord and I have felt a profound commitment to the Christian faith. Because of this, within my possibilities, I want to be faithful to the dictates of my conscience."

The Rettig Commission concluded that between 1973 and 1990, 815 people died, illegally executed or from torture, and it confirmed that 957 people disappeared after arrest. Another 508 cases presented to the Commission were outside its mandate; in 449 cases they received only a name, insufficient to carry out an investigation.

The Commission's results include only those who died; many thousands more passed through the hands of the DINA and the CNI during their "operations". They live with the effects every day, perhaps none more scarred than those whose only path out of the pain was to join their torturers, consciously trading the lives of close friends and comrades for their own.

In 1992, Investigaciones locates Osvaldo Enrique Romo where he's been hiding in Brazil. He's extradited to Chile, where he faces trial for his role in the forced disappearances of his victims. He has announced he will "co-operate" with justice. It's not clear exactly what that means.

After he was arrested by the FBI and taken to the United States, Michael Townley talked. Mariana Callejas, his wife, spoke at length and often afterward. For different reasons, Juan Muñoz Alarcón, Luz Arce and Andrés Valenzuela eventually regretted what they'd done and also spoke, their words adding faces and names to the anonymous civilians who appeared at doorways in the night, who vanished at dawn. Those who talk fill in many of the blanks in the stories of survivors. Some ghosts can be laid to rest. Many relatives continue to suffer the eternal treadmill of grief and resignation, doubt and guilt.

And there are others who worked in Chile's police services, perhaps the majority, most of them soldiers in active service, who don't regret what they did during military rule, either because they believed in what they were doing, or because they were at least convinced that they gained more than they lost. Few of these have wanted — or dared — to speak out. Eventually, there was to be one, rather spectacular, exception.

Chapter seven

MURDER AMONG
STRANGERS

VIÑA DEL MAR 1981

The murderer of strangers has probably always been among us. However much we may wish to dismiss him as a freak, an aberration, or an accident, his tastes and desires are part of the human repertoire, the human experience, and the human capability. Nor must we dismiss him and his behaviour as meaningless, for mankind is a gregarious and social species, and anything its members do has some social meaning.

Their aim ... is a kind of sustained sub-political campaign directed toward 'the timelessness of oppressions and the order of power'. But their protest is not on behalf of others, only themselves; their anguish is trivial, not profound; and they punish the innocent, not the guilty.

ELLIOTT LEYTON, *HUNTING HUMANS*

She grew up on a steady diet of stories from World War II – of the French resistance, gas chambers, the partisans. She even met Leopold Trepper, the "director" of the Red Orchestra, a network of disciplined, creative spies that worked against the Nazis in the Second World War.

Her father was an anarchist, expelled from fourth year law in the midst of a student strike. He ended up working for the railroad. "He was a very cultured man," she tells me, and "Yes, I think he was happy." He cuddled and coddled her and taught her about poverty and social justice and rights.

She studied and then taught journalism at the University of Chile at the height of the student rebellions in the late sixties, when Chilean society was bubbling with change and the rhetoric of revolution. "The alternatives were to follow Che Guevara and join the MIR, or become a com-

munist. I, too, was a 'real' revolutionary." She joined the Communist Party.

In those years, the early seventies, the best thing she ever did was an exposé of conditions in the maternity wing of a public hospital, experienced when her first daughter was born. Prostitutes who'd just aborted, women suffering miscarriages, mothers giving birth were crowded together in the same room. Auxiliary staff ruled like autocrats, beating women in labour who didn't follow orders. Episiotomies were done with rusty razor blades. Worst of all, women would do anything to keep on bleeding, so they wouldn't have to go home after the mandatory three-day stay.

After the coup, Agustín Edwards, a fervent supporter of the military, owned three of Chile's four daily newspapers; the military had taken over the four television channels and assumed direct or indirect control of numerous radio stations; newspapers controlled by political parties were shut down and their properties confiscated. From then on, it was as if the media set out to discover what can happen to a society whose media don't cover the news. Even after censorship was officially lifted, the self-censorship of the press and the censorship of the owners, who almost without exception supported the country's new authorities, managed to turn the media into a sieve pressing out all but the most irrelevant of news. And censorship wasn't really lifted: new publications required governmental permission to be set up and those already existing could be shut down, their staff imprisoned or kidnapped or simply killed.

Football and foreign news headlined coverage day after day, while news of what was happening in Chile shrank to official government news releases, printed verbatim. Editorials often dealt with events a century earlier, and were signed by writers who used pseudonyms like Personne, Sherlock Holmes, Filebo. A fistful of pages of police news, foreign news, the latest speech by the Generals, would be followed by sixty pages of football, tennis, car and horse racing, puzzles, tarots, lottery results, astrologers' predictions, a couple of comic strips and, in the cheaper tabloids, a cultural section which consisted of extensive (dis)coverage of the latest *vedettes* to hit town.

Still, reading old newspapers is perhaps the closest we ever get to travelling through time. Flipping through *Las Ultimas Noticias* from 1979 carries me back to sounds, sights, smells from my first visit: the sound of a gunbattle nearby, late one night, cars gunning their engines, brakes squealing and the crash of metal on cement; the sight of newspapers the next day, covering the kiosks on every street corner, containing nothing about bullets or car crashes, robberies or arrests; the smell of fear, more suffocating than the thick smog. The media's noisy silence rubbed nerves raw.

I slowly realized that the absence of information, commonly shared through the daily news media, is one of the most frightening things that can happen to a modern society. The constant barrage of an official version of reality which bears no resemblance to what you know makes you feel fuzzy-headed, as if your glasses are on upside down or someone has just cracked your skull and you won't recover for a long time.

In 1973 she lost her job, her house, and to avoid losing her husband, she left Chile for France. She started working in the print shop of a large municipality. They switched her to the purchasing department. She took some law courses. In three months, she headed the department. In 1978, she left her husband and France and returned to Chile. In 1979, she started work as the manager of Chile's National Builders' Association. Later she'd change jobs, become a teacher at the Chilean-North American Cultural Institute. She no longer considered herself a journalist.

On June 4, 1979, huge red headlines announce the defeat of a soccer team and the triumph of a tennis player. *Las Ultimas Noticias* (LUN), Agustín Edwards's morning tabloid, includes a guide to national entrance examinations to Chilean universities, and a story about a "mentalist" who claims to know where a missing girl is. The next day we're treated to an exclusive interview with Nicaraguan president Anastasio Somoza and on June 6th, we learn there's a state of siege —in Nicaragua. Small type mentions the "kidnapping of Rodrigo Anfruns. They're looking for two women."

Two days later, the Anfruns disappearance is big news: "FATHER'S ANGUISHED CLAMOUR: 'GIVE ME BACK MY SON, I'M WILLING TO DEAL WITH THE KIDNAPPERS'." A round-cheeked six-year-old face, fringed by straight blond hair, smiles out at the reader. "Leave him in a supermarket, a school, in the city centre," begs a subheading. "If someone's after revenge, they've got it," says another. "I appeal to the most intimate heart of these people to give my son back." "The parents of Rodrigo Anfruns live hours of anguish ..."

I am learning to read between the lines. The word "revenge" flashes like a red warning light. I read on, searching for clues and meet Rodrigo's teachers, his schoolmates, his grandparents. Rodrigo's absence sits down to breakfast with readers throughout the country, fuels lunchtime gossip and haunts the purgatory in darkness when sleep won't come. He could be our son, our nephew, our younger selves and he is lost out there where we can't comfort him. On Sunday, June 10th, the bishops plead: "FOR THE LOVE OF GOD, RETURN RODRIGO TO HIS PARENTS ..." An anonymous phone-call leads to the discovery of a shoe in his grandparents' house — one of the pair he was wearing when he disappeared from the street out front. What kind of a macabre cat-and-mouse game is this? On Thursday, there's a picture of Rodrigo at a school party, dressed in a suit and tie, dancing with a girl in a long dress. He looks vulnerable and you'd like to give him a hug, wrap your arms around him and breathe in the scent of his hair. "THE NEIGHBOURS ARE NERVOUS," a cutline tells us. So are we. The next day:

"DREADFUL OUTCOME OF RODRIGO'S KIDNAPPING: COMMOTION FOR THE KILLING OF AN INNOCENT CHILD ... EVERY CHILEAN HEART DRESSED IN MOURNING." "All we who are mothers have lost Rodrigo ..."

Thirteen pages of details follow and readers scan them like detectives, searching for death's limits, the borders of danger, so that we may prevent our loved ones from crossing them. The body was found near his grandparents' home, *covered with shrubs and earth.* Two detectives enter the family home, there's sobbing minutes later, *everything's finished.* We read *unanswered questions* and we learn that *Rodrigo Anfruns symbolizes a most excruciating case of pain and anxiety collectively shared.* We sift each page, search for instructions on how to live with horror, escape unharmed.

"Signs of cigarette burns on the boy's upper lips and on different parts of his body" head an article in which the paper brags about publishing the autopsy report "before it had even reached the hands of the civilian police". *Cigarette burns?* The autopsy reveals the child was starved and tortured, before dying. "His nails and fingertips show the purple colour of people who die from suffocation, as do his eyes, staring terribly out of their sockets ..." A macabre and telling controversy has begun.

Amidst the funeral coverage (ALL SANTIAGO WEPT, FAREWELL RODRIGO, GOD WILL GIVE RODRIGO ETERNAL SPRINGS) reporters weave a new net to hold our interest. They begin with a character sketch of sixteen-year-old mentally disturbed "PPV", accused of raping and killing Rodrigo in an outburst of uncontrollable passion. Although juvenile offenders' names may not be published, we're treated to interviews and photographs of his parents and finally a photograph of PPV himself.

The case will drag on so long we'll eventually learn his full name, Patricio Pincheira Villalobos.

But on the days following the funeral ceremonies he's still PPV, even though we catch a glimpse of his school career lurking among the "Condolences from His Excellency [Pinochet] to the Anfruns Family" and the DRAMA OF THE PARENTS OF THE YOUNG MURDERER. But it's a brief cutline under "the pathetic photograph of his parents and grandparents ... during the funeral" that echoes our unease: "*Contradictory versions have come forth about the killing.*"

Investigaciones, Chile's civilian detective police force cling to the official version, elaborating with the aid of the press. PPV and Rodrigo were playing, PPV attacked, the body was lying in a lot near his grandparents' home for the entire eight days the boy was missing. But the Carabineros, Chile's uniformed police, insist that Rodrigo was killed shortly before the body was found. The autopsy supports their version. Newspapers begin to publish Investigaciones' gruesome explanations of how the antibiotics he was taking, the type of soil the body was placed in, and the cold weather combined to prevent normal decomposition. Eventually the director and deputy of the morgue will be forced to resign. One receives anonymous death threats on his unlisted telephone, just minutes before receiving reporters.

A pall of fear settles over the country. Fear. Yes. "Dread, fright, alarm, panic, terror, trepidation, meaning painful agitation in the presence or anticipation of danger. Fear ... implies anxiety and usually loss of courage," my faithful Webster's tells me. Fear, being "an unpleasant often strong emotion caused by anticipation or awareness of danger".

Directors of schools and day-care centres issue special instructions to their workers. Parents arrive early, hover anxiously outside the gates, just in case. Whatever the reason for Rodrigo Anfruns' death and no one doubts there was a reason, it had nothing to do with the boy himself.

No one misses the headlines' silent subtext, their hidden threat. People exist who commit the worst of crimes against total strangers. They don't get caught.

All the while she "worked on other things too. In the opposition. I mean, I did my day work and at night it was a whole other thing. And I was at peace with myself. Until a new director arrived and wanted to make me head of communications."

He insisted. She lasted a month. Then came the secret police report. She was fired. There was a strike to support her. She was arrested, raped, tortured, suffered the knowledge her young daughters had been left alone. When she got out, she sent her daughters abroad for safety. And went to work on a new opposition magazine called Cauce. *But a lot had to change before* Cauce *could even be born.*

Opposition magazines appear, quietly at first, with small readerships: in 1976, a newsletter called *Apsi* starts to publish; the Vicariate of Solidarity's periodical, *Solidaridad*, comes out for the first time; in 1977, *Hoy*, published by the Christian Democrats, and *Análisis*, put out by Christian Democrats and left-wing party members and independents, appear.

Newspapers are having a hard time in the early eighties. The government still frowns on all but the official version of political news and sports do get boring. Crime, of course, is always big, and seems to have a new lease on life. *La Tercera, Las Ultimas Noticias,* Radio Cooperativa and Radio Chilena are starting to slip in the odd spot of political news, often disguised as crime coverage. The border between political and delinquent crime is often hazy. Brief articles, sometimes just an odd turn of the phrase, convey messages from a shadowy other world that floats under the surface of the government's version of reality.

Shades of George Orwell's *1984*, from 1973 onward, a permanent double vision which fosters insecurity, a clinging to impossible official versions so we don't fall out of the safe, everyday details of our lives.

"TWO UNKNOWN BODIES DISAPPEAR IN SAN CARLOS CANAL."

"VEIL OF MYSTERY AROUND KILLING OF WOMAN"; "DETECTIVE WHO KILLED WOMAN ARRESTED"; "DETECTIVE WHO KILLED SECRETARY HAS ANOTHER DEATH ON HIS SHOULDERS"; "5000 PESOS BAIL: [DETECTIVE] TURNS OVER A NEW LEAF".

"SINGER CARLOS MORAN FOUND DEAD. POLICE RECKON HE DIED OF DROWNING. THE FAMILY, DOUBTS."

"THE HANDCUFFED FUGITIVE TELLS US ALL – He says he doesn't know who or why they're trying to arrest him". (*A mysterious white pickup truck, used to transport a group of men who say they're police, has two men on tenterhooks. "When I saw I was handcuffed and they were putting me into their white truck I thought they were going to kill me and I fled. I've become a wild beast, pursued for I don't know what crime.*")

FREE BUT SCARED, WORKER WHO DISAPPEARED.

HE WENT TO WORK AT THE DAY-CARE CENTRE AND NEVER CAME HOME, "Parents search desperately for 18-year-old son who disappeared in strange circumstances."

THE DRAMA OF THE DECAPITATED MAN OF TENGLO ISLAND. (We're told the victim drowned, losing both hands and head thanks to *"heavy blows from his body hitting the rocks, due to the sea's violence ..."*)

Even members of the regime's secret police disappear: THREE YEARS AGO EX DINA OFFICER'S TRAIL LOST.

Throughout January 1981, in the small town of Viluco, a *killer couple* seduce their victims with a *briefcase full of money* and leave their lifeless, broken bodies on the railway line.

Even so, the editors aren't satisfied. "THE CRIME OF THE SUMMER HASN'T YET BEEN ESTABLISHED" and with delight the article recalls the "celebrated case of Pham Van Loc, an Indochinese, who in January of 1931 killed the French artist Charles de Witte, engraver for the Casa de Moneda, by offering him pastries poisoned with cyanide. Phan (sic) Van Loc, Chancellor of the French Embassy at the time of the crime, did this for the love his victim's wife had inspired in him." The killer then escaped police, starring in "an authentic adventure novel that impassioned" its Chilean audience. "Something like this or of this level should happen in our burning summer of 1981. We're waiting."

We don't have to wait long, in fact, "something" has already happened and will continue to sell newspapers and alarm readers for years.

While in France, she spent most of her free time visiting concentration camps. She wanted to know, had to know, why. The conclusions she came to are long and complex, but she boils them down to this: "That we all have a black and a white inside ... Every organization runs the risk of excesses, of errors. That your fanaticism and your strength prevent you from seeing that you don't have a monopoly on what's right. That they don't let you see that there are other human beings who think differently from you but are valuable, are important, have values similar to yours."

She believes her most serious error was to have yielded to that fanaticism in a given moment. Sometimes she asks herself what would have happened if the Popular Unity had triumphed over the military, instead of vice versa. She left the Communist Party in 1984.

Viña del Mar – The Sea's Vineyard, a city of green lawns and stately

avenues, whitewashed walls and even whiter mansions. Luxury condo-
miniums garnished with hanging plants look out over the metallic waves
of a burnished pewter sea or crowds of fashionable teenagers, pullulat-
ing on a background of warm sand lapped by sapphire waters. The
Casino with its Greek pillars looks more dignified than Chile's square new
congress. Coloured lights flash among the branches of the trees along a
main street lined with glass, steel and plastic cafés, ice-cream parlours
and soda fountains. A large natural reserve houses a spectacular collection of plants and trees and hosts Chile's "International" music festival
every summer. It was here that a handful of Army and Naval officers
planned the 1973 coup and it was here, in the Santa Inés Cemetery, that
Allende's widow, Hortensia Bussi, hurriedly buried her husband's
remains in a family grave which never bore his name.

Just a few minutes down the coast from Viña is Valparaíso, Chile's
most important port, the place where the poor live, the work gets done
and the Navy has its main base. Unlike Viña, Valparaíso smells of sweat
and stale urine, and its downtown of curving, narrow streets harbours a
dangerous strip of bars and whorehouses which have delighted sailors
from around the world almost since the city's founding in 1535. But
Valparaíso possesses a beauty as delicate and fleeting as winter sunshine.
Its elevators soar through the rocky foothills of Chile's coastal mountains, cable cars pull people home from work, staircases wind mysteriously upward through old adobe and clapboard houses, as enticing as an
Escher painting.

Viña is Chile's favourite showcase, the tanned, smiling face the country likes to show the world. But it was in elegant, airbrushed Viña that
Chile's most famous psychopath preyed on couples making love on
shadowy cliffs, under bridges, in lonely woods.

On August 5, 1980, he attacked Enrique Gajardo and an unknown
woman, while they were parked in his Austin mini, killing Gajardo with
a .38-mm revolver.

On November 11th or 12th (there are two versions), two killers shot
Dr. Alfredo Sánchez Muñoz. One dragged him from the car and propped
him bleeding against a tree, while the other raped his fiancée, Luisa
Bohle, a nurse. Her evidence established that the killers were at least two
men, working together. Afterward, she staggered through the bushes until
she found help and both were rushed to hospital, where Dr. Muñoz died.

On February 28, 1981 the killers attacked and killed Fernando Lagunas, owner of a small trucking company, and Delia González, a prostitute. Police believe she died because she recognized one of the killers.

Three months later, on May 26th, they shot Luis Morales and stole his taxi. That same night, Jorge Inostroza Martínez, a bricklayer, died from bullet wounds while his companion, Margarita Santibáñez, a secretary, was raped in the presence of her small daughter in the backseat of their car.

On July 28th, the killers flagged down another taxi and ordered the driver to stop in a lonely underpass. There they shot him in the back, throwing his body into a ravine. Upon returning along the same road, they found him staggering along the road, seeking help. They killed him and threw his body over the same cliff. Hours later, they attacked and killed Oscar Noguera Palacios, a bank employee, raping his companion, Ana María Riveros, a teacher.

On November 1, 1981, two young people were the last of the psychopaths' official victims: Jaime Ventura and Roxana Venegas were found dead under the Capuchinos bridge in the heart of Viña del Mar. The photograph of their lifeless bodies, face down in the sand, papered newsstands the next day.

Mass hysteria is of course unleashed, flogged by media desperate for headlines that will increase sales. Frightened couples spot suspects on Santiago's Santa Lucía Hill, outside schools, even under water. "Apprentices" are captured throughout the region surrounding Viña as well as in Santiago. Editorialists preach warnings at illicit couples; police officers recommend motels; cartoonists sketch lurid scenes of perverts preying on loving twosomes.

Newspapers theorize, analyze, dramatize. One publishes a special clip-out form consisting of two eyes over a caption: "Hunt down the Mirón [watcher] before he hunts you down," followed by a space for the reader's name, address and information about the Mirón. At the bottom of the form: "Only 68 days until he kills again!"

Maps, funeral photographs, the testimony of survivors. Many readers believe the crimes are politically motivated. Reports that one of the killers told bank employee Oscar Noguera Palacios that he was being shot for being a "sapo" (spy) reinforce the political theorizing. Rumours that Jaime Ventura and Roxana Venegas were killed while painting anti-regime slogans abound. The government appoints special investigators who travel from Santiago. As with the Anfruns case, Carabineros and Investigaciones compete.

Luis Eugenio Gubler Díaz is a successful businessman in Viña del Mar. He's married to Mariana Herrera Echegoyen, in turn, the daughter of a naval captain and a former mayor. His father, a very important man in Chile, enjoys a close friendship with General Augusto Pinochet. Nevertheless, on March 3, 1982, the Director of Investigaciones announces that the "psychopath" is Luis Eugenio Gubler Díaz. The head- lines crow. But days later they do a shameless double take. Some even have the nerve to pretend they knew it all along. The Carabineros' élite investigating squad, OS-7, presents two, low-ranking police officers to the courts as the "confessed authors of the ten killings". Jorge Sagredo and Carlos Topp Collins are detained and indicted. Gubler goes free. The president of the Chilean Supreme Court appears on all TV channels and radio stations to apologize to the Gubler family — and blames the press for Gubler's ordeal. Heads roll.

The two cases are never combined, the three accused are never brought together. Gubler heads back into private life and relative anonymity. The two Carabineros — officially ex-Carabineros now — are tried and sentenced. On January 26, 1985, they face a firing squad.

The avalanche of words spent on covering the case is nothing com- pared to what the rumour mill does with it. Within days of the arrests "everyone knows" that the killers are part of a freelance death squad, formed before the coup and officially sanctioned afterward; that a gang of sons of wealthy families with unusual sexual tastes is involved; that the government's highest authorities have been blackmailed to ensure Gubler's release; that the Carabineros, Sagredo and Topp, followed the orders of someone more intelligent and powerful than they.

The advantage of travelling backward through time is when doubts assail you, you can leap ahead to the answers page, if you happen to know one. On my own answers page is white-haired Monica González, forty- three years old, tall, with shocking blue eyes. Husky voiced and decisive, she seems to have lived by Virgil's maxim, *Let us die even as we rush into battle, the only safe course for the defeated is to expect no safety.*

When a friend managed to convince her that she really was a jour- nalist, she went to work on the magazine *Cauce,* an opposition weekly that started to publish in 1984. She broke the story of General Pinochet's new luxury mansion in the exclusive Lo Curro neighbourhood of Santiago;

of his well-appointed country house in Maipo Canyon; of the dubious business interests of his daughter Lucía and son-in-law, Julio Ponce Lerou. And then, in August 1984, just before a State of Siege silenced opposition magazines for months, a strange man appeared in *Cauce*'s reception area, insisting he wanted to see Monica González. The secretary nervously waved at her to leave the room, but she turned to face him. "I'm the person you're looking for. What do you want?"

The names of detainees and murder victims that Andrés Valenzuela recalled that day were not unknown to me, she writes in her book, The Secrets of the Joint Command. *Theirs were the faces; voices and laughter of those with whom I'd shared the beautiful days of youth. Suddenly those faces and those voices flooded my retina and my ears. I tried to concentrate on his story, on the questions which would indicate whether it was true, but I couldn't take my eyes off his hands: large, slender. I stared at his fingers, while a cold voice told the story step by step of the kidnapping, torture and killing of José Weibel. The fingers sped up their incessant, violent motion and suddenly I found myself shouting: "How could you do it? Tell! How?" For several seconds, the only sound was my crying.*

The man was one of the first and most important of the regime's deserters. She took his testimony, persuaded him not to commit suicide, and, when the regime shut down opposition periodicals, she published the interview abroad. Contraband copies stubbornly found their way to Santiago, bringing painful relief to the relatives of the disappeared whose cases it clarified, providing hard evidence of the crimes of the regime's secret services to anyone interested.

Monica González disposes of years of tabloid purple prose with one breath, confirming that the Anfruns case was political. She takes a long drag on her cigarette, then says, "The boy's grandfather, a retired Army colonel, had discovered the DINA/CNI's intervention in the post office and the existence of a criminal network that was stealing money. He decided to put an end to it. [The kidnapping] was their revenge."

Digging, trying to find what my friend Dr. Juan Manuel Pérez, a psychiatrist who worked for many years with the regime's victims, calls "that little sore in your mouth, the one you keep trying to touch with your tongue, as if by touching it you can somehow limit this dreadful, painful thing. It begins here, it ends there." He forms a small box with his hands. "That leaves you with all this space," a broad sweep of his arms through the air between us, "that's free of the horror."

But there was no limit, no end to the contradictory, significant, revealing details. The story was enough to drive a nation of between-the-lines-readers insane, a pack of lies painstakingly built into a delicate castle of air, ruthlessly shielded by the Chilean courts.

Who is the "principal suspect" or LGD, as the newspapers coyly label Gubler, once the courts have seen fit to release him? A psychiatrist speculates that "this may be an individual who suffers from sexual frustration and through rape satisfies his desires." Or he may be a schizophrenic suffering from "destruction of his personality". Others agree that "it's very easy for this type of subject to go unnoticed in society." Photographs reveal a balding, brown-haired businessman, whose slightly bulging eyes stare intensely at the camera over an indeterminate chin.

Friends say that Gubler has a "strange personality ... aggressive, violent and boastful". Some found him "tranquil, normal" but others say when he was small he killed cats for pleasure, that "we always called him the madman, because he had strange ideas. One night he beat up a 'gay' for staring at him. Another time he destroyed the window of a friend who was setting up a delicatessen shop, 'because it was vulgar'." "These nuts formed a sort of youth patrol some years ago. They went around scaring couples in Sausalito, Concon, Las Salinas. At night. But they did it for fun." "It's true. It was an exclusive group who collected porn movies and spent time in a friend's apartment in Reñaca [an exclusive beach resort]. —With women? —No, not that I remember. Just *pisco*, whisky and smokes."

In the case of the psychopaths, there is no answers page, even today, a decade later as I write this. There is, however, a former police commissioner, Nelson Lillo, the man who hand-picked a team of men to investigate, the man who went through every .38-calibre weapon in the region, until he found the one he was looking for. Thirty-eights are used primarily by the Chilean police, members of the Armed Forces and a few civilians. Luis Gubler, wealthy, confident, well-connected, personally presented his gun for the review. But when investigators found it strikingly similar to the weapon used in four of the murders and asked Gubler to return it for more tests, he refused. By a stroke of luck, they searched his car and were able to seize it.

A decade later, Lillo told José Cayuela, a journalist, that he'd "never seen a case like Viña del Mar. There was no reason the victims should die and the author didn't particularly want to kill them ... It was by chance, anyone could die. ... it was a spectacular case, a case of incomparable psychopathy."

For Nelson Lillo there were fifteen killings committed by the same group, not ten, because "in all of them bullets appear that were shot from the same weapon used in Viña del Mar."

Death squadrons, "sinister, with different strange affinities, not very normal, not very common", existed in the area, but for him the crimes were a "product of a psychopathy and had nothing to do with their homes or their social relations. The victims weren't chosen for any particular condition nor their political connections. ... [The killers] considered themselves superior to the rest and the system. As they themselves demonstrate they were part of a police organization and proceeded with a sense of absolute impunity. The one who for me — not the courts — was the main author, was so sure of himself that he personally offered the murder weapon to Investigaciones for checking."

Lillo tried to explore the psychopaths' thoughts: "We reckoned that the intention of the crimes was to divide the couple. In every one of the cases there were couples in communion, in an attitude of love and the murderers wanted to separate them. Because in their own lives the authors didn't achieve this satisfaction, of being loved. And they had such envy that they wanted to finish off the couple. To do this it wasn't enough to dissolve the connection; rather, they killed the man, eliminating one of the players and leaving the woman alive. That was their main purpose, to eliminate the loving relationship. The other was to dispose of people at will.

"The method consisted of lighting up the scenario with headlights and wherever the light fell, that was the couple that would be the victim. It didn't matter who they were. The two Carabineros went in and proceeded.

"I think that the subject that I handed over as the main author participated in all the crimes in the same way: pointing out the victims. And the Carabineros proceeded, not so much as mercenaries, for money, but rather because they were submitted to another's will; they let themselves be managed. They were used to this, the same as others are used to giving orders."

His interrogation of Gubler was "the longest of my life. He's a capable man, dangerously intelligent."

Investigaciones' official report to the courts reveals the fruit of Nelson Lillo's eighteen-hour conversation with Luis Eugenio Gubler Díaz.

"After we explained to him the system for tracing bullets [Gubler] admitted having committed the crime in which Lagunas Alfaro and Delia González Apablaza were killed. ... on that day, he left his house at night and headed for the Marga Marga estuary and then had a mental blackout.

"He then remembers being in his house where he realized that the revolver he was carrying had been fired, exhausting the ammunition, for which he hugged his wife and began to cry.

"From then on his wife, Mariana Herrera, began to suspect that he was the author of the crimes under investigation. He added that he remembered having entered the Chapel of the French Fathers' School ... a block from [where the killings took place]. There he'd spoken with a priest by name of Pelaya, thin, bald, elderly, who had recommended that he calm down. Then he only remembers having been in the chapel, having broken something, cutting one hand, leaving for his house where he found himself crying at his desk. There he also realized that his Diamondback long .38 revolver had been fired, was dirty and smelled of gunsmoke.

"Upon being asked who the co-author who'd participated with him in the homicides was, he answered it was his friend Guillermo Morales Anabalón, Customs Agent, whom he'd known from infancy.

"He said he thought he was the author of the rest of the killings, but doesn't remember, because he has memory blackouts.

"He then retracted what he'd said and denied having committed any crime."

Detectives retraced his steps that night and discovered that someone had entered the chapel in question, broken a window and taken a priest's ornamental robe, which later appeared on a busy street. Bloodstains on that robe matched Gubler's blood type and he had a scar on his right hand. The priest Gubler mentioned hadn't been to that chapel in years and hadn't seen Gubler since he presided over his marriage with Mariana Herrera. Detectives also searched Gubler's home where they found a clippings file and notebook, with details on the crimes that only the author could know. Witnesses recognized a leather jacket and glove taken from another of Gubler's houses.

The Carabineros' official report contains details of the killings from police officer Jorge Sagredo's confessions. Although Sagredo contradicts himself often, the basic facts coincide with those known about the murders. For the first killing, Sagredo said he and Topp Collins took a bus and then walked to where Enrique Gajardo and his friend had parked. For the second, they met under the palm trees in Viña's central square and then walked up to the Sausalito Lagoon where they killed Dr. Alfredo Sánchez Muñoz and raped Luisa Bohle. Sagredo said he alone killed Fernando Lagunas and Delia González. Together they killed again in May and July. And he said he was alone when he attacked and killed Roxana Venegas and Jaime Ventura in November. But he later claimed he hadn't participated in either the Lagunas or the November murders. And witnesses said after Ventura and Venegas were killed they saw two men run along the railway and drive off in a jeep.

A second investigating unit within the Carabineros actually confirmed Sagredo's alibi, that he was sleeping off a drunk the night of the last killings. The officer in charge was forced to resign.

The investigating judge never resolved these contradictions: he simply accepted Sagredo and Topp and their confessions.

In October 1984, *Cauce*'s cover announced in inch-high orange letters: "TOPP COLLINS IS INNOCENT, Sagredo is guilty, but only of part of the conspiracy ..." The *victims'* lawyers were campaigning to save Sagredo and Topp from execution. If they died, the lawyers argued, the truth might never be known.

Inside, Sagredo spoke of six psychopaths: two Carabineros, Gubler and three others of high social standing. He said that he had been promised that if he declared himself crazy he'd be free (and rich) within six months. Three months later, he and Topp faced the firing squad together.

There were other crimes around the same time: a union leader, Tucapel Jiménez, was shot and knifed to death in February 1982, just weeks before the psychopaths were arrested in 1985, Carabineros kidnapped three professionals whose bloodless bodies appeared in an empty field near Santiago; a young woman from a wealthy family was raped and killed and a wealthy young businessman was accused, but later released.

The battle of the versions continued between the Carabineros, Investigaciones and the secret police. Often the results were straightforward cover-ups, sometimes involving strategies which would make any future clarification virtually impossible (for example, the fake suicides of key witnesses who were then blamed for the crime in question, thus disposing of two problems with one ruse). But sometimes, one or the other service would lay the foundation for investigations that were reopened after the military handed over power to elected authorities. Sometimes, they led to real "solutions", opening doors once barred shut against those few judges willing to attempt justice. In 1992, investigations of the Letelier, Prats, Leighton and other crimes engulfed some of the regime's most dedicated servants in cases that threatened to reach judgement and sentencing. The regime's parliamentary supporters proposed to subordinate Investigaciones to the Carabineros. The proposal failed, but the government's attempt to take the Carabineros out of the Armed Forces was also defeated.

The existence of two police forces with overlapping duties led to contradictory versions even before the military coup in 1973, but the militarization of the Carabineros and the government's manipulation of both forces after the coup exacerbated their differences dangerously.

"What [the government] did was to rely on one service's consent and complicity, while the other investigated. And whichever wasn't being used would discover the truth, but charges were never followed through, because there was no justice," says Monica González. "And because the policy of state terrorism was to use them to compromise each other."

Corruption had been minimal among Chilean police officers before the coup, but afterward it began to affect their ability even in apparently straightforward criminal investigations. "The politicization and the instrumentalization of these services worsens with the arrival of people who aren't appropriate for this work but come in solely because of their loyalty and a capacity for brutality which is useful to the regime. This corruption spread to other groups.

"Because obviously, if you work hard, for a low salary, and you see people beside you who work little and earn a lot more, in the end they corrupt you," says González.

"The years pass and they arrest, torture and kill in impunity. The press doesn't talk, judges don't investigate, there are secret prisons and everyone knows. They themselves have worked in them and there isn't a single judge who dares to enter one. Impunity becomes the norm.

"This man who is at the very bottom feels a power that he's never had and will probably never have again and that is a very special drug, because there's no vice more dangerous than power. And a moment comes when the repression drops and he's moved back to ordinary criminal work. And he needs emotion. And he no longer fears recognition. He runs into someone else, they join together and decide to do some 'work' that will bring them – emotions.

"These are people from poor families who've always been at the bottom, who've received humiliation, blows, hard work, low pay. And the Carabineros is without doubt the part of the Armed Forces with the worst inferiority complex. They've always been the poor, foolish brothers."

"Psychopaths," Dr. Juan Manuel Pérez, my psychiatrist friend tells me, "are people who don't follow the norm, who are always against everything, are incapable of generating long-term close relations with other people. They can't stand anxiety. It breaks them up. They can't stand to postpone their desires. They're explosive in their feelings. They express rage, sexuality, sadness easily, and experience sudden mood swings. They're pretty unpredictable.

"And sometimes, if they're submitted to more or less heavy environmental pressures they may develop small psychotic episodes, that is, they lose their sense of reality. And that is serious. Because the world is full of this sort of 'borderline' personality. They're not necessarily bad people. I've known colleagues who if you analyze them meet all the criteria. A guy who hasn't a stable partner, with three kids from different women, who's never happy with what he has, who's just bought a very big car which he can't afford, who's involved in all kinds of strange businesses, who's suddenly capable of breaking the law a little. And you say to him: 'But what you're doing is illegal!' and he says no.

"There's also the narcissist. He surrounds himself with people he considers his inferiors and they're always flattering him.

"What's popularly called a psychopath is really a mixture of these narcissistic, borderline types, combined with an antisocial personality."

Psychopaths usually work alone. But in Chile, people in the security forces were trained to torture and to kill in company. "There's something basic that makes people reject causing death to another human being, so that turning someone into a killer is quite a job," says Pérez. "I think that's easier to do collectively. If I see others doing something, I feel better doing it too. And that's the way torturers are trained. In general, the torturer begins on the periphery, taking notes, moving prisoners to their cells and then, according to people who've studied this, with the first blows they pass the point of no return."

Sex: "From what torturers themselves have told me, the rape of women in the midst of blows produces a sensation that's very hard to achieve, a sort of addiction. By possessing women through violence the torturer feels a power —" Monica hesitates, then forces herself to finish, "— it seems he experiences an orgasm like never before. So when he makes love normally he doesn't feel it and he wants to feel it again. It's like cocaine. That's why I say it's a very dangerous *drug*."

The old cliché about absolute power occurs to Dr. Juan Manuel Pérez and to Monica González. "I'm thinking about why absolute power corrupts," says Pérez, "and I think it's because the things one can do with power are somehow legitimate. Power legitimizes oppression, subjection. We grow up in a society where someone's either superior or inferior, man or woman, master or disciple, big or little, blond or dark, whatever. It's a society that's so dichotomized that there's always the perspective of the chicken-coop law — you know, the chicken above shits on the one below and to avoid being shat on you have to climb to the top of the coop.

"In this sense, absolute power can lead to someone who has some kind of imbalance to do these things. Because somehow, it makes that person, those activities legitimate."

Elliott Leyton, in his chilling study of serial killers, *Hunting Humans,* warns that madness "is not like cancer or any other physical ailment ... it is a culturally programmed dialogue." Those who indulge in this dialogue are "alienated men with a disinterest in continuing the dull lives in which they feel entrapped" and "they add the joy of sex to their adventure."

It's hard to believe that the psychopaths who preyed on Viña for so long were simply maddened individuals whose actions coincided with a particularly violent episode in Chilean history. And it's hard to ignore that, until their eruption in that hitherto summery paradise, there were many Chileans who were willing to accept certain extremes of cruelty for social 'peace'.

Serial murderers tend to appear when societies are in crisis, when established social roles are threatened and one class feels it is in danger of losing long-established privileges. During the late-nineteenth and early-twentieth centuries, writes Leyton, most of the famous murder cases involved members of the middle class, often, although not always, "killing the failures and the unruly renegades from the system, and doing so with obvious pleasure", acting as "enforcers of the new moral order".

Allende's Popular Unity government that ruled Chile from 1970 to 1973, with its forty-point program promising everything from milk for poor children to genuine agrarian reforms, began a process of social upheaval which the military coup was intended to reverse. Elliott Leyton's prediction that when "a single class ... is most threatened (when its rights are challenged by another class, its legitimacy questioned by a discontented proletariat, or its new-found status imprecisely defined) ... we can expect to find some members of that class beginning to fantasize about killing members of another class" rings true for Chile in the decade preceding the psychopaths' appearance.

The competitive ethic which dominates modern Western societies and the urban growth that turns neighbours into strangers also favour the development of a potential killer. The pillars of Chilean society – the Catholic Church, the Army, a rigid class system – load the dice against outsiders who set out to improve their social position.

"[Multiple murderers] may be statistically rare, but ... they are no freaks," says Leyton, who considers them the logical extension of central themes in their culture – worldly ambition, success and failure and "manly avenging violence."

Leyton excludes from his study the men whom governments deliberately train to torture and kill, on the grounds that these men are bureaucrats, motivated by personal ambition and not the perverse pleasure that killing can provide. Perhaps this is a mistake. Certainly the Viña killers fit his description of "the multiple murderer [as] a profoundly conservative figure who comes to feel excluded from the class he so devoutly wishes to join. In an extended campaign of vengeance, he murders people unknown to him, but who represent to him (in their behaviour, their appearance or their location) the class which has rejected him ... With varying degrees of explicitness, the multiple murderers see themselves as soldiers: small wonder then that they feel neither remorse for their victims, nor regret for launching their bloody crusades."

What about the role of the media? They enthusiastically advertise the killings – even when they aren't occurring – as if to goad the murderer(s) into action. Monica González says any newspaper, anywhere in the world would have covered the psychopaths the way the Chilean papers did. But Dr. Juan Manuel Pérez says that the "phenomenon took advantage of a moment when the dreadful was absolutely present", and that the impact of the Viña killings at that period in Chile's history was completely unlike the "normal" reaction to a sensational crime.

"In those years, faced with any killing your first question was always:

where's the political motive? No one could believe that a murder happened for no reason. It had to have a political motive and soldiers were likely behind it."

There is no other known case of serial murders of strangers in Chilean history. The psychopaths scared people. Not just because of the arbitrary nature of the killings or the fact they occurred in a comfortable, complacent city like Viña del Mar, but because they were overwhelming evidence of the corruption spreading through Chilean society. People who could silently justify political killings ("it's them or us," "they're all communists, subversives, delinquents, etc.") suddenly felt vulnerable.

In March 1982, a mental health expert who preferred to remain anonymous, told *Hoy* magazine that "until now the anaesthesia that most people apply as a survival strategy" was to react to news of an arrest or a death with the attitude "well, they must have done something wrong." That changed after the investigation of the Viña psychopaths and a second crime in the northern city of Calama. There, a bank manager and a security guard helped secret police agents to rob the bank where they worked, under the mistaken impression that it was a test of bank security. Investigators eventually discovered the truth and a few remains of the manager and the guard, who had been been blasted to pieces in an isolated spot in the desert. *Hoy*'s mental health expert said that the combined impact of the two sensational crimes was a completely new attitude: "people identify with the victims: 'it could have been my son, my wife, my brother, me.'"

The publicity demonstrated something else. The screaming headlines, the melodramatic posing and the endless stirring through the compost of pathos and squalor produced fertile ground for a protest that eventually forced Chilean police, and behind them, the government, to find culprits, to try and punish them. Whether it was the "true" story or the "whole" story was never clear. But there had to be something. The significance of the fact that pinning the crimes on a pair of Carabineros was the best that the police could do was not lost on newspaper readers.

"People are beginning to talk to the people around them because they know now that silence won't protect them and because they see that the institutions which provided security have been invalidated," the health expert added.

Does fear, that dense, smoky fear that choked so many critical voices, have a limit? Did the authorities, the secret police, the pro-regime media go too far in their attempts to manipulate fear as a means of social control? Did the psychopaths set off another, contradictory tide, repelling the regime's supporters? In some societies, multiple killings of strangers may be a sort of "accident", the result of attitudes and tensions which national mores and values unconsciously generate. What happened in Chile reveals that the ability to kill strangers can be deliberately fostered, but once these "skills" are unleashed their limits are frighteningly unpredictable.

I am always relieved to find her alive, and whole.

At the height of Chile's national protests, in the depths of repression that always succeeded them, she continued to live a "normal" life, in a small bungalow at the edge of the Hermida Shantytown on Santiago's eastern edge. Anyone could have mugged her, knifed her, run her down to rob her of her money — or her increasingly dangerous voice. She simply carried on. Her car was bombed. She received death threats. She didn't talk about it. Doesn't talk about it now. She carries on. And she still receives threats.

She set high standards for the few Chilean periodicals willing to criticize the regime. While she was on its staff, Cauce *became the kind of muck-raking, investigative thorn in the authorities' side of which the American legend I.F. Stone himself would have been proud. An opening salvo in* Cauce *was often echoed by a volley of similar investigations in other magazines. Released from prison one day, she immediately published the story of a fellow prisoner who discovered that her rape during interrogation had resulted in pregnancy, a pregnancy revealed when she started to haemorrhage from a miscarriage, also the product of beatings.*

Her influence grew, still grows. The week before I visited her at La Nación, the newspaper where she then headed the Department of Investigations, she had twice been called up by a judge to give information on the inner workings of the regime's secret services.

She laughs when I tell her I'm amazed that she's still alive, says simply, "Me too." What makes her happiest is "not ending up full of resentment or hate. Because a lot has happened to me. If I had to face judgement, I would do so in peace. Faced with a dilemma, my convictions, my principles were important.

"I've been able to listen to torturers and killers, to understand what happened to them. I think they are also part of the truth."

Chapter eight

IGNACIO

SANTIAGO, PLACES UNKNOWN 1981–1987

Let him who desires peace, prepare for war

VEGETIUS

June 15, 1992: Five years ago today, Ignacio was walking toward his mother's house on a crisp fall morning. A car pulled up behind him and a man hanging out the window shot Ignacio in the back, killing him instantly. Last night I spoke to Cecilia on the phone. Cecilia is in her forties, small and plump, her round cheeks sag slightly, pulled down by a grief relentless as gravity. She has a high, nervous voice which she battles to hold steady. But the pain speaks through her voice even when she strains against it.

For weeks, Cecilia and I have been trying to arrange an interview. The first time, Cecilia lost her voice. Now her throat has recovered but nothing else is quite right. She loses her temper easily, is irritated by the pressures of her work as a librarian, a mother, a daughter-in-law. Every year, this cycle repeats itself, as remorseless as the changing seasons. Cecilia is Ignacio's widow.

Ignacio's death made it possible to talk about what Ignacio had been doing. Those of his comrades-in-arms who survived face more difficult choices. Although no one wakes up to fear mixed with the morning smog any more, they must remain dressed in silence, disguised by pseudonyms. I don't know what Ignacio would have decided, faced with those same choices. He died before they ever became possible. His family believes he died making choices possible again.

Ignacio was tall, with pale skin stretched across a bony oval face, freckles sprinkled over a slightly prominent nose. He had short curly hair, private green eyes and if anything looked conservative. He studied economics at the university with my husband, Patricio, and he married Cecilia, who worked in their faculty library. He had a small son who was delicate and (we thought) over-protected.

We saw each other a handful of times, but a strong empathy sprang up between us. Ignacio had an eager, hungry intelligence, was one of the few Chileans I met to ask perceptive questions about Canada, its political system, the ongoing friction between French and English, Native people. We'd gather at their apartment or ours, feast on cheap clams, home-made yogurt, white wine, and discuss world politics until the sun started to wink through the venetian blinds. He and Cecilia were among those friends we were always meaning to see, delighted to meet by chance and when together we enjoyed an easy intimacy as if we spent every weekend together. From our conversations we deduced that he had a growing interest in the military.

Earlier this year, *La Epoca* carried a large colour photograph which seems to represent the current view of the organization Ignacio founded and eventually died for, the Manuel Rodríguez Patriotic Front (Frente Patriotico Manuel Rodríguez), FPMR. In the picture, a FPMR spokesman appears in a skirmish with Carabineros, his head thrown back, his eyes rolled back into their sockets. He looks like the devil incarnate. Just as many of the relatives have made heroes and martyrs of their dead, the new mythology has reduced FPMR members to madmen and delinquents.

Ignacio doesn't fit. I need to map the unnamed territory he has become, the choices he made and what they may have meant. I am not alone in this.

Adriana, Ignacio's mother, sits across the dining-room table from Patricio and me, slender and nervous, longing for a cigarette. She wears a simple but formal red-and-black silk suit. Her white hair curls elegantly away from a smooth, pale face with lovely bluish green eyes: Ignacio's eyes. Since his death five years ago, she has been interviewing all those who knew him, trying to piece his life back together.

Adriana looks the essence of fragility, but her life has been a bitter struggle. She and her first baby, Ignacio, lived in a cramped apartment with her parents until they died. With the burden of a difficult marriage weighing her down, she raised two sons virtually alone. Life gave her the joy of their achievements. And an unyielding strength. While Ignacio lay dying in the street, police wouldn't let her near. She convinced herself she wasn't looking at her son, and went on an errand. Later the control shattered.

Adriana's son was sensitive. When nuns told his grade one class that Jews had hung Christ on the cross he ran home crying. He was also generous. One Christmas he spent hours inventing gifts for every member of the household, including the dog. And he was stubborn: once she found him stuck among the branches of an enormous fig tree, unable to climb down, refusing to call for help.

He grew sharp and plump and liked to argue, especially about politics. He got good grades anyway. He persuaded his father to leave the conservative National Party and support the Popular Unity. He liked to dance. He loved his friends. He never told them about his difficult, sometimes violent life at home. He acknowledged his mother's bone-wearing sacrifices with a glance, a gift, a fistful of flowers. He never fought at school. He never let his own son play with toy guns.

He inherited his mother's eyes, her strength, the determination to take everything to its logical conclusion, a quality that can produce heroes, martyrs or serious mistakes.

Because I can't talk to Ignacio, I manage to find one of his comrades-at-arms. Even in 1992, two years into Chile's new democracy, I must use a pseudonym, "Eduardo", for this dark-haired, dark-eyed, energetic man. Like many, Eduardo idealizes his youth, but not every generation grows toward maturity in a moment of profound social transformation. Not many adolescents identify so wholly with a political project.

"I started high school just as the Popular Unity government began," says Eduardo. "There was a tremendous increase in political, cultural, sporting and artistic activities. Little by little my adolescence became intertwined with everything that was happening. We painted murals all over the city. In the summer, we volunteered, building dams, teaching people to read ..."

Ignacio, Eduardo and 80,000 other young Chileans belonged to the Communist Youth. Both Ignacio and Eduardo grew up in families which struggled to provide a good education and a fruitful future. They felt the poverty around them, children begging, shoeless children, hungry children, sensed that this could happen to them. They staked their hopes on the Popular Unity's program. For two years, it looked as though it would become reality. But during the government's third year, violence grew.

"For the parliamentary campaigns in 1973, there were people with bullet wounds, chases in the streets, attempts at sacking the headquarters of left-wing parties. We reached a point where we could only go out in groups, for fear of attack."

Popular Unity's supporters increasingly came to blows with members of the MIR (Left Revolutionary Movement), over the question of armed struggle. MIR, inspired by the Cuban revolution and the civil wars in Central America, advocated the use of violence to overthrow "bourgeois democracy" and thus ensure justice for the poor. Led by Dr. Salvador Allende, the Popular Unity argued that they wanted revolutionary change through democratic institutions.

"Sometimes we were involved in skirmishes, because young people are passionate and we were tremendously so. If we experienced an aggression, we fought back," says Eduardo. "But I never saw a weapon while I was a member of the murals brigade. It was unthinkable."

"There are days when everything goes badly," writes Adriana. The alarm doesn't go off, the children are late for school, the parents for work, the toast burns, the car won't start, traffic looks bad. What to wear? Not the grey pants and the red sweater – she wore them the day the tanks surrounded the Moneda, the presidential palace, demanding higher salaries for soldiers. There's nothing else. The bus lurches along streets with spring flowers timidly appearing, past the Military Academy where troops are lined up in front, practising, she supposes, for the military parade the next week. Traffic worsens: another demonstration, she thinks absently, as she hurries along on foot to her government job.

But she turns a corner and the street's deserted: cordoned off by the Carabineros. Tanks surround the Moneda. In her office, the radios blast out military marches. Desperately she retraces her steps. "People are silent, pale, hundreds of soldiers everywhere, armed to the teeth, their machine-guns ready. On one corner I run into two Carabineros listening to a radio. What's happening? *A coup d'état. The armed forces have taken power.* I felt like crying."

At home she finds her husband, slumped in an armchair. Ignacio marches in, leading a squadron of school friends, armed with sticks, stones, a worker's hard hat.

Adriana makes the improvised militia dump their "weapons" in the backyard. A neighbour's son reports them to a military patrol. Soldiers surround the house, poking machine-guns through the windows. An officer sends the children home. Eventually Ignacio's father will leave Chile, but the family stays. Adriana writes: "No one sleeps. Nobody's hungry. Afterward, orders to go back to work. Nothing has happened here and everything's normal. Our glorious Armed Forces splash in blood."

In March 1974, Ignacio starts university and Adriana returns to finish law school, after a twenty-one-year interruption. She watches her son come and go, always busy. She overhears him on the telephone, giving his friends advice when they fight with their girlfriends or face problems at school. She knows he still thinks about politics. She believes he no longer acts. But she has anxiety attacks: sometimes her heart beats so fast that the bed vibrates as if in an earthquake.

What she avoids knowing: that he's part of an underground Communist group and he's doing things like getting the first guitar brought back onto campus, convincing people to sing again, having sex for the first time, getting crabs, blushing terribly when he asks a friend for advice. Later he'll work behind the scenes, supporting festivals of music and theatre and art. He'll be arrested several times, paying the price for the opposition's early, naïve resistance to the regime.

Ignacio graduates with honours and receives a scholarship to study at the United Nations' Institute in Santiago. He'll go on to teach, debate options for facing Chile's foreign debt. One day, he will tell a friend that he can't go on talking and not acting, encouraging people to protest and watching them get killed.

A companion remembers him then: "He was enthusiastic. He wasn't sad, but I never saw him laugh out loud. With a nice house, no economic problems, maybe he could have laughed more, enjoyed more, gone to more parties. But I think he felt a tremendous responsibility.

"I felt a lot more capable after the [Manuel Rodriguez Patriotic] Front's actions. I felt the dictatorship was smaller than it looked, that it could be attacked, beaten. Before that it was like a cancer, like one of those diseases you get and can't do anything else but sit and wait for it to kill you."

Although his critics insisted that General Augusto Pinochet's military coup was an abrupt break with a hundred-year-old tradition of democracy, Chilean politics have see-sawed constantly, often violently, between authoritarian rule and ever-broadening participation, from the time the Chilean-born Spanish settlers fought for and won their independence from Spain in the early 1800s. Chileans are well-versed in their own history. The events and the heroes of the battles for independence and the ensuing years of political conflict profoundly influenced events during the military regime.

Pinochet shored up his own reputation using the prestige of General Bernardo O'Higgins, the bastard son of an Irishman and a southern (Chilean) lady, who led the resistance to Spain during the early 1800s and eventually, after multiple defeats, carried the country to victory and independence in 1818. While Pinochet held up O'Higgins's name as his banner and his justification, his critics went rummaging through history, searching for the national symbols that could embody their cause.

There was a song, sung by a band composed mostly of students from Ignacio's faculty, in the late seventies, when singing in public became possible again. With a gentle, lilting melody, "The Road to Til Til" describes the last moments, circa 1818, in the life of Manuel Rodríguez, a hero of Chile's wars for independence, 1810-1818. In the song, a woman is watching a band of soldiers drag him away. He holds his head high. He gives her one long, last look.

> His clear eyes among the sabres
> His laughter hides secrets intended for me ...
>
> They say his name's Manuel
> That they're taking him to Til Til
> That the governor doesn't want to see
> his gentle figure in the glen.
>
> They say that in the war he was
> the best and in the city
> he shone like a thunderbolt of freedom.

It is difficult to separate Manuel Rodríguez, the man, from the legend that turned him into a kind of Robin Hood. Above all, Chile's Robin

Hood is dedicated to a political cause, his country's freedom from Spain.

According to respected Chilean historian Richard Latcham, Manuel Rodríguez grew up poor. As a rebellious boy interned in convent schools he learned to slip through locked doors, pass unperceived through crowds, improvise disguises and go his merry way. He loved horse races, bull fights and betting and he used to read while others enjoyed their afternoon siesta. Even in prison, he could usually arrange a night out, dancing, drinking and making love. He used to place cigarette butts in keyholes to frighten the credulous into thinking they were small spirits, glowing ominously in the shadows.

While independence armies regrouped in Argentina, Rodríguez spied and organized undercover in Chile. In his book, *Manuel Rodríguez*, Latcham describes the scene: "At night, the hills come alive with mysterious messengers. A far-off bonfire seems to indicate something with the telegraphy of its flaming signals ... Dark shadows slide along ridges and rivers are no obstacle. Rodríguez is in Colchagua and his web of messengers is being woven throughout the central valley."

Robberies to finance the cause, bold strikes at the royalists' very hearts, persecution by the dreaded Talaveras regiment, the history of Manuel Rodríguez kindled flames which cast shadows 150 years long over Pinochet's Chile. On one occasion, Manuel Rodríguez, with a huge price on his head, pushes his way to the front of a crowd just as the Spanish governor pulls up in his carriage.

"The coach sparkles, covered with stained glass, its inner seats softened by rich tapestries and luxurious cushions covered with silk and brocade. Marcó greets his functionaries and sinks into the incense of admiration, while a workman doffs his hat, humbly opening the luxurious golden door. The bejewelled magnate leaps to earth, contemptuously throwing a silver coin to the servile pauper," who is none other than Manuel Rodríguez.

Women love him, according to Latcham. "Even though people in general have no system, no constancy nor resources, each of these chosen women is worth all the men put together," writes Manuel Rodríguez. And he seduces them with silk scarves and fine gifts. One day in 1817, he attacks the village of Melipilla, where he liberates co-conspirators and celebrates with card games and moonshine. He attacks San Fernando, escaping along the Tinguiririca River.

Latcham calls Rodríguez "the first sincere democrat to appear in Chile's little political world" and observes that Chile's working classes

remember him to this day. In the eighties, the Manuel Rodríguez Patriotic Front successfully recruited "Popular Militias" named for their hero,
primarily in the working-class areas, the *poblaciónes.*

If Manuel Rodríguez had lived in the late 1800s, argues Latcham, during
the rule of Diego Portales (another of General Pinochet's historic models),
"he would have been an opponent of the great minister's authoritarian
policies." And if he'd lived under Pinochet? In 1986, the main headline
on the cover of an FPMR publication was: "Just like in Maipú in 1818:
The Patriots Will Crush ANOTHER TYRANT, Yesterday Marcó del Pont
and his Talaveras, today Pinochet and his CNI-DICOMCAR." In 1988,
Raúl Pelligrín, the Front's top commander, and Cecilia Magni, another
leading commander, died fleeing along the Tinguiririca River, the same
one which had sheltered Manuel Rodríguez, escaping from the royalists.

As Pinochet considered himself the incarnation of O'Higgins and Portales, an authoritarian figure key to the development of the Chilean
republic, his opponents slipped their fingers around the banner of
Manuel Rodríguez and marched on, in an unnerving replay of political
conflicts, born with the Chilean republic and never resolved. Patricio
Manns, a gifted Chilean writer and author of "The Road to Til Til", served
as the spokesman for the Manuel Rodríguez Patriotic Front in Europe for
many years.

After independence, Manuel Rodríguez fell foul of General Pinochet's
model, Bernardo O'Higgins, and in 1818, he found himself back in jail.
As fall chilled into leafless winter, a secret organization plotted to dispose
of him. One guard refused to shoot him: "If you ordered me to execute
him, in the presence of the corps and in broad daylight, I would obey
you weeping; but in criminal darkness I will not."

The official announcement of Rodríguez's death doesn't differ much
from those that followed the 1973 military coup: "... three days after the
Cazadores de los Andes Battalion left this capital ... Alvarado reported
that ... Rodríguez grabbed a knife and threw it at the officer who, in
self-defence, used his pistol and killed him with one shot."

Wars for Independence, for Rights. And Wrongs. War is as much a character in this book as the people themselves. Whether there was a war or
not, whether that justified all that happened ... As a civilian, brought up
in a country at a time remarkably free of war, with only my mother's
nostalgia for the tinny voices of wartime singers and my father's stories

of hiding under tables during bombing raids, I feel helpless in the face of so many experts. A "larval civil war", a "subversive war", an "embryonic" war, a "patriotic" war: Do these terms really mean something, or are they merely the kind of expert patter that professionals use to confuse?

General Alejandro Medina argued that the military had acted, on September 11, 1973, to prevent a war, to pull a country threatened by war back together and to put it on the right track. To this day, Chileans still debate whether there really was a war in Chile. What is clear is that one side, the military, was convinced there was a war, and acted accordingly. In 1985, General Pinochet scolded journalists: "You still aren't convinced that this is a war between Marxism and democracy." In 1988 he reminded the whole country that "This is a war to the death."

And yet, what is a war, really?

"War," said Karl von Clausewitz, who is studied in military academies around the world, Chile's among them, "is nothing but the continuation of politics with the admixture of other means."

In the words of a retired Chilean Army colonel, written in 1977, war, is "the source of all arts ... the source of all great virtues and abilities in men. In war, all great nations have learned exactitude of thought; they have improved at war and been weakened by peace ..." In any war, the professionals of war, the generals, hold all the cards.

But, as Genaro Arriagada, a Chilean political scientist who specializes in military studies, writes: although "war has its own grammar, it doesn't have its own logic. The logic of war is politics." And he adds, quoting von Clausewitz, "The political proposal is the objective, while war is the means, and the means can never be considered separately from the objective."

The coup turned the inflamed rhetoric of the Popular Unity years, with its talk of defending – or fighting – the government to the death, of arming the workers or the farm-owners, or whoever to defend their "god-given" rights, into genuine acts of war: the bombing of the presidential palace, the massive incarcerations, trials by council of war, summary executions.

It could have been a short war, though.

In 1991, the National Commission for Truth and Reconciliation concluded that the Armed Forces achieved effective control of the country in very few days. Military actions were, in fact "minimal; irregular in terms of their location, form and weaponry employed; uncoordinated and without the least probability of success." Alejandro Medina, one of the "war's" top generals, confirmed with great pride that the military had Santiago under control within days.

Nevertheless, once unleashed, the juggernaut continued. Words are a poor substitute for weapons. The war was very one-sided.

Of the more than 1,200 people killed or disappeared in the three months following the coup, only thirty belonged to the police or armed forces. One was a civilian detective accidentally shot by a conscript; another, a conscript killed by members of the Air Force. More than half died on September 11th itself: four during the siege of the Moneda, three in an exchange of gunfire with workers defending a factory, six fighting in the Santiago *población* La Legua, two from snipers' bullets, one trying to stop civilians from escaping to Argentina, two more when a subordinate shot them for supporting the military coup.

Of those who tried to defend the presidential palace from the military uprising, fighting one of the few genuine battles, Salvador Allende committed suicide, as did one of his advisers. The rest of Allende's twenty-nine supporters disappeared after soldiers took them away. Forensic scientists eventually identified the remains of some among the bones dug up in the General Cemetery's Patio 29.

The vast majority of the coup's early victims disappeared after arrest, were executed, died from stray bullets, or were found dead. Three are known to have died fighting. Throughout the country, the deposed representatives of the Popular Unity government peacefully handed over power to the new authorities; most of those on the military's "wanted" lists gave themselves up. Eduardo, like many of the young people who would later form the Manuel Rodríguez Patriotic Front, was among them. Seventeen years old, he watched a man die of electric shock. Torture left adults he knew in wheelchairs. "I watched them pull people's teeth out with pliers. I was unusually lucky," he says again and again. "I still have all my teeth."

Others weren't so lucky. Although the newspapers faithfully parroted the regime's version of events, many suspected and some knew firsthand the truth behind headlines like "Seven Extremists Die In Six Confrontations". They watched in hopeless frustration as the media lied, the courts refused to act, the police denied all knowledge of kidnappings, arrests, disappearance. Victims began to break under the fierce tortures and soon the number of those being tormented in secret detention centres reached the hundreds. A survivor, Hugo Rivas, tells of a meeting with his Communist Youth contact in 1976. "We knew there was a real possibility that the DINA could arrest us. We were afraid we would give people up under torture. I told him I wanted to carry a weapon. I preferred falling in the street to the risk of being arrested and tortured." He waited in vain for his contact, Carlos Contreras Maluje, at their next meeting.

Rivas never saw Carlos Contreras Maluje again. He had been kidnapped by the DINA, Manuel Contreras's dreaded secret police. During interrogation he denied all knowledge of the Communist Youth until his torturers stripped off his blindfold and he found himself surrounded by most of the Central Committee. He realized then that they had been betrayed and he figured out who was responsible. He convinced his jailors that they could capture yet another leader by following him to a contact he'd set up before his disappearance. They agreed and followed him to his meeting. But Contreras, shouting of betrayal, begging for help, threw himself under a bus. The contact got the message. Contreras got shot the same night. Witnesses, including a police officer, noted the licence plate of the car which had carried him off. Eventually, investigation revealed that the car belonged to Air Force Director General Enrique Ruiz. Three months after Contreras's death, the writ for habeas corpus in his case was approved.

Usual civil law was not applied. Nor were the Geneva Conventions, originally adopted by the Red Cross and ratified by countries around the world, Chile among them, which define rules for the treatment of the wounded and prisoners of war.

Chile's military authorities justified the irregularities, the permanent states of siege, of emergency, of "danger of perturbation of the internal peace", arguing that an invisible enemy was stalking the country.
Manuel Contreras, the creator of the DINA, Pinochet's first secret police, said, "We were the Army of the Shadows and with the motto 'we'll fight in the shadows so our children can live in the sun' we carried out a permanent fight against the clandestine war triggered by hypocritical Marxism." And added, "We won."

But did they? Lieutenant-Colonel Alberto Polloni, of the Chilean military academy taught that the goal of war is to "destroy the [enemy's] military might and, if possible, submit it to the will and customs of the winner, making it serve his own cause," specifically through the "annihilation of the enemy's armed forces", "conquest of its vital zones", "the occupation of the adversary's capital", its isolation from potential allies and the "complete defeat of the enemy's allies".

The MIR became the first target. Once it was virtually dismantled, security services took about a year to decimate the Communist Party's leadership. By 1977 the "war" could have been over. But it went on. "First [the idea was] to stop terrorism, then possible extremists and later those who could conceivably become extremists," an ex-DINA agent later admitted.

A century ago an American senator said that war's first casualty is truth. The price for Chile's shadow wars was the credibility of the country's main institutions: its police force, its army, its media, its political institutions and, above all else, its justice system.

The regime employed "acts of violence". And, as one prominent businessman who had organized underground activities against the Allende government acknowledged, the military occupied "vital zones". However, instead of "annihilating" the enemy, sympathy for the opposition grew. And year after year, the United Nations condemned the Chilean government for widespread human rights violations.

The Rettig Commission records three deaths in 1979 of police or military personnel. In 1980, six. In 1983, nine; 1984, fourteen plus one civilian; 1985, nine, plus two civilians; 1986, nine, plus six civilians. Instead of "destroying the enemy's military might", after seven years of shadow boxing, the military's sparring partner stepped down off the wall. It borrowed a name, a personality and justification from Chilean history. Suddenly Chileans were very close to having a real war, a civil war, tearing their country apart.

This was no victory for the Armed Forces. But the FPMR didn't win either.

For "Eduardo", detention and torture were "like receiving a degree, the confirmation of my ideas about what a military dictatorship was, what fascism was. I came out thinking 'I have to fight the dictatorship to the death.' It was hard to even begin."

In university, Eduardo, Ignacio and countless others had lived with a potent mixture of fear, frustration and the need to act, and they searched for examples of what they could do. They didn't have to look far. They had grown up reading about the resistance during the Second World War, and saw their country, "being occupied by an army just like Europe in times of fascism, so we have to liberate it.

"Fear is a natural reaction in all animals," Eduardo says, "especially people, who experience fears that are more sophisticated and are able to provoke more sophisticated fears too. But fear has a limit. You reach a point where your own needs make you overcome fear.

"I remember walking through downtown in early 1983, seeing people pick up pamphlets," Eduardo says. "If the police came, they'd whistle against them. And if the police tried to arrest someone, people would defend him. There was already an attitude of rejection, of rebelliousness and incipient confrontation. That was a great lesson for us and we realized that we could organize and lead that force against the dictatorship."

Eduardo, Ignacio and other young people may have argued in favour of armed resistance to the military regime, but the decision to create a professional military force that might ultimately confront and break the Chilean Armed Forces was made by Communist Party leaders exiled in Moscow. The Chileans were trying to learn from the experience of Nicaragua, Cuba and El Salvador, where the Communist parties failed to support successful rebellions against the local oligarchies and wound up out of power when the rebels triumphed.

In 1980, the Chilean Communist Party's General Secretary Luis Corvalán announced the "deepening" of party policy to include armed resistance. The announcement touched off fierce debates and split parties throughout the Chilean left. The Communist Party's own leaders never acknowledged this as a radical change to their former pacifist stance. The membership argued, largely in private, seeking definitions for new terms like "popular rebellion" and "insurrection". In the early eighties, some of the Communist Youth's most committed cadres founded the FPMR (Manuel Rodríguez Patriotic Front), supported by the Party's contacts around the world. Neither the Communist Party nor the FPMR ever officially recognized the Party's paternity, producing an ambiguous public relationship which led to some of both organizations' most serious errors and would eventually turn the FPMR, like the Chilean Armed Forces themselves, into a military robot without a political heart.

While politicians argued, party members were sent out onto the streets to implement a policy for which they had little preparation: intellectuals attempted minor acts of sabotage, students and *pobladores* fought off sophisticated police weaponry with stones and home-made gasoline bombs. But the growing defiance on the streets wasn't all the result of deliberate political decisions. When the Copper Workers' Confederation convoked a national protest for May 11 1983, the overwhelming enthusiasm in working- and middle-class communities astonished no one more than the organizers themselves. In later protests men in business suits and formally dressed women joined protesters as they tore up cobblestones, the grills over drains and concrete blocks to improvise barricades against police buses. People began to rebel of their own accord, dragging their "leaders" behind them.

When the lights suddenly went out during a protest in 1983, people cheered. The FPMR was making its debut.

"I never killed anyone. But I fired many times: within the context of some urban action. There weren't all that many. Because the best organizations are those where as much as possible you don't fire a shot. Often it's not even necessary to show your weapon. If you're blowing up [electric] towers it's a military operation but not necessarily a confrontation. There's no need for [guns] unless you're spotted by enemy forces. Sometimes there are people who get in the way by accident: that is what is so awful about using a weapon."

A year of military training in Cuba, with few opportunities for writing home, for news of family. They live in modest but comfortable houses, three or four to a room. They're allowed personal belongings, photographs. They all use false names. Eduardo calculates that only three people ever knew his real identity. Two of them are dead.

Day and night they study strategy, underground work, intelligence, tactical operations, ideology, ethics, personal security, loyalty: never abandon your companions or the organization. The officers don't impose, punish, pressure. They teach, educate, convince. There's a modest graduation at the end of the course, "an intimate thing, not like the rigorous military graduation that's generally known". Some go on to experience real fighting in Central America. After basic training, Commander "Ernesto", José Joaquín Valenzuela Levy, served as a captain in the Sandinista Army in Nicaragua before returning clandestinely to Chile, where he directed the ambush on General Pinochet. He was one of those found dead, the day after Ignacio, in a house on Pedro Donoso Street.

Back in Chile the everyday routine of family and the occasional visit with friends is interwoven with contacts on busy street corners or in secluded houses, the planning of operations, supplying combat units with cars and weapons and money, placing bombs under electric towers, kidnapping "enemy" representatives to show their vulnerability. They commandeer delivery trucks and distribute food to the poor. They occupy radio stations and international press organizations to transmit their opinions. They interrupt regular radio and even television broadcasts. They use forbidden words, speak of the unspeakable. There's power in that, especially for those who don't agree with them.

At first all goes well. The FPMR members are like Mao's proverbial fish swimming among people who look on them as heroes or at least an option, suspending judgement. They recruit easily in the impoverished working-class communities, the *poblaciones*, and among university students who've grown up under an authoritarian regime. Unemployment is 30 per cent. Costs have risen and spaces in universities have shrunk, leaving many feeling they have no future. Curfews on vehicles severely limit night-life. Even private parties are suspect.

People are tired of being frightened. They're hungry. They want something at least to hope for. I remember in 1983, making the slow climb up the hills of Peñalolén, past flaming barricades. As women and children clustered round and ragged youths chanted, an elderly woman stormed at me: "They say we're armed. We're not armed. Where on earth would I get a weapon? We don't even have the money for a pot of beans!" In the leaping light of the fire, her brown eyes snapped: "But I'll tell you, if someone gave me a gun, I'd use it!" Students rework an old Popular Unity slogan and chant: "The People, Armed, will never be defeated." *Pobladores* shout: "Let's die fighting, from hunger no way."

A former Junta member, General Gustavo Leigh, who had been ousted during a power struggle with General Pinochet in 1976, warns that the plebiscite on General Pinochet's continued presidency will be as phoney as the one which made him president. Jorge Ovalle, a lawyer who once advised the military government, writes in *Cauce*: "Today our homeland is a land of violence. And a violent government can't stop it, but only increase it. Only in democracy and in freedom will we be able to destroy it, calming spirits through the reconquest of lost rights."

Civil disobedience is the opposition's chosen strategy and the FPMR often seems like an ally. It becomes the focus for secret police activities, at times deflecting attention from grassroots leaders and traditional politicians. The few political leaders who begin to lift their heads and their voices reserve judgement on the FPMR. Its blackouts arguably make the streets safer for demonstrators on nights of protest. It clearly tries to avoid civilian deaths, concentrating on sabotage and harassment. The FPMR tries, within the military framework it has adopted, to fight ideas with ideas, but it also attacks "military" targets, police stations, bases, secret police headquarters. Most of its victims die in armed confrontations, but there are mistakes, deaths, innocent victims, among them a thirty-two-year-old train conductor who tries to stop FPMR members who had taken over his train for an "armed propaganda" activity, and a physiotherapist who drives past the US consulate just as a car bomb explodes. Other armed groups appear, among them the Fuerzas Populares Rebeldes Lautaro, who specialize in approaching police officers, shooting them point blank and taking their weapons.

In 1986, the FPMR begins to plan its boldest operation: the ambush and killing of General Pinochet. Both Eduardo and Ignacio help choose who will lead the attack. "We all wanted the chance to punish the tyrant, but some had more rights than others. Most were the children of people who'd disappeared or been executed after the coup." They argue about what to do if there's a child with General Pinochet when they attack. In the end, his grandson is with him. The attack goes ahead.

The discovery by authorities on August 6, 1986, of a massive smuggling operation in Carrizal Bajo by the FPMR to bring weapons and ammunition into Chile doesn't change their plans. Several of the leaders are arrested, tortured so intensely they lose their memories. Chileans' initial reaction is total disbelief. They cannot conceive of an armed movement of this magnitude in their country. An opposition magazine publishes a cover story suggesting that the whole thing is a hoax.

From a military point of view, the operation against General Pinochet is brilliant, prepared with audacity and grace. Its execution is marred by mistakes that show the Front has inherited some of the flaws, as well as the strengths, of its hero, Manuel Rodríguez. A triangular relationship and a romantic last night violate security norms, leave clues. So does a last swig of Coca-Cola before battle.

José Joaquín Valenzuela Levy commands the ambush operation, seconded by "Comandante Tamara", Cecilia Magni, a young Chilean woman whose upper-class origin serves the FPMR well. With the aid of Cesar Bunster, then working as a doorman in the Canadian Embassy, she rents several vehicles and a comfortable house up in Maipo Canyon, an hour's drive from Santiago. The house is on the route that General Pinochet typically takes back into the city after a restful weekend up in the canyon.

None of the twenty five "combatants" who gather in Stone House for the attack know what they have been called together for, until Valenzuela Levy gives a small speech one morning in late August 1986. He announces that their "mission" is to "make the tyrant, Pinochet, pay with his life, for the thirteen long years of crime, misery and shame". Solemnly, many with tears in their eyes, they intone the FPMR's anthem: "Like the shadow of living memory/ Manuel Rodríguez returns to frontal combat/ tall and hard as an unending lightning bolt/ against the same immemorial tyrant ..."

But Pinochet returns to Santiago earlier than expected and the ambush has to be postponed a week. By Friday evening, September 5th, all the FPMR's fighters have once again gathered in Stone House. On Sunday, after listening to a recording of Salvador Allende's last speech, originally broadcast during the coup, almost thirty FPMR members settle in for a tense afternoon of waiting. Juan Moreno Avila manages to chug down an icy Coke, only to discover the glue covering his fingerprints has come off. Although he wipes the bottle with a cloth, the print remains.

At 6:20 that evening, the FPMR receives the signal that Pinochet's convoy is coming down the canyon. Four squadrons set out in a Nissan Blue Bird, a Chevrolet truck, a Toyota Land Cruiser, and a Peugeot station wagon towing a mobile home. At a narrow stretch of highway, flanked by a steep cliff reaching upward on one side and a sharp drop down into the canyon, the car jerks sharply across the road, blocking it just as General Pinochet's Mercedes, flanked by police on motorcycles and in cars, drives into sight. The machine-guns thunder in the narrow canyon. Some of the police officers throw themselves over the cliff, then can't get back up again.

An FPMR fighter leaps onto the road, less than a metre from General Pinochet, who is hunched over his grandson in his armoured car. The fighter fires a LOW missile launcher, but the missile fails to explode. Corporal Oscar Carvajal jams the car into reverse and backs out of the ambush. Five members of General Pinochet's escort die.

Six years later, sitting on the edge of his chair, Eduardo gestures with brusque pride as he argues that the attack on General Pinochet illustrates another element of the FPMR's training that differentiated them from their opponents: the use of firearms with discrimination. "The Black Berets were neutralized and disarmed as was the civil guard formed by the CNI. All twelve or fourteen of them could have died, but their lives were pardoned because they had surrendered."

He considers this "a great lesson for those little lead soldiers in the

Chilean army who are tremendously brave when it comes to unarmed people but when they're in conditions of equality they're incapable of fighting. War is war," he adds, but "there are minimal norms, a form of conduct that respects the human being."

General Pinochet attributes his survival to the divine intervention of the Virgin of Carmen, patron of the Armed Forces, whose image he claims to see drilled into the bulletproof windows by machine-gun fire. Others suggest the missile was either faulty or fired from such close range it didn't have time to explode.

With sirens screaming and red lights flashing in a realistic imitation of the secret police, the attackers barrel out of the narrow canyon and shoot past a security barricade lifted in their honour. They desert their vehicles in Santiago's sprawling suburbs, dispose of their weapons, change their clothes and slip back into their regular lives. The perfect crime. But.

There are other victims. During curfew hours the night of the ambush, "unidentified civilians" drag four men known to oppose the regime from their homes and riddle them with bullets. A fifth escapes, thanks to the quick reaction of his neighbours. No one can quite believe that someone in Chile could seriously challenge the government's military might. There's speculation that the CIA did it, or Pinochet himself to unite the Armed Forces behind him. In the days that follow, opposition leaders hidden in safe houses condemn the ambush, criticize the FPMR. Or they're trooped before the military prosecutor for interrogation.

A few days later, Maria del Rosario Pinto, a telephone operator, remembers placing a call from Maipo canyon to Santiago, for an attractive blonde foreign woman and her male friend. She also recalls seeing this woman leave Stone House, which had served as the FPMR's headquarters. The police trace Isabelle Mayoraz, a Swiss woman, after finding love letters from Marcial Moraga, one of the attackers, and a photograph of them together in Viña. There is a postcard from him after their break-up. The police find Moraga and arrest him.

The fingerprint on the Coke bottle leads the police to Juan Moreno Avila. He, in turn, reveals that, in flagrant violation of security norms, four of his companions are set to jog around a local park. They are all arrested.

In total, errors – due to pride, love, carelessness – lead to the arrest of eleven participants in the attack and nine sympathizers. Nevertheless, of the twenty-five people who acted directly and the estimated one hundred to two hundred who assisted them in some way, often without knowing what exactly they were involved in, most remain unknown, untouched. Until after José Joaquín Valenzuela Levy was found dead, in the house on Pedro Donoso Street, the CNI and General Fernando Torres Silva, the Army's head prosecutor, did not know he had commanded the famous attack.

In fact, according to Patricia Verdugo, a journalist, and Carmen Hertz, a lawyer, who together wrote *Operación Siglo XX*, a book about the ambush based on direct interviews with those involved and testimony that formed part of the investigation, most of the arrests during the investigation were thanks to the labour of Chile's regular police, the Carabineros and Investigaciones detectives. The CNI, the political police, whose very existence the government constantly justified by the potential for crimes like the one against General Pinochet, contributed hundreds of detainees, many of them well-known political leaders, and tens of thousands of pages of detailed information on their activities worldwide, and very little else.

The FPMR's failure was as spectacular as its goal. "Because it failed, because of the deaths that followed, the ambush created absolute panic," says Monica González. "It made people withdraw from everything." And because the Communist Party had always defended the FPMR, "the discovery of the weapons made the rest of the opposition cut off all ties with the Communist Party, isolating it."

Opposition strategists recoiled. The importance of one force in society having a "monopoly on arms" became key to discourse. The Communist Party, under tremendous pressure from its own ranks and worried allies, secretly tried to dissolve the Front. But the young people, who had trained and conspired and risked and sacrificed, refused. What became known as the "Frente Autónomo" (the Autonomous Front) was born. General Pinochet's "war" and the left's "armed resistance" had taken on a dynamic of their own.

Ignacio, Cecilia tells me, didn't like to talk about the conflicts that followed the birth of the Autonomous Front. "Once he said that he was hurt by the [Communist] Party's attitude and that this thing had to go on, that it was no joke." Eduardo denies there was a split, saying one officer left the leadership, but the organization remained intact.

In essence, the Front was a military organization with some political preparation, originally designed to support the Communist Party's strategy for a Nicaraguan-style insurgence. When the Communist Party withdrew, it took its political leadership and its resources with it. The Front held on to its organization, existing weaponry and infrastructure. It was a divorce that left the means without a clear political objective and the base of support necessary to move toward it.

Security became a growing problem. Cecilia and Ignacio talked about what to do if he were captured: "Take Lucien and Adriana and run, fast, because otherwise they'd catch us and torture us to make him talk." But if he were killed, "there was no danger. I had to tell the whole truth," says Cecilia. Officially, they separate and he rents his own place, but he spends most weekends with Cecilia and Lucien. When he's on an operation, others phone her with messages: "Ignacio's fine." "Ignacio says he loves you." "Ignacio sends you a kiss."

Between operations, they try to maintain a normal life, go to movies, birthday parties, visit friends. One day they fight because he doesn't make it to a wedding where they're supposed to meet. "I was furious," she remembers. "The next day he said we should separate, that I had a right to rebuild my life. He hardened himself, packed a suitcase, told me not to worry about Lucien, or money. I knew I didn't have to worry about those sorts of things with him.

"I grabbed the suitcase, hid it and said Ignacio, no. It took me five hours to convince him that that wasn't what I wanted."

Both Cecilia and Eduardo speak of the CNI, the secret police, having a photograph of Ignacio months before his death, of Ignacio knowing that they had him identified and that there was a serious risk. Instead of plunging further underground he took on new responsibilities in the Front. He continued his life as father, husband, son.

Cecilia and Ignacio spend their last weekend together racing from one commitment to another, barely meeting, fighting bitterly. In the end she throws the worst insult she can think of at him: "You're nothing but a bloody soldier!"

"He fell silent and I started to cry and I said Ignacio, you know I love you and I need you anyway. And he said you're right, I am a soldier. And every day I have less and less time ..." Her voice breaks. "Later, I realized that he knew that at any moment he might not see us again."

After the fight, a passionate reconciliation, a quiet walk through Santiago's older streets planning to buy a house, remodel it little by little. He leaves that night and the next day she goes to work as usual. In the afternoon, a mutual friend phones, asking about Ignacio. She leaves the library, pretending she's going to the washroom, and runs to a newsstand. Before she can look at the headlines, a friend takes her arm and firmly steers her to his car. The first thing they do is go to a pharmacy to buy tranquillizers.

We learn of his death when a nightly newscast shows security agents pawing over his almost naked body, while the announcer describes yet another "armed confrontation" between "delinquent terrorists" and Pinochet's secret police. By the next day, twelve are dead.

In the days that followed, horror unfolded with the drama of a multiple murder and the mockery of an official explanation that was obviously false. Today, we know that the CNI, the secret police, broke into Julio Guerra's apartment and shot his eyes out. They riddled Patricio Acosta with bullets as he crossed the street. They kidnapped and tortured José Joaquín Valenzuela Levy, Ricardo Silva, Ricardo Rivera, Manuel Valencia, Ester Cabrera, Elizabeth Escobar and Patricia Quiroz. And they executed them in the CNI's headquarters on Borgoño Street. After they moved the bodies to an empty house on Pedro Donoso Street, an agent strolled through the rooms, shooting each one yet again. Just before dawn they inundated the little house with bullets. They called it an armed confrontation.

But we also know that the last two, Juan Enríquez and Wilson Henríquez died fighting. Together, they resisted the CNI, while their companions, including a woman with a small child, escaped over the roofs of working-class homes in southern Santiago. Juan Enríquez died in battle. Wilson Henríquez managed to reach a neighbour's backyard. There the CNI found him and shot him in the head.

"Eduardo" saw Ignacio's photograph in the afternoon paper, but "I felt convinced that it wasn't him." Eduardo had lived and argued, eaten and fought at Ignacio's side, but he knew only his pseudonym, Benito. "I had an emergency contact — the guy arrived and said, 'we thought you weren't going to make it either. Your chief is out. The dead are Benito, Arturo, Ernesto, Tamara, Gustavo and Juan Carlos.'

"For me they had been immortal. They were people with a very special magnetism, the sort of people who change history, like José Miguel Carrera, Bernardo O'Higgins, Fidel Castro, Che Guevara. I broke down and cried."

They were virtually his entire unit: top Front commanders and new recruits. To this day he doesn't understand how they could have died that way, although he has received an official explanation. Nor does he know why he survived. He ponders, looks away. "I had good military training. But all my companions are dead."

It is September 1987 and I am taking my son Camilo to day-care. We walk down the stairs of our apartment building and, as usual, he races on ahead of me, out the door and around the corner. I walk into a strangely silent street; even the birds have flown. I look around for Camilo and see a helmeted soldier, machine-gun ready, on the corner. And across the street. And on the next corner. And the next. Under the budding trees, soldiers are searching every house. And my son? Fear closes my throat. I force myself to walk to the corner and turn it. And there he is. Whole. Confused by the way small toys, easily mastered in play, have suddenly grown giant.

Ignacio died ten weeks ago and the Autonomous Front has kidnapped Colonel Carlos Carreño. The soldiers will search thousands of houses in Santiago. General Fernando Torres Silva, a special military prosecutor, will use every means to find Carreño. Torres's tactics will include the broadcast of images obviously filmed during torture sessions of a young woman confessing to the kidnapping. He will harass the priest who carries out negotiations between the family and the Front.

In November, my colleagues and I will visit the población *La Victoria. The ransom for Colonel Carreño is truckloads of food to be distributed among the poor. In many ways it seems like a quixotic Front operation. But local organizers refuse to co-operate and hungry men and women mob the trucks. Bottles of oil break and spill. Rice, sugar, flour litter the streets. Children, crying bitterly, run behind the trucks, trying to scrape food from asphalt. I feel ashamed to watch.*

The Front moves Colonel Carreño across two borders and releases him in Brazil. This is quite a military feat, but politically the kidnapping backfires. Carreño is quickly silenced when he speaks well of his captors. Back in Chile, he's shut up in the military hospital. Eventually he's released — and retired.

If anything, the kidnapping pushes leaders of the Christian Democrats, Socialist and smaller left parties away from civil disobedience, toward negotiations with the military regime. The Communist Party disagrees with a strategy based on negotiations, but can offer no alternative. Bare-

ly two months later, most of the opposition's leadership, starting in
February with the Christian Democrats and ending in August with the
Communists themselves, will accept the regime's constitution on its own
terms and stake their futures on the presidential plebiscite it offers.

Monica González believes the turning point for the FPMR was the failed
ambush and the debate which followed. "There's analysis, conflict and
some sectors withdraw their support. And that makes [those who remain
in the FPMR] harden. And that conflict results in a militarist current and
they take refuge in their trenches – that's what happens to the military.
The harder they're hit, the more they hide in their trenches."

In *El pensamiento de los militares,* his book about the Chilean military, Genaro Arriagada says that militarism is a glorification of the military's role in governing society, and calls it a "suicidal tendency", a
"psychological catastrophe in three acts". Some of his observations also
apply to the Front. Militarism's worst error is that it eventually turns on
itself and "tries to realize its ambitions at the cost of members inside its
own society. This," Arriagada warns, "leads to open or veiled civil war.

"The militarist, trusting too much in his own army, doesn't perceive
that culture, history, the social movement are following other paths, foreign or even decidedly contrary to official military rhetoric. Thus, the
successful military movement of a first period, deprived of its social
impetus, dries up, fossilizes, until its 'stiff and threatening figure' is
nothing more than 'a corpse inside the armour.'"

Monica González says that initially "the Front showed that state terrorism, security groups and the army are vulnerable, it's possible to fight
them." That's why they chose Manuel Rodríguez as their symbol, she adds,
"because [at first] people felt it was impossible to fight the Spanish troops,
but then with cunning, little means but conviction, they defeated them.

"The Manuel Rodríguez Patriotic Front had a lot of charisma. To get
in you had to swear that you were willing to sacrifice everything. And
that's the generation, the structure and the conception that corresponds to
the Front's first phase. What comes after is the militarist conception in
which already the cost of deaths and sacrifices made, the harshness of the
life they were living, makes people develop a callus and they forget those
feelings of utopia, romanticism, always involved in a revolutionary
movement, because those feelings can make you a target, are weaknesses."

People like Eduardo, the young men and women who initally joined the FPMR did so not because they viewed soldiering as a career or even an activity they would like to engage in. They wanted to find a way out of the political dead-end created by the military government and then get on with the rest of their lives. But little by little, this began to change.

Monica González noticed this first in an interview with "José Miguel", Raúl Pellegrín, a top FPMR Commander. "It was just before he died and he was surrounded by his general staff. I asked them to leave. Because "José Miguel" would say he had absolutely no interest in being a soldier, that his objective was to forget weapons. But his second-in-command said, No, I want to wear a uniform. To her, this argument was an exact reflection of what was happening to the FPMR at that moment. One side was "taking itself apart, recycling itself and trying to partici-pate in this transitory democracy that we have." While the other wanted to go on using guns.

"Things changed," González says thoughtfully ... "When something happened and you didn't know if it was security organisms or the Front, then something was very, very wrong."

Was Ignacio's life a waste, his tenacity a fatal flaw? Cecilia says that in a peculiar way, even his death was part of the endless planning he never failed to carry out. If he had to die, the way he died left his family suf-fering but safe. He did not face torture, nor risk giving up precious information about his fellows.

Two years after General Pinochet reluctantly stepped down as presi-dent, the Front continued to carry out "executions" and kidnappings, this time for ransom. Another armed organization, the MAPU Lautaro, became more active than ever, shooting Carabineros at random to "recover" weapons; setting off bombs; participating in robberies. The MIR split, with most members preferring to return political "struggle" to a peaceful, unarmed arena. Communist Party members deserted it in droves, many because of its inability to recognize its own errors. Some criticized the Communist Party for creating the Front; others for with-drawing its support. Still, it managed to win almost 7 per cent of the votes in Chile's 1992 municipal elections.

Where would Ignacio stand, if he had survived? What would he be? I look at "Eduardo", who sacrificed six years of his life in the belief that that was the best he could do for his country. After Ignacio's death, he left the Front for security reasons. While his friends are buying houses, raising children, enjoying in some cases the prestige of posts in the new government, he struggles to survive, moving from one odd job to another. Unlike the men he fought against, "Eduardo" is not protected by the Amnesty Law. A specially appointed judge continues to gather information about the Front. At any moment, "Eduardo" could find himself surrounded by police agents. Or dead.

He doesn't regret what he did, but he now believes that by 1988 Chile was "a country that was tired of death. Our way was one of enormous sacrifice, risk, suffering. The great choices had already been made. We should have recognized that to triumph our [political] project had to have the support of the vast majority. In the end, it was displaced by other projects that had more support. We have to accept that."

Monica González says Chileans were never as brave as they thought they were. "There's an impressive lack of ethics when we look at ourselves in the mirror." And she remembers an interview with Patricio Aylwin when she asked him why he dropped civil disobedience in favour of negotiating with the regime. "He said, because I was wrong. I thought Chileans were brave, but they're not.

"You have to be very brave to say that." She adds, "I lived with that lyric discourse during the Popular Unity government and it led to failure. To think that everything was ready to resist the onslaught. And nothing was prepared. I think the same thing happened to the Front. Young people were prepared for battle but nothing was prepared for them to resist what followed.

"There are a lot of dead young people. And that's what's terrible. The people who created this are there with the same old political conflicts. They don't recognize a single mistake, not one defect, no connection with or complicity in their deaths."

Is it surprising that some Chileans, most of them under thirty, many of whom had suffered arrest, torture, the death of someone close to them, finally responded by taking up arms? Isn't it surprising that there were so few and that it took them almost ten years to do so?

Neither side won Chile's shadow war. Some believe the FPMR shortened Pinochet's stay in power, others argue that the Front strengthened his hold. Some say the Front inspired them, gave them strength; others were clearly terrified.

The FPMR's strategy was based on the belief that Chileans would rise up and follow them to victory, if only the Front provided the leadership and the weapons. They gambled on Chileans' courage, on many being as good as their word. But any initial enthusiasm for the Front faded or was dashed by its mistakes. And like the dictatorship's, the FPMR's martial rhetoric also frightened people.

Perhaps more than anything else, the discovery of the arsenals in Carrizal Bajo in 1986 showed Chileans a nightmarish future, one symbolized more by the prolonged civil war in El Salvador than the victory of the Sandinistas in Nicaragua.

As television cameras panned along the endless rows of more than three thousand M-16 rifles, one hundred and seventeen rocket launchers, 179 LOW rockets, two million cartridges, eighteen hundred bombs, two thousand grenades, three thousand kilos of explosives, forty eight hundred detonators, how not to visualize the bloodshed and the carnage they could produce? Was it cowardice or good sense that made many Chileans, whatever their political colours, shrink away from that future and seek yet again for a peaceful solution to their historic conflicts? The potential conflagration made democracy look awfully good, martial rhetoric sound very empty.

And the costs of the shadow wars are all too with us. There are the dead: 132 members of the Armed Forces; 19 Frentistas; 2,128 men, women, children. And the costs that numbers can't express.

Adriana's voice thins to almost nothing, as if the air itself were speaking, all cracked and swollen, parched as desert earth.

"There's no pain like the loss of a son. Sentimental problems are very hard. The loss of parents too, but children are born programmed for the loss of their parents. No one's born prepared to lose their children.

"It never occurred to me that he might be involved in something military, because he was a pacifist above all else. He never liked weapons. He hated war. He knew that it was difficult to talk with machine-guns. Yet, in those circumstances, he became convinced that it was unavoidable, the only way out.

"I've always thought that I would be incapable of surviving my sons. They have been the reason and the purpose for my existence. They have been all that really interested me in life. And they were my only source of happiness. I am amazed to find myself alive.

"Human nature is incomprehensible."

Chapter nine

SOWING
THE WIND

WASHINGTON, SANTIAGO SPRING

O! it is excellent
to have a giant's strength, but it is tyrannous
to use it like a giant.

SHAKESPEARE, *MEASURE FOR MEASURE*

You're born in Washington on January 7, 1961. You grow up engrossed in the scores of Senators and Redskins baseball games. At Easter you hunt for eggs; on Memorial Day you run in competitions organized by the neighbours. You spend weekends with your family in the Shenandoah Valley. Lots of families live between two cultures in Washington. You do too. Your father's away a lot. Your mother teaches Spanish. You learn Spanish and behind your first country there's a second, the shadowy presence of sunny Christmases, cousins' laughter, mischief, horseback riding on the beach.

Your father's strict. He wants all four sons to go to the military academy, as he did. You and your brothers don't eat dinner with your parents. Sometimes, public reality tears the private fabric of your days: the day Robert Kennedy was shot, McGovern launched his candidacy, or Nixon won. You discuss these events with friends, but most of your life runs a smooth course between school (private and Catholic), holidays on the east coast, visits to Atlantic beaches. You watch the anti-war movement, civil rights marchers, hippies. Neighbours go to war, return. You ask a lot of questions. Your hair grows. Your father complains. You fight. Your mother teaches you songs by Peter, Paul and Mary, The Beatles, Pete Seeger. You learn to play the guitar. You think it's good that people don't want to go to war.

One day, the holiday country, the family country, jolts closer. Your father's become ambassador in Washington. Now you know you're different from your friends. It's not common for nine-year-olds to meet presidents. You ask more questions. Your father's away a lot.

Then, one piece of the family after another climbs onto a plane and heads off into an unknown future. One day, you climb onto one yourself, leave Washington's spring and step into Santiago's fall. You miss your friends, eighth grade, the girls you liked, the girls you thought liked you. But the marches are exciting. Gradually, you feel at home. When the trees outside your new apartment bud lush and pale, your father arrives. It's September – fall in Washington, spring in Santiago. The family is whole again, surrounded by unpacked crates, the fragments of transition.

The next day your father leaves early. An aunt arrives. The radio's always on. No one knows where your father is. Suddenly, this matters. Days pass, then weeks, months. You learn new rules. You speak about some things to some people. You don't speak to others. You keep a lot to yourself. The Air Force takes over your school and wants to expel you. You fight to finish the year. Your father's imprisoned, your mother under house arrest. Your father, the newspapers tell you, is a thief. You're furious. And helpless. You see a corpse pulled from the river as you cross a bridge on your way to school. Your father's moved to the Air Force Academy. You pass it every day on your way to a new school. One day, you, your brothers, your mother, an aunt, your grandmother, enter the Academy. Your father is pale, thin. Your father is alive. You have learned to be grateful for this.

Beyond the greetings, your parents must talk. This means sometimes you and your brothers must be very quiet. Sometimes you must make a big fuss. When he's transferred to a camp, visits become rituals. Your father is moved to an island in southern Chile. Your father's friend and fellow prisoner dies of unnatural causes. You remember his death. You remember the funeral. What you miss most about Washington is the feeling you were safe.

The family breaks into pieces. First, your father's expelled, then a brother; then your mother, another brother, you. The whole family meets again in Venezuela. From there, "home" to the States. But now you are in exile. This is hard to explain. "Oh Chile, that's in Mexico?" your new friends ask. You think they live safe in the empire's heart, oblivious to anything beyond it.

You've always assumed there's an invisible wall between your two worlds. You've gone back and forth, but not much else has. In Santiago, you were a bright, observant boy. In Washington, you're a typical east-coast teenager.

This begins to break down, but you don't see that at first. At the most you're aware that encouragement, interference, has travelled from Washington to there, but nothing's come back. Washington remains immune. The stately white buildings still stand majestically on their immaculate green lawns. They still promise safety, security, a place where normal can't be turned upside down from one day to the next, where people's insides aren't suddenly spilled out. Life keeps death in place here, neatly shelved away in cemetery rows. Cemeteries are relentlessly kept out of the picture.

But now you realize something's changed. Your two lives, two languages, no longer co-exist. Something unspoken shoots back and forth, silent and tense between them, it won't leave you in peace. You're still technically an American citizen. You go back to school. Find a girlfriend. But her parents don't like you. Still, you go steady. You fight with your mother and your father, you go to proms, to high school. Then it's September again, spring in Santiago, fall in Washington. One day you're called out of class. You rush to hospital. Your mother hugs you and says: "I don't want you to come out of this hating."

Your two separate independent worlds, with their separate words and separate rules and separate values, have collided in the shape of a car that explodes, blowing your father's legs off, cutting the throat of a young American woman he was driving to work. Her new husband was left staggering through smoke and dust, the sharp stench of explosives.

The men who had spent money, written articles and held conversations in low voices with military officers in a country their fellow citizens had barely heard of did not expect the bombs they'd encouraged in one land to echo so lethally in their own. And the men who gave the orders, seated in plush offices in safe and solid white buildings surrounded by neatly manicured lawns, the men who had held their silence through bombings and deaths in other countries, will react to this one. But you don't know this yet. What you know is that your girlfriend's parents won't let her attend your father's funeral.

Copper. The word doesn't resonate like gold or silver; it doesn't bring echoes of greed and myth, the bitter exhilarating struggle of lonely miners sifting rivers and shifting landscapes in search of precious metal; nor does it appear in endless quotations from poems; the historic epoch which copper defined is better known as the bronze age. There's no "copper rule" that I know of. Although coppery hair has sometimes been praised, it's more often associated with witches. The copperhead is a poisonous snake.

Delicate strands of copper continually bind Chile's fate to the United States, sewing the seams of union so tightly that any attempt to sunder them has brought violence to both.

The relationship began with the US consul supporting Chilean independence from Spain. After independence in 1818, British investment grew, and by 1849 about fifty British companies controlled most Chilean exports, and from 30 to 40 per cent of Chilean imports came from England. A Chilean historian, Francisco Encina, says that "What resulted in these years was not, as usually suggested, an intensification of international trade. Rather what occurred was an exploitation of the Chilean economy by foreign interests. They traded 60 per cent of their goods, at least, for silver, gold or copper ... avoiding the customs house. Luxury goods went down in price while the price of articles of primary necessity which the country did not produce went up ... Between 1823 and 1830 some three or four thousand foreigners ... sucked the blood from the Chilean economy ... while 95 per cent of the Chilean people had retrogressed to the lifestyle of the last third of the seventeenth century."

By the 1850s, nitrates were an important ingredient of fertilizer; Alfred Nobel would soon discover their importance in making explosives. The deserts between Peru, Bolivia and Chile were full of guano and nitrate deposits. Tensions escalated and, in 1879, Chile went to war against Peru and Bolivia. Chile's triumph brought a Peruvian monument, the Victory Fountain, and left it sitting in the main square of Valparaíso. Bolivia lost the mineral-rich Atacama desert, which became part of Chile, along with its access to the Pacific Ocean. Chile's victory also cleared the way for the country's transformation from a small agricultural country into one of the world's major producers of minerals. The Chilean government denationalized the nitrate industry, benefiting mostly British companies. Some observers considered this a payoff for British support of Chile during the 1879 war.

As the century turned, American investment grew from US$5 million in 1900 to almost US$200 million in 1914. The First World War pitted Chile's two main trading partners, Germany and England, against each other. Nitrate production, which before the war accounted for 25 per cent of Chile's GDP and employed more than 5 per cent of the Chilean workforce, dropped 60 per cent, turning Chile's northern production centres into ghost towns. The United States', entering the war in 1917 increased the demand for Chilean raw materials, but Germany was developing a synthetic nitrate which would undercut Chilean nitrate forever.

By the war's end, American investors controlled more than 87 per cent by value of Chilean copper production, which had mushroomed from 31.4 million pesos to 132.8 million pesos during the war. American involvement brought personnel, technology, capital, machinery and cultural influence. In 1925 it also brought the Kemmerer Mission to reorganize Chile's economy along US lines, with a central bank, legal regulation of banking structures and centralized monetary policy. The police forces were united under a sole, hierarchical leadership, responsible to the Ministry of the Interior.

As the war drew to a close, the economic difficulties that floated in its wake threatened to sabotage Chile's political stability, as one president after another elbowed his way to the head of the line, only to fall over the cliff. Arturo Alessandri Palma left his mark during his first presidency (1920-1925) in the form of the 1925 constitution that ruled Chile until the coup, but was eventually ousted.

Conflicts continued and, in 1932, six different governments struggled to control Chile in one, 102-day period. Marxism, Liberalism, Social Catholicism and Fascism all touched off chords in different sectors of Chilean society and by the end of World War II, the Cold War had arrived. US agents and diplomats worked to directly influence the course of elections, labour unions and other social organizations, while the socialist countries in Europe, particularly the Soviet Union, funded and influenced Chile's Communist and Socialist parties.

The 1938 victory of the Common Front coalition, led by the Radical Party's Pedro Aguirre Cerda and including the Communist and Socialist parties, posed an interesting dilemma for US policy toward Chile. The government needed new resources to finance development of national industries, but tax increases were unpopular. American diplomats settled upon a cautious program of loans, credits and investment for projects which did not directly threaten US interests, at the same time as they supported government members who opposed the Marxists.

This proved successful, as the government's Corporation for Industrial Development (CORFO) became key to Chile's economic improvement throughout the next four decades, financed largely by US Export Import Bank, EXIM, credits. Most of CORFO's capital investments went to purchase American materials, machinery, technical assistance and consultants. Brian Loveman, the author of a study of Chile's economic and political history, concludes that "Although CORFO's policies directly threatened the position of selected American firms, its overall effect was to greatly expand the market for imports of United States capital goods, in addition to placing Chilean policymakers in a vulnerable position vis-à-vis decisions made in Washington, DC."

Copper formed the tough flexible core of this connection. During World War II, American ownership of Chile's copper mines meant that Chilean copper was subjected to a price ceiling, a situation that cost Chile – and saved the United States – an estimated US$100 million to $500 million. After the war, the US recession kept prices down, and, when the outbreak of war in Korea might have pushed them upward, new price controls were promptly imposed.

In 1946, Gabriel González Videla won the presidency of Chile, with the support of the Democratic, Communist and Radical Parties. He faced a deficit of more than a billion pesos, aggravated by declining prices for copper and nitrates. His first government included three Communist ministers; US pressure began immediately, through Chilean conservatives. As tension increased, the US ambassador cabled the US Secretary of State: "Chile is [a] key country in the struggle against Communism, and I feel that we should make every effort to overcome the present impasse."

Pressures, threats, negotiations, culminated in "The Law for the Permanent Defence of Democracy" in 1948, which outlawed the Communist Party, striking almost 30,000 voters from an electoral register of 631,257 people. The law allowed authorities to purge the union movement, forced elected Communist Party members underground and resulted in massive firings of party workers. Thousands were expelled from company-controlled towns and camps, among them María Nélida Sánchez who would later be among the founders of La Victoria. Loyal friends and readers smuggled the poet Pablo Neruda, who was a senator for the

Communist Party, across the Andes to safety in Argentina. As those expelled struggled to rebuild their lives, far from the Andean communities that had been their homes, the American copper company Anaconda announced that it planned to invest a further US$130 million in the mine at Chuquicamata and the American EXIM Bank agreed to provide substantial economic assistance.

This US strategy created the paradox of a government-sponsored corporation closely allied with the private sector. Brian Loveman observes: "Credit to agricultural and industrial interests from CORFO often entailed negative real interest rates; that is, inflation more than counterbalanced the interest rates, making credit a subsidy to debtors. Externally financed economic modernization was oriented toward importing capital goods for industry and labour-saving farm machinery, and [it] thereby strengthened the position of employers, especially in agriculture... Moreover, private investors achieved a dominant voice in the three major industrial complexes originating from CORFO initiative – the Pacific Steel Corporation (CAP), the National Petroleum Corporation (ENAP) and the National Electric Corporation. Key stockholders included Kennecott Copper Corporation and influential members of the National Society of Manufacturers."

Conflicts followed as Chilean attempts to develop industries through CORFO met with opposition from American companies. "Most of all," concludes Brian Loveman, "disparity between what copper exchanges might bring the nation and what they actually provided in foreign exchange led groups on both the Right and the Left to resent, if not attack openly, the American copper firms."

In the fifties, economic crisis brought another American trouble-shooting mission to Chile, Klein-Saks, which recommended reduced currency emissions, wage controls, credit restrictions, government cutbacks, the elimination of government subsidies and removal of price controls. New laws reduced taxes on the American copper companies, increasing profits, while wage controls reduced workers' buying power and eventually led to rioting in Santiago in 1957. A detention camp in Pisagua made its debut, under the command of an army captain, one Augusto Pinochet, and labour leaders and communists were imprisoned for the first time in a barren enclave between northern Chile's Atacama desert and the Pacific Ocean. In 1957, the alliance which had swept Carlos Ibáñez del Campo into power collapsed and Jorge Alessandri, son of Arturo Alessandri Palma who governed in the twenties, crawled to power in the 1958 elections with 389,909 votes, 33,500 more than his nearest competitor, Salvador Allende. A year later, Fidel Castro led Cuban rebels to victory against the corrupt dictatorship of Fulgencio Batista, raising the stakes in US/Chile relations to an unprecedented level.

Playing one-pack solitaire you lay out the cards face down in orderly piles. Only the top card of each is uncovered. *Order,* by colour, by numbers, is the *method.* But the *goal,* the only way to win the game, is to *reveal* all the cards. Often, this is impossible from the moment the player deals. But you only discover this by playing out the game. I play solitaire when I'm stuck in the midst of a chapter. Organizing, ordering. Turning over people's lives – organizations – like cards.

In 1975, the Church Commission, a Select Committee of the US Senate set up to study governmental operations with respect to intelligence activities, published a report on its findings regarding Chile, called *Covert Action in Chile, 1963-1973,* turning over many a crucial card. The Church Commission revealed how in the early sixties top White House advisers and CIA personnel formed a special "Electoral Committee" to prepare for presidential elections – in Chile. The United States spent US$4 million on secret projects to ensure that Salvador Allende wasn't elected. It also contributed US$2.6 million – half the cost – to the campaign of Christian Democratic candidate, Eduardo Frei Montalva. Frei Montalva won with an absolute majority of 55 per cent.

Frei Montalva's platform of "Revolution in Liberty" dovetailed with the US's new strategy for Latin America, the "Alliance for Progress". Not surprisingly, it depended heavily on assistance from private and public US sources. In fact, the United States poured more than a billion dollars into Chile between 1962 and 1969, the highest per capita rate in the continent. American banks also opened special short-term lines of credit in Chile's favour. In 1964-65, the American Aid program accounted for almost 15 per cent of Chile's national budget. Aid contributed significantly to improvement of Chile's national education system, the reduction of infant mortality rates, and progress in the National Health Service. It also strengthened American influence and brought pressure for agrarian reform that threatened the rich landowners' historic control of the countryside. Hardline conservatives were often as anti-US as the Communist and Socialist parties, a paradox which contributed to the unanimous vote to nationalize Chile's copper industry in congress in 1972.

The Chilean government was far from a puppet whose strings were tugged by Uncle Sam. By the late sixties, Chile was one of the most urban, most industrially developed countries in Latin America, with a high rate of literacy (almost 100 per cent) and a social security system which, after decades of social conflicts, provided important benefits to most of the population. After the instability of the mid-twenties and early thirties, elected governments had negotiated political changes through a bicameral congress with considerable success, giving the country forty years of experience solving political and social conflicts through democratic means.

After 150 years of independence from Spain, the Chileans also enjoyed a strong sense of self, of nationhood, founded largely on a thriving culture with roots in both the oral traditions of its main native groups and a folkloric past rooted in Spain. Strong economic ties with Germany and England in the 1800s and England and the United States during the 1900s did not limit the Chileans' determination to cut their own path through the twentieth century. Throughout their history, the Chileans had borrowed ideas, technology, goods and money from foreign powers with vested interests in their future. In turn, foreign governments meddled, adjusted, negotiated, influenced. Both sides received benefits and blows from this situation. In the sixties, some Chileans began a process of unprecedented closeness to the United States even as others struggled for independence harder than they ever had before; in the extreme and dangerous intimacy of this relationship, the ingredients for disaster fused.

Poring over texts, the words flying up at me like Alice's cards when Wonderland got rough, a steady voice murmurs in my ear, a slim face rises again before my eyes, streaks of grey hair dignifying an intelligent forehead, framing a face of understated, undisputable authority.

She's a corporate lawyer, perhaps the most experienced, certainly among the most powerful in Chile. Daughter of a Carabineros general, she grew up in the north, in Viña del Mar and Santiago. She studied law at the University of Chile in Valparaíso and graduated in 1954. But no one really wanted to hire a woman lawyer. Finally, as a favour to her father, the head lawyer at Anaconda's Chile Exploration Company hired her, inventing the job of legal secretary. For a year she worked as a clerk, making notes, filing and organizing. In 1958, she took a leave of absence and studied at New York University's Interamerican Law Institute. There she learned a little English and a lot about the Anglo-Saxon legal system; Chile's is based on the Napoleonic Code.

As the CIA, the US government, and American corporations became increasingly active in Chilean politics, Laura Novoa began a professional career that placed her at the centre of battles over copper.

"Between 1954 and 1970 I noticed an intense change, gradual but accelerating, of antipathy toward the American companies," she says. "At the start when I said I was the lawyer for Chile Export doors would open for me, but around 1970, if I said that I would receive insults, 'how can you work for a foreign company?' A climate was being created by some political parties ... which reached sectors who weren't necessarily leftist, of animosity toward the American firms. They were looked at as having despoiled the country, taken out many profits, and not behaving responsibly.

"Their taxes went higher and higher. Tax reviews became more [obsessive]. They rejected all the expenses which the companies claimed so the work that had to be done to reclaim these costs was atrocious. Parallel to this, Frei Montalva's government began to seek – through very tough negotiations – the creation of mixed companies. The first of these was El Teniente in which the Chilean government [purchased] 51 per cent and Kennecott Copper took the remaining 49 per cent. The advantage of this treatment, which was called 'Chileanization', was that it was accepted voluntarily and as a result it was a system in which everything was regulated."

In 1969, the Chilean government formed similar mixed corporations to control the Chuquicamata and Salvador mines belonging to Anaconda and the Andina mine, owned by the Cerro Corporation. That same year, the CIA's local office in Santiago began to develop contacts within the Chilean Armed Forces, to "monitor" coup attempts.

Like Laura Novoa, Orlando Letelier graduated from law school in 1954 and bright strands of copper wove through his life too. In 1954, as Laura Novoa was settling into her new position in the Anaconda Copper Company, Letelier went to work in the Chilean government's Copper Department. As Novoa organized files and prepared notes, Letelier researched the regulation of the mining, sales, marketing and shipping of copper. Unlike Laura Novoa, in 1958 both Letelier and his wife, Isabel Morel, supported Salvador Allende's election campaign. Former friends accused them of "betraying their class"; he was fired and they were forced to move abroad. In 1959, first Orlando Letelier, then his wife and three sons, moved to Venezuela and then to the States, where he worked for the Interamerican Development Bank. His dream was that the IDB and the Alliance for Progress might lead to a genuine and fair integration of the Americas, North and South. His youngest son, Juan Pablo, was born in Washington in 1961.

In the 1960s, Letelier had strong suspicions of the CIA's growing intervention in Chile, but as a seasoned economist and diplomat, he was convinced that Chile needed allies in America and that it was not only possible, but necessary, to find them. As Letelier carried on his efforts in Washington and within his own party, the US government was pouring millions of dollars into its secret game in Chile. The year 1970 and a new presidential election rolled round, and the US invested from US$800,000 to US$1 million in Allende's defeat. The CIA, with the full co-operation of Chile's oldest national newspaper, *El Mercurio*, blitzed the media with articles, editorials and news. For a while, the CIA's local office generated more than an editorial a day, for an audience of more five million people. Polarization became extreme.

The month before the election, a National Intelligence Estimates report predicted that state participation or open nationalization of copper was inevitable. On September 4, 1970, Allende won with 1,075,616 votes to Jorge Alessandri's 1,036,278. The Christian Democratic candidate, Radomiro Tomic, came third with 824,849 votes, perhaps because, as the US Senate's Church Commission speculated in 1975, CIA organizing on behalf of Frei Montalva in the 1964 election both left the Christian Democrats with an inadequate structure for grassroots campaigning and damaged the party by its association with the United States.

Laura Novoa lived in the midst of that polarization, stimulated to a frenzy by the CIA's propaganda machine and anti-Allende Chilean media. She looks back with a mixture of disbelief and wonder.

"Perhaps I became unnecessarily hardened," she reflects. "At that time, aside from having clear ideas about what was right or wrong, I didn't really participate [in politics]. But maybe because I was working with American companies and had seen what they'd done in the mines and how valuable it was – to a point I think the Chileanization process traumatized me. I began to form the idea that all our political management was unnecessarily aggressive and unproductive.

"I was confused, but I began to worry about what was happening. When President Allende was elected I was a fanatic who supported – I don't know what – but it was anti-Popular Unity [the governing coalition, led by Salvador Allende]. I had been educated by my father in a rather simple system in which the president of the Republic, if he is elected, must be respected no matter what. He's a symbol. And although I could participate in a march against the Popular Unity, I could never have insulted the president – it was pretty contradictory."

The society that had produced these values was disappearing. "Everything was violent, aggressive, everything was life or death, at least verbally, because the violence had a tremendous effect on the rupture of our peaceful co-existence. It had no limits. And it was us, our society that was like that."

When Frei Montalva's government carried out the Chileanization of copper, Laura Novoa had expected to be replaced as head of the copper mines' legal affairs department. Instead, Anaconda recommended her, the government approved, and she became head lawyer for the combined mines of Chuquicamata and Salvador. With Allende's election, she was accused of having an "American spirit". She persevered in her job, on principle. When the communists at the Chuquicamata mine asked her to leave, she requested a personal interview with Allende.

"I'm not going to say that I found him nice, but he did have the courtesy to listen to me. I had lists of signatures – I'd begun in such a low post, as a woman –and the result was that people respected me a great deal, because I was a good worker and had a lot of support, even from people in the Popular Unity.

"So I met Allende and said, look, I've come to talk to you because you're Chilean and I'm Chilean too and I think copper has to be as important to you as it is to me. I think your people are making mistakes. They're firing people for reasons as absurd as the accusations they've made against me. It's true that I worked in Anaconda but the truth is I work for copper and for Chile. I don't work for the Americans."

On this chill July day two decades later, on the tenth floor in the imposing marble building that today houses Codelco, the state-owned copper corporation she helped to create, Novoa relives her interview with Allende, and it is as if I am hearing his voice reply. "'I've just appointed someone to manage the copper situation. He has very good criteria and will know how to act appropriately.' And this was true," she concludes. Her life continued to revolve around copper.

As Laura Novoa prepared opinions, background documents, advice concerning the future of the nationalized copper companies, Orlando Letelier often sat on the government's side of the negotiating table. His quick, open mind and seemingly inexhaustible capacity for work could do little to staunch the flood of orders from the White House that were contributing to the growing violence in Chile, but it did win him knowledgeable friends and contacts, along with a deep fund of experience.

In February 1971, Salvador Allende appointed Letelier his ambassador in Washington. Upon presenting his papers to Richard Nixon, Letelier studied every word in Nixon's acceptance speech: "I am sure you will agree, Mr. Ambassador, that no nation can in good conscience ignore the rights of others, or the international norms of behaviour essential to peace and mutually fruitful intercourse. For our part this government and this nation stand pledged to mutual respect for independence, diversity and international rights and obligations."

It sounded reassuring, but Henry Kissinger's comments to the press were not: "Now it is fairly easy for one to predict that if Allende wins [the congressional ratification vote] there is a good chance that he will establish over a period of years some sort of Communist government. In that case, you would have not an island off the coast, which has not a traditional relationship and an impact on Latin America, but in a major Latin American country who would have a Communist government ... So I don't think we should delude ourselves that an Allende takeover in Chile would not present massive problems for us, and for democratic forces and for pro-United States forces in Latin America and indeed to the whole Western Hemisphere."

The US Senate investigation carried out by the Church Commission, of US covert activity in Chile, reveals that the US's analysts did not believe their own propaganda about the dangers of Chile "going communist". The report quotes from State Department memos, CIA reports and National Intelligence Estimates (NIE). Nevertheless, as I reread the Church Commission's revelations, I am haunted by the cards that remain hidden. Castles of cards, fragile abstract constructions of what went on beyond the reach of the Church Commission – the questions it couldn't answer, the fatal chinks through which blew the cold winds of corruption, impunity, the marked cards that stack the deck against anyone who picks it up and deals. Playing solitaire, you think you hold all the cards. You think you're the only player. But the cards themselves are playing against you, mute, blind in one eye, seeing all with the other.

Nixon and Kissinger seem to have been convinced that the Allende government seriously threatened the US government's interests – around the world. But who convinced them of this? Not their own intelligence experts: as the efforts of the US and its Chilean allies became more frantic, the National Intelligence Estimates actually became more reassuring. As early as September 1970, a CIA memo noted that the US had no vital interests in Chile; that the world military balance would not be significantly altered by Allende's government; and that Allende's victory would probably not cause any alteration in peace in that region. In October, the CIA sent out a memo to prop up the justification [for a coup] that "you'll surely use, the pretence that you're saving Chile from Communism."

In August 1971, a National Intelligence Estimate (NIE) concluded that Allende wanted to effect social change within the constitution, that he preferred to avoid a confrontation with the US. It also noted that Allende was unwilling to subordinate Chilean foreign policy to any foreign power and that the presence of Soviet troops in Chile was unacceptable to both the military and to Allende himself.

In June 1972, a new NIE reported that the government was respecting the results of election in student, labour and other organizations regardless of who won and that Allende continued to desire friendly relations with the States and to exercise caution in his relations with the USSR.

In August 1973, a last NIE reported that Allende had not consolidated a Marxist regime. While most low-income Chileans believed their living standards had increased, a growing polarization of Chilean society was undermining the country's ability to compromise. Allende kept communications open with Washington until the end.

So why, that question again, were Nixon and Kissinger so worried about Allende's attempts to build socialism through the ballot box in a small Latin American country whose population at the time was less than ten million? Where were they getting their information, if their own intelligence evaluations were hardly cause for alarm? The only clue is a quiet breakfast between White House advisers Kissinger and John Mitchell, and the CIA's loyal friend in Chile, *El Mercurio*'s owner, Agustín Edwards. The breakfast took place just eleven days after Allende's election and before his ratification; it was arranged by Coca-Cola president Donald Kendall. What did Agustín Edwards tell Kissinger and Mitchell over breakfast that morning? Something bloodchilling enough for Nixon's shrill orders to "make the Chilean economy scream", issued to the CIA head Richard Helms that same afternoon. Nixon also ordered the CIA to approach the Chilean military directly and try to organize a coup to prevent Allende's ratification in a congressional vote.

The US mobilized around the world and Christian Democratic governments and the Catholic Church pressured Frei Montalva to accept a manoeuvre that would have put him back into power. He refused. But co-operation between the CIA and *El Mercurio* and other Chilean media continued to sow predictions of a fearful future: within weeks of Allende's victory, the CIA had journalist agents from ten countries in Chile or on their way there; eight more supported them from bases in five other countries. During this campaign, which lasted until October 24th, 726 articles, radio and television broadcasts, editorials and other informational products resulted from the agency's activities. Between October 5th and 20th, the CIA had twenty-one meetings with key military and police officials in Chile, assuring all those inclined to organize a coup of the support of the United States. The US Ambassador Edward Korry was authorized to tell the Chilean armed forces that all US military aid would cease if Allende were elected, a threat which did not materialize (in fact, US military aid increased significantly both during the Allende government and immediately after the coup).

On October 22, 1970, a Chilean general, who had received considerable encouragement from the CIA, tried to kidnap the commander-in-chief of the Chilean army, General René Schneider, the articulate defender of a theory which had kept Chile's Armed Forces democratic for decades. The "Schneider doctrine" defended the principle that Chile's military forces owed their allegiance to the constitution – and the democratically elected government. General Schneider, a major brake to pro-coup elements, was gravely wounded and died shortly after the Chilean congress formally ratified Allende's presidency. A loyal friend and follower replaced him, General Carlos Prats.

Both Kissinger and General Alexander Haig told the Church Commission that coup attempts were suspended after Congress ratified Allende's election on October 24th, but CIA agents' comments suggested the contrary. The CIA compiled information relevant to a coup, including lists for arrests, key civilian installations and personnel in need of protection, along with contingency plans that the government could use in the case of a military insurrection. According to the CIA, this information was only for Agency use and was never given to the Chilean military.

Orlando Letelier returned to Chile in May 1973, as Minister of External Affairs. When, in August, pro-coup army generals forced the resignation of General Prats from his dual posts of Minister of Defence and Army commander-in-chief, Allende appointed Letelier Minister of Defence.

Letelier stepped into the position as General Augusto Pinochet swore to uphold the constitution as Army commander-in-chief. General Prats thought him loyal. Letelier told his wife, Isabel, that Pinochet "gives me the creeps. He's flattering and servile, like the man in the barber shop who runs after you with a whisk broom after you've had your hair cut and doesn't stop sweeping at your back until you've given him a tip. He's constantly trying to help me on with my coat and always trying to carry my briefcase."

Orlando Letelier settled in. Laura Novoa went on strike against the government. On September 10th, Letelier and his family held a cheerful housewarming party in a new and comfortable apartment near the city centre. Novoa spent September 10th securing the release of a youth arrested for "public disorder".

"The next day he was free," she remembers. "Nothing happened to him; he spent the night in jail. That was all. That was the difference between those who were arrested before the 11th and what happened after."

Only when she heard airplanes dive-bombing the presidential palace the next morning, did Laura Novoa realize that this was not what she wanted. "Perhaps it was very ingenuous, but I expected the military to take power peacefully, to remove President Allende, but to put him on a plane and then to act accordingly. That is, to put things in order, to say this will last a certain length of time. I suddenly realized that this was going to be terrible."

She also remembered a brother-in-law, with whom she had fought so bitterly that they stopped attending the same family gatherings. He worked in CORFO and supported Popular Unity.

"I don't know what happened to me, but that day any difference I ever had with him disappeared, and I realized that I had to help, that we had had a children's quarrel, that all that verbal violence, all those fights in family parties, calling each other fascists, all that was foolishness. Suddenly I realized that this was something very serious, that people's lives were important. That same day I left a card telling him that he could count on our help. He was on the first lists and was arrested.

"From then on, when I wasn't working on copper, I concentrated all my efforts on having this person taken out of the country. Finally we got him out."

The experience brought her firsthand knowledge of a reality that her family and friends refused to see.

"At first there was a spontaneous brutality unleashed, a product of the atmosphere [of] great hatred, polarization, a society where there were two groups and some wanted the others to die. So those who won acted with the psychology of the winner of a war.

"No one reacted. No one wanted to know. No one cared what happened to those rotten Popular Unity members. If they were killed, so much the better; if someone made the effort to torture them, better still and if someone pulled out their fingernails, well, [you said] you couldn't be sure — but you knew it was true. That terrible atmosphere lasted a year, a year and a half. It was a sort of gigantic wave that swept away a whole society."

September is a month laden with symbols in Chile. It starts on the 4th, the day Chileans traditionally elected their national president and it culminates in a four-day weekend of empanadas, red wine, apple and grape ciders, circuses, fairs and games and kite-flying, along with a massive military parade, all to commemorate Chilean Independence from Spain. Not surprisingly, there's also a major army anniversary slipped in among the general patriotic fever.

The military officers who led the coup wasted no time incorporating September 11th into the national catalogue of patriotic symbols. They declared it a holiday, Chile's national liberation, its second independence. A shiny new coin showed a winged woman, her hands breaking free of chains. They remodelled a square across the Alameda from the bombed-out Moneda, Chile's main seat of government, and installed an "eternal freedom flame". The square, a huge concrete wasteland, is partially enclosed by the Armed Forces' national headquarters and national defence buildings, a subtle comment on the sort of freedom the military intended. As Laura Novoa woke up to the rattle of gunfire and explosions, Orlando Letelier was standing in what would one day be Liberty Square, demanding entrance to the Ministry of Defence he officially headed, with all the authority he could muster. Guards promptly arrested him.

Four blocks away, the US Embassy was monitoring the coup's results. In the months that followed it would report that about 5,000 people had died; 50,000 been arrested and "interrogated". By early 1974, 10,000 people in protective asylum were leaving Chile for resettlement; another 50,000 raced for the borders and the illusion of safety in Argentina and Peru. Of Chile's population of 10 million, an estimated 100,000 experienced death or arrest, one million exile.

Orlando Letelier was among them. During the long months of imprisonment, first in the basement of the Ministry of Defence and later in the frigid snows of Dawson Island near Punta Arenas, he had plenty of time to meditate on what had happened to his former companions from military school. "Each soldier is a prisoner in all situations," he concluded. "Each private has a corporal above him, each corporal is observed by a lieutenant, and each one is trying now, because of fear and terror, to show that he's more violent than the others, because he knows that if he doesn't, they will apply the sanctions to him: there's a verticality of terror ... softness, acting human, could lead them to real harm."

And the Americans? Two died, victims of the coup, swept up at random by the maelstrom of violence or, some speculate, deliberately killed to silence damning information on the US government's participation. Because although the US Senate's Church Commission proved the White House had ordered a coup attempt in October 1970, it never established that the American government actively participated in the 1973 coup. The Church Commission demonstrated that propaganda campaigns, economic destabilization, co-ordination with US companies, indirect and direct financing of Allende's violent and non-violent opponents were all part of the effort to get rid of Allende. But conversations between US military officers and a young reporter, Charles Horman, in the days following the coup, suggest that the United States contributed more than moral support to the Chilean military officers behind the coup. Horman and a friend, Frank Teruggi, mysteriously disappeared. A friend later identified Teruggi's body in a Chilean morgue. Horman's wife and father spent frustrating weeks searching for information on his fate, until authorities finally confirmed his death.

Here the game is lost, I'm forced to deal again. There's no more Church Commission, only hints, quotes, speculation, the occasional fact turned up by investigations of the Chilean secret police's crimes. The CIA slips behind the cards, becomes the cards, playing themselves out against knowledge, resolution.

There's no doubt that the CIA knew of the coup beforehand. Afterward, with the suspension of civil liberties and political parties, funding for CIA activities was drastically cut and most anti-Allende projects were cancelled. Covert operations focused on improving the military regime's image, along with maintaining access to government leaders. The CIA contributed to the Junta's early economic plans and maintained its media influence. It also renewed its contacts with Chilean security and intelligence services.

The CIA had helped develop the intelligence arm of the Carabineros in the sixties and later encouraged the Military Intelligence Service (SIM) to turn its attention to "counterinsurgency programs" within Chile. Upon seizing power, "Pinochet, on the advice of the CIA, asserted the need for a full-scale secret police that was under his personal command, independent of any military structure and charged with the coordination of the other intelligence agencies," say John Dinges and Saul Landau in their book, *Assassination on Embassy Row*. The CIA had already encouraged the development of similar forces in South Korea, Brazil and Iran. Pinochet put Colonel Manuel Contreras in charge of what was to become the most powerful secret organization in Chile.

According to a former member of the DINA, the secret police, interviewed by Dinges and Landau, "At the beginning of 1974, he (Colonel Manuel Contreras) had a full set of plans and six months later he had built an empire. I thought he was some kind of genius to have built up such a large, complicated apparatus in such a short time – then I found out how much help he got from the CIA in organizing it." This same source indicated that DINA agents were trained using CIA instruction and procedural manuals.

The CIA admitted to the Church Commission that the Agency worked to help Chile control "external" subversion. Given the activities of the DINA's External Department, this has turned out to be quite an admission.

Chapter ten

OF DWARVES
AND GIANTS

WASHINGTON, SANTIAGO 1976, 1989

We are like dwarfs on the shoulders of giants, so that we can see more than they, and things at a
greater distance, not by virtue of any sharpness of sight on our part, or any physical distinction,
but because we are carried high and raised up by their giant size.

BERNARD OF CHARTRES, DIED CIRCA 1130

In 1974, the military government finally exiled Orlando Letelier, thanks
to pressure from a prominent Venezuelan politician, who was a close
friend of Letelier's, and Letelier soon returned to the United States where
he proved a credible and diligent opponent to the regime. The contacts
he had sown as ambassador came to fruition, and he began to build up
considerable support for the regime's opposition. After a conference in
Mexico, the Popular Unity's exiled leaders appointed him their representative in Washington.

In the years that followed the coup, the defeated Popular Unity parties
were particularly bitter about the Christian Democrats' refusal to compromise with them. The Christian Democrats' obvious assumption that
the military would hold power only temporarily, then hand it over, probably to Eduardo Frei, the former president, fed the bitterness. Few political
leaders would be able to bridge these differences and unite efforts to
defeat the Junta. Orlando Letelier was quickly becoming one of them.

Laura Novoa took refuge in copper. "As an open supporter of the military government and a good opponent to the Popular Unity, I was reap-

pointed head lawyer of the now government-run copper company. We worked to pull everything back together."

A year later, obsessed by her sense that the American companies should receive compensation, she completed a brief on the subject just as the military government appointed a negotiator to come to terms with those companies. By 1974-75, the regime had "cleaned up the past.

"Now the politicians say what we did was a mistake; but we called it a success because those affected accepted the fact that the mines weren't returned [to the American companies] and because the sums agreed upon were based on the regime established by Allende's constitution and the amounts paid were really prudent, not to say advantageous, for the Chilean government.

"Afterward, I was put in charge of organizing the new copper corporation, that is, to reorganize all the nationalized companies whose administration under the UP [Popular Unity] had been precarious and inefficient. And the current National Corporation of Copper of Chile was put together through a law which I participated in."

With the military in power, the symbolism of September took on new overtones. In 1974, General Carlos Prats was in exile in Argentina, putting the finishing touches on his memoirs and corresponding with former colleagues, concerned about the direction the military regime was taking. On September 30th, a car bomb destroyed Prats and his wife, eliminating a dangerous threat to General Pinochet's growing power. The next year, a founding member of the Christian Democratic Party, Bernardo Leighton, was making important strides toward uniting Popular Unity and Christian Democratic party members in exile in Italy. He was also convincing the Italians of the importance of showing strong opposition to the Chilean regime. One September evening, he and his wife were gunned down as they arrived home after a stroll. They survived their crippling injuries, but the political unity that Leighton had been so close to achieving did not.

September 1976 came round and Orlando Letelier was informed that he'd been stripped of his Chilean citizenship — a symbolic gesture, to be sure, but one that cut to the bone. On September 18th, he and Isabel danced their last *cueca* together; on September 21st, a car bomb blew off his legs and killed him. Flying metal cut the throat of Ronni Moffit, an American friend riding in the passenger seat. Her new husband, riding in the back, leapt out, screaming over and over: "DINA did this! DINA!"

Details of how much the CIA helped to build the DINA's external network remain unknown, as does the extent of CIA knowledge of DINA's subsequent operations. But judicial investigations in the United States and Chile have since thrown other cards onto the table. There's a sudden glut of information, the easy ordering when every card falls into place and the solitaire reveals how Manuel Contreras, head of DINA, the powerful secret police, set out to build a powerful international network and largely succeeded. His shadow army linked Italian fascists nostalgic for the total solutions of World War II, CIA-trained Cuban nationalists disillusioned with the US after the CIA "abandoned" them, and intelligence organizations in Argentina, Chile, Paraguay, Venezuela and other Latin American countries in a powerful web of mutual obligations, information sharing and murder, as surely as Chilean copper wire carried conversations across mountain ranges, under oceans, past horizons.

Until early 1977, when the Carter administration changed top personnel, CIA head General Alexander Haig enjoyed a cordial relationship with Manuel Contreras and received him at headquarters in Langley, Virginia, in August 1975. The State Department also knew that in 1976, two Chilean agents applied for visas to enter the United States using false Paraguayan passports. This was detected by the US ambassador in Paraguay, George Landau, who photographed every page of the documents and later rescinded the visas. Contreras then sent two different agents to the States using the same names and they phoned the CIA directly. Although they were in Washington barely a month before Letelier's death, the CIA showed no apparent interest in their mission.

The man who built and mounted the bomb that killed Letelier and altered an electronic paging device which set it off was a blond American whose family followed their businessman father to Chile in the sixties. Michae'. Townley could never seem to win his father's full approval. When Allende was elected, Townley formed a squadron of Fatherland and Freedom fighters that eavesdropped on governmental phone lines and blew up strategic targets. After the coup, all Michael Townley wanted was to serve his leader, General Pinochet, and win an officer's commission in the Chilean Army. He had tried to convince the CIA to recruit him on at least three occasions, but the Agency appears to have done no more than maintain the contact. To this day, Townley calls Letelier's killing a mere confrontation between one soldier and another. The fact that Letelier was never armed doesn't disturb him. Goebbels, too, fought with ideas, says he.

The Letelier and Moffit families, staff from the Institute for Policy Studies where Letelier and Moffit worked, and several American journalists rode the investigation like a horse, whipping it over seemingly unsurmountable barriers, driving it on when it seemed permanently bogged down. It was a hard ride, as FBI agents and lawyers in the US Attorney General's office favoured other theories. The possibility of a sexual motivation – the Leteliers had been separated – was their first choice. Through sympathetic media, the CIA propagated the theory that Letelier was killed by the Chilean left in a macabre scheme to create a martyr that would damage Pinochet's reputation. Investigators chewed this over until it was more hole than theory. State Department employees contributed to these digressions by filing away George Landau's memorandum about the Paraguayan visa incident and the photographs it contained. When those photographs reached the hands of US Attorney Eugene Propper, the investigation focused on the DINA and entered the home stretch. They hit the pages of Washington newspapers and wire services carried them to Chile and *El Mercurio*. Within hours, people who'd met Townley were shakily dialling reporters.

The fact that the Chileans had carried off a bombing in the heart of Washington provoked the wrath of many who worked for the crime's resolution with genuine passion. George Landau, who had first stared uneasily at Townley's photograph on a visa application in Paraguay, was US ambassador in Santiago when Townley's name became public knowledge. Together with US Attorney Propper and FBI Agent Robert Scherrer, he bluffed and threatened the Chilean military government, and convinced the Chileans that they needed a scapegoat and that Townley would fit the bill nicely. On April 8, 1978, Investigaciones detectives hastily bundled him into a car and rushed him to the airport, where Scherrer and Propper handcuffed him and accompanied him onto a plane.

Loyal to his Chilean masters to the end, Townley required written permission from his "senior officers" in the Chilean military before he would testify in the United States and he still swears General Pinochet knew nothing of the assassination plan – a difficult assertion given the crime's importance and the fact that Pinochet was Contreras's direct – and only – superior officer. In the ensuing years, American police have tracked down most of the Cuban exiles involved in the murder plot. Townley served forty months of his ten-year sentence and was released on parole, to a new identity and a new life, somewhere in the States. A special commission awarded US$12 million to the Letelier family for their loss, which the civilian Chilean government agreed to pay.

In Chile, the Letelier case has become a major test of whether the victims of human rights violations under the military can expect any justice from Chile's compromised legal system. (Retired) General Manuel Contreras and his righthand man, Colonel Pedro Espinoza (still in active service), are on trial. It remains a tough and dangerous battle between the pro-military courts and an independent investigating judge, supported by the family and all those concerned with the case's results.

The Letelier case showed just how much influence the US could wield. At the time, it was one of only a handful of governments supporting the military Junta. Inside Chile, US advisers and friends were encouraging economic restructuring and were playing down human rights violations. But Contreras's methods had given Pinochet unprecedented power over the military as well as civilian Chile and many of the regime's political leaders were anxious to have him removed. When the US threatened to cut off relations if Townley weren't handed over, Contreras's opponents within Chile saw their chance to depose him.

Even before Townley's expulsion under pressure from the United States and some Chileans, General Pinochet announced plans for turning Chile into a "protected democracy" and began restructuring the DINA, firing about one thousand agents and creating a new organization called the Central Nacional de Informaciones (CNI). In November 1977, Pinochet replaced Contreras with another Army general whose intelligence-obsessed father had actually given him an encoded name. General Odlanier Mena (his first name is Reinaldo spelled backward) assumed control in conditions that more closely resembled gang warfare than a bureaucratic change. General Contreras packed his files, with details, many of them unsavoury, about the lives of hundreds, perhaps thousands of Chileans, into boxes and shipped them abroad, a kind of insurance policy which many feel is still in effect today.

Barely a week after Townley's expulsion, in April 1978, General Pinochet was swearing in a new cabinet, the first one to have a civilian majority. Hernán Cubillos, former righthand man to Agustín Edwards and a man who'd co-operated closely with the CIA's propaganda mis-

sions in Chile, took over the Ministry of Foreign Affairs. A new deal, a
new game began.

The Letelier case marks an important shift in US policy toward Chile. It
was too blatant, too dangerous a threat to be ignored. Its resolution led
to the strict enforcement of a new American law suspending sales of US
military equipment to Chile. The regime's use of CIA techniques to carry
out its own political agenda around the world earned it a severe and
public slap on the nose from the United States government.

But the fine strands of copper, braided now with gold and silver continued to wind their way from one continent to the next. Behind the economic policies bringing poverty and unemployment to Chile's precarious
poblaciones were the economic theories of yet another American. Chile's
suppression of civil, human and labour rights made the country an ideal
laboratory for the neo-liberal ideas of Chicago economist Milton Friedman. Pinochet, surrounded by graduates from the University of Chicago,
fully supported the economic model they were determined to implement
in Chile. From 1976 until 1983 (at least), the human rights versus economics dichotomy ruled, and US policymakers favoured economic over
human rights, publicly praising the economy's advances as they employed
"silent diplomacy" to convince the regime to ease up on its opponents.
Although the US abstained on some international credits to the Chilean
government, it was with full knowledge that the excess of petro-dollars
on world money markets would make private credit a secure alternative.

As economic ties between the two countries buzzed, Laura Novoa
mourned the decay of a legal system she was brought up to love and
revere, and looked hopefully for signs that with an elected government
back in power, that would change. "Just recently," she told me in 1991,
"the military court sanctioned a police lieutenant who, during a protest,
arrested four boys who weren't doing anything violent, had them beaten,
stripped and thrown into a canal. One of them drowned. This was proven
and the officer punished. If that had occurred in the beginning, if the
military or non-military courts had acted with that kind of rigour, I think
the Chilean situation would have been very different."

The military government started out harshly, but "pure in the sense
that they had the best intentions. What happened afterward is that
groups within the Armed Forces – and that's why you can't contaminate
the entire institution with this – began to act under the pretext or the

conviction that to clean our society, for the common good, it was indispensable to eliminate whole political sectors. I don't know if this is because of what they call the doctrine of National Security, but there's no doubt that was the ideology behind most of the brutality that was committed. And this was managed by very small groups of people – I'm sure that many military, police, aviator and naval officers didn't even know because the Armed Forces' system is so vertical, so authoritarian. At the same time, if something becomes known, the *esprit de corps* is such that everyone defends [the institution]."

National Security. The Rettig Commission, of which Laura Novoa was eventually a member, called it the doctrine of counter-insurgency, and described it as a no-holds-barred guerilla war between the USSR and the US that each country was fighting within its own borders and worldwide. The doctrine reflected the training that Latin American armed forces, Chile's among them, had received from the United States, including covert actions, interrogation techniques, "special" deaths, ambushes, survival techniques which often included carrying out cruel or degrading acts, that "accustomed students to retreating ethical limits".

The doctrine of National Security provided the ideological foundations for the coup and gave the military the ruthless logic they required to pursue their goals. For American policy makers it was one of the considerations that justified their continued support for Pinochet.

A US ambassador in Santiago, James Theberge, taught a course on National Security at the military institute. Theberge's was the blank face of the King, covering a pile of hidden aces, or so many people in Chile felt. No one missed the significance of the American government's support for the military government in the face of worldwide condemnation. Sometimes the United States seemed to be the last strut propping up the façade of the Pinochet government's legitimacy: the former Popular Unity parties and Christian Democrats levered away, trying to knock it down.

After the Copper Workers Confederation called for the first national protest against the military regime and, rather to the surprise of organizers and almost everyone else, disgusted citizens filled Chilean cities with the clanging of empty pots, cheerful marchers and excited professionals honking the horns of their spanking new cars throughout middle-class neighbourhoods, rumours flew that James Theberge was in trouble, that he'd confidently predicted the protests would flop. As the protest movement began to provide the cover for an urban guerrilla movement, US policy makers became increasingly concerned.

And what was the CIA doing? There were rumours again: that the CIA had detected the Manuel Rodríguez Patriotic Front's arms smuggling operation; this was officially denied. In the early hours after the ambush on General Pinochet's convoy, no one could believe that a Chilean opposition group had the discipline and the resources to carry off such an operation. The CIA? An army squad, disillusioned with the regime? Those rumours proved false, but the CIA remained a presence, haunting Chilean politics.

By 1985, changes were seeping slowly through the adobe walls of Chile's political world. Embittered, many say, by the regime's reluctance to improve its image, Theberge finally left Chile and in yet another September, in Washington, he lunched with the man who would replace him. This was a tall, loose-limbed fellow with the crooked nose and irregular features of a boxer. He was also a gifted American diplomat, an expert player of games of solitaire in countries as diverse and complex as India, Rumania, the USSR. He knew which cards not to touch, which to uncover. In November 1985, Harry Barnes arrived in Santiago.

He dealt again.

Boston, 1993, in an Au Bon Pain restaurant near Harvard University, I sip on orange juice and coffee, try to ignore the classical music in the background, and listen to Harry Barnes's version of his tour of duty in Chile.

I was born in Minnesota of German and English extraction. My first name's Harry, after my father. We were a generation or so removed from farming. My father was really a land speculator, grandfathers were both ministers, but there was a small community, a couple of hundred people, so everybody did some farming. One day when I was home on vacation, my father called me and said someone from the foreign service is back in town, why don't you go talk to him. So I did. It sounded interesting, so I pursued it.

In September 1973, I was in Washington, working in what's called the Executive Secretariat of the State Department. There are several senior positions ... the Executive Secretary has two deputies and I was one of the two, and each of us had big chunks of that management, for a good part it's information management you might say, to see that material needed for decisions is provided on time and in a useful way. Or to carry out instructions of the Secretary and Deputies which lead to par-

ticular actions again often in the form of paper, such as options of courses of action, or suggestions for actions or policies.

There's a section of the secretariat called the operations centre, sort of the nerve centre of the State Department as far as information's concerned. And the secretariat proper which works on things that are a little less time sensitive or requiring something more in the way of thought and development. We shifted back and forth between those two. I was in charge of the slower paced part [on September 11, 1973], but some months earlier, when I was still working on Operations (the faster paced part) there was a bulletin that came in about rumours of a coup in Chile and one of my colleagues who had worked then with the group which managed the operations centre recalled some years later that he had phoned me in the middle of the night to say there was something brewing in Chile. The actual coup part, no, I don't remember being involved in it. I probably would not have been, given what I was doing then.

I knew a certain amount [about Chile before I went there] because of the attention that was paid in the United States, particularly at the time of the Church Committee investigation, although I was overseas at the time. And I knew something because of my interest about human rights matters.

My approach was essentially to try to immerse myself in the context and then when I thought I was beginning to understand something to draw up some hypotheses, what I thought might be a program, or some objectives, for the time I was going to be assigned to that country, and then the third step was to try and see if I could develop a consensus among the people with whom I would deal in Washington. [For Chile, my objectives were:] first, supporting an early return to democracy. Second, promoting a much greater respect for basic human rights. And third, an emphasis on an open free economy.

I met Jim Theberge in Washington. We had lunch one day at the State Department and talked for some time. My sense was he'd come to the conclusion that it was important for the United States to be somewhat more explicit about what was important for us. I guess that if he'd stayed on, he might have been more outspoken. My sense was that he was somewhere between frustrated and disillusioned, that he thought that the approach that he was taking would produce more in the way of understanding and results on the part of the government and it had not.

I think there was beginning to be some change of perception. There was a change of personnel in Washington. Elliott Abrams who'd been the

*Assistant Secretary of State for Human Rights and Humanitarian Affairs
had been named to be the Assistant Secretary of State for Latin American Affairs and brought to that new job experience with the Chilean
question in human rights fora. I remember comments he'd made earlier
on about the frustration he encountered in dealing with Chilean representatives, so he came into his new job with at least questions, reserva-
tions about the Chilean government on human rights matters. His
deputy, Bob Gelbard, who was responsible for our relations with South
America, had at an earlier stage been involved in Washington in dealing
with economic questions and dealing with Chile and had a good sense of
the country and problems, but also felt that economic policies were not
sufficient justification to remain uncritical of other aspects of the Chilean
government's behaviour.*

*I [also] made it a point to get to know people in the Congress who were
critical of government policy toward Chile to get a better sense of why
they were critical, what problems they saw and also to get to know people in the human rights non-governmental positions for the same reason.*

*Attitudes varied from the conviction that this made sense to some
scepticism, "well try it and we'll see what happens". The scepticism
could be from one side or another – some people who thought that the
economic side was particularly important and could be supported, the
free market approach, people who weren't so certain how far one could
go on the human rights side, or should go. And people on the other hand
who thought the emphasis should be very heavily on the human rights
and democracy side and weren't so sure that could be linked up with the
economic approach.*

*I found the [Chilean] government, I think, confused by me. Not quite
sure whether they should be nice or not nice. They went back and forth
some. The people in the opposition on balance willing to give me and
our approach at least the benefit of the doubt, although there was some
puzzlement about how the US could be in favour of the Pinochet government's economic approach but critical of the Pinochet government on
human rights and democracy.*

*I tended to see [Pinochet] a couple of times a year on sort of set
occasions, [for example] around Christmas time there was a reception for
the diplomatic corps. On the whole, in public, [he was] polite. The other
occasion was the annual international trade fair, where he would tour*

various pavilions. I guess he came to our pavilion [three times] and my job as the ambassador was to sort of escort him around.

There was also an instruction at one point — because I'd still occasionally see him when I took visiting American dignitaries — that I should be cropped out of any picture [leaving] just the personage who was visiting and Pinochet. There was a period when Pinochet apparently put out an instruction in 1988 that I should be kept at a distance and there was a cartoon, I think in La Segunda, *that showed me standing at the gates of the Moneda, with the gates firmly shut. [He chuckles.]*

I fairly quickly got caught up in what turned out to be the death of Rodrigo Rojas, the burning of the two of them, with Carmen Gloria [when detained by a military patrol during protests in July 1986]. Obvious reaction of shock that anyone could have been set on fire. Went to see right afterwards one of the priests who'd been very much involved and again also relied on other members of my staff. When we got word from friends at the Human Rights Commission that there was going to be a memorial service, my wife and I talked it over and just concluded that this sort of behaviour was something that you had to register publicly as being beyond the pale. He was not a US citizen but his time in the United States was such that I thought there was an American point, so to speak, as well as a more general human point that could be made.

The only demonstration [I saw], if you want to call it that, was the funeral, when the guanacos *[water cannon] came after the crowd. Those of us from the diplomatic corps who were there were invited outside for the service, but the press of the crowd was such that whoever was supposed to come get us never made it. The next thing we knew the service had started, we could hear it through the loud speakers, so we watched what we could through the windows. Then saw the crowd starting to mill around, which didn't make sense for a service, it was only then— it was my wife as a matter of fact, who spotted on one angle the approach of the* guanacos.

Paradoxically for my own situation, the approach that I advocated in terms of US policy was strengthened because of something that came out of the burnings, namely Senator Helms's visit to Chile and his strong attack on me as an individual, but [also] in effect, the policies we were following. There was a clear identification with a return to democracy, respect for human rights. And the revulsion in this country [the US], opposition to Helms's opposition, make my position much stronger.

I found no shortage of people with whom I could talk, a fairly broad spectrum. I decided I would not seek out anybody in the Communist Party. Essentially a conviction that it would not be helpful to my principle mission; that is, if I appeared to be associated with the party, various questions [would be raised] about the basic democratic thrust of what I was trying to do; and second, because, at least at that point, and the whole time that I was in Chile, it seemed to me that the party had an approach which didn't contribute anything to trying to find any lasting solutions.

Over time [I] developed certain patterns, for example, you may have known Marilyn MacAfee; she would organize periodic lunches at her house with people from radio and TV, writers, journalists, editors and we would just talk about an hour and a half or two hours off the record and the ground rules were only that we both got chances to ask questions. That is, I got the chance to ask them what was going on in such and such a thing, where I had trouble understanding and they asked me what the United States was doing and not doing.

As an individual mathematically there's just so much you can do. You've got to select. Hope your selection is somewhat judicious and relevant. Also you've got to rely on other people whose judgement you might trust. What I attempted to do was also to get something of a cross-section in two ways, one by going outside the capital. Spending some time, a couple of days a month, somewhere in the regions. Secondly, used time in Santiago to talk with people connected to non-governmental organizations, relied here both on people on my staff who had Chilean friends and acquaintances with connections, plus American non-govermental groups – for example Americas Watch, Amnesty International's human rights side, with the Interamerican foundation which worked with small groups.

This tended on the whole to confirm the sense of significant problems despite the economic prosperity on a certain level. There were other levels of society where things were very tough. It also confirmed the sense that Chileans were resourceful. Could work together in the face of serious difficulties. The soup kitchens, for example, the ability to help one another in the poblaciones, *that type of thing.*

My own sense was that a more coherent approach by the opposition might have produced better results than going back to the protests. There

Matilde Urrutia, widow of Chilean poet Pablo Neruda, who won the Nobel Prize for Poetry before his death in the wake of the 1973 coup, during a gathering at his tomb in Santiago's General Cemetery in the early eighties. After elected government resumed power, the graves of both Neruda and Urrutia were moved to his beloved home on the sea's edge in Isla Negra. *(Photograph: Patricio Lanfranco)*

top
A delegation of Canadian unionists, Margaret Wilson, Jean Claude Parrot, Ron White, meet with Rodolfo Seguel, then president of the Copper Workers Confederation in 1984. *(Photograph: Patricio Lanfranco)*

bottom
A solitary candle lights a street vendor's display of illegal publications that kept alive the songs of Violeta Parra and Victor Jara, 1983. *(Photograph: Patricio Lanfranco)*

top
The cable cars of Valparaiso. *(Photograph: Patricio Lanfranco)*

bottom
Welcome to Colonia Dignidad in 1987: the front gate, complete with electric porter system and a barbed wire fence are unusual among Andean farms and ranches. *(Photograph: Ines Paulino)*

above
On a university campus, the Christian Democrats' symbolic arrow and the left's militant fist share two sides of a cement column, 1979. *(Photograph: Patricio Lanfranco)*

right
On September 29, 1983, the Cardinal Silva Enriquez land occupation began when women and children staked out their square of ground, erecting improvised tents with blankets and any other material that came to hand.
(Photograph: Patricio Lanfranco)

above
With help from professional and union organizations and foreign non-government organizations, the "squatters" built houses of wood, 1984. *(Photograph: Patricio Lanfranco)*

left
Female volunteers, belonging to organizations headed by the wives of the members of the military Junta, parade down the Alameda in front of the Moneda, to show support for General Pinochet, 1981. *(Photograph: Patricio Lanfranco)*

above
Flaming barricades and flimsy banners
mark the resistance of young people
who fight police under a drawing of
the face of Dr. Allende. *(Photograph:
Patricio Lanfranco)*

right
Lake Sagaris covers a demonstration at
the University of Chile Faculty of Law,
during anti-government protests in 1985.

*were of course a couple of other things which made it more difficult for
the opposition. The arms caches for example. The assassination attempt
on Pinochet. The only role that the US played [there] was in terms of
helping to identify the types of weaponry and therefore the likely origins.
We provided some experts in that respect.*

*[The discovery of the arms cache] underlined the complicated nature
of the situation. Even though numerically there was a very small number
of people involved [in the Front], there was a violent side that I don't
think commanded much popular support, [but] it still could reinforce the
Pinochet approach, which saw no case as being democratic and could
undercut any efforts by the democratic opposition to try and become a
viable alternative.*

*I was not the only one of the foreign ambassadors – I'm thinking now
of 1987 – who in one form or another were trying to get the message
across to the democratic opposition that they couldn't expect to get significant understanding or support in various ways from democratic countries
outside of Chile if they couldn't show that they were committed enough
to organize themselves to represent some sort of a united route ... but I
think the logic of the obvious was also fairly clear to people in Chile.*

*In a shorter time frame I didn't think [there would be a civil war] but
I did worry that if the opposition couldn't organize itself effectively,
couldn't present an alternative, then, you could get a continuation of the
Pinochet regime and the corresponding frustration, even though it might
in a sense be the opposition's fault, would still turn out to constitute a
motive for people providing a tacit support to a more violent approach.*

So the Front, possibly against its own intentions, influenced things
toward a more peaceful solution?

I think so.

*Scepticism was probably the greatest with people in the business
community. They were so convinced of the rightness of the economic
approach that they were troubled by any criticism of the government on
other grounds. I think one of the accomplishments I tend in retrospect
to feel particularly positive about was what I sensed as a significant
change, at least among some leaders of the business community,
particularly at the time of the plebiscite that business, should I say
stability, or business prospects did not have to be tied to a military
dictatorship, that this could thrive in a democratic society as well, or
at least there was a chance of that. So there began to be more in the*

way of dialogue between people in the business community, politicians, labour union leaders.

One knew what the constitution said and one could figure out the latest date that the plebiscite might take place, but the question of what was necessary before that to create some conditions for some sort of participation was a fairly frequent theme in the series of conversations I had with the 1986/87 Minister of the Interior, Ricardo García, and as it began to look as if there would be some actual decree laws setting up the framework, then it did seem as if there might be something there that could be used.

I don't think I was the only one, obviously, but I was part of the sentiment saying in effect to use this [the mechanism of the plebiscite] for all its worth. I thought there was enough sentiment in the country that would give Pinochet a significant vote in his favour that, unless a boycott were really massive and represented a clear and firm conviction on the part of the opposition, Pinochet would not only win mathematically but that he would win in effect psychologically.

But the first condition I felt was for the democratic opposition to decide whether it was capable of forging some sort of a consensus, that is, developing the processes, the consultative mechanisms, the mutual confidence so they can decide anything.

That it worked, in spite of some initial scepticism and that it worked as well as it did, yes, I was quite impressed.

Some things I still don't understand: for a referendum you don't need political parties. But the feeling that this was somehow in the Chilean tradition. If I were more cynical, cynical isn't quite the right word, probably if I were more imaginative, I would think that it was a conspiracy on somebody's part, a pro-democratic conspiracy, to persuade the regime that there had to be political parties and somehow that got through.

There were certainly people in the regime who I thought were, in their own lights, in a democratic business. They wanted a return to a recognizable democracy. They could have felt that the coup wasn't only necessary but desirable, that Pinochet had accomplished a lot in various ways and so on, but that was not the same thing as thinking that the Pinochet government ought to go on indefinitely, so to that extent I think they put their weight behind seeing that the plebiscite was indeed an open and fairly conducted act.

The rumours at the time [of the plebiscite] were that the government

*alternatively feared or hoped that the Frente [Patriotico Manuel
Rodriguez] or their people on the extreme would stage demonstrations
and try to take advantage of the anticipated opposition victory to get a
massive demonstration going and the government therefore had to be
prepared to cope with the sort of violence that would come out of that.
Some of the rumours were to the effect that the government would use
this as an excuse to suspend the counting and somehow invalidate the
results. Till it was over it wasn't over; you couldn't be absolutely sure.*

*One of the questions I ask myself fairly often [is why so much American
interest in Chile]. I can only talk about the period I knew directly. I don't
really know if it's valid before or valid since. My analysis at the time
was that there were a couple of factors, not in order of importance. Certainly there had been the earlier economic ties, copper was part of it, but
then you had the nationalizations. I think in the American business
community that pays attention to what goes on in the rest of the world,
there was a very favourable impression created by the free market
approach that came in the seventies. It was not tarnished that much by
the collapse in 1982, because the recovery was relatively rapid.*

*On a second level, much less positive, in fact, very negative, was the
whole human rights side. And a feeling there that the abuses in Chile were
particularly outrageous given the country's democratic tradition. There
was also a domestic political angle, among Democrats in Congress in
particular, that there was a feeling the Reagan administration in its first
term was reversing the position developed on human rights by the Carter
administration and probably because of the role that was perceived that
the United States played in the overthrow of Allende, a sense that it was
only worse that the United States was not supporting respect for human
rights in Chile. So there was a sense on that side, a combination of guilt
and I would say outrage, sorrow, regret and a variety of aspects.*

*For all of the good economic policies, Pinochet didn't seem to care
that much about − call it the atmosphere, call it the context − in which
Chile reached the United States ... even those who were in favour of the
economic policies, they found it embarrassing many times to have this
sort of regime promoting those policies.*

*[The Letelier assassination] was a thread all the way through. Again,
the people who were supporters of the economic approach tended not to
give that much attention; those who were concerned about human rights*

took it as a particular affront to the United States because it happened here. And felt there was a particular obligation on the part of the US government somehow to see that the people responsible for the assassination were prosecuted.

Clearly what happened in Chile is essentially what Chileans were able to accomplish. [For us] it was possible to chart out an approach and to stick with it for a couple of years and I think on the whole play a somewhat useful be it marginal role in what turned out to be a very positive outcome. As an outsider, it's good to be on the side that won and won in a meaningful sense. Because I think that for all the differences with any other country that you could name, what the Chilean experience demonstrates goes back to the maturity of Chileans.

What's important about the Chilean experience is that it does show what a people is capable of and does speak very well for a long democratic tradition. If Chileans hadn't been able to recover their democratic heritage I think that would have had very serious implications for many other places in the world.

Of all the assignments we had, each in its own way brought a lot to all of us in our family, but in terms of the sense of being involved in something quite, quite moving and fairly historic it's hard to beat that period in Chile. Particularly that last year.

It demonstrated to me, speaking here as an American, that the United States is able at least on occasion to be supportive in times of stress in ways which are compatible with what I would consider our own basic values. I went to a lecture yesterday afternoon in Harvard, given by the author of this new book on Kissinger, where there was a discussion of morality and power, characterized by Kissinger, but also more broadly in American history over the last couple of decades. Turned around it was a question of how much morality and how much of our values are possible or tolerable in questions of the national interest. I think that one can, one has to bring in questions of values [his husky voice deepens], how you bring them in and how effectively is very tough, but I'd be among those who feel that you can't leave them out.

My experience in Chile in a sense confirmed that you can not only not leave them out, but that you must bring them in.

You return to Washington to study Economics and Politics at Georgetown University, graduate, return to Chile. During your first detention, your name, Juan Pablo Letelier, brings you special abuse from police, but nothing worse. You join the Socialist Party. You climb steadily through the same spheres of power your father knew. Many of your companions are sons and daughters of his friends. You marry. Have children. They turn mealtimes into minor riots. You let them. Your hair is still long, at least by Chilean standards. You speak Spanish with a slight accent. Sometimes English words break through the smooth surface of your "mother" tongue.

Your impression is that your political beliefs stem more from the rational point of view than a material need to have those points of view. On October 5, 1989, you're among those who hug and beam and celebrate the opposition's victory in the plebiscite. On December 11, 1989, you're elected to a seat in Chile's Congress.

Now you watch your old homeland from a distance. The dual vision of your upbringing serves you well. In fluent English, you say:

"I think that if there are pressures in this new context, things will not occur as they occurred in US foreign policies in the late sixties and early seventies. There will be a large area of permanent tensions, which are due to the fact that we are a small country, that we have national interests which are very important and which are contradictory to US interests. Today Chile is in a lot better condition to diversify its foreign relations, diversify its commerce, its foreign investment. Now, that opens an external front which is very different from the sixties, in which the US and Chile's foreign relations were very concentrated. We were very dependent on the US.

"I have no doubt that in the Chilean left there's a different reading and understanding of American society, with a capacity to differentiate what the society is all about, the social actors, the different roles of Congress versus the Executive branch, how one can find allies depending upon what the topic is under discussion.

"One has to assume that we're a growingly and consistently and inevitably interdependent world. In external relations, the US can't continue saying that they're the fathers of free market, international commerce, and still remain most protective and most insensitive to those who are making open commerce a reality. One perceives that the US as well as other developed countries are consistently protectionist, [applying] the law of the funnel – the large end for them and the short end for less developed countries. I would like to see more equal relations. I favour participating [in a Free Trade agreement] based on certain conditions: that Chile not become the sweatshop of the US and its transnational industries. We want to compete.

"The US today is not Chile's only option."

A friend's rough sketch of Orlando Letelier, your father, in the Dawson Island prison camp in 1974, has watched you from the wall of every office you've ever occupied.

Chapter eleven

LA VICTORIA

SANTIAGO'S SOUTHSIDE 1957,1983

There was a married couple who had a son who was in the Navy. One day their boy came to see them. The father was a very humble man and the mother too. They were very good people. So the father starts to talk about what's been happening in la Victoria in the protests — how is it possible that they do all these things, killing people and so on? The son stares at his father and says, look Dad, if they tell us to kill our father because he's a Communist, then we must do it.

And the father says, Son, would you do that?

Yes, he answers. Because if I don't, they'll kill me.

Then the father says, but that's impossible! It's incredible that you would prefer to kill us to avoid being killed yourself.

That was how badly they'd brainwashed him. And the father was so hurt — well, he always drank, but after that he got into it seriously and he used to say "my son said he'd kill me, how can this be?"

One day he got very drunk and he crossed into the airport and the soldiers yelled "no!" and he yelled "yes! I'd rather you killed me than my son." Like that. Desperate. He died that same year with that great pain. His son never returned to ask his pardon, not while he was alive and not for his funeral either. And the mother always remembers.

That was the worst thing about the coup. Whole families became enemies.

It begins as a one-inch newspaper story on the front page of a section in

El Mercurio in May of 1983: the Copper Workers' Confederation has called for a National Strike. A what? In the midst of hunger marchers beaten down by enthused riot police, in the midst of funerals, and of my growing knowledge of the Catholic cult of the dead, in the midst of the muffled outrage of families and human rights organizations, and of almost no other outrage, the Copper Workers have called for a National Strike? I look up federation headquarters in the phonebook and head downtown, to a rather dark, unfriendly building on MacIver Street. On the sixth floor of a poorly furnished office I'm made to wait for the newly elected president, a fellow new to Chilean politics, with the burly, rather pear-shaped figure I'll soon learn is typical of miners.

There I learn that the Copper Workers' Confederation, the spoiled élite of Chile's working class, famous until now for striking against the Allende government in the early seventies and producing one of a handful of pro-regime union leaders, have elected a new leadership. In their general meeting they voted to hold a National Strike, which, by the time I visit, they have changed to a National Protest, set for May 11, 1983. Their declaration clearly states that the problem is not simply changing one law or another but rather, "it's a whole economic, social, cultural and political system, which has surrounded and limited us".

The instructions for the protest day are straightforward, borrowed, in fact, from tactics that middle- and upper-class housewives had used to shame the Allende government during the early seventies: keep children home from school, don't shop and at 8 p.m. honk horns and bang empty saucepans to symbolize the disastrous effects of the government's economic policies.

Early on the evening of May 11th, a strange silence descends on the city. Our apartment has a small balcony overlooking the street and we've opened the door in case anything happens. At eight o'clock sharp, a distant ringing floats in from the pale night sky which curves like an inverted bowl over the city, reflecting its lights, refracting its sounds. We step out onto the balcony and the clank, clank, clank of someone banging a pot rings out nearby. Another joins in. It's then we realize how used to silence we have become, sitting speechless on subway cars, or nodding noncommittally at taxi drivers' eternal monologues. Now the silence is being broken, first by a metallic trickle running downtown, running to the north, south, east and west of us, swelling until a cascade of sound is pouring through the streets the way winter floods have swept over bridges, turning pavement into riverbeds. From nearby Plaza Italia rises an excited chorus of honking horns and suddenly the whole city seems to be lifted out of itself by the clamour of spoons slamming steel.

We turn on Radio Cooperativa and hear that police are shooting tear-gas bombs at the middle-class apartment buildings at Tomás Moro and Fleming streets. The phone rings. Chavela calls from the middle-class neighbourhood of Nuñoa and we can hardly hear her for the din. A friend has told her of gunshots on the roundabout near her house. Ernesto phones, exhilarated after driving through Providencia: the high-rise buildings roar with the thunder of saucepan drums and whole families are out in their cars, honking and grinning and celebrating as if Chile had just won the world series.

I was born in the Teniente camp, in a housing project [near the copper mine] called Coya. At eighteen I had to leave, because of the repression of González Videla. My father had worked in different places, on the railways, then as an electrician, and he ended up taking care of the sluice gates at the main dam. He'd been there for more than thirty years. ..

My great crime was having worked for González Videla's election; we worked as the Communist Party, as the youth. We were young and there was a girls' group. The camp was small, there wasn't much to do. So we felt happy working for González Videla, especially when he was elected. I was thirteen then. We never measured the consequences. And we liked it because it was a disciplined party, a mixed party where women were respected.

But when he was elected, the first thing he did was persecute the Communists. Leaving was very hard. There were caravans of people who'd been fired, with nowhere to go, like us.

The way rain dispels the clogged, muggy sensation of humid, grey days and clammy nights; the way it washes away the smog and clouds and suddenly the mountains emerge, craggy and white, floating above the city; the way everything looks suddenly sharper in the clear dry light; by the next morning Santiago has changed irrevocably. We all know this instinctively. Something essential has changed and the fear has lost its hold. It's still there, but it's not in control any more. People grin as they emerge from their houses, nod a greeting at neighbours they've ignored for years. There's an excited buzz to conversation on the subway. People walk with a new looseness and confidence, as if their bodies have been released from an invisible straitjacket. Not everyone comments on the events of the night before, although some do. But everyone knows what happened. How big it was. Surely there are many who are alarmed. But in the morning sunlight they've drawn in upon themselves and disguised their fear, for the first time, for the time being.

Three days after the protest, the government retaliates with a massive search-and-arrest operation in several of Santiago's *poblaciones*, poor communities on Santiago's south side. Just after midnight, soldiers and police surround the entire area. At 5 a.m., loudspeakers order thousands out of their beds. All men over fourteen are arrested; women and children must stay inside their homes. Often searchers break into houses, carrying off valuables and so-called evidence of subversive activities. The men stand, often scantily dressed, for hours in open fields or sports arenas, heavily guarded. Some are beaten. Most are released by day's end; others are arrested.

The newspapers, *El Mercurio, La Segunda, Las Ultimas Noticias,* all belonging to the Edwards family, and *La Tercera* begin their campaign uncertainly. Before the protest, they focus on Pinochet's threats to punish the organizers. Afterward, there has been no national protest. There have been "events", "manifestations", "detainees", "two dead", "incidents", "disturbances". "Politicians refer to Wednesday's Events", "Unofficial balance of arrests and wounded" "Montero: To the Courts Protest Instigators (Government blamed common delinquents and extremists for the disturbances the night before last)". As the protests persist, the pro-regime media increasingly focus on the violence, the confrontations with police, the burning barricades in the *poblaciones*, all the poor, working-class communities that ring Santiago and most Chilean cities, large and small.

But the media's lost credibility will become one of the government's greatest liabilities. As the protests continue, the regime will resort to the same tactics that protest organizers use, papering the streets with crudely drawn flyers. They'll scrawl pro-government legends and threats across miles of whitewashed walls. And no one will care. Because suddenly news travels on its own frequency, we are the news, we make the news, we know what's happening because it's all around us, on the streets, in our homes. Late at night when curfews silence normal city noises, the protest will roll upward like smoke from an inextinguishable fire.

After that I moved to San Antonio where I worked in a rayon factory. I met my compañero *and we got married. I was nineteen. He was twenty years older. After they fired us for trying to organize a union, we came to Santiago. We lived in one room for several years; that's where four of my daughters were born. But the owner didn't pay her taxes. So we began to look for somewhere to live. We looked for over two years. Finally we put up a* mejora *beside the canal. We lived there for a year and a half, until there was a big fire that burned down forty houses. A month later, the canal itself caught fire, because someone threw a live coal into it. We already knew about these empty fields and some of us were exploring ways for us to live there. The only way was to take them ourselves.*

Every month now there's one day when I gird myself with my tape recorder and set out for the city centre, to watch police clobber demonstrators who stage lightning protests on street corners, then dissolve into the crowds of office workers and shoppers. Stomach tight and lungs shrinking with advance knowledge of tear-gas and water-cannon jets laced with acids, I walk or run among them, watching, recording, reporting to the different media in Canada, the United States and England who suddenly take notice. At night, more rounds in friends' cars, recording the honking, the banging pans and increasingly the chants of small columns of protestors who stream out of their buildings and homes and march around their own neighbourhoods where they feel reasonably safe.

In June, the initial euphoria is still high; in July, bonfires and burning tires have joined the protests; in August, the Minister of the Interior resigns and is replaced by Sergio Onofre Jarpa. He once belonged to the Chilean Nazi party, helped organize the 1973 coup, but he was also a senator and a leader of Chile's "old-time right" and people see his appointment as a sign that some kind of negotiation will be possible. The Christian Democratic party re-emerges from clandestine shadows, putting itself at the head of the "Democratic Alliance", a heterogeneous assortment of centrist and splintered left parties. But August's protest shows a desperate attempt to return to the recent past. The government ships in 18,000 troops from all over Chile to occupy Santiago. As I drive around the city in the early evening, I see the heavily armed figures, their faces painted black, lurking behind trees, lying in ditches, aiming their pistols and machine-guns and automatic rifles in every direction.

Five minutes before curfew I race home. Patricio and I stand on the balcony, listening to the familiar drumming. Then a terrible knot forms in our throats as explosions, gun shots, enormous anguished wails well up. The next day, I numbly scrutinize newspapers, sorting out facts in quick succession for a report to *The Globe and Mail* in Canada. "Police and troops continued a series of savage attacks on Chilean civilians on the weekend," I begin. "Doctors working with human rights groups called on the International Committee of the Red Cross to intervene on behalf of thousands of people who they said had been beaten, shot, tear-gassed and burned by Government forces."

A doctor reports treating a group of young men for severe burns: "police had rounded them up as they got off a bus, stripped them, beaten them and forced them to extinguish a bonfire." "There were also reports of soldiers and police stripping people, tying them to posts and using them for target practice with heavy stones."

Yet the new Minister of the Interior is promising elections and a Congress before the 1990 target date, although he says the opposition's leaders have "marked exhibitionist tendencies" and emphasizes "We're here to do serious things, not worry about some people's fantasies." An ex-Junta member criticizes the Army's role in the repression and a general who led a coup attempt in 1968 adds his voice. Air Force General Fernando Matthei says his troops were not involved in the repression. "It's time political debate was allowed in Chile again," he adds, promising that "all democratic groups, even those who don't agree with the Government, are soon going to find a way of expressing themselves as legal political parties."

My article appears on *The Globe and Mail*'s front page, between a photograph of women protesting and the "morning smile": "Now, son, there is a wonderful example for us in the life of an ant," a father points out. "Every day the ant goes to work and works all day. Every day the ant is busy. And in the end, what happens?"

Unimpressed, the boy replies: "Somebody steps on him."

So that was how we came to risk ourselves. The land belonged to Mrs. Ochagavía but she didn't grow anything on it. The homeless were living in a church behind the Montecarmelo vineyard and from there the church moved them to the San Miguel stadium. This was in October, the night of October 30, 1957.

We saw that things weren't very well organized so we women orga-

nized ourselves. It was drizzling and very foggy and we had covers to protect at least the children. We started out at one in the morning, with a cart. The carts were all lined and we wrapped up the horses' hooves too so they wouldn't make sound on the pavement. Everything was very quiet. And there where Feria Avenue is now there was a narrow dirt road with blackberry bushes on either side.

There was a caretaker and we cut off his phone so he couldn't call police. We cut the fence and went in with our families. There was a silence so large that I got scared and thought, "we're the only ones here." I thought this deep inside, but I didn't dare speak. And then the Carabineros came up with their trucks and spotlights, on horseback, everything.

Then they turned on the spotlight and we saw how many we were. There wasn't room for a pin. The Carabineros told us to leave and set their horses on us and we brought the flag so we planted the flag in the ground and we put our things around it and they pulled up the flags and kicked them. They attacked with sticks and everything, but when the people from the municipality arrived, the Carabineros calmed down and the next day we spoke to Monseigneur José Maria Caro and he spoke to the wife of the president [of Chile, Carlos Ibáñez del Campo] and she spoke to her husband and they let us stay. So we got ourselves organized, put up a huge tent to receive everyone who came. There were 30,000 of us, all without homes.

In spite of a child shot in the head while doing her homework, of a mother killed while serving her family dinner, of guards shutting a cemetery and not allowing the funeral processions of the victims to enter, Patricio believes the government will fall before Christmas. On September 29th, my twenty-seventh birthday, we decide to start a family. I realize I'm pregnant a month later, as I strip off tear-gas and water-cannon drenched clothing after covering the opposition's first "legal" rally. From then on, my unborn child, Camilo, accompanies me to protests, rallies, *poblaciones,* stamping his feet to the rhythm of anti-government chants on more than one occasion.

His conception is not the only event that marks September 29, 1983.

At dawn, two thousand homeless people steal into an empty field on Santiago's southern edge, improvising tents with blankets, planting flags, just as many of their parents did thirty years before. The police surround them and offer them a deal. If the men leave, nothing will happen. "We didn't want fights," one of the leaders says afterward "so all of the men withdrew." Once the men leave, police attack the remaining old people, women and children. Fighting lasts all night, but finally, on their fifth charge, the homeless triumph and stay. Between them, the Campamento Silva Enríquez and the Campamento Francisco Fresno, as they become known, house more than 20,000 men, women and children, *allegados* who haven't fit anywhere for too long.

"We have nowhere to go," a young woman says. "They won't accept us back where we came from." And if the police return, "They can shoot us all. We're not moving." The fifty people around her nod agreement.

Almost a month went by before they came to take the measurements and we began to organize block by block. Each representative attended her or his people to make sure they had everything they need. There were also several deaths, we had to go to the Hogar de Cristo for services. Students from both universities helped a lot. I was happy. The years of sacrifice ahead didn't matter, because now at least we could say this is ours and we could make it what we wanted. I went to work in [another factory] and my husband started selling newspapers on the street and we could live on that. We had six daughters and a son. The family was pretty large but thank God we never lacked for anything. That was our life during the first years of the población.

Between 1983 and 1985, different opposition groups will organize fourteen National Protests against the military regime. One hundred and thirty-one people will die during those protests, the vast majority shot by police or anonymous civilians in cars or vans, who circulate freely, even during curfew. Said the Rettig Commission: "Death reached people not previously chosen by those responsible; not sought for because of political party membership or specific personal relationships. Children and the elderly, youths and adults, men and women, participants in the acts of protest and people indifferent to them, died. All they had in common was their immersion in a reality of acute political confrontation." Among the dreadful absurdities of that period is the case of José Osorio, twenty-seven years old, a former sergeant-major. During the national protest on August 11, 1983, he called to soldiers on guard in his community to ask them to stop the pot-banging of his neighbours. The soldiers ordered him to leave his house with his hands up, then to keep walking. A corporal approached and shot him in the back.

In 1983, opposition leaders call for a great national consensus around the voluntary resignation of the military regime, followed by a provisional government, the election of a Constituent Assembly, an emergency economic plan, the immediate restitution of social and political rights. Protests include a broad range of peaceful tactics: work stoppages, sit-ins, assemblies, marches, slowdowns, horn-honking, boycotts of schools and stores, closure of offices and shops.

From the fourth protest on, confrontations between marchers and police become increasingly common, as do occupations of university campuses, bonfires and flaming barricades in the *poblaciones*, blackouts, sabotage, sacking of foodstores, armed attacks on police stations.

A pattern for protest days establishes itself: around midday, the demonstrations start in the city centre; by the time I'm hurrying home to file my first reports, I'll pass student demonstrators overflowing into the streets, battling police who try to push them back behind the fence around their faculties. I usually have a couple of tense hours to write and file reports before rushing out for at least one round of the city. Sometimes I can tape a few minutes of the pans before curfew turns the city into a jail whose inmates have been locked up for the night. During curfew, we hardly dare to stand for a few minutes on our own balcony. Sometimes a car races by and we know that it's the secret police. Almost always, "unidentified civilians" shoot from moving vehicles during curfews. Almost always, this happens in *poblaciones*.

Población. The word is usually translated as shanty-town and *pobladores* are called "shanty-town dwellers". This doesn't work for me, when I try to give them and their complex history of pride and craft and painful errors the brisk three-word summary required by the average news report. I remember the images these words conjured up when I lived in Canada: thin, ragged figures with flies on their noses, ruthlessly trimmed of their own history, their present lives, to fit within a cliché that the modern television viewer in a "developed" country can classify and forget by dinner.

When the *allegados* invade two empty fields, I face more translation problems: the *allegados*, the "added" ones, the ones who live the daily humiliation of not having their own kitchen, their own bathroom, their own bed to lie down in, their own floor under their feet. Well, in English they're squatters, aren't they? People who take over other people's land by "squatting" on it.

They don't see it this way, and watching them, listening to their stories, I can't either.

Throwing my mind back, I finally reach a place where a different strangeness hits me — the strangeness of there being empty land where a homeless family can't hope to pitch a tent. What a long way we've come from our nomadic past to this sedentary "civilization", this world, where the homeless literally have (as the Chileans put it) nowhere to drop dead.

How to explain this to my legalistically inclined, primarily Anglo-Saxon audiences in Canada, the United States, England? The land belongs to somebody. And others, these needy Others, insist on using it. But they don't squat, they are literally building dreams.

One day I sit at a chipped table in the Población La Legua, listening to the history of Santiago according to the *pobladores*, which is like hearing the Bible being retold before it was written down. "First came La Legua," one woman with spotty teeth sings out, grinning with pride. "My parents were here —" "We put up our *mejoras* ..." "*Mejora*", the word they use for the fragile wooden shacks, comes from "better", suggests a euphemism, subverted.

"Then came La Victoria," a man adds, his eyes lost in visions of blankets and plastic sheets dotting an empty field, damp children with runny noses playing beside a flimsy structure they already call home.

"La Victoria", the Victory. They've named their community for that rainy moment when the ragged banners marked a corner of the earth as theirs. I sense they've named it for the future too. In its time, this "Victory" was a revelation to both the homeless and the powerful of Latin America, an example to be followed or crushed. During the protests, La Victoria becomes a symbol of resistance; but the name remains a promise too: many reach for it blindly in the dark nights when bonfires close access roads, rocks answer bullets and, like the flags, the bodies of the dead are raised by the living.

There were always problems here. They never forgave us for taking the land. Everything we have was hard to get. For example, water. First we had to cross the road to get it. Then we had a tap on each block. There were fights because everyone wanted their water first. Then running water in our homes. Electricity was another problem. People from La Legua gave us the posts and the wire too. We stole the current for a while.

Maria Nélida Sánchez Escobar tells the history of La Victoria as if she were chanting an epic poem. Small and plump with dark currant eyes, a shy voice and a hearty laugh, her story and her family mix God and Communism, praise for the Yankee owners of Chile's copper mines and surprise at the betrayals of earlier "progressive" Chilean governments. Her *compañero* of almost fifty years of labour and local organizing died recently. The pain flows gently through her voice, blending with a soft strength.

Her home is the living child of this struggle, a small, one-storey wooden building with a tiny built-on kitchen and a cupboard-sized bathroom. Through a curtain I sense another room, with a TV set on. The furniture is worn, the walls and shelves covered by small adornments, some of them religious. But the great beauty of her home is her grown-up daughters who stroll in, their children tumbling across the floor, her son, Renato, who comes to visit with his small son. There is a gentle watchfulness in all of them, even here in their own home, even now, in 1992, two years after an elected government took power. They hover at the doorways to the garden or the kitchen, listening to the cadences in their mother's voice, slightly protective, nodding agreement on occasion.

Maria Nélida's son, Renato, was a teenager when the coup occurred. "For a kid like me, who'd been working since he was six years old, I'd realized what the [Popular Unity] government meant. For the first time I saw a government concerned about giving us culture. Once a month we had tickets to the municipal theatre to see a play or listen to music." After the military coup, "This was stolen from us."

Like most boys his age, he'd always felt "a certain admiration for what it meant to be a soldier". That also changed, after the coup. He remembers the *población* being bombed, then strafed with machine-gun fire, then mass detentions. After the coup, the government changed the names of La Victoria's streets. Ramona Parra Street, named for a young Communist girl killed in struggles earlier in the century, became General Oscar Bonilla. The Chicago Martyrs reappeared as Lieutenant Ramón Jiménez. Unidad Popular was baptized Sargento José Wittlin. Karl Marx became Carabinero Esteban Cifuentes.

From then on, Renato's day began early, with school from eight to one. There were spies among the pupils and "We weren't allowed to meet much in groups. We'd get together in the street and then a patrol would appear and we'd disappear." At fifteen, he added factory work to his schedule, from 2 to 10 p.m. He watched as a supervisor abused

young girls. "There was a lot of fear, no more games. We had an inspector who'd been in the army and he would make us march."

More than anything else, the protests that broke out in 1983 and carried
on for the rest of the decade were the outpourings of rage, passion and
courage of a generation who had looked ahead into their futures and seen
nothing. University and high-school students, the young people in the
poblaciones, children in school uniforms, their socks falling around their
ankles, their ties askew, danced and chanted in the steets, in the city
centre during the day, in poor, middle- and even some upper-class communities at night. All night. Tired of marching around school yards, listening to the endless lists of everything they couldn't do, or shouldn't
do, frustrated by a society that ignored them, except when it came time
to apply discipline, Renato and his peers took resistance to the military
regime out of their leaders' pockets, and, for some time, made it their own.

The protests' first victim was a taxi driver, Andrés Fuentes, shot while
peering through his gate at one of La Victoria's dusty streets. Subsequent
visits jumble together, but seem to always take place at dusk, under
heavy grey skies, the thick air of an impending storm blasted not by
rolling thunder but the explosions of machine-guns and tear-gas cannis-
ters. I remember reaching La Victoria one night in a carful of journalists,
when the sky had already darkened into twilight. A police bus was
parked on a sideroad. Around the corner, officers in bulletproof jackets
fired steadily at a ragged squad of youths who hurled insults and rocks
from their stronghold several blocks away.

On another occasion, we gasped as we watched the local priest, Padre
Pierre DuBois, throw himself in front of a police bus to prevent it from
entering the *población*. Fighting started, he argued, when the police
entered the area; they were a provocation to the *pobladores*. During a
protest in September 1984, his companion Padre André Jarlan died when
a police bullet cut through the wooden wall of the second-storey room
where he was sitting, reading the Bible. They were aiming at journalists,
hiding in the chapel. By the time the protests ended, seven people of La
Victoria had died from anonymous bullets.

But Maria Nélida laughs with relief as she remembers the first
protests. "I think young people always act. My friend here [she gestures
to Renato] arrived several times with grapeshot in his back. A daughter
of mine in her forehead. Because they'd put up barricades and stones

and things and, well, [the police] would shoot, and [fire] tear-gas. I couldn't hold them back and tell them not to go, because I thought it was a way of unloading all the impotence, the rage we all felt. I did think it was absurd that we were fighting with stones while [the other side] had bullets, though."

Renato didn't hide at the garden gate, waiting for death to find him.

"The important thing was to change the government," Renato says. "To defeat the dictatorship, any way we could. It started with a rock. Every street had them. We stopped [the police] from entering that way. After, weapons started to appear, and with weapons, things were very different."

"When did that begin?"

"In 1986," he says, with total certainty. "Not just here, but in several *poblaciones*. It's a step that had to be taken. When we started to throw rocks we became more enthused because there was an urgent need for change, because we had no jobs, no chance to go on studying, so things went from bad to worse. We began to paint murals on the walls, to hold fund-raisers for prisoners, to march along the Alameda. Every protest here brought one or two deaths."

"And you weren't afraid to die?"

"After a while, no. Because there was a slogan: to die fighting, not from hunger. It was something that overwhelmed the rational. There was nothing to lose. Life is something that's on loan to us too. Once they threw [tear-gas] bombs into my house. He [he gestures toward his small son] was a baby and my daughter was just a little bigger. They were suffocating. I took them and went to the police station. But I went in and yelled, "you hurt them! You save them!""

"And how did they react?"

"They gave them mouth-to-mouth, they put a ventilator on them. And they said it wasn't their fault. How could they throw a [tear-gas] bomb inside a house? What house here has no children? I lost my head and went in thinking if they kill us, they kill us. That's it."

And Maria Nélida remembers Padre Pierre Dubois. "The day they expelled the priests they put on quite a show. Very early in the morning they cordoned off everything and began to shoot, first in one direction, then another, because they knew the padre would come out, and he did and that's where they took him. One time I saw a soldier was going to shoot him in the back and we called him, we called him," her voice fills with anguish as she remembers, "Padre!"

"And the Padre turned around and said, 'But man, how can you do this?'"

In the early eighties, as the protests roll like great waves across Chile's major cities, Santiago's older *poblaciones* are large urban villages, brooding in the backyards of skyscrapers, computer-controlled buildings, modern architecture's tricks with mirrors. The occasional two-storey building breaks the solid line of one-floor wooden huts and adobe houses, on muddy, hole-filled roads where children play as adults stroll, chat, plod, pun, mourn, advise. The paint from better times is faded now, but if I stare hard enough I can superimpose yellows, oranges, blues, mauves, reds, greens on the faded walls before me. I can recapture others' memories of communities that were poor but proud, with decent health care and public education, the hope of university for the smart son, occasionally a daughter.

These are not Brazil's *favelas* or the temporary shacks thrown up to house migrants from the country. People built them thinking of the future, convinced this would be their niche in a world which calls them the *postergados* (the postponed), *the marginados* (the marginalized), *los pobladores,* (those who populate). The new paint, the larger room, the brick bathroom, the proper kitchen hover like ghosts over these *mejoras.*

As the *poblaciones* fade, life in other parts of the city is radically changing. Santiago, with four million inhabitants – a third of the national population – remains physically and politically the centre of Chile. The main universities, the seat of government and the headquarters for most major corporations nestle into this hollow in Chile's central valley. Concrete, asphalt, adobe and wood cover Chile's best agricultural land. A visitor arrives at a modest but functional airport and drives into the city along the Alameda, Santiago's main street. Its name means "poplar-lined" although it's been many centuries since the poplars disappeared. And the street itself was once an arm of the Mapocho River, cut off and paved over early in history.

Following the Alameda you reach the city centre, which by the eighties is full of pedestrian malls lined with stores selling radios, stereos, VCRs. After standing for years at the city's heart, a ruinous monument to the violent destruction of democracy, the presidential palace, the Moneda has been repaired. Inside, General Pinochet and his wife have their office suites. The modest door Allende used has vanished.

In Plaza Italia, now called General Baquedano Square, the Alameda changes its name to "Providencia" and becomes packed with exclusive boutiques, American-style restaurants, fashionable doctors, the military hospital, climbs forever upward through Apoquindo, ending in Las Condes (The Counts), a sprawling zone of brick and stucco houses with fine green lawns, walls topped with broken glass and luxury appointments.

The people who live behind these walls, whose dogs bark fiercely if you approach the gate, whose voices are barely audible on their speakers if you touch the doorbell, drive shiny, new Mercedes, BMWs and Jaguars. They whip along paved roads to work in high government positions, in the top posts of Chile's many, recently privatized corporations, in banks rescued from disaster by the military in 1982. Many are high-ranking officers, integrated into civilian society through their multiple posts in government, private corporations, public and private universities. In 1988, at a soup kitchen, I ask a young girl what she'd like to be when she grows up. "A military officer," she answers.

This is the world that economist Joaquín Lavín celebrates in his book *Revolución Silenciosa*, published in 1987, after four years of protests and funerals. Chile in the eighties will be remembered, he proclaims, as "the decade of English lessons, the introduction of computers in education, the boom of courses and seminars, the increase in scholarships abroad, and the intensive apprenticeship of economics via the mass media."

Anyone who criticizes the new economic model is part of a backward-looking minority who can't stand to see Chile finally grow up without them, a potential or real terrorist, an eternal taster of sour grapes. The vast majority, Joaquín Lavín believes, are excited about the new computers, the private pension programs, the export-driven economy and the "professionalization" of the fight against poverty.

Joaquín Lavín is so thrilled with the new Chile that his book is mainly a list of changes and he doesn't waste space arguing why they're positive. He'll run for election to Congress in 1989, "a fighting cock", and lose, but in 1992 he returns to the hustings as the mayoralty candidate for the snobbish, *nouveau riche* district of Las Condes and wins.

Chile is becoming a developed country, he argues, thanks to the "dramatic change in the world economy which has gone from the 'industrial era' to the 'information era' in a few short years; a deliberate policy of integration into the world, initiated in 1975 ... broadened Chileans' horizon by giving them access to information, technology and consumer goods ... and an atmosphere that has favoured individual initiative, creativity, innovation, audacity and enterprise."

Among the marvels this has brought: Oscar-winning movies are shown in Santiago within weeks of the ceremony; two million homes have TV (and children watching TV are a wonderful "new market"); the "vineyard boom" has brought high salaries to the north; there are 445,000 more cars on the streets than fifteen years ago. A housewife shopping at the Almac supermarket can now choose from among 15,500 items, 10,000 more than in 1974.

One million people per month stroll through the glittering hallways of the Parque Arauco and Apumanque shopping centres. Land around the northern city of Copiapó, worth US$50 a hectare in 1977 costs US$10,000 ten years later. Export-oriented agriculture now covers most of the country. "The export of blackberries, with its multiplying effect on pickers' income, has had explosive growth: from US$90,000 in 1984, it jumped to US$2 million in 1986. In the picking [everyone from] children of five to grandfathers of seventy work." Chile, he adds, has the largest pine plantations in the world. Its fisheries are thriving, with new salmon-cultivating industries building in the south.

Lavín contrasts an old-fashioned economic model which is slipping into decay, with the fast-paced success of the export and information-driven economy. He doesn't often mention the *poblaciones,* where more than half of Santiago's people live, although he's excited by the discovery that "children from the *población* La Pincoya are considerably more creative with a computer than children of the same age from high-income neighbourhoods. This experiment was carried out after the Municipality of Conchalí bought 29 Ataris for its schools."

He's also delighted with the massive book "sales" of the early eighties – 33 million over four years, but these turn out to be special, cheap editions of dictionaries, encyclopedias and classics required by schools, handed out free to bolster the sagging readership of conservative, pro-regime magazines. Beethoven's Fifth Symphony reached 200,000 pairs of hands through the same strategy. And the Lord Cochrane Company has become one of Latin America's largest publishing firms, exporting magazines like *Viva, Disneyland, Mickey [Mouse], Donald Duck, Uncle Rich* and *Playboy.*

Those twenty-nine Ataris for the 36,000 students of La Pincoya now mean that "the children of Conchalí, Las Condes, Renca, Chile Chico, Providencia or New York sit down in front of the same machine and learn, from the same age, to handle the same 'mouse', the same language which moves around the same screen."

Whether the Almac supermarkets offer 15 thousand or 15 million new products isn't very relevant to Maria Nélida and her family. After we talk, they invite me to share tea with them and are absurdly grateful when I add a bag of sweet buns and cookies to the bread and margarine they've put on the table. This is their main evening meal.

Not surprisingly, Eugenio Tironi's book *Los Silencios de la Revolución (Silences of the Revolution)* tells a different story. A social scientist linked to non-governmental organizations which absorbed many of the academics barred from the military-controlled university system, Tironi focuses on what has become a central image for Chileans opposed to the regime: the two Chiles.

"The revolution which began fifteen years ago, meant from the start a cruel and profound tearing apart of Chilean society," he begins. "And today it continues to mean pain and frustration for all those who haven't received its benefits and who don't see any perspective for that happening. To forget this reality – which is, indeed, silent – is a risk which could cost a nation a great deal of additional suffering."

He defines modernization, a term often used by the military's economic advisers, as "an emancipation from the factors which limit individuals and societies from guiding their own destinies", and he complains that the "obsession for success and dogmatic superiority are the most evident symptoms of a revolution condemned to stagnation. ... Anyone who tries to call attention to those whose dignity and interests have been wounded by the changes are persecuted or denigrated with the worst epithets. In this way, revolutions become monstrous creations which devour societies, since, to live and to grow, every society needs to be capable of integrating past and present, change and continuity, 'winners' and 'losers'."

Tironi describes how the military government's planners have deliberately moved ("eradicated" was the word they used) 28,703 poor families (about 187,000 people) from "camps" in mixed-income communities to isolated fields on the city's rim, putting them out of reach of most jobs and the better social services available in well-to-do areas. Tironi's careful follow-up reveals that these communities have experienced disproportionate growth in delinquency levels. Many of those who participated in the Raul Silva Enríquez and the Fresno land occupations were moved to La Pintana. Between 1982 and 1984, La Pintana received 22 per cent of the "eradicated"; delinquency climbed 59 per cent. Whole buildings have been stolen(!), dismantled brick by brick. La Pintana has seven telephones, one for every 22,000 inhabitants, and no post office. There's limited bus service because 63 per cent of the roads are unpaved. And while there's almost a car per person in the wealthy shopping and residential area of Providencia, there is just over one per hundred people in La Granja on Santiago's south side.

Tironi also cites studies which show that general poverty has increased, from 17 pere cent in 1970 to 45 per cent in 1988. Real wages have dropped. Unemployment has soared. By 1986, eight out of ten families in the *poblaciones* consume fewer calories than recommended by the World Health Organization; even so, food takes 70 per cent of family budgets. A 1985 study finds 6.5 people per house in the *poblaciones,* compared to a national average of 4.2; 41 per cent of homes have more than three people per bedroom, compared to 21 per cent twenty years earlier.

Joaquín Lavín's *The Silent Revolution* hits the bookstores in 1987 as part of the regime's campaign to win voters' approval for another eight years of General Pinochet. From the start, General Pinochet and his supporters are sure their strategy of singing the economy's strengths while beating down the opposition will succeed.

From 1980 on, the government had programmed Chile's political evolution with military precision. In 1980, a plebiscite – with no voters' lists and no guarantees for opposing viewpoints – approved a new Constitution to replace the 1925 version suspended in 1973. This Constitution includes controversial "transitional" articles, which legalize the repression of the press and civil liberties. It also provides for a presidential plebiscite to be held in 1988.

At first, some political leaders try to convince General Pinochet not to run. Others propose allowing several candidates, arguing that this way General Pinochet would have a better chance. But the General, shut off from reality by a sycophantic court of followers, none of whom dares to mention that the Emperor may be wearing no clothes, is so sure of victory that he exchanges his stern, uniformed commanding presence for that of a fatherly autocrat in a grey suit, smiling down on his children from billboards stretching from north to south. So confident is he that, after complex negotiations, both the pro-government parties and the opposition have access to fifteen minutes of television every night. The Electoral Service is rescued from sixteen years of mothballs and dust. Juan Ignacio García, until now second in command, is promoted to director of the Electoral Service (the former director is now a comic in commercials for luncheon meats). Voters' lists are painfully reorganized and millions of Chileans line up to sign their name and stamp their thumbprint on the official registry which will dictate who can vote.

The fifteen minute "no" program is an instant hit, whether it precedes or follows the pro-Pinochet "yes" spot. While General Pinochet's supporters focus on the chaos – a mother fleeing terrorists' bullets with a baby in her arms is an early image – that will be unleashed if the opposition wins, the "no" campaign's symbol is a rainbow of cheery Andean colours, representing the broad spectrum of political parties which have finally united. With catchy music, brief interviews with famous public figures, romantic riders on horseback waving rainbow flags, the "no" program focuses on reassurance. Vote "no" and things will change, gently but surely in favour of democracy. Vote "no" and no raging hordes will be unleashed. Vote "no" and the little, old lady who has barely enough change for a tea-bag and a bun can hope for more. The relatives of the disappeared dance their lonely *cueca* on television for the first time in sixteen years. The mother of a popular soccer player reveals that she was tortured.

The unspoken has travelled from silence, to the lime-painted walls of country and city streets, to national television. Fifteen minutes' worth of the "other" reality: in the wasteland created by years of pro-regime commercials, talk shows and news programs, those fifteen minutes have the impact of a lush, tempting oasis.

Eugenio Tironi's *The Silences of the Revolution* is also part of the plebiscite campaign. As exiles return and opposition newspapers can finally publish, the two Chiles do battle: Joaquín Lavín's technological paradise oiled by privatization and an overweening respect for private property, versus Eugenio Tironi's lament for the losers and his claim that only by recognizing their existence and taking publicly funded steps to ameliorate their situation can Chile hope to build a decent future for its people. Human rights are a key issue for many, but even more important are the everyday issues of health care, education, work.

Public polling companies spring up like mushrooms. Even the police get involved; not surprisingly, General Pinochet comes out on top of their poll.

In rural areas, in the *poblaciones*, at first there is fear, rumours that there will be cameras in the voting booths, that retribution will come yet again, from incensed landowners or employers or government bureaucrats who can punish by withholding much-needed subsidies. But slowly, as the campaign proceeds, enthusiasm grows for the gamble that Chileans just might defeat a dictator through the ballot box. It's a very Chilean gamble. On the day of the plebiscite itself, Chileans from the *poblaciones*, from isolated villages, provincial cities and Providencia, travel by foot, by car, by horse, by rowboat, many dressed in their Sunday best. They line up solemnly to vote, standing for hours, hushed or speaking in the low tones reserved for sacred occasions.

There is an almost mathematical equation that has become synonymous with the political role of the *pobladores*. Eugenio Tironi sums it up as: poverty = frustration = violence. This, according to both the regime's scare campaigns and the left's idealization, is what made the *pobladores* the "motor" of the protest movement as it purred or roared or putt-putt-putted along from 1983 to 1987. More than the workers who called the first protest, the *pobladores* and the university students led the marches, lit the bonfires, battled with police and made Chile virtually ungovernable for a military government whose internal unity was beginning to crack.

But in a rare empirical study, Tironi surveys *pobladores* and constructs indices of "orientation toward violence", "frustration", "adaptation/resignation", comparing them to other social sectors. His results show that "orientation toward violence indices for marginal groups don't differ significantly from those of middle-class people. What is more, the orientation toward violence appears as a learned attitude and not the direct result of a frustrating situation and even less the result of high levels of poverty. Most *pobladores* tend to assume adaptive attitudes and fall into a state of resignation."

Tironi concludes that the protests are a response to a coercive, repressive State, rather than an attempt to seize wealth directly. Poverty may produce nothing more than passivity. But, if those affected act, repression from the State tends to elicit a violent response, while participation may, perhaps, produce solutions.

"In other words," Tironi concludes, "the *pobladores* are interested in the protection a State of Law offers them, along with the opportunities for integration that democratic political institutions open up ... This reveals neither ingenuousness nor romanticism, but rather a fine sensitivity to identifying conditions which bring them closer to their final objective: the abandonment of their marginal condition."

When the opposition gambles on being able to beat the regime at its own game — the plebiscite — it is really gambling on two levels. In the short term, that it will win the plebiscite; in the middle to long term, it's gambling that it can return to building an old Chilean dream within the framework it will inherit from the military.

This dream is expressed in a study Tironi cites in which two-thirds of Chileans describe the Chile they aspire to as "a civilized, cultured nation which, in spite of not being rich, allows all its inhabitants equally to live a life of dignity", a vision which La Victoria once embodied. From the thirties to the seventies, Chileans progressed steadily toward moulding their society to this image, preferring "the values of sobriety, education and democracy" over "a country with a high standard of living, but large social differences" or "a nation with high indices of equality and wealth, but a poorly educated, uncultured population".

As the battle between Lavín's and Tironi's books suggests, the plebiscite was also about Chileans' willingness to sustain this goal or pursue a different vision. In theory, the unpretentious but dignified version of Chile has triumphed.

Tironi adds that while a new democracy would be unable to solve the problems of poverty and the frustration it may produce, "that won't awaken the violence of poor urban groups because that's not what they expect from the transition to democracy. What they expect is the end of a coercive State ... If it achieves this, urban marginals could become the mainstay of a new democracy and not, as is often feared, a threat."

On the spring day in 1992 as I talk with Maria Nélida and Renato in La Victoria, images of yet another police invasion of their community are weighing on their minds. September 11th, the anniversary of the coup, has taken place the week before, and *pobladores* who commemorated with a march faced the same tear-gas and clubs used by the military government.

They add this to their own personal list of grievances: Renato is a former political prisoner. His problems began on October 22, 1988, almost two weeks after the opposition won the plebiscite. Carabineros arrested him, accusing him of participating in a combat group. After three years in prison, the Supreme Court sentenced him to 61 days and he is currently free – on bail, because he faces more charges. "[The prosecution] is asking for a sentence of one hundred days: they want me to go back to jail for another hundred days ..." he says, bitterly. In the meantime, stamped across the papers he needs to get a job is a message: "on trial: anti-terrorist law". With help from a church organization, FASIC, and financial assistance from Holland, he's studying to be a food handler at the National Technical Institute.

Renato and Maria Nélida don't feel they have any more clout than they did under the military. I ask them what they think of the way the politicians took over the leadership of the protest movement. Maria Nélida hesitates, but Renato has no doubts.

"[Pinochet] should never have carried on as the commander-in-chief of the Army. There were secret agreements, deceit, commitments made abroad by some leaders. There were political leaders who suffered in exile, but others conducted politics from behind a desk, like kings. And they harvested the sacrifice, the deaths of pobladores, in all the poblaciones."

"I'll never believe Mr. Aylwin," Renato adds. Disillusionment hardens his husky voice. "He came here, beating his chest, kneeling in our church and promising that we would be out of jail within a year. And here we are, just recently out of jail, with the trials still on, these trials which should never have happened. Because if we assumed a fight in a given moment, it was because of a moral commitment that we had as Chileans." His voice expresses amazement that anyone wouldn't understand this.

"But the government doesn't have too much strength, does it?" I ask.

"They have to have the political will. The government, with all the forces it has between the Concertación [the government coalition of Christian Democrats, Socialists and other parties] and the left parties, has the necessary strength to overpower the right ... This government promised before the whole world that [the political prisoners] would be freed. They talk of a lesser evil–"

"And isn't it a lesser evil?"

"But they should have taken the chance on a different outcome, to really get rid of Pinochet, throw him out of the country."

"Like Nicaragua?"

"It could have been."

"But it could have been like El Salvador too?"

"It could have been."

"A long civil war?"

Maria Nélida breaks in: "No. Please."

"But I tell you, these groups keep acting the same way they did in '85, '86, '88." And he argues that while he disagrees with what some of the armed groups are doing, the government is using "the same repression, exactly the same or worse than the CNI, the regime's secret police". Passion blurs and rents his voice. "I have a friend — it's a fact, they showed on television. He was in prison with me, more than a year, Fabián. Perhaps he made a mistake. But they made a big show of his death on television, all day, to show his death, which was an execution, that was plain to see. But they justified it: they're terrorists and must be killed." His voice thins to almost nothing, as if skating over his own death. And he accuses the Investigaciones and Carabineros of continuing to torture.

"Do you have a case?"

"Yes. Right now. Alvaro González Meneses. He was arrested about a month ago. I went to see him because we'd been in prison together. They burst his fingers, pulling out his nails. In Investigaciones. The persecution is the same. I worked in a night job; Investigaciones went every night. Psychological tortures continue and they're the same or worse than before ... They themselves say they're not the CNI, they're real professionals.

"So you find yourself asking, was there or was there not a change? This opposition was good for something, or wasn't it? Today many people say if there hadn't been an agreement between the left and the Christian Democrats maybe this would have been different. Maybe a civil war as you were asking. Maybe we would have achieved little in ten years. ... Maybe it was a lesser evil. We'll have to see what happens in the next elections."

"But I won't ever give my vote to a Christian Democrat again," Maria Nélida breaks in. "Because, as my son says, they didn't keep their word ... We're conscious that this is a transitional government, that things take time. That's fair. But what I see here is that Pinochet is ruling, the same as ever. We still can't speak freely in the street, the way we are talking here."

"Why not?"

"Because you're exposed to being picked up afterward. Because there's spying on what people say and later they're arrested and accused of being terrorists ... This scares me. On the bus I never talk. I say yes, no, yes, nothing more because I don't have confidence. That's one of the things I learned with Pinochet's regime."

"Yes," Renato agrees. "You can't trust anyone. Look, I live a block from here, my aunt lives next door and she's caught men in the morning, watching my house. Men in rags with perfectly kept nails and a vocabulary that's too good for someone who lives on the street. She asks what they're looking for and they ask about the gentleman who lives next door. All this because I'm an ex-political prisoner.

"That's why I say I don't believe them. They speak of "reinserting us" but who guarantees us reintegration when the government sets the same dogs on us as before? Now the names are different, that's all. What guarantees does this government provide so we don't take up arms again as they ask? Who guarantees we'll be able to live in peace or have a decent job to feed and educate our children? I say what I think because they tortured me once and they can do it again for all I care. It doesn't matter to me."

Renato argues long and passionately that people will realize, that the revolutionary movement, that higher levels of struggle ...

His mother, Maria Nélida is not so sure. "I don't like the idea of weapons much, I've always been a pacifist. I don't think we're prepared to suffer the way they did in Nicaragua. We weren't even prepared for the coup, we couldn't even—" anguish breaks her voice "defend the government we had, the government of Salvador Allende. If we'd been prepared, this would never have happened. I don't know if it's cowardice, I don't know. It scares me a lot.

"I think maybe we should get organized. We have a bad habit, we Chileans. We can get used to things ... I'm unhappy with this government. I gave my vote — well, it was the only way we had of getting rid of Pinochet. But the disillusionment is very great when we see him walk into the Moneda as if it were his house. The same thing, last week, for the 11th: celebrating with a 21-gun salute, he says it was a war, that he's giving homage to his martyrs. What about the people's martyrs, hundreds of thousands, and they're still finding the bodies?"

Today, in La Victoria, life goes on much as it did a decade or two or three ago. A definitive victory — that modest, dignified, cultured country which lives in most Chileans' minds — seems further away than in the sixties or early seventies. But in the meantime, they continue to celebrate anniversaries, light, survival. They continue to build. "Pavement committees" have charged each household about US$30, one-third of the monthly minimum wage and, with the government making up the difference, the streets of La Victoria are soon to be paved, not with gold, but with something worth almost as much: asphalt.

A municipal decree has restored the streets' old names. The walls are splashed with murals, reproach, demands. Waiting for a bus to take me home to my own neighbourhood, where we take pavement for granted, phrases echo in my ears.

"I'm proud of being from La Victoria. Many people call us terrorists, delinquents, but you'll never find a more affectionate place."

"I would never leave. Maybe it's the huge effort to make this grow, a huge love toward all this."

"Yes, there has to be consensus."

"The people 'outside' are very cold."

"Yes, there has to be consensus."

"All our lives, covered with mud, how could we not live a little better?"

"Yes, there has to be consensus."

"I used to belong to the Front. Now I'm president of the committee to pave our block."

Chapter twelve

TINQUILCO

SOUTHERN CHILE, CHRISTMAS 1988

The valley sinks below us, houses, trees, cattle, and the long, green pastures shrinking, as if we were taking off in a hang-glider rather than winding up a narrow mountain road perched between terror and beauty — my terror of heights, the beauty of wild flowers into which we might fall.

Within this mountain's peak in Chile's southern Andes, about twelve hours from Santiago, lies Lake Tinquilco, a huge bowl of water, fringed by *araucaria* pine and enormous cathedral-like *coigüe* trees.

Two years ago my husband and I bought a small tract of land at the end of this lake from don Fanor Castillo. I thought it meant escape and solitude. Instead, it's been a gentle initiation into the meaning of names and time.

Don Fanor is a lord of sorts and doña Delicias his lady. Rich in land and animals and children, they live in a two-room cabin, eking out a living on the edge of the twenty-first century. Fanor's family has been here for thirty years; Huerquehue National Park, which hugs his land like a great fur wrap, has been here six. In summer, the children roam it freely. They spend winters down the mountain in a boarding school. When times are tough, older children are "loaned" to distant relatives. Times are always tough.

Relying on oxen for transport, don Fanor has built a modest empire, including an electrical turbine run by a waterfall. Lightbulbs gleam softly at night and his sawmill produces boards and shakes, along with a moderate income, expanded by campers and the occasional sale of livestock.

How we travel up the zig-zagging road to Tinquilco varies. Sometimes it's a long trudge up the steep mountainside, punctuated with sighs and exclamations as each twist in the road reveals a new view of the valley. Sometimes don Fanor meets us with the horses and we ride upward in clouds of dust, amidst their sneezes, snorts and the jingling of tackle. This visit, the four of us – my husband, Patricio, his son, Jaime (twelve), our son, Camilo (six) and I – travel in style: a rented car. We top the last rise two days into summer, tired and dust-caked. Below us the lake gleams darkly, wind gusting across it and dying with the sun.

We bump over the ghost of a road which takes us to Fanor's gate and eagerly climb through wild mint and squealing turkey chicks toward the cabin. Don Fanor's and doña Delicias's welcome seems less warm than usual; their baby cries when Patricio shakes his head in greeting, although the baby smiles and flirts outrageously with me.

I spend the next day washing a winter's harvest of mouse droppings from dishes and shelves, hauling water up from the river until my back aches. The wild fuchsia are out, bleeding hearts dangling from twisted branches above the river. I search for humming birds and recognize a sort of wild holly, with orange, bell-like blooms. The sky vibrates a bright, cobalt blue. The sun is hot, the breeze from the river cool. I couldn't be happier.

I worry, though, about what we have done to offend don Fanor and doña Delicias. Have we stayed away too long? There's no guidebook to Tinquilco's social rules, only a fragile web of dependencies and the need to fit in without breaking any threads.

Doña Delicias drops by with soap powder. She holds the baby, wide-eyed and attentive to every shift in the murmuring river, the soft notes of our voices and the long rests between words.

"*Sí pués*," her voice hums, when I exclaim at how big the baby is. I have learned, since I first came here, that Chile's southerners always use a gentle questioning lilt at word's end, as if doubting, even as they say "yes", whether anything is as absolute as the word suggests.

Together we admire the cabin, which has now spawned a series of imitations.

"Imagine that," she says, shifting the baby. "Don Patricio managing to build it and don José [she nods at the neighbour's lot] barely able to build a roof. And him from the country and all." Don José from down the mountain, also bought from don Fanor, but seldom visits.

A piece of the eternal puzzle of our relationship slips quietly into place. We are the city people who bought the land and came trundling in with our grandiose plan for a cabin. Aladino, the carpenter from a lake at the foot of our mountain, quoted us a price so high we had to build ourselves. By summer's end, after I'd left and Patricio was bravely hammering away in the rain, Aladino would come and help on his days off. Work is a common language here. As is need.

Aladino — Aladdin of the lamp. He has been magical for us, changing from the flint-faced tradesman to the genial host who stood serving glass after glass of *chicha*, a raw apple cider of varying alcoholic grade (according to the bottle, of which we had by then gone through several) in the middle of Delicias's warm cramped kitchen, one fall night.

Anecdotes circled like hawks, the ritual laughter getting heartier with each repetition, until the neighbour on my left suddenly raised his glass and pronounced an ingenious rhyming couplet. Aladino rhymed back. For half an hour they thrust and parried in a witty, verbal duel called "*payas*".

These are the rhymes and songs which Chile's *recopiladores* spend their lives chasing down and recording, then performing in city cafés. In the 1960s they formed the basis for the music of Violeta Parra, the mother of Chile's New Song Movement. After the 1973 coup, exiled musicians sang this music around the world.

Delicias's name means Delights. She's thirty-one, three years my junior. I look at her neatly combed, slightly squared head, the baby in her arms, four older children never far behind her, two girls being raised in Concepción, a city six hours north of Tinquilco. She seldom leaves Tinquilco, even to visit her family "down below".

She once showed me how she takes raw wool and twists it into yarn using a wooden spindle (which I can only associate with fairy tales) and then knits it into winter warmth.

Canadian-born with ten years in Chile's largest city, Santiago, I am doubly strange to her. I come and go as I please, spending up to three months away from home, leaving everything in my husband's capable hands. As a writer, I earn my living with my mind. I can't cook, am a mediocre sewer and have few life-making skills.

We sit on the beach, watching swallows dive. We seldom look at each other, observing instead how the wind ruffles the silver-plated lake. She tells me how she met Fanor.

"He came to my wedding with my first husband," a brief, (ironic?) smile moves through her gaze and past us. Swallows soar and plunge. A fish flops. I ask what happened to her first husband.

"He got lost," she says in the singing voice she uses for all brief facts. "He went into town and didn't come back."

"And you never found him?"

"They say maybe he's in Argentina." The swallows' wings glint white, flash black, in the setting sun.

"The worst was his family. They blamed it on me. His death," her voice doesn't change. "The detectives came. They used electric current. I don't remember anything after that," she smiles slightly, as if this were a joke on someone.

She sold his oxen, built a house by her mother's. Later she and her four children moved up the mountain to live with don Fanor.

Delicias has taught me that we name our children for our hopes: Sara (the *princess*, who works as a maid in Concepción); Alexis (*healer*, who lives in Concepción too); Samuel (*who hears God* and works from dawn to dusk); Luisa Daniela (an *herb* and *courage*); Fanor, Jr., spoilt, coddled lord and heir. Gilberto Iván, whose name has still be to registered in the nearest town. Verónica, *the cloth with Christ's face impressed upon it, a cunning flick of the matador's cape, the black shawl Chilean women wear.*

One afternoon, Verónica (eight) and Luisa (ten) are sitting in our cabin alternately chatting and blushing, the baby bouncing from one knee to another and to mine when they tire.

Patricio caresses the guitar and launches into a song about how fathers always want sons and weep when they have daughters, but end up loving them and crying at their weddings.

By now I've noticed that only the girls are considered, when children must be sent to relatives for raising. The boys are kept on hand to work. They earn their keep.

As Patricio's voice swells, the girls turn toward him and the music illuminates the longing on their faces. Luisa's perhaps is mostly curious, but Vero's so hungry she finally turns away.

I had always thought that Verónica was from Delicias's first family, that like Samuel and Luisa she was adopted by Fanor, but not particularly loved.

I had always thought that Fanor, Jr. was so favoured, because he was his father's oldest child. Today I've realized that Vero is Fanor's eldest, but she's a girl. Now I see her in a more nebulous no-man's-or-woman's land: Vero with her gnomish face, the toothpick angles of her elbows.

We have chosen to spend Christmas here in Tinquilco. This has limited our gift-buying and time spent burning our feet on the hot Santiago pavement. The greatest gift is Jaime's presence: this is his first Christmas with us. On Christmas Eve, Camilo, Jaime, Patricio and I feast together, then head outside to watch for Santa's sleigh.

Because of the mountains, the sky's dome is black and small, but crowded with stars, little pinpricks of light between our darkness and a distant brilliance.

"We'll know it's Santa," Camilo explains, "because he'll cross the sky quick as a flash."

We watch the stars glimmer peacefully, Patricio and I, with a sinking feeling. We're about to head back inside when a star sizzles across the sky. "That's him!" Camilo shouts, dancing with excitement. "We have to go in and see the presents."

We rush inside after him and there they are, piled in the corner. Six years old and after tonight, he believes in Santa Claus more firmly than ever.

What is the magic of this place? Why do we come here? I consider the idea that I may be searching for my pioneer past or some other (quintessentially Canadian?) grail. But my parents were recent immigrants. And I certainly don't come because I like to pee in a potty, haul water on my head or hack houses out of trees.

We are reading the Narnia books with Jaime and Camilo. Patricio is discovering them for the first time and I am revisiting a country to which I often escaped in childhood. Our lips shape Lewis's universe of mist-swaddled forests; trees whose spirits speak and dance and some-times do battle; river spirits, who rise to flood the earth in anger, or save it from drought.

We read into existence a world where causes have yet to be lost and innocence is still protected by mysterious forces. Wonder abounds.

This world is deliciously immediate. Sometimes we pause in our read-ing and look out the window and don't know where we are. Rain drums on our roof. The children run for shelter in Narnia.

After Christmas, we decide to visit one of the region's thermal baths, about an hour's drive from Tinquilco. A roadside sign promises a "historic site" but all we see are cattle grazing in endless fields sunning among flowering brambles. I joke about the fields being historic sites, then realize they are. These fields were once Mapuche territory. For three centuries, the Mapuche successfully resisted the Spanish conquest, as they'd earlier resisted the Inca. The neighbouring town of Villarrica is built on the site of a Spanish fort, burnt by the Mapuche in an offensive which established borders around hundreds of kilometres of territory and forced the Spanish to respect them. In the 1800s, the newly independent Chileans crushed several Mapuche uprisings and shipped in mostly German "colonists" to occupy the land.

There is still a large native population in this region. But here around Tinquilco only the native names seem to have survived, identifying places, fears and rituals, and adorning the luxury summer resorts for Chile's millionaires.

The Huife Hotsprings cost a bundle. As we drag ourselves out of the car blinded by the hot sun and walk across rocks that burn through our shoes, we feel a little crazy, heading for hot water.

The luxury hotel is a strange (but typical) blend of German alpine style covered by Chilean *tejuelas* or shakes. Beyond, a frigid mountain river runs alongside two scalding green pools.

We settle awkwardly into deck chairs and survey a never-never land of scrubbed families in fashion's latest summer co-ordinates, speaking French, German, Japanese, a smattering of English, *un peu d'espagnole*.

In our borrowed car, this is an hour's drive from Tinquilco. For years it meant a hard day's journey with oxen for don Fanor. We come for fun. He comes to buy winter oats from a nearby farmer.

The country people still open their homes to strangers, even if now they often run *pensiones* and charge a small fee for their warmth. They spend all year anticipating the tourists, but they receive little respect in return.

Day or night, the sons of Chile's wealthiest families race flashy BMWs down the narrow country roads, showering pedestrians with dust. They run over chickens and dogs and the occasional human being. They fill small-town streets with their shouts and garbage. They race their boats across the lakes and their plumbing taints the waters. They use the local people like the servants they've left at home. They consider this their right.

It rains the night before I am to leave my family and Tinquilco and continue southward. I'm worried the road will become impassable. I lie awake, timing the pauses between showers as if we were involved in some peculiar sort of labour to bring forth sunny weather.

It's New Year's Day and before I leave we have been invited to don Fanor's and doña Delicias's for an *asado*, a roast kid, culled from their herd.

"The baby has a hernia," Delicias tells me. "The doctor saw it. He said we'd have to operate. But we did a secret ..."

"A secret?" I ask, hoping to be included.

"Yes. A secret," she answers, hesitates. "When the moon is waning, you take the baby, yes, and you trace his foot like this, with the *canelo* branch. And then you take it home and hang it in his room. He's getting better," she says, confidently.

Where did she learn her secret? The *canelo* is the Mapuches' sacred tree. I look again at her long dark hair, the high cheekbones. I sit watching her shuffle an array of kettles from one part of the wood stove to another, pouring cold water in and hot water out, measuring rice into a huge pot. We don't talk much but our solitudes curl like smoke together, explore each other cautiously.

The food's delicious. The company better. In the air fragrant with woodsmoke, other smells, other sensations mix. This exists now, I think. This is their present, not my past.

We are visitors, pilgrims who come for healing. We like this place, because here there is time for the present. These people, who seem so different, vibrate with the same clear air, the lake gleaming in the rain, the clouds unwinding on the high rocks of the Andes.

They are no simpler than city people, their lives no easier. I think of Delicias walking down the mountain, her arms shielding a sick baby.

Out in the smoke-shed, Patricio and don Fanor tend the kid, turning the roasting lance. This cooking method was born in the Mapuches' straw-thatched *ruca*, surely? People drinking *chicha*, talking and later singing and building stories around the central fire.

How old is this tradition? The fattened lamb, killed to greet the prodigal son. The Inca's living sacrifice. We celebrate our friendship, the cost and worth of being here together. Death's presence crackles over the fire, soon to be defeated by and savoured on our tongues.

Outside, rain dashes across the lake toward us, an invisible army of noisy, rushing feet.

Chapter thirteen

NGUILLATÚN

QUINQUÉN, TEMUCO 1881, 1992

Ancient old man, ancient old woman, we're travelling this earth / May the Mapuches not end my God is saying / May the Mapuche women carry on / Help us God the Father / You who kneel above in the skies / You mother too / Give us our food, our fate / We are suffering a lot / I walk with you God the Father / You give me this power to beseech / Our Father who art in heaven / Our Mother also / Who watch us from above / You made me machi / You told me: "Have no shame you will be among your sisters" / Help us ancient old man, ancient old woman / May those who wander abroad return and walk on their earth and see their family, you are going to be a machi, you told me that's why I'm here / You gave me all this understanding / Help us Great Father, Great Mother / We must love each other / we are of one Father only and one Mother only / God says he hears many contradictory words / That is why our family wander outside our country / We are suffering a lot, that's why we're asking you my God to help us / May all those involved with the President finish / We want to be at peace with our family / That's why we ask you Ancient old man, Ancient old woman / to look upon us, to help.

PRAYER OF THE MACHI ANTONIA CHANQUEO

Two-month-old Daniel wakes me at five a.m., rooting among the blankets, looking for breakfast. I slip him inside my sleeping bag and the two of us wrestle with the layers of sweaters that have attempted to keep me warm through the icy night in a tent in a field high up in Chile's Cordillera de los Andes.

Finally, Daniel and nipple connect and he starts to pull warmth and

*food and comfort into his belly. I become aware of the sounds outside —
horses hooves galloping through dust, drums vibrating against valley
walls, a voice chanting, caught and multiplied in the riders' throats,
answered by echoes flying among rock. The image of the araucaria, the
strange pine of the high Andes with its spirals of spiky branches sweeping upward in an eternal, optimistic greeting flashes across my mind's
eye. A strange excitement stirs me in spite of the frost which has colo-
nized my bones. The sensation of milk flowing into the baby's mouth and
of sounds reverberating through the valley combine: inner and outer
worlds become one.*

*Outside the tent, frost coats the landscape, like moonlight poured
from the icy sky. A procession of paired riders on horseback whirl by.
Their green and yellow flags billow in the wind over the chanting voices
and the steady thunder of hooves.*

A young foal, leggy, the colour of melted toffee pursues the riders.

A larger-than-life bronze statue of Pedro de Valdivia, Chile's own
Conquistador, rides through Santiago's central square on a gigantic
horse. A few blocks away, a statue of Lautaro, the Mapuche who killed
Valdivia stands on top of the Santa Lucía Hill. The figure is actually
modelled on a native of the North American plains. Chileans' views of
the people who have inhabited their country since long before the conquest are a contradictory morass of idealization and contempt, a telling
mixture that says more about Chileans' own identity crisis than the
nature of the Mapuches' tenacious struggle for survival which has lasted
now for five centuries.

There are people in Chile today who will tell you the Mapuche no
longer exist. Nevertheless, in the 1992 census more than 900,000 people
declared they were Mapuche. And in Chileans' eternal quest for who
they are, they turn often to their native people and particularly the Mapuche.
A speech at the Military Academy one day in 1987 was typical of this
attitude. A new generation of cadets had just passed their first eight weeks
of training, among them one Julius Caesar, the grandson of then military
president Augusto Pinochet. The whole family was on hand for the ceremony, which consisted of considerable marching back and forth to Prussian
marching music, in Prussian uniforms, using the goose-step; the blessing,
by the military chaplain, of the cadets' recently awarded ceremonial dag-
gers; and a series of fiery speeches, including one which began:

"Cadets, you are the living expression of the most genuine merit of a race without equal in the entire world. Every event, every moment Chile has lived through, has brought it wonder and tribute ..." This was no mere rhetorical device. The history of Chile is often reduced to a string of battles, victories and defeats at the hand of foreign and, later, internal "enemies". In 1944, General Indalicio Téllez published a book called *Una Raza Militar (A Military Race)* which argued that the Chilean "race", the product of the joining of the Spanish Conquistador with the noble Araucanian warrior, had an extraordinary talent for making war. General Agustín Toro Dávila begins his study of Chile's military history with the Araucarian (Mapuche) army.

Biologically, for what it's worth, Chileans are more of a Spanish/native mix than they acknowledge, with the blend, typically the product of rape, occurring early in the Conquest. Dr. Francisco Rothhammer, a Chilean born of German parents, educated in liberal German schools influenced by post-World War II reforms, uses his position as an inside-outsider to study the drama of Chileans' relations with their "other" selves. Rothhammer began as a dentist, with a passion for anthropological and genetic research which he cultivated during post-graduate work in the United States and other Latin American countries. In a study of four Chilean cities, Santiago, Valdivia, Valparaíso and Temuco, he concluded that upper-income Chileans (about 10 per cent of the population) had 27 per cent indigenous genes; the middle class, 35 per cent; lower income, a little over 50 per cent. In Temuco, an eight-hour drive south of Santiago, the percentage of indigenous genes went as high as 70 to 75 per cent, reaching 96 per cent among more isolated groups.

"We don't know a great deal about when or how fast the process of genetic integration between the Spanish and the indigenous peoples was," he added. "What is clear is that the relationship was between the Spanish men and indigenous women, because at first there were few Spanish women in America." The first fifty arrived in 1583 and the first party, 4,000 altogether, of settlers that included women, arrived between 1601-1630.

The shiploads of adventurers that flocked to Latin America after Columbus' arrival in 1492 were a far cry from the religious radicals who tackled the more hostile shores of North America. Miguel de Cervantes called the Americas "a refuge and haven for Spain's *desesperados,* a church for rebels, a safe-conduct pass for murderers, a shovel and cover-up for gamblers."

Chilean writer and anthropologist Sonia Montecinos argues that the rape of the native woman by the Spanish fortune hunter has become the archetype in a society where single mothers raise their children, who often suffer from the stigma of the bastard. "The symbolic vacuum of the Pater in the *mestizo* imagery of Latin America was eventually supplanted by a powerful and violent masculine figure: the *caudillo*, the soldier, the guerilla," writes Montecinos. For her, the continent's identity, "which today seems to be a fracture ... is nothing more than the confirmation of a cultural synthesis, ambushed by its own negation."

I did not know exactly what a Nguillatún was: only that it is one of the Mapuche's most important ceremonies. My friend Helen and I drove twelve hours from Santiago to attend this one, in the Pehuenche community of Quinquén, high up in a canoe-shaped valley in the Chilean Cordillera de los Andes near Argentina. To get here we had to drive four kilometres underground, following an old railway tunnel cut through the tons of rock that form the southern mountains. We hurtled along the railway tracks lined with rough planks through a darkness barely penetrated by headlights, water pouring down.

As we left the tunnel, we saw two enormous stone fireplaces with high chimneys standing in an empty field, facing each other across the ruins of what was once an imposing house. Between them, a stone staircase marched resolutely upward into thin air.

Past the clapboard houses of a small town, as we began our climb toward Quinquén, we stared dumbly at miles of slopes devastated by logging, trunks scattered like broken toothpicks over the mountains' massive flanks. At sunset, we drove through a ghostly grove of silvered trunks, all that a fire had spared of a forest of araucaria pine. A full moon struggled to rise above the dead branches.

The Temuco office of the Special Commission on Indigenous Peoples, the CEPI, in the south of Chile, is empty when I arrive first thing in the morning, but halls soon fill with the gentle hubbub of a genuine meeting place. One of President Patricio Aylwin's first actions was to create the Special Commission on Indigenous Peoples, to change existing laws and to plan development to improve their economic situation. Of the twenty poorest communities in Chile, ten are Mapuche.

More than half of the Commission's twenty-two-member council members are representatives of native communities: the Aymara and the Atacameños of northern Chile; the Rapa Nui from Easter Island; the "Fueguian peoples", a scattering of survivors of the Selknam, Yamaná and Ona in Chile's extreme south. By far the largest group are the Mapuche, concentrated in what, until just over a hundred years ago, was their own independent territory. The Commission's director is José Bengoa, a researcher of Chilean origin whose history of the Mapuche people is praised by the Mapuche themselves. Commission members explained to me that Bengoa had been chosen as director because he was seen as a credible arbiter between the sometimes conflicting interests of Chile's different native groups.

In the thirties, many Mapuche left their communities in search of work in the cities. There they faced discrimination and abuse, without the support of their communities and traditions. Many opted, at least on the surface, for trying to pass as non-Mapuche. In the countryside, however, hundreds of communities or *reducciones* have kept the Mapuche's language and traditions alive. The CEPI has chosen a system of self-definition to identify people of native origins. Because the Spanish keep both parents' surnames, most people of native people origin have at least one indigenous name.

The man in charge of the CEPI's Temuco office is Víctor Hugo Painemal, born and raised in Temuco by a Mapuche father and a Chilean mother. He's an accountant whose main political activity up until 1983 was in Chile's largest political party, the Christian Democrats. He knows some Mapudungun from visits to relatives in rural communities, but he is a Roman Catholic by religion and recognizes that he feels awkward when asked to participate in traditional Mapuche ceremonies.

"I got involved in this out of necessity more than anything. My father was very dedicated [to the Mapuche cause]. For me, the Mapuche problem has a cultural and religious element, but more than anything else it's a social problem, because of the poverty, and a political problem."

The Pehuenche were key to the Mapuche resistance. Guardians of the high cordillera, magnificent riders, they controlled the passes between Argentina and Chile, and thus communication between Mapuche on both sides of the Andes. Rebels often escaped through the mountains. Then both governments joined forces; the Mapuche lost their escape hatch and eventually their independence.

The Pehuenches used to summer here in Quinquén, but after the last rebellion this harsh refuge became their permanent home.

The thirty families of Quinquén often wear blue jeans and running shoes, store-bought mantles and brightly patterned polyester head-scarves. But I hear Pehuenche parents correcting their children in fluent Mapudungun. They skilfully round up and butcher the young bull and sheep which are roasted on vertical stakes during the weekend's ceremonies.

Their main food is still the araucaria *fruit, a two-inch long, banana-shaped nut, which can be boiled, roasted or ground into flour. They call the* araucaria *tree the* pehuén *and their name means people of the pehuén. A tree forms the altar around which the Nguillatún's ceremonies take place. Among the offerings gleams a pile of the reddish nuts.*

Víctor Hugo Painemal is the product of a long tradition of Mapuche participation within Chilean society. Already in 1903, newspapers reported political meetings inside Mapuche communities; many identified with the new, liberal Democratic Party. Others were conservatives. The integrationist forces founded the "Caupolicán Society for the Defence of Araucanía" in Temuco in 1911, whose two main goals were the defence of the Mapuche and education. In 1924, a teacher named Francisco Melivilu became the first Mapuche to be elected to Chile's National Congress.

Succeeding generations continued this tradition and successfully opposed a 1927 law which would have divided native communities. Venancio Coñoepán, the grandson and son of pro-integrationist *caciques,* became Minister of Lands and Colonization in the Ibáñez government in the fifties, the highest post so far achieved by a Mapuche.

José Bengoa argues that "without this ability to integrate themselves into national politics, there's no doubt that their situation during the twentieth century would have been different, and very possibly the destructive tendencies of the turn of the century would have become extreme."

But the debate over integration began early and is far from over. In 1916, Manuel Aburto Panguilef told thousands of listeners in Temuco's main square that "Our race has lived abandoned to the rough waves of a sea of daring thieves, who've never hesitated to rob from the Indian; first they robbed his women, then they tried to steal his freedom, his animals, and finally his beloved earth ... In spite of these thieves and murderers, we won't die!"

In the twenties, Panguilef's Araucanian Federation organized an agitprop theatre group which travelled from town to town, singing, dancing, interpreting dreams and recovering Mapuche rites, as well as fighting for the land and direct representation before Chilean authorities. Visits to major cities produced strong ties between the Federation and the growing working-class movement, represented by the Workers Federation of Chile (FOCH). Although he was pro-indigenous and firmly opposed the division of their lands proposed by other native leaders, Panguilef also believed they should have their own representatives in Congress.

Fifteen thousand Mapuches attended the 7th Congress of Panguilef's organization held in Temuco in 1927. During the 11th Congress (1932), his movement declared a new "Indigenous Republic" would be possible "only with an effective alliance between indigenous peoples, peasants and workers ..." When Marmaduke Grove declared the country's short-lived Socialist Republic in 1932, Panguilef was one of three members of the Junta formed in Temuco. After its failure twelve days later, Panguilef's movement waned considerably, but its influence is still apparent in the ceremonial discourse of the old caciques, the Mapuche's leaders, and the *machis*, their traditional wise people.

We were stopped twice at police checkpoints on our way to Quinquén. Questioned about the purpose of our visit, I used a Chilean shrug and open-ended phrasing which could mean anything. The policeman looked curiously at us, but waved us on. Helen suggested I say we were going camping next time. This kind of subterfuge was routine during the military regime, but surely things are different now there's an elected government? We agreed, in theory, but were all too conscious of the distance between theory and practice. Times had changed, but who wanted to test how much?

Throughout the Nguillatún, police on large horses and in official jeeps "visit". As the ceremonies are ending, a police jeep will cut through the ceremonial circle. Their attitude insists they are still the real authorities here, that the decision on whether the Nguillatún ends peacefully or in unequal battle is still theirs.

"For the Mapuche, the dictatorship didn't begin with Pinochet," Painemal told me. "It began a long time before, during democratic governments which simply did not listen to our demands. They tried to integrate, to assimilate, but there was no respect."

Víctor Painemal expected the CEPI, with its representation from native organizations and governmental ministries (some of which also chose representatives of native origins) to be different. Of the eight existing Mapuche organizations, one had supported the Pinochet government and did not participate in the Council; a second, demanding restitution of all Mapuche lands between the Bío Bío and Chile's extreme south, co-operated with the CEPI on some issues. The remaining six were full members.

"We have a very high degree of autonomy from the government and we have opted for an indigenous perspective. I'm speaking even of Bengoa, who has studied this area in depth. He is not neutral. Our attitude is clearly one of defending those who've never had a defence before."

In its first two years (1990-1992), the Aylwin government showed an exceptional interest in native rights. José Bengoa estimates that about 100,000 native people participated in assemblies to define a new law recognizing Chile's original peoples as founders of the Chilean nation and granting them rights and special benefits. The draft presented to congress in October 1991 was virtually identical to that finally approved by a national congress of indigenous representatives. If the law is approved, it could put Chile into the forefront of countries with positive indigenous legislation and provide the framework for solutions to many ongoing problems.

"We have to look within ourselves as well and we don't have well-trained leaders at the moment," said Painemal. "We want bilingual education, but how? Or intercultural, fine, we need a project, but they don't know how to prepare one.

"During the dictatorship, we made demands, shouted, we want freedom! But now that we have freedom we have to define what it's for, what we want to do with it. We can make proposals, because today the authorities are listening. But the movement is suffering from a lack of proposals. It has to be involved in everything, including science."

With Daniel in my arms I watch the wiry men pulling a lasso, at the end of which dances a black bull. They wrestle it to the ground and cut its throat, then patiently saw and cut and divide it among the thirty families of Quinquén, all descendants of the Meliñirs, the family that originally took refuge in this valley.

A little later, don Ernesto, a slim blue-jeaned Pehuenche with a blind white pupil in his right eye, invites me to share his family's lunch and we walk through a wooden archway into the inner circle of the ramada, a long semi-circular frame divided into separate spaces for each family

and covered with branches. These open onto the inner side of the semi-
circle where the araucaria *altar has been placed.*

A bonfire burns in front of each family's space. The night we arrived,
the Pehuenches were busy settling in. Thirty fires sparkled like a neck-
lace against the night's black skin.

High up in the cordillera, about a hundred kilometres north-east of
Temuco, stand the last large groves of a tree unique to Chile, the *arau-*
caria pine, whose thorny trunk shoots as high as fifty metres into the
air, its branches curving outward like umbrella spokes, covered with
bristling dark green leaves. My husband shouted with surprise when we
came upon *araucaria* in exile in Vancouver's Stanley Park during a visit
in 1981. I first saw one in 1964, when I was eight and lived in England:
we used to drive past it on the way to visit my grandparents in Woking.
The trees, shooting their bristly, fountain-like branches in every direction,
looked weird among the fragile English flowers, behind neat English
hedges. The English call them "monkey puzzle trees".

But the *araucaria* or *pehuén* doesn't look absurd in the high mountain
valleys of the Andes. Whether they thrust skyward from their precarious
footholds on rocky cliffs or spread in regal stands along yellow hills,
they are an ancient part of a landscape which changes only through
conflagration, usually fire, although logging is more and more common.

The *araucaria* are incredibly slow growing: it may take them twenty
years to reach four feet. Nevertheless, for most of this century logging
companies ruthlessly clear-cut mature trees. Their activity has threatened
the survival of both the trees and the people who depend on them.

For two days, the bonfires smoke and people move freely about, greeting
friends with a handshake, sharing meals and hot, sweet sips of mate
(pronounced ma-tay), which is drunk through a metal straw.

Don Ernesto's wife, doña Rosalía, is in charge of the mate. *She pours*
the herb, which looks like fresh oregano, into a small tin cup, adds sugar
and hot water. She tastes, spits and stirs, then refills and passes it to a
guest. Several sips and the liquid is gone. She fills the cup again and
passes it along.

Mate *tastes like very strong tea and its rituals are multiple and com-*
plex. There's even a book on the etiquette of mate, *which is a popular*
drink in the Chilean and Argentine countryside. I loved it from the first

sip, but have had to stifle my Canadian good manners. I always want to thank whoever's serving the mate *– but "thank you" means you don't want any more.*

When it's time to eat, don Ernesto pushes the tip of the roasting skewer into the soft earth and hands me a knife. I lean forward and cut off a piece of lamb, then pass the knife along.

They called them *títulos de merced*; they were deeds bestowed upon the Mapuche from the 1880s onward. *Merced* may be translated as benefit, award or mercy, although it's hard to find those elements in the deeds system. The procedure was simple. A *Comisión Radicadora* or Locating Commission identified an area of Mapuche land use (usually their agricultural lands, rather than the larger expanse used for grazing animals, gathering and hunting) and gave the community involved a deed establishing its ownership. Sometimes, Mapuche leaders approached the Commission to obtain the deeds. Or the Commission travelled to Mapuche communities.

But after the defeat of the Mapuches in their last rebellion in 1881-82, whole communities fled from their traditional lands in more accessible areas near the coast, taking refuge with other communities higher up in the mountains. Although the Commission functioned for thirty-seven years (1883-1920), a Chilean historian of the period estimates that as many as a third of Mapuche families were simply never "located". In other cases, a Mapuche group composed of different communities received only one deed. This was what happened to the Meliñirs of Quinquén.

In 1910, a *título de merced* was granted to Paulino Hueiquellán and 144 other members of his family, among them one Manuel Meliñir who married Sofía Ñanco Chahuina. Even before they officially received the deed, the Meliñirs had already spilled over into Quinquén. Legal documents establish that the family lived and grazed their animals in the Quinquén Valley as early as 1906, eating mainly the fruit of the *pehuén,* the *piñón,* which they roasted, boiled or ground into flour. Nevertheless, the Chilean government auctioned off most of the land in the region, selling Quinquén to Guillermo Schweitzer.

According to research by Zorca Moreno, the Meliñir family carefully saved a scrap of paper given them by Guillermo Schweitzer for generations, in the belief that it certified their ownership of Quinquén. In fact, it simply stated that Manuel Meliñir had cared for Schweitzer's herds for ten years.

The lack of official papers didn't affect the Meliñirs for years. They did not know that over time a series of deeds transferred a poorly defined area around Quinquén from one owner to another until in 1953 a 6,870-hectare ranch ended up in the hands of Andrés Lamoliate.

In January 1961, during the conservative government of Jorge Alessandri, the Meliñirs applied to the "Indian Courts" for the expropriation of Quinquén as provided for under Law 14,511. This law empowered the president to expropriate lands owned by third parties but occupied by native communities, in favour of the latter. In spite of legal documents, a cemetery, fences, homes and a chapel indicating their long residence, the courts rather surprisingly ruled against the Meliñirs in 1967.

In 1971, the Meliñirs again tried to establish their legal right to Quinquén, this time using the agrarian reform laws passed by the Christian Democratic government of the late sixties and applied by the Popular Unity government which had taken power a year earlier. The Agrarian Reform Corporation (CORA) planned to make the area a national reserve in order to protect the *araucarias* and guarantee the Pehuenches their homeland. At the beginning of 1972, an agreement was signed granting the Meliñirs permanent use of about 1,970 hectares of the valley for grazing their animals, along with the right to harvest the pine nuts. But this was abruptly suspended after the coup.

Even so, information from within the military government indicates it originally planned to divide the communally owned land into small plots granted to individual families. However, on September 4, 1974, the government returned the property to Andrés Lamoliate. Although in 1977 the Minister of Agriculture, Jorge Prado, expressed concern for the 150 members of the Quinquén community, on July 25, 1985, the Galletue Society created by Andrés Lamoliate applied to the courts to have them evicted.

In 1986, regional authorities investigated the possibility of moving the Pehuenche to a nearby ranch, but it didn't work out. Complicating the whole process was the question of the *araucaria* pine that covered most of the valley. On February 9, 1976, the military government prohibited the cutting of the rare tree as a conservation measure. The Galletue Society took the government to court, questioning its authority to limit the Society's right to exploit their property and eventually achieved a settlement of more than US$15 million. The government responded on October 9, 1987 by allowing the logging of *araucaria* again, under the mistaken impression that this would release it from the obligation of paying. When this didn't work, it delayed payment so long that it was the civilian government that signed the first cheque.

In the meantime, the Temuco Appeals Court had overturned Judge Oscar Viñuela's decision that the Meliñir were permanent residents of Quinquén and therefore could not be evicted. In 1990, just months after the civilian government took power, the Supreme Court upheld the Temuco courts decision in a rapid resolution which left defence lawyers with no chance to prepare their case. The Galletue Society applied for an eviction order.

Desperate, the Pehuenche community leaders wrote President Aylwin. He suspended logging of the *pehuén*. But the problem of the land remained. In September 1990, the Special Commission for Indigenous Peoples, CEPI, announced its support for the Pehuenche, criticized the Supreme Court's decision, asked the new government to negotiate to buy the property, and recommended expropriation if the Galletue Society refused. Negotiations quickly turned into a battle of estimates of the property's value. On May 8, 1991, the government made Quinquén and 100,000 hectares around it a National Reserve, but during the winter (June-September) of 1991, only the snow saved the Pehuenches from eviction. In October, their lawyer achieved a six-month stay of action, but by summer, January 1992, when I visited with my two-month-old son, they were promising to die fighting for their land. For a while it looked as though they might have to.

On March 2, 1992, the government and the Galletue Society reached an agreement. Chileans gasped at the price, US$6,150,000, on top of the more than US$15 million already paid for the trees the Society had not been allowed to cut. Mariela Vallejos commented in *La Epoca*, "just as a family gives all that it can to protect the life of a threatened son or brother, so Chileans have recovered Quinquén."

There are hundreds, perhaps thousands of cases as complex: just a short journey down the Bío Bío River valley, other Pehuenche lands are threatened with flooding from a hydro-electric project under construction. Communities are divided, with some supporting the project because of the jobs. In Temuco and the surrounding region, the *Consejo de Todas las Tierras* (Whole Earth Council) has proposed a claims approach to solving the Mapuches' many problems and they've led occupations of properties they say rightfully belong to them. The Council's leaders have faced trial for using an approach which has led to negotiations between native peoples and governments elsewhere in the world. Other Chilean Mapuche organizations have criticized this persecution, but nevertheless don't support the Whole Earth Council's approach.

Sitting around a table in the Special Commission for Indigenous People's Temuco office, wreathed in veils of cigarette smoke and spring sunshine, a revolving group of about fifteen Mapuche agreed on their problems but not the solutions. For the CEPI's communications co-ordinator it may be time for the Mapuche to stop talking to *huinca* (non-Mapuche) journalists. "If there's no commitment, we don't co-operate," he said. "For the Mapuche, the fruit of these five hundred years as far as communications go has been nothing. We continue to be used for different aspects, be it cultural, religious or historical." But he also conceded that it was "good that people from different countries are concerned and also let us know what's happening internationally.

"Newspapers, radio stations, they always show the Mapuche as something folkloric. Especially in the past fifteen years, they put us in the best photos on the front page in full colour, saying: 'This was the Mapuche people.' They treat us as if we're part of the past and that has been tremendously negative because we exist, we have our own language. Unfortunately, we don't have our own journalists."

José Maliqueo accused political parties of dividing the Mapuche. "Political parties always appoint Mapuche, but then they don't do anything. Today it's we ourselves, who live in the communities, who must become the protagonists."

José Cayupe, an accountant and Christian Democrat party member, passionately defends the opposite view. "We don't leave our communities for the adventure of it," he says, "but rather to get an education and build a better life. We get to the city and we realize that the Mapuche are poor, often because they don't know their real possibilities. When you realize that this injustice exists, morality demands that you defend your people."

A young law student, Dionisio Rapiman, is critical of both the legal and education systems. "The laws have always covered the land, not the peoples, not our rights. The education we receive at school and university isn't an education. It's the technification of the human being so that he'll fulfil a certain function. Many of those who receive scholarships stay in the city; they don't go back to their communities. They forget their people, so the Mapuche themselves remain in the same situation."

Rosendo Huenuman, a former member of congress exiled after the military coup and trained abroad as an agricultural technician, adds: "Education is designed from outside the reality of the Mapuche, as part of a policy of assimilation. From primary school through to university, the Mapuche doesn't graduate with the idea of returning to his community and sharing his knowledge. He graduates with a *huinca* [white European man's] mentality and that's why few return."

"It is the duty of every Mapuche to participate in the elaboration of a political project, but from the perspective of Mapuche society, to remove political party colours and speak with honesty and respect."

Doña Rosalía, like most of the women, is small and plump and very shy. She has a long oval face with downcast eyes I find sad and she works very hard. Don Ernesto tends to order her around, with short, sharp phrases in Mapudungun. Their family includes an adult son and daughter and four small children, but their winters are childless, because the children must attend boarding school in a valley down below. Their oldest daughter, Sofía, also lives down in the valley below, where she works as a housekeeper. When her mother was sick over the winter, the family had a hard time contacting her to tell her help was needed at home. Modern life has forced difficult choices on the Pehuenche: both work and study mean sacrificing family and the tight knot of community.

I ask about women in the Mapuche community, and the men, who have been the most vocal, start to answer, but are interrupted by Ana Catrileo. Slim and shy, her eyes have remained downcast throughout the hours of conversation. During the initial round of introductions, she refused to identify herself and only now has she gathered the energy and resolve to launch not only into the conversation but into a direct confrontation with the men.

"The Mapuche woman is very shy and afraid to talk," she says firmly. "The Mapuche are very *machista;* they think women should dedicate themselves to their homes and nothing more."

Their voices talk on, thick and rich as the cigarette smoke that frames their faces, elaborate as the gestures which underline their thoughts. Sandra Atinao, a university student, complains about limited scholarships – perhaps an appeal to the international community could solve this, she proposes tentatively. José Cayupe doesn't believe in international support. "When the Conquistadors arrived, they never respected the values of Mapuche society. I think the Chilean State and society are in debt with this people. This is something Chilean society has to do, because with the heritage which the Mapuche had in those times, with all that land, there's no reason we should be waiting for alms of any kind.

"But our effectiveness depends on how much influence the Mapuche have from within. This is why we must get an education, without losing our traditional values and above all our unity. I have my convictions; that's why I belong to a political party and it's not to privilege that party but rather the reverse. Even so, I think the unity of the Mapuche is over and above political ideologies and religions."

Dionisio Rapiman doesn't mind a brother going to hospitals with "some *huinca* sickness. But I don't accept that he goes to a [non-Mapuche] herbal doctor, because he has stolen all his knowledge from the *machi*. Now they say that the *machi* is a witch, but for me, this concept of the witch or wizard doesn't exist. It belongs to the West, which divides things between good and evil. But within Mapuche philosophy, there are two energies: the positive and the negative that, when united, allow a new being to exist.

"We need to look out more for nature itself, which means that I, as a human being, have a role to play, that I am no more than a tree, no more than an ant. What does development mean after all? What sort of development is it to fill our pockets? Or those of a few others? For the Mapuche, that doesn't exist.

"In our homes, we are educated to respect not just other people but also the things around us. For me, I don't need a photograph of something, because all of nature is in my eyes."

The Mapuche community of Nueva Imperial doesn't look very different from a typical Chilean country town, except that it is so much poorer. The buildings are well-used, like old shoes that someone else might have thrown out long ago. The people in the streets are typically short and stocky, no more than five feet tall, with thick waists and hips which remind me of those dolls that can be knocked over but always pop up again.

The women wear white or coloured handkerchiefs around their heads. Old cars are propped by sidewalks; horses pull wagons along the cracked pavement. The town is a reminder that not all Mapuche communities are involved in dramatic conflicts over land tenure or the building of dams. Nevertheless, life remains a complex journey through a maze of legal, political and social dictates essentially hostile to their language, customs, existence. These are the "ordinary" problems of survival for the communities of southern Chile, the Aymara and the Atacameño in the north, the Rapa Nui on Easter Island.

Our guide is an employee of the Special Commission on Indigenous People, don Gabino, who takes us through town to a muddy lane where we park the jeep. On a hillside with grass so lush it's almost fluorescent, we hear the sounds of hammers. Rounding a corner we see a large wooden framework for a new schoolhouse, one result of the hope which is beginning to germinate more shyly than this radiant spring.

Behind the wooden structure built to meet Chilean standards, *rucas*, the traditional Mapuche dwelling, perch on the hillside, watching over bright meadows toward the silver highway of the Cautín River. These *rucas* will be used for workshops, a builder tells us. Each is about twenty feet long, with rounded walls and conical thatched roofs, the traditional living space of the Mapuche since before the conquest. One has walls made of adobe bricks which will last, even in southern rains, for more than thirty years; another has concrete walls; a third is wood. Each building, from the modern school to the variations on the *ruca*, seems like a testimony to the Mapuche's ability to borrow, to adapt, to rescue what is best from their own and other cultures.

When the school finally opens, we learn, the education will be bilingual and bicultural. The Mapuche and *huinca* children who study here will learn more than the official version of the Pacification of the Araucania. Nor will they, as their counterparts in the northern Andes do, learn their ABCs from a textbook set on the Santiago subway.

Five men, with feather head-dresses and blankets folded around their hips, dance around the araucaria, *their dance imitating the mating dance of an Andean ostrich, alternately aggressive, shy, flirtatious, stomping ahead or turning back. The women sit, backs straight, legs pointing toward the* araucaria. *Some wear traditional head-dresses of brightly coloured ribbons. Most wear the straight skirts and long aprons common to women in traditional communities. They chant to the beat of a resonant skin drum, while the men, blue circles and upside-down tridents painted on their bare chests and legs, dance.*

A ewe and a ram, two horses and a young bull spend the ceremonies tied to posts beyond the araucaria. *The high cost of animals has saved from sacrifice all but the bull I saw dancing at the end of its rope.*

Between each family's dance, riders on horseback circle the ramada, *the branch-covered frame that shelters the thirty families, at a fast gallop, filling the air with the jingling of tackle and small bells, creating a minor earthquake. Saffron-coloured dust pours through the openings in the* ramada, *covering everything. For a moment, the horsemen truly seem to harness the elements, to control the earth's huge, shaking, irresistible power.*

Alone in my tent, when night has made the world disappear and it feels as though it might never come back, I realize how important these rituals are and begin to feel I miss them from my own culture. The difference between those who dwell inside and outside is more than distance, time, the gap between country and city. Our survival strategies are often imposed upon us, rather than the product of collective invention.

Leaving Nueva Imperial, my husband and I and don Gabino turn off onto a sideroad and take a "ferry" across the Cautín River. Wide as the Saskatchewan River where it runs through Edmonton, the river's distant banks are joined by a ferry that is little more than a log raft guided by a cable which stretches from shore to shore. By shortening or lengthening the cables at either end of the ferry, the boatmen ensure we're propelled across. Where the current slows by the shore, they use long poles to prod us along.

A fellow passenger, with a wizened face and the pungent halo of chronic alcoholism, asks for a ride "a little ways up the road".

"How far?" we ask.

"Oh just to the crossing where the school is," he says. He must know we have no idea where we are. "I have a few things to carry, very heavy, for the house I'm building," he adds. The little man looks so frail it's hard to imagine him getting himself up the road. We nod helplessly and make space in the front seat.

"Just a little bundle," he adds as he leaps nimbly in and out, loading parcels into the jeep until he can barely squeeze himself on top. Most contain five-litre bottles of wine, although later my husband and I will argue over whether one, at least, was paint for the new house.

The "little ways" takes us along the Cautín River and then jogs slightly inland, through a puddle that disguises lake-like depths under a silvery veneer of rainwater. The four-wheel drive pulls us through and we carry on for miles of bare, muddy road, lined by leafless poplar and the early-flowering aromos. In the dimming light we pass cattle grazing green fields, the turnoff we'd planned to take and clusters of low buildings which are the homes, sheds and extra rooms of the Mapuche who work these lands.

Finally we reach our passenger's destination. He invites us in for a drink, to celebrate his new house, but the darkening afternoon makes us refuse. As we back out of his lot, I glimpse a straw-thatched *ruca* hunched in a row of modest wood cabins.

We drive back and turn down the lane we'd passed earlier. Don Gabino introduces us to doña Adela Curaqueo, who dries her hands on a cloth and greets us, while her husband, don Aureliano, finishes feeding the pigs. Both are a good foot shorter than me and my companions, with the rounded bodies and cheeks, dark brown eyes and hair common to most Mapuches. In the waning light it's hard to see more than the wrinkles and warmth of their smiles, to feel the rough dry surfaces of the palms they press into ours.

Inside her neat cabin, doña Adela heats up the wood stove and bustles to set the table, pound garlic with a stone crusher and mix a savory egg mixture which she serves with home-made bread and instant coffee. A loom of straight young trees, strung with handspun wool covers one wall. Strands of black, grey, brown and occasionally red trace an intricate geometric design in what will eventually be a poncho. I kneel beside it, amazed by the way such slender threads can form a thick blanket. She crouches comfortably beside me, her left hand deftly selecting threads from a thick cluster, while her right passes a wooden shuttle between them, then blocks them down, forming more of the pattern.

She has studied the art of spinning, dying and weaving wool all her life, but few are willing to learn nowadays, she says. Both she and don Aureliano speak Mapudungun, but it's hard to keep it up, even between themselves. Their daughter, who lives in Santiago, is also a craftswoman, but none of their children speak Mapudungun. Doña Adela knows and sings many of the traditional Mapuche songs and plays the *kultrún*.

She asks us if we believe in God and our muddled replies launch her into the story of don Aureliano's near-fatal illness, shortly after the 1973 military coup, when many doctors in state-run hospitals had been arrested or were in hiding.

"He had an operation, here," her hand slices through her midriff, just over her liver.

"For gallstones?" don Gabino clarifies.

"Yes. They sent him home here just a couple of days after the operation. At first he tried to get up and work as usual. You know, there's always lots of work on the farm. But then he felt sick and finally couldn't move. We took him back to the hospital —" it took them most of a day to find a driver and a vehicle to take them to Temuco, thirty minutes away by car.

"He was almost gone. They'd sent him home with no instructions for tending the wound. At the hospital they had to operate again. I prayed and thought, if he survives, God really does exist."

Just across the river to the north, Temuco's lights glitter and pulse like a starry sky, captured and bound to the earth. Hundreds of kilometres south-east, electrical current and voices buzz along wires, all the way past Villarrica and Pucón, to the shores of Lake Caburgua in the Andes' lap.

But here in doña Adela's two-room cabin, nightfall brings a thick darkness that swells around us like rising water. She hurries to a corner shelf where she keeps her candles. When they're lit, when she's managed to prop them up on windowsill, table and shelf, she sits and talks on from the shadows, spinning raw wool into thread using a single spindle, which twirls like a ballet dancer on the rough planks of the floor.

In mid-afternoon, men and women gather before the araucaria *to celebrate the* rogativa, *the requests which are the Nguillatún's essence. As the* lonco, *their leader, speaks in Mapudungun, people alternately stand and kneel. Then, to strains of accordion music they link hands, forming circles of men within circles of women, each moving in opposite directions. The circles tighten until they're almost crushed together, then relax. Finally, the participants form a small procession around the* araucaria, *chatting in a friendly, relaxed way.*

Their solemnity, as they kneel and stand to the rhythm of the lonco's *Mapudungun, moves me. I feel both humbled and grateful, surprised that on the edge of the twenty-first century I have been able to see this, that it's real. Like the host and wine in the Christian mass, the meat and* mate *we have shared during the Nguillatún is a pledge of loyalty binding all those present.*

I am struck by the beauty of praying before a live and life-giving altar, formed by the araucaria. *I feel Daniel's small body moulded over my heart. I incline my head and fill my lungs with his still-newborn fragrance. As I listen to the dying notes of the drums, I can't help adding my own requests to theirs.*

Chapter fourteen

ALVARO VALENZUELA/ JULIO CORBALÁN

SANTIAGO 1985, 1995

My scale of values, in this order, is: God, the fatherland, family, honour,
justice, freedom, loyalty, peace. National security is the fatherland's Security,
first value of man, after God.

ALVARO CORBALÁN CASTILLO

For weeks my desk has been covered with books, clippings, photographs, notes about the organization that began among the snarled acronyms of Army, Navy, Detective, Carabineros and Air Force Intelligence; that did battle with the Joint Command; that emerged as the DINA, was reborn as the CNI and carries on within the DINE, the Army's Intelligence Department. I pin blue squares of paper to them, trying to sort them into some kind of order, but they are as entangled as the roots and vines of Chile's southern forests, swinging between one tree and another, twisted, perilously alive. The red tongues of a forest fire can withdraw so deeply into those ancient trees that the fire survives the deluge of winter rains, travelling along the root system until the hot sun turns the vegetation to tinder and the fire conspires with air to ravage again.

In the midst of this disorder, I try to spin together the threads of the life of the Army's representative who started work in the Joint Command; the man said to have led the operations on Fuenteovejuna and Janaqueo streets in Santiago; the manoeuvres that ended Ignacio's life and the lives of eleven others; the man indicted for "fraudulent bankruptcy"; the man imprisoned for murder; the man who launched a pro-Pinochet party; the man who threatened to take to the hills; the man who lived behind a high wall, defended by armed guards; the man with the guitar; the man whose wife says the guards are "to protect the children"; the man who frightens people, who charms, who leads, who talks at length; the man of many names, whose interviewers begin by asking: who am I talking to? Meaning, what is your real name? The man who's proud of everything he's done. The man who denies everything. The man who once called himself, Alvaro Valenzuela; the man who answers to: Alvaro Julio Corbalán Castillo.

He was born on December 14, 1951; his father was an agricultural engineer and his mother a writer, journalist and piano player. Fourteen years later he entered the military academy where he is remembered for his ability to charm even the most rigid of his superior officers, staying out late to play the guitar at private girls' schools in the wealthy Santiago neighbourhood where the Military School is located. In 1970, the year Salvador Allende assumed power, he chose to specialize in Artillery. In 1971, he attended a forty-five day course in Fort Gulick, School of the Americas, in the Panama Canal zone. Like General Medina, he was then stationed at the Artillery regiment in Linares. From there he went to the Pudeto Artillery regiment in Punta Arenas, where he accidentally killed fifteen lambs, which the troops happily ate. Writing in a Santiago newspaper *La Nación*, Manuel Salazar calculates that somewhere between 1971 and 1972 Corbalán entered Army Intelligence.

In 1974, he signed a contract to tape a record with the Odeon company, but decided to take a basic intelligence course instead, in the village of Nos, near Santiago. He was assigned to the Army's Intelligence Corps, and in 1976, he specialized, taking time off to compose the Intelligence School's anthem: "We're sons of the school of silence ..." He became the Army's representative in the "Intelligence Community", co-ordinating operations with the Air Force's Edgar Ceballos Jones, the Navy's Daniel Gimpert, Agustín Muñoz of the Carabineros, and Roberto Fuentes Morrison of the Air Force. Sometime between the end of 1976 and the beginning of 1977, he achieved his first big triumph: with the help of an Army chaplain, the Spanish priest Felipe Gutiérrez, he infiltrated the administrative structure of the Santiago diocese of the Catholic Church, at that time the only refuge for Chile's growing legion of victims of human rights violations.

As a captain, in 1978, he was part of the preparations for war with Argentina, travelling abroad constantly to set up a secret service network, under the cover of a travel agency, Cordillera Tour. But the next year, Lieutenant Colonel Roberto Schmidt Sanzi, then commander of the Army's Intelligence Corps, discovered he'd misused funds. He was sent to General Carlos Forestier, Army vice-commander. *La Nación* reports that there he declared that one intelligence agent was worth a whole division. This could have cost him his career, but Corbalán reminded his superiors of "what he knew", and was promptly dispatched to the CNI.

In 1980, after a lengthy battle with the former DINA head Manuel Contreras, the CNI's director was replaced by General Humberto Gordon, a heavy-set man who took to Corbalán with enthusiasm. With Gordon's support, Corbalán reorganized the CNI's operative structure into units with names like Apache, Blue, Yellow and Green, responsible for different political groups, one of which pursued and finally eliminated the top leadership of the Left Revolutionary Movement, MIR – on Fuenteovejuna and Janaqueo streets, in September 1983. The name "Alvaro Valenzuela" appeared in the press for the first time, identifying the man in charge.

In the report in *La Nación*, Manuel Salazar has described Corbalán as a man who could work long hours and recover with just four hours of sleep, who didn't drink or smoke, who ate lots of fruit and milk products, but had a weakness for Fanta and Orange Crush. During his years in the CNI, he trained his men in the art of cat-and-mouse pursuits, stretching operations out over time to make more money out of them.

These perquisites were in addition to "war booties" that is, money and valuables seized during operations. Salazar mentions a film by the CNI of the operation on Fuente Ovejuna Street, the same one with the bullet-ridden house, the almost naked-bodies of a young woman and two men, the pitiful display of "subversive" material and weapons that I had visited with my colleague from Radio France. The film reports that the police seized only US$3,000, from one of the MIR party members killed during the attack. The MIR leadership, however, claim that briefcases hidden in the house were full of money.

A week after the operation on Fuenteovejuna Street, "Julio Corbalán" founds a new political movement, "Avanzada Nacional". On September 11, 1983, the movement's founders climb San Cristobal Hill, singing their anthem: "Avanzada, for the fatherland/ always alert, always true,/ A trumpet from our past/ shakes our skin ..."

Another special report in *La Nación* traces the movement's intellectual parenthood to Chileans and Europeans who admired the "Iron Guard" or "Légion of St. Michael the Archangel", which fought with General Francisco Franco in Spain and co-operated with the Nazis. A Chilean magazine, inspired by these ideas, called *Avanzada,* was published by a bombing expert and saboteur during the Popular Unity government. Among the magazine's mentors was a prominent lawyer, Sergio Miranda Carrington, who, during the nineties, defended General Manuel Contreras when he appealed the sentence for his role in the killing of Orlando Letelier and Ronni Moffit, in September 1976.

This attempt to mobilize a broadly based public movement in favour of General Pinochet's presidency was short-lived however. By the end of 1983, some of Avanzada Nacional's supporters were struggling to get rid of their main political officer, Julio Corbalán. A splinter group broke away, but failed for lack of funding the next year.

In 1985, shortly after heavily armed men acting in broad daylight kidnap Manuel Guerrero and José Manuel Parada from the school where their children study and Guerrero also teaches, and their bloodless bodies, along with a third man's, have been found in an empty field, Alvaro Valenzuela's name crops up again. A CNI report blames the Carabineros' Intelligence Department, DICOMCAR, for the crime. The CNI report is leaked to the opposition magazine, *Análisis*. The Carabineros blame Alvaro Valenzuela.

At the same time, Valenzuela's "political" work continues apace, with a signature campaign supporting General Pinochet, whom he considers Chile's greatest "soldier, statesman, patriot, Christian and father". The CNI's director, General Gordon, heartily approves of this campaign, which is to express Chileans' support for the legitimacy of the military government, but he wants to see results before he hands over the appetizing sum of 20 million pesos (about U$66,600). The campaign culminates in a formal presentation of the petition to General Pinochet and his wife, Lucía Hiriart, complete with breakdowns by region and sex, provided by computer expert Eugenio Fourt Guzmán. Years later, in February 1991, a special report in *La Nación* estimates that of the 265,000 signatures accumulated during the campaign, around 5,000 were legitimate. The rest were culled from lists of housing-subsidy applicants and pressured public-service employees.

In spite of its success, the signature campaign almost costs Corbalán his post. Anxious about what the general's approval could mean for Avanzada Nacional's future, Corbalán insists on attending the ceremony with General Pinochet, in open defiance of an order from General Gordon. During his celebration speech at a restaurant hours later, Corbalán bursts into sobs and reveals he's been fired from the CNI. A week later, he's back in his office at the CNI's headquarters.

In 1987, the name Alvaro Valenzuela is murmured again in relation to the killings of Ignacio Valenzuela and his companions, known at first as the Corpus Christi killings, then "Operation Albania", then "Operation Elephant". As 1988 draws to a close after the opposition victory at the polls, Alvaro Corbalán emerges in an unusually lengthy interview published by the magazine *Cosas*.

The *Cosas* interviewers describe him as a sharp, intelligent man of multiple talents, a former "important officer" in the CNI, now a full-time politician. For four consecutive issues, Alvaro Corbalán expounds his views of Chilean society, General Pinochet and politics in general. He admires many of Chile's historical figures: the Mapuche, Lautaro; liberation generals Carrera and O'Higgins; the conservative statesman Diego Portales; and above all, General Pinochet. He reveals his love for the classical composers Liszt, Chopin and Mozart, along with modern performers like Frank Sinatra and Paco de Lucía and he talks about the writers he likes (Gustavo Becker, Manuel Magallanes, Pezoa Véliz).

He considers September 11, 1973 the date of Chile's Second National Independence and he believes that the "real" human rights situation in Chile should have helped General Pinochet to win the plebiscite. The cases listed in reports by Chilean and international human rights organizations (many of which are simply Communist fronts, he says) are disproportionate exaggerations, insignificant in the light of how uniformed personnel and their families and innocent victims have suffered. Chileans who voted "No" to General Pinochet's presidency are guilty of ingratitude. He believes they will correct this mistake.

When the *Cosas* interviewers ask his position in the CNI, and how he came to hold it after a negative evaluation while in the Army, he denies he was ever negatively evaluated; intelligence officers are always "élite", he emphasizes.

"How and why did you become head of Operations of the CNI in circumstances in which it should have been a colonel? What consequences did this promotion bring?" they ask.

"The position of Director of Operations doesn't exist, so I never held it. Neither did the custom of appointing a colonel, since it would be strange to appoint a high officer to a non-existent position. Since there was no director and no appointment, what consequences could it produce?"

"Specifically then, what was the position that you held in the CNI?"

"Specifically, I've not been the head of Operations, and it is not good to reveal the functions or organizational positions that Intelligence has in Chile to terrorists for the modest sum of 600 pesos [the cost of the magazine]."

For Alvaro Corbalán, the Armed Forces and particularly police services are white blood cells defending the social body from dangerous disease. Terrorists are atheistic cowards "utilized by foreigners, who deny God, the Fatherland and their own family for foreign ideologies that they themselves don't even understand". The only terrorism in Chile comes from the left. Only a poorly informed foreign correspondent could think otherwise, he adds.

Has Alvaro Corbalán ever made a mistake? It's hard to say. In one of the *Cosas* interviews, he calls errors and successes "two phases of the same process called mission. It would be vain on my part to draw up a balance between successes and errors."

He thinks terrorism should be fought through parental influence, the de-politicization of the Church, education, respect for Chilean values, compulsory military service. He considers his new political career the logical continuation of his "defence of the permanent values of our nationality" and "nationalism", he says, "is immortal, the cultural and socio-political root of man, the Fatherland's identity." "Liberty," he will clarify in his third *Cosas* interview, "comes before democracy," which is "only a method for obtaining it and when it falls into the wrong hands, it destroys freedom."

"A nationalist society," he expands, "is an inspiration which, without name and surname, is carried by each Chilean, by each person in his conscience. It desires a humanistic society where personal values are above any ideology, technology or system. It also aspires to [have] an integrated, united society, that can show itself to the world with its own identity, where the foreigner is absorbed without deformation. Of course, it desires a society that respects its roots, its historic past, its traditions, not to anchor itself in contemplative immobility but rather to learn and strengthen itself. It also aspires to a real democratic society that's not politicized where intermediate bodies allow the participation of all social sectors and make more fair the relations between businessman and worker. Finally, every good Chilean looks [critically] upon the old division of centre, left or right, that allows all kinds of poses and camouflage. The nationalist set of ideas is popular and is above these obsolete schemes."

Nationalism, he concludes, "is a superior value system".

Asked how he can guarantee that he won't use military methods in the political arena, he explains that both have been inseparable for thousands of years. "Weapons become decisions, actions images; but the military methods remain there. I don't guarantee going back in history and making everything begin again without military influence in the civilian arena, or vice versa."

Corbalán's comments to the *Cosas* interviewers are lavishly accompanied by photographs showing him shaking hands, sitting at a podium, sharing the limelight with prominent Chileans, some of whom might have preferred not to appear. In his second *Cosas* interview, he warns that "the loyalty which today brings me to public silence could bring me tomorrow to unmask situations and people for the good of the fatherland's interest and the president's." By the last interview there's a sarcastic promise to former associates that he won't publish any more photographs "for now".

A few months later, he's news enough for *El Mercurio*'s prestigious Special Reports section in the Sunday paper. Their top interviewer, Raquel Correa, takes him to task, but only after he looks her over in the Military Club, where they chat for half an hour. Finally, he whisks her from the club to Avanzada Nacional's nearby headquarters in a new Volvo, followed by his bodyguards in a similar car.

"This could well have been a play," she writes afterward. "Sometimes a drama, at others, a comedy. "A very solemn stage. Enormous velvet curtains, walls covered with fine panelling. In these salons, some three decades ago, Teresita Pereira Larraín gave the most luxurious dance of the season.

"Now, there's no more music, nor girls in lace, nor waiters with silver trays; rather, [there are] men who move among the shadows, who appear and disappear as if by magic; obsequious, silent, with alert stares." Correa compares him to Omar Sharif, with "eyes, brilliant as fire", a neatly trimmed moustache. She describes him as he tries to be polite, sitting

flanked by flags of Chile and Avanzada Nacional, with a photograph of
General Pinochet behind him.

When Correa pulls out her tape recorder, he moves for his own, but
she stops him and he asks her pardon. Then she begins, asking his name
and insisting on seeing his national identity card. Although everyone by
now refers to him as Alvaro Julio Corbalán Castilla (with a final "a"), the
card actually gives his mother's surname as Castillo, as if, even now, with
so much known about him, some last detail must be changed. He justifies
the false names with an argument that has become automatic: citing
famous writers, among them Plato, who used pseudonyms. He compares
his move, from the secret police to political leader, to that of George
Bush, who headed the CIA, or Gorbachev, who worked with the KGB.

When she asks if he's armed he stands up, opens his jacket and twirls
around to demonstrate that he's not, although he admits he keeps "a
personal weapon and some others which I won't name" in his car. He
refuses to say if his car is armoured or not. "Dangers must be fought
with equivalent arms," he adds. When the photographer finishes and
prepares to leave, he presses a button to unlock the door.

"How do you explain that a retired Army Major with an income of
120,000 pesos [US$400] can have the following goods: a summer house
in Papudo, a fortified mini-palace in El Arrayán with a pool, sauna,
Jacuzzi, a private corps of body guards with AKA machine guns, a fleet
of late model Volvos?"

The beachhouse belongs to his mother, he replies, and as for his house,
"While I was abroad I saved enough to buy the land about ten years ago
when the sector was pretty empty ... Little by little I began to fix up my
little site. I bought the bricks ... in the Infantry School's factory which
was much cheaper and allowed me to build a fence somewhat higher
than normal. Photographs taken from the hill across the way – where
people habitually go to photograph my installations – make it look like
a fortification."

He adds, almost as an afterthought, that he is a partner in a security
company, a transportation firm and several other businesses.

"Have you killed anyone?" she asks him, point-blank.

"That question bothers me."

"I asked General Gordon the same thing when he was director of the
CNI. And he answered it with no problems."

"I've never killed anyone. And security services don't kill either. In some situations, the terrorist, whom you can't pick up just by ringing the doorbell and asking permission, forces an agent to act in an inevitable way."

"And you never confronted terrorists? You never participated in an assault on a 'safe house'?"

"When a situation like that is produced, a proper trial is carried out as corresponds in a State of Law. I've never been in that situation."

"You weren't involved in the 'confrontation' in Fuente Ovejuna, nor the Janaqueo operative, nor the one called 'Operation Albania'?"

"No."

"... What is your moral position on torture?"

"I reject it absolutely. I find it despicable. I'm a Christian. I believe deeply in my country, in the family, in God. Never in my life have I acted in any activity against my principles! I don't know of a case different from mine among the people I had close to me or to whom I had access. What is more, I feel absolutely proud to have had the privilege to carry out the most noble activity that a person born in Chile could have: the defence of its sovereignty, of the fatherland, national security!"

In 1990, a year after his interview with Raquel Correa, Alvaro Corbalán is the ex-president of Avanzada Nacional. He holds forth at a news conference, carefully dressed with a tie pin in the shape of a curved military knife, announcing that the "irregular, dirty, subversive war that can't be fought with regular forces" is still in effect, making special police forces necessary to fight them. He is prepared to take up arms to defend "our institutions, our constitution" in the unlikely event that the Armed Forces are overcome, "in which case I would carry out the defence of my fatherland throughout the whole national territory, as should every citizen of the Republic including my critics."

Asked about human rights, he says that if anyone has the right to raise the issue, it was the military government, and he adds that he hopes that the Rettig Commission for Truth and Reconciliation, which has just begun work will meet its goals, although he fears that the Marxists will turn it into a "commission [of] vengeance and resentment".

By November he's been charged with the fraudulent bankruptcy of the Santa Barbara Transport Company and he's not allowed to leave Chile. Ana María Acevedo, a reporter from *La Nación*, visits his house. She stops in front of a brown gate, "behind which there were two guards dressed in black, one of which was carrying an Uzi sub-machine gun". Alvaro Corbalán isn't in, the guards say. When they ask permission to take a photograph, one guard says no.

"But this isn't military property," she argues.

"For me, this is military property," he answers.

"Are you a soldier?"

"I can't answer that."

"You don't look like a soldier because you have long hair."

"Some soldiers have long hair."

When they insist on their photograph, the guard warns they'll be stopped, and the film taken from their cameras.

In interviews, Julio Alvaro Corbalán Castilla or Castillo is confident, an active man who speaks in a mocking tone verging on insult, a retired Army officer, a political ideologue, a future candidate. He finds a precedent for everything he's done in world politics, in the fight against illness, in the war between good and evil, communist-terrorist-killers and the Armed Forces of Peace and Order. In spite of the lost plebiscite, he believes General Pinochet will run in the elections and win. All other presidential candidates are "cadavers".

But on December 14, 1989, his party wins no seats in Congress; a Christian Democrat (the party, he has said, whose members wear two watches, so they're never sure what time it is) wins the presidency, heading a coalition of centre and left parties, including many of those persecuted by the military. Soon afterward, the CNI is officially dissolved. Alvaro Corbalán and close to a hundred men vacate the headquarters of the secret police, scattered around the city, and head for Corbalán's house where they form the Augusto Pinochet Ugarte Special Brigade, whose financing and operations remain a secret.

On March 11, 1990 his candidate, General Pinochet, rather sulkily hands the presidential sash – and political power – to Patricio Aylwin. Ten months later, Alvaro Corbalán is in jail, sharing the same patio with members of the Manuel Rodríguez Patriotic Front who threaten to kill him.

He's not there for long though. According to Alejandra Matus of *La Epoca*, Corbalán's wife asks General Pinochet to intercede. A few days later, Corbalán begins to complain of headaches. The physicians from the Legal Medical Institute and the penitentiary order observation and minor examinations, but a doctor from the Military Hospital diagnoses congenital narrowing of the aorta, which requires a complex battery of examinations. Safely ensconced in the Military Hospital, Corbalán enjoys the assistance of a private secretary, free access to a telephone and other comforts.

Rolando Fernández, a lawyer representing the case against Corbalán, complains that this is interfering with the investigation. Twelve days later, Corbalán's lawyer, Alejandro Barros, says he's tried to escape, racing down five floors of stairways before being stopped in a guarded area on the first floor.

The second time, says Barros, who left Corbalán's case a week earlier, he used "sheets and blankets knotted together. This way he tried to slide out the window of his room on the fifth floor, but upon arriving at the fourth floor he was caught by a patient who gave the alarm." When the room is searched, the guards find a new pair of shoes, a religious outfit, a short-barrelled loaded weapon and three boxes of tranquillizers.

Both the Military Hospital and Patricio Hidalgo, Corbalán's current lawyer, deny the escape attempt.

Pressured by media questioning of Corbalán's lengthy stay in hospital, the judge responsible requests a report, then goes on holiday. A week later, a source in the courts explains they won't press for the explanation "because if there's anything to inform us of, it's their job ..."

Barros soon finds himself in the Military Hospital, due to a diabetic crisis. In the days following his remarks to the press, he has received death threats and the announcement that a bomb would explode in his home, so perhaps he's relieved to be safe in hospital for a while. A retired military officer and a former member of Avanzada Nacional, Barros says he won't refer to Corbalán any more.

A source in the Military Hospital has told *La Epoca* reporter Alejandra Matus that several women have attempted to visit Corbalán in his sickbed. According to this source, nineteen-year-old María Carolina Fourt became hysterical when denied access to Corbalán's room. Two months later, a report in a Santiago newspaper describes her mother as "prey of an intense panic", shut up in her luxurious home. María Olga de la Cruz has accused Alvaro Corbalán of being involved in her daughter's running away. Now she's confiding to a *Tercera* reporter that she's received death threats and "if anything happens to me, you know who did it."

She adds that she knows some terrible things and for this reason her daughter is being used to keep her quiet. However, the daughter herself announces that she's living with her father.

"My old lady got unbearable four years ago when she got into politics," says María Carolina Fourt. "She changed 180 degrees, as a woman, as a mother and as a wife. She separated from my father and then she started on me."

María Olga de la Cruz was a founder of Avanzada Nacional. She's a former mayor appointed by the military regime. Her ex-husband is Eugenio Fourt, once a business associate of Alvaro Corbalán's, in fact, he's involved in the same fraudulent bankruptcy case which has put Corbalán in jail.

A week later Alvaro Corbalán is in top form during a special luncheon organized by his supporters. "I don't resort to exile, nor do I ask protection from Vicariates," he tells about a hundred of General Pinochet's most loyal followers. "I've been the target of all sorts of infamies, slander, defamation, persecution. They have tried to compromise me with any irregularity that's occurred in our country."

He denies ever having been a partner of the Santa Bárbara Transport Company and adds he never had any signing powers. "With renewed energies, my spirit and my freedom are at the disposition of nationalism, justice and truth. ... I'm here before you, at the disposition of the courts and I prefer to die in the frontlines to being healthy in the rearguard".

What was the Santa Bárbara Transport Company? According to Rolando Fernández, who files the charges against it, it was "a paper society, conceived to provide financial support to the ex-head of Operations of the Central Nacional de Informaciones (CNI), Alvaro Corbalán Castilla" and he adds that the firm paid the salaries of Corbalán's twenty-odd bodyguards. Their names are on Santa Bárbara pay-slips; several also appear on the CNI's payroll, leaked to the communist newspaper *El Siglo* in April 1990.

The company was legally created on June 28, 1988, a family affair whose main partner was José Mario Guillén Zapata, the third husband of Alvaro Corbalán's mother. The other partners were Eduardo Núñez Bories, personnel manager of the Credit and Investment Bank, and his wife, María Josefa Barón Jiménez, a real-estate agent.

Eduardo Núñez Bories's stepbrother, Jorge Vargas Bories, headed Corbalán's bodyguard for a while and is a former CNI agent. According to

Rosemarie Bornand, a lawyer in the Catholic Church's human rights department, in 1979 Vargas Bories participated directly in the tortures which caused the death of a university professor, Federico Alvarez Santibáñez. Vargas Bories is supposed to have participated in "Operation Albania" in 1987, the operation in which Ignacio was killed, along with eleven other members of the Manuel Rodríguez Patriotic Front. *El Siglo* describes Vargas Bories as he walks through the house on Pedro Donoso Street, accompanying Francisco Zúñiga while he fires into the seven dead bodies. Francisco Zúñiga, a former Carabinero assigned to the CNI, appears as a manager on Santa Bárbara's organizational chart as drawn up by a partner, María Josefa Barón.

The Santa Bárbara Transport Company seems to have got off to a good start. It landed a juicy contract for moving 5,000 tons of slag a month for the state-run copper corporation, Codelco, and on the strength of the contract, it convinced Chile's State Bank to lend it one and a half million dollars. No mean feat given that the usual procedures – requiring guarantees, guarantors, financial backup and records – seem to have been waived completely. Not only that, but when the chips were down and the company was going broke in March 1990, the State Bank hurriedly processed and conceded a new loan to Santa Bárbara, just days before General Pinochet handed power over to the elected government. The man responsible for these marvels, according to the Santiago newspapers, is Eugenio Fourt, once married to María Olga de la Cruz. He is also the computer wizard who impressed General Pinochet and his wife with their supporters' signatures.

When payments made by the state-owned copper company, Codelco to Santa Bárbara are added up in 1990, they come to a rather generous 500 million pesos (US$1.6 million). The money is definitely gone, but 300 million is unaccounted for. Most of the company's records disappear shortly after the trial begins.

The company's crash is all the more resounding when the widow of a murdered Santiago businessman accuses Alvaro Corbalán of being involved in her husband's killing. Isabel Pizarro tells judges and press that her husband was shot when he demanded that La Cutufa, an illegal finance company associated with the CNI, return millions of pesos he'd deposited. Judges in both the murder and the illegal finance company cases have ordered Corbalán to testify, but the only evidence is inconclusive: Isabel Pizarro's declarations and Corbalán's business cards, found in the murdered man's car.

Intrigued, even the staid *Mercurio* reports that both cases, that of the illegal finance company known as La Cutufa and the Santa Bárbara Transport Company, will eventually be combined: "... when what happened with the millions Santa Bárbara couldn't justify becomes known." Santa Bárbara "could have transported the 'merchandise', to pay the Cutufa's interest of over 10%."

And the *Mercurio* cites the lawyer Fernández asking himself: "could it be pure coincidence that the person who managed all of Santa Bárbara's monies, Mrs. María Josefa Barón, has the same lawyer as the principal accused in La Cutufa, Patricio Castro?"

But Alvaro Corbalán says he was never anything more than a Santa Bárbara employee, denying other witnesses' claims that his stepfather and the other owners were fronts for three former CNI agents. And there is no legally notarized document proving Corbalán's ownership, although there are letters from Vargas Bories pleading with him to come up with the money to cover the company's growing bills.

Rolando Fernández also asks that Corbalán explain: "how it's possible that persons who worked in his personal security group received their salaries from Santa Bárbara Transport ... that he acquired a Nitzuko telephone switchboard and a computer, both installed in his home, that were billed to the Santa Bárbara company ... that he acquired monthly gas coupons from Copec to use in his private cars and escort vehicles, gas that is billed to the company ... that he's owner of a Chevrolet pick-up truck, model Chevy 500, that is listed under the name of the A Fondo publishing house (belonging to Avanzada Nacional) used by his security personnel ... that his mother's property in Papudo was remodelled and enlarged with valuable materials ... with bills to Santa Bárbara ..."

Among the company's debts is a four-million-peso cheque to Francisco Zúñiga's — by then — ex-wife. Zúñiga himself commits suicide in December 1991. Embittered friends and relatives accuse Alvaro Corbalán of having made himself rich; some repeat accusations that he headed the "Operation Albania".

But all this means nothing to Corbalán. In October 1990, he writes *La Epoca* claiming his accuser's background "removes any seriousness from this presentation". The case will be resolved in the courts, he says, and adds: "I'M A LOVER OF JUSTICE AND I'M SPEAKING THE TRUTH".

As 1991 ends, the Santa Bárbara trial drags on, but Alvaro Corbalán is
out on bail; in fact, he's even gone to Argentina and come back. He's
ordered to testify and twice fails to appear before Judge Sergio Patiño,
who issues an order for his arrest on January 20, 1992. At 1 a.m. on
May 13, 1992, detectives track him down and arrest him during a meeting in his car with his lawyer, Patricio Hidalgo. This time the charge is
homicide, in relation to a case, the headlines announce, "about which it
is prohibited to inform". Chilean laws allow judges to ban news coverage
and they've chosen to do so in the case of Tucapel Jiménez, a union
leader who originally supported the military government, but who had
begun to reunite the union movement when he was suddenly and brutally killed in February 1982.

After the arrest, Corbalán's lawyer emphasizes that his client has
been "treated with great respect" and "everything was excellent". He
adds that Corbalán is aware that "he's been the object of a machination
to involve him in something he has nothing to do with. His participation
in the CNI was of a preventative nature and he never went out on the
streets." Where he is imprisoned at present remains a mystery. As a
retired officer he can be held in a military unit: the day after his detention, Alejandra Matus of *La Epoca* speculates he's in the Army's
Telecommunications Centre.

Five days later the judge rules Corbalán is to be tried for the killing
of a carpenter in Viña del Mar, Juan Alegría Mundaca, whose suicide
was faked to cover up the killing of Tucapel Jiménez. A former CNI
Agent, Patricio Roa Caballero has testified against Corbalán. Corbalán's
lawyer says that detectives bribed witnesses. One of Alegría Mundaca's
neighbours has recognized Corbalán as a man she saw in the area
around the time of the killing.

Corbalán answers, "I can only tell you that I think justice is blind in
these instances. Happily the lady who recognized me, according to her
in Valparaíso, didn't see me coming out of the building where Kennedy
was assassinated. Otherwise the United States would be requesting my
extradition. But we nationalists can stand slander and have patience ..."

The Army promises to pay for Corbalán's defence. The government
expresses disagreement. Genaro Arriagada, who is both vice-president of
the Christian Democratic Party and a political scientist who has specialized in studying the Armed Forces, tells Radio Cooperativa that the

Army should stay out of the case. "One would feel much better," he says cautiously, "if the Institution were to say: you, sir, who are accused of the murder of the carpenter Alegría Mundaca, and through that of the crime of Tucapel Jiménez; you sir, if you're found guilty of these events deserve the worst condemnation from the Army, because you learned nothing in the Military School, nothing of military honour."

On May 17, 1992, a special report in *La Nación* summarizes what judges, journalists and lawyers have been able to piece together in relation to the existence of a special unit within the Central Nacional de Informaciones employing about forty men, from the Army, Carabineros and Investigaciones, along with civilians. This special unit is believed to have carried out the operations which led to the deaths of Tucapel Jiménez (February 1982) and Juan Alegría (July 1983); the killing of four people in revenge for the ambush of General Pinochet's convoy (September 1986); the deaths of twelve people during Operation Albania/Elephant (June 1987); the disappearance of five Front members (September 1988); the killing of MIR leader Jecar Neghme (September 1989). Among the key pieces to the puzzle is the testimony of ex-agents and confessions of some who are already detained.

"CNI agents will never pardon the head of the [CNI's] Department of Civilian Personnel for giving the newspaper *El Siglo* the complete structure of the organization, and a list of almost 1,000 names, published in April 1990," the report adds.

Three days later, the Army announces it has changed its mind: Corbalán will have to pay for his own defence.

Chapter fifteen

CAMILO'S FIRST
DAY AT SCHOOL

SANTIAGO 1990

Changing countries is a kind of death, followed by that most dubious of experiences, resurrection. Nothing comes with you. You come to realize how your personality, your work, your past are a shape in the air, held in place by how friends and family and others see you. Your language is the form your country takes in your mind. You make it yours. It makes you who you are. When you leave it behind, leap into thin air, arrive stripped of your past in a new country, there's no space waiting for you. You have to make one. You walk down the streets thinking you see a familiar face, from school, from your hometown. And realize over and over again that that's impossible. Here you know no one. No one knows you. You barely exist.

My education in North York (Toronto) public and high schools, followed by university in British Columbia, came with me though. It was a strange sort of education, the kind that many would frown on as "useless". I studied the regular curriculum throughout primary school, but took advantage of sixties experimentation with programming and a semester system to study mostly humanities in high school: French, English, German, Spanish, Creative Writing, the Modern Novel. Instead of taking Mathematics, I studied Investment Analysis. I dropped History and Geography after grade 10, and fulfilled the Social Science requirement with a course on Canadian law. In university, I studied about the most useless program imaginable, that is, least likely to lead to gainful employment and graduated many years later than I should have with a Bachelor of Fine Arts in Creative Writing. At the time, I saw university as a space to figure out what I wanted to do with my life and a time to acquire the necessary tools, although I wasn't really sure what they might be. My parents, fortunately, were tolerant: they helped with expenses and put up with me when I dropped out for a while, just four courses away from my degree. "If it makes you happy," my mother used to say. It did, oddly enough.

My rather spotty education gave me a good base in languages, and like most footloose foreigners in a new country, in Chile in 1981 I started to teach English. A friend gave me some contacts in the Canadian media and suggested I do some reporting. When the protest movement against the Chilean military regime erupted in 1983, reporting became my full-time job. All of a sudden, I was sending reports to *The Globe and Mail, The Times* of London, the CBC, BBC and NPR (National Public Radio), Canadian television's (CTV)'s nightly news broadcasts. My education served me in good stead. It literally saved my life.

March 12, 1990. Camilo, curly-headed, five years old, is off to his first day of school, the day after the official inauguration of Chile's new democracy. Our ears are still ringing with the notes of the national anthem, while the images of the inauguration of a new era still dance before our eyes, among them, Pinochet grimacing with distaste as he hands over the tricolour presidential ribbon to his elected replacement, Patricio Aylwin, now President of Chile. Newspapers' front pages this morning carry endless photographs of dark-suited cabinet ministers, lined up like boys in a school choir. Chile's national TV channel has ceased to be the official mouthpiece of the Pinochet government, and is trying very hard to become an independent, BBC-like, publicly owned medium. We watch long shots of crowds of grinning Chileans, who lined the streets of Valparaíso and Santiago, cheering and fluttering their flags. Unfortunately, the sharp, choking fumes of tear-gas still seem to hang in the air, too. As Aylwin's convoy raced into downtown Santiago, along the Alameda Bernardo O'Higgins toward the presidential palace, the Moneda, a small party of youths provoked skirmishes. It was business as usual for police. Rather than encircling and controlling the trouble-makers, they shot toxic clouds of tear gas into the crowds. Thousands of men and women, the elderly and children coughed and cried, as the water-cannon stampeded them blindly in all directions. Patricio, excited by memories of political rallies from the past, took Camilo along, thinking he would be initiating him into a new phase of Chile's history, where it would once again be safe to celebrate democractic practice in the streets. After battling against the water-cannon jets and choking on tear-gas, Camilo was not impressed.

As a family, we hope and expect real changes, above all, genuine investigations into the human rights violations that have occurred, the kidnappings, the murders and disappearances. We would like torturers taken off the streets, or at least off the government payroll. We would like those most responsible to go to jail. The world according to our values has been upside down for seventeen years. Theft and murder have been rewarded with physical comforts and social standing. This goes against everything we were taught in school, at home, in the public, shared world of modern societies. We want compensation for survivors, special assistance to victims' children, but above all, social recognition that certain crimes remain wrong, whatever the circumstances. We share these expectations with many.

We've been preparing Camilo for school for weeks, talking about the importance of arriving on time, of paying attention, of learning everything he can in order to understand the world better and become everything he's capable of being. School starts at nine. By 6 a.m., he's waking us up, washed and fully dressed in his new school uniform, a navy blue knit jogging suit with a lavender T-shirt, a compromise after hours of discussion among parents and the director of his new school.

At the school we gather, twenty proud and slightly nervous parents, dressed in business suits, blue jeans, brushed wool skirts or T-shirts, depending on our occupations, each of us in our own way having to come to terms with what it means to have a child in grade school. The transformation from being children ourselves to having them was a major landmark in our lives. Now we've watched our cherished babies become grade-school children; their transformation has in turn changed us. We each shoulder our responsibilities for our children in different ways, knowing we must love them even as we launch them into the world. As they begin their formal education, we are learning to let go and hold on, in a delicate dance that we will seldom feel we have mastered.

Our children line up at the entrance to their new school, which is also their former day-care centre. The *tías*, "aunties" or day-care workers, welcome each with cries of surprise and admiration: how much they've changed, how grown up they look. On the steps up toward their patio and their newly painted and furnished classroom, the *tías* have placed paper stepping stones, which each child must navigate alone.

The first "stone" holds a diaper, representing their state when the day-care first received them; the next a potty, a major step toward independence for parents and child alike. The last offers a pencil, the promise of literacy, freedom and obligations. Each child takes a deep breath and hops from one to the next. At the end, their companions welcome them with laughter and applause. We parents linger behind, trying not to let the tears of pride and loss trickle down our cheeks.

The last of the fourteen children hops her way into grade one. On the patio, our children line up before us, joining hands. We, in turn, form a half-circle facing them. Our eyes on theirs, our elbows touching those of our neighbours, we all sing the national anthem, together, for the first time. In the early years after the coup, opponents to the military regime refused to sing the anthem, while its supporters sang with vehemence, adding a second verse about "courageous soldiers" saving the fatherland. During the protests in the eighties, anti-regime protesters reclaimed the anthem, belting out lines about "Chile will either be a graveyard for the free, or an asylum for the repressed" and "Sweet homeland, receive our vows" with defiant emphasis.

Today, we sing shyly together, glancing sideways at the other parents, as if we have never met before. The only political message is one of unity and pride. It's as if the music is slowly waking us from a long and terrible dream. We look at each other, and I realize that beyond the ceremony and the rituals the day before, something has really changed. Each day from now on will be subtly and completely different. We can say different things to each other, provoke different reactions, do and feel and live things differently. I realize from the snatches of conversation that float in the air around me, mostly about yesterday's inauguration, that many of these parents, whom we've "known" for as long as five years, opposed the regime, but we have never spoken of this before. It's equally clear that the parents of Rafa, Camilo's best friend, and María Jesús, Camilo's first girlfriend, supported the regime and are worried about the future. Round-faced, sharp-featured Daniel, Matías's father, cracks a joke about the kids looking like a line-up of cabinet ministers and we all laugh at once. The sharp divisions, born of moral condemnation and fear on both sides, are no longer necessary to survival.

All this floats in the air as our children receive small baskets of dried flowers, mementos of their first day at school. They walk into their new classroom, sit at their desks, receive their first notebooks. We parents stand around talking or hover at the windows, snapping pictures. Gradually it dawns on us that it's time to go, we have no role here. We drift off, secure in the knowledge that our children are going to get the best education possible, one that we all hope will bring them success, happiness and security for the rest of their lives. But life is a series of chapters that refuse to end happily ever after.

Camilo was conceived after my birthday in September 1983. The joke at the time was that Pinochet would eat the Chilean meat pastries, empanadas, that characterize September's independence celebrations, but he wouldn't be around to munch on Christmas cake. All around us people were comparing the protest movement, student and workers' strikes to the flood of popular protest that washed away an earlier Chilean dictatorship, led by General Carlos Ibáñez, in the thirties. Democracy seemed close enough to touch. As my son quickened in my belly, so did hope. We grew confident that our son would grow up in a country where normalcy was once again, well, normal. But as the protest movement waned and General Pinochet demonstrated his extraordinary ability to cleave to power, our debates about Camilo's education grew increasingly desperate.

"I always went to public school and that's good enough for me," we'd say to each other, with false bravado.

For both financial and moral reasons we believed that public school was the best choice. But when we confidently announced this at an informal gathering of parents one evening, the result was shocked silence. A day-care worker, Mary, was the first to react. Her eyebrows hit her hairline and her thin hands shot here and there as she told us that there was no way we should put Camilo in a public school.

"Public schools have changed," she said. The single earring that she always wore in her left ear, a colourful view of a hillside street in Valparaíso, shuddered with emphasis, as if an earthquake threatened devastation. "The children have to march and salute the flag, every day. They're taught to behave like soldiers. Camilo would always be in trouble. They'd expel him the first time he spoke back to a teacher, whether he was right or not."

273

Other day-care workers and parents joined in and thus began a debate which was to become constant at dinner parties, Chilean barbecues, after the men had debated their recipes for cooking sausages and beef to a turn and the women had finished gossiping while they sliced up the tomatoes, around bonfires in the wilderness, anywhere middle-class parents gathered with a few minutes to chat. Upper-class Chileans had no qualms about placing their children in élitist private schools, often affiliated with a foreign "colony", the English, the Americans, the Italians and the Germans being the most popular. Working-class Chileans had no choice: it was the local public school or nothing. (Often, it became nothing, as they could not afford the extra costs. Although classes themselves were officially free, the required uniforms, parental association and other fees could be prohibitive. Or the children attended but failed to learn, because they were too hungry to concentrate.)

In the end, our option for a good Chilean public school became obviously absurd. By the time Camilo was ready for school, public schools no longer existed.

For two decades, each newly elected Chilean government had concluded that the educational system was in crisis and sought solutions to the overcrowding, high desertion rates, the overly bureaucratized, unparticipatory school system. But for middle-class families, a reasonably good public school was usually close by, and through the Christian Democratic government's reforms (1964-1970) a decent public educational system developed throughout Chile, measurably increasing access for city and rural children alike. During those six years, enrolment in the eight years of primary education increased by 65 per cent, reaching the level recommended by UNESCO.

The Allende government's proposals for educational reform died with his government, but the military government could not escape the crisis. By 1979, 80 per cent of Chilean students attended public schools, causing serious overcrowding. The regime's policy makers criticized a lack of appropriate texts and materials, along with the inadequate training received by Chilean teachers.

The three pillars of the military government's educational reforms were decentralization, restructuring and privatization. Education should teach Christian Humanism, the military's ideologues ruled, and the Doctrine of National Security. My dictionary doesn't define National Security, although it does include National Socialism. Definitions or not, the military regime's supporters went ahead and built their ideological muscles around a backbone of National Security.

One educational researcher summarized National Security as a doctrine in which "the State provides for the conquest or defence of national objectives in spite of antagonisms and pressure; the State has the capacity to impose its objectives on all those who oppose them, and, as a result, is *capable of destroying all adversary forces and making national objectives triumph.*"

In the early eighties, the regime began a massive privatization program of the entire educational system, by handing schools over to the municipalities. This could have been a great step toward local control in a democratic country, but in Chile the city governments were political plums, awarded to loyal supporters of General Pinochet. Not only that, but the municipalities often handed over administration of schools to private societies. Periodically scandals would erupt and it would be discovered that the private company had pocketed the education subsidy, leaving schools in disrepair and paying teachers pittances.

The military regime's approach to solving Chile's chronic crises in education plunged the middle class into a crisis of its own. Horrified by the declining quality of public education and without the purchasing power of Chile's wealthier families, middle-class families like ours spent endless phone calls, meals and conversations trying to ensure our children's futures. Most were much more sensitive to another aspect of Chilean/Santiago society that we, as outsiders, tried to ignore (Patricio being from Punta Arenas, me from Canada): the importance that contacts made in university, high school and even primary school could have for a future career.

The school system became a front from which we were constantly receiving battle reports. I remember passing a school in the La Florida suburb of Santiago on my way to work the first year I was in Chile. Puzzled by the military music blaring out of loudspeakers, I eventually discovered this was part of the children's morning march routine. A friend told us of the horrors of trying to keep track of forty children in his grade four classroom. Administrators reviewed the attendance records and would sometimes falsify them, because government subsidies were based on attendance. It was more important for him to keep children coming to class than to teach them the material for which he was responsible. News from a rather expensive private school: the classes were forty strong and the children had hours of homework every night, which teachers would correct during class, cutting short teaching time and ensuring even more homework the next night.

Foreign-language training at some of the private schools could be very good. But the values that children imbibed with the language were a problem: snobbery, class differences being the most common. The German schools, inspired by a post-World War II ethic, taught charity, if not social justice, but the discipline was said to be extreme. One of the best private schools, with small class-sizes, flexible curriculum, tennis courts and a swimming pool, would have cost us our entire monthly budget. Costs for any private school, even a modest one, included registration fees, materials, monthly school fees, accident insurance, uniforms, parental association fees.

The variety of choices seemed huge, but in the end it all boiled down to price. Eventually I felt my son's future was being held to ransom: if we didn't pay, he wouldn't get the education he needed to face adulthood and survive with a minimum of happiness. And even if we did, I had the feeling we might end up creating a snobbish, urbane monster who had little understanding of the complicated works of everyday survival.

In the meantime, Camilo's (private) day-care centre seemed like an oasis. The day-care workers or *tías* (aunts) as they were more commonly called, proved excellent. Not only were they well-educated university professionals but they also loved children, a combination which I had feared difficult to find. Each level had a university-trained *tía*, a technical school graduate and one or two auxiliaries. They worked so well together, it took us some time to realize there was quite a sharp hierarchical difference between each level. During his day-care years, Camilo took workshops in theatre, modern dance, painting, folk dancing, nature and ecology. He formed strong friendships and all of the children thrived. It was intimidating to think of all this coming to an abrupt end, just when we felt it was most crucial for him to enjoy learning.

When the day-care owner, Vicky, suggested adding grade one and committed herself to going at least as far as grade four, we were all relieved. This solution was particularly attractive to my husband, Patricio, and I, because Camilo was technically too young to start grade one, and Ministry officials were no longer flexible about age requirements. After four and a half years in day-care, Camilo was eager to learn to

read and we were afraid that another year in kindergarten would turn
him into a serious disciplinary problem. He was stubborn and outspoken
(like both his parents) and we'd encouraged him to defend himself, fearing that he would end up in an authoritarian public school, where
teachers sometimes abused children physically.

But one sunny winter afternoon in July, our children's teacher, Elizabeth, pulled me aside when I went to pick up Camilo. Peering nervously
around, she murmured that the school had not filed for Ministry approval
and would therefore not get it in time for our children to legally pass
grade one.

"I'm not supposed to be telling you this," she said, looking nervously
around, "but I feel responsible to the children." After four and a half
years, we considered the owner of the day-care centre a good friend. At
a loss for words, I searched Elizabeth's pale face, the skin taut over high
cheekbones, her narrow eyes behind old-fashioned wire-rimmed glasses.
She was obviously as uncomfortable as I. And she was nervous that the
day-care's administrator, or Vicky's daughter, a frequent visitor, might
notice our conversation. Later I would learn that Elizabeth had been
fired and blacklisted for organizing teachers against the military regime's
policies in state schools. She and her family had barely survived on
earnings from odd jobs and handicrafts. This was her first job as a teacher
in many years.

That evening I mentioned our conversation to Patricio. "Oh, Vicky'll
have something up her sleeve, I'm sure," was his response. We were all
accustomed to having to go around regulations. That was the way most
things got done. But we expected official word, with a proposed solution,
and when none was forthcoming, Patricio approached Vicky.

"She's on her way to Mexico," he told me that night.

"Mexico!"

"Yeah. Something about a brother who may be coming home."

"What about the school?"

"She said not to worry, she has a solution."

We began to worry.

Two-thirds of the way through the school year, we found ourselves desperately searching for a school that would accept a dozen grade one students.
We organized into teams with other parents and went off to interview
directors at public and private schools. Someone would get a tip from a

friend and away we would go. Most wouldn't even consider taking the whole group. Several proved too expensive or too rigid. Finally we found a modestly priced private school, with small class-sizes and an independent learning system. It had no library and only a rudimentary gymnasium, but it would even hire Elizabeth. We decided to give it a try.

A month later, the parents of children remaining in the day-care centre had to organize to get the buildings cleaned up, toilets fixed, proper supplies bought for the children. The *tías* went on strike for decent working conditions and wages commensurate with the fees charged parents, their education and their dedication to the children. By the end of the year, the *tías* who for us had symbolized the quality of our day-care centre had been fired or forced to resign. Meanwhile, our children were deliriously happy with grade one in their new school.

To a large degree, it was the military government's sweeping changes to the educational system and other social services that finally mobilized a disenchanted middle class. The regime's economic policies seriously reduced middle-class incomes, often by freezing them at below inflation rates. A modest income when you have access to a good, free public education system, health care and social services isn't so bad. But middle-class Chileans watched their incomes effectively drop, even as the regime's reforms to health, education and other social services caused a notorious decline in both quality and accessibility.

One of the biggest surprises of the anti-government protest movement when it started on May 11, 1983 was the participation of middle-class Chileans tooting their horns along Providencia Avenue, the glittery shopping area that had become a symbol of the military government's economic policies. In the apartment towers of Carlos Antúnez, in the heart of Providencia, people hidden in their kitchens started nervously banging their pots, only to discover that next door the neighbours were doing the same thing. Soon hundreds stood on their balconies, banging and whooping and cheering in a movement which took Santiago and, ultimately the whole country, by surprise.

In 1986, the Chilean doctors' organization, horrified by the decline of the health care system, raised a united, critical voice and, with other groups, founded the National Assembly of Civil Society, la Asamblea Nacional de la Civilidad. They called a two-day national strike in July of the same year. The Assembly included members of almost all Chile's professional associations, high-school and university students, women's groups, native people, the National Workers Command. These representatives' political persuasions ranged from independent, through conservative (but anti-regime), Christian Democrat, socialist, to communist, and they were united for the first time ever.

When the regime sent the entire strike leadership to jail, people joked about schools for dissidents behind bars, but the sight of respected members of society being dragged off to jail further deepened the chasm between the regime and many former supporters.

The arrests that July weren't the most shocking event. On the first day of the strike, a taxi driver found two teenagers staggering along a deserted country road. Their clothes were charred, their skin turned to ashes, and they were barely conscious. The burning alive by a military patrol of Carmen Gloria Quintana and Rodrigo Rojas, a Chilean-American back in Chile trying to discover his roots, became an international symbol of how arbitrary and extreme cruelty could become when protected by a dysfunctional justice system and the State. Both the massive funeral of Rojas, who died, and Quintana's struggle for life and then rehabilitation, became powerful symbols for Chileans' overwhelming determination to oppose and defeat the regime.

The thought that the lives of these children we had worked for and worried and wondered over during years of constant effort and sacrifice could end in one horrific moment, shot, beaten or burned alive, was too appalling. The gap between ordinary Chileans and a government that not only defended the military patrol responsible for the burning but later promoted the commanding officer, Lieutenant Pedro Fernández Dittus to Captain, widened visibly, and not even the pall of fear which the burnings cast over the protest movement could paralyse it.

The Rettig Commission report concluded that, "The human rights violations of recent years and the high degree of social tolerance [of these], seem to demonstrate that in Chile during the period in which these violations were committed, there was not a sufficiently firm national consciousness of the imperious duty to respect human rights. We believe that the education of our society did not successfully incorporate these principles into our culture."

B.F. Skinner said that an education is what survives after the learning's gone. After history's endless spider web of dates and deeds has disappeared, after great writers' names have dissolved, unloved, on the tips of children's tongues, after the palaces of formulae have collapsed into crumpled, hard-to-hold-onto bills, what remains are the spine-cracking hours spent seated on an unpadded chair, bruised knees crushed under a desk, listening to voices droning, and the seemingly endless ritual of silence. No questions asked. No blows. Teach us to sit still. Teach us not to care.

In December 1994, a UNICEF study covered by the Chilean press reported that 63 per cent of Chilean children are beaten by their parents, with 34 per cent suffering serious injuries. One out of four children suffers from malnutrition, when measured by size. Two hundred thousand children have been abandoned by their families. One out of four Chilean families is poor. One out of four urban dwellers don't have the benefit of proper sewage facilities. There are 40,000 cases per year of teenage pregnancies. One woman out of every four is beaten by her husband. One out of three is subjected to psychological violence. Experts estimate there are 175,000 backstreet abortions in Chile every year. The women who must resort to them often get tried and sentenced for murder. Their male partners do not.

In the school system, 30 per cent of children drop out before they've completed the first eight years of education. Only one out of ten children from poor families masters school materials satisfactorily. Teachers complain that they spend as much as a quarter of their class time on discipline. Blows, threats and coercion in the school are merely a continuation of what goes on at home.

A National Commission to Modernize Education, presented a report to President Frei in December 1994. Few argued with its scathing evaluation. At the primary level, national testing has revealed that three out of four students from the poorest half of the population don't understand what they read and possess less than half the skills required of their grade level. Thirty per cent drop out; 12.3 per cent repeat; it takes students an average of 5.35 years to complete four years of schooling.

Chilean students study less than 800 hours a year, compared to 1,177 in Taiwan, 1,073 in France, 1,053 in Switzerland and 1,003 in the US. Teachers dictate material while students memorize an encyclopedic quantity of information, much of which will be obsolete by the time they graduate.

Chile's new democracy is five years old today; if it were a child, it would be starting kindergarten. Perhaps this is where the changes will finally begin. But the signs remain dangerously ambivalent. Toward the end of 1994, Captain Pedro Fernandez Dittus was finally condemned to 600 days in prison, less than two years, for the two lives he ignited like incendiary bombs in July 1986. General Manuel Contreras and his right-hand man, still in active service, Brigadier General Pedro Espinoza, have been sentenced to seven years and six years in jail, respectively, for their role in the killing of Orlando Letelier and Ronni Moffit in Washington in 1976. In January 1995, Contreras and Espinoza were forced to plead their appeals on national television, to record ratings, a first in Chilean history. Under intense pressure from the military, the government announced it would build a special military jail. A military court recently applied the amnesty to seventy-eight cases of human rights violations that occurred during the military government.

The report by the Rettig Commission, which investigated the human rights violations, emphasizes the key role that education must play if Chile is to avoid repeating the multiple tragedies of military rule. But Patricio Donoso, a philosophy teacher, asks how we can teach human rights as basic values, when the debate over justice for rights victims remains unresolved. "The reconciliation of this nation remains pending," he writes, in a weekly newspaper column. "Our experience in schools and with teachers has shown how painful the wounds opened during [the military] period remain and how weak is the pedagogical proposal related to forming the values of those who are educated.

"To speak of the search for justice within the limits of what is possible is, in fact, to admit that justice, and thus, the values on which society is founded, cannot be achieved ... To make this explicit is to make explicit that there is a correlation of forces involved and to accept that this determines the values which one should assume. In this case, the values we are trying to teach as educators remain suspended in the air, because we cease to talk about values, rather, we're talking about powers," writes Donoso..

And he asks: "Perhaps we should change the objective of education and, instead of forming persons, aspire to form good negotiators and beings who know how to find good niches in the power structure? Perhaps we should educate within the limits of what is possible and relativize the values of new generations, so that if the market and the economy demand the depredation of the environment, the alienation of persons, the routinization of work, and so on, we orient the educational system in this direction? What educational heritage do we want to bequeath to future generations? How can the educational system be credible in its formation of values, if society sends out ambivalent messages on this subject?"

Years after General Pinochet handed the presidential ribbon to President Aylwin, we no longer worry about the cruelty that could destroy in an instant the children who have cost us years of sleepless nights, trips untravelled, sacrifice. Our children's futures continue to be held hostage, their education a Pandora's box we're forced to open, and deal with.

In September 1993, I visited a school in a middle- and lower middle-class neighbourhood on the south-east side of Santiago, in the municipality of Macul. With assistance from UNICEF, the school was trying to change the way teachers behaved in the classroom, after twenty stagnant years. I sat in as a group of women teachers evaluated a workshop where they had explored their own feelings of self-confidence and knowledge. Sylvia, a vivacious bespectacled blonde woman led the conversation, prodding and encouraging and warmly welcoming every small discovery. When the session was over I listened to a litany of what was wrong with the school system. Mostly, it boiled down to resources: lack of laboratories, classrooms, space. I asked them about human rights and received twelve blank looks and a few stumbling replies, no, not here ... They shifted nervously on their chairs. What had human rights to do with *them*, their hastily controlled faces seemed to say.

The classroom I visited was large and comfortable, with windows on both side walls, a blackboard covering the front wall behind the teacher's desk. The children's colourful posters and paintings livened up the walls. Forty or so boys and girls sat in their neatly pressed grey and blue uniforms. Their desks had been clustered into groups of six. Sylvia, the same blonde woman who had led the teachers' workshop, was giving an English class, working with a television advertisement for a popular soft drink. The process included evaluating the message and how it is put across, followed by a creative re-enactment, all this in English with a group of rowdy nine-year-olds, many of whom had learning disabilities. It was hard going, but as the children gathered in their groups, chattering and jotting down notes, Sylvia moved briskly around the room, asking questions, encouraging, complementing and gently chiding. Throughout, the children's regular teacher sat at her desk, a large woman in sombre clothes, her dark hair disorderly and her face grim.

Once or twice she barked out orders or remonstrances at the children. Her whole being exuded hostility. After the class was over, three or four boys vied for the pleasure of carrying Sylvia's books back to the teacher's room.

Sylvia's class was the result of a special program to bring more creative methods into the classroom, to encourage children to participate, to become protagonists of the educational process rather than the passive recipients of a huge quantity of information. She didn't seem very different from the public-school teachers in Toronto when I was growing up, but it was clear from my conversations with teachers, supervisors and others that she was very different from the average public-school teacher in Chile. A week later, in the rural city of Castro, I spoke with a teacher discouraged by the widespread physical abuse of children in the municipalized school system.

"They get beaten at home and beaten at school," she told me, "and if you talk to the parents about what goes on at school, most will simply say 'go ahead and hit them.'"

Aware of this reality, we had told Camilo, "No one, NO ONE, no teacher or director or anyone else can hit you, ever." We had long forgotten this conversation, but even at our small, relatively advanced private school there have been some conflicts. When Camilo was in grade three, a new science teacher quickly won herself a reputation for being grumpy and hard to work with. One day she threatened to hit anyone who stepped out of line. Camilo, another mother told me, stood up and said that if she did that, she'd have his parents to answer to. Another child requested a meeting with the director, who spoke to the teacher, and from then on relations quickly improved. In most schools, the children would have been expelled.

In the years following the return to democracy, the Ministry of Education implemented MECE, a special improvement program aimed at the country's poorest schools. Another pilot project, which includes Chilean-made software, is bringing modern technology, computer networks and electronic mail systems to some of the poorest schools, including those around Temuco, with a high percentage of native students. A special library program has put thirty basic books on the shelves of every classroom. Teachers and students join together to compete for special projects funding, for activities that included school newspapers, radio programs and the like.

In 1994, the Ministry of Education planned a special program integrating the theme of human rights into different subject areas rather than having one course on the subject. *El Mercurio* conveniently skipped over twenty years of Chilean history, attributing this policy to Chile not wanting to fall behind the rest of the "modern" world.

Critics, particularly those associated with the former regime, oppose these changes. They are afraid that ideology will be slipped into children's minds, disguised under the lamb's skin of human rights. They warn that this has been a "sensitive issue" in Chile over the past quarter century and there's a "risk of valuing human rights from a short term perspective". Teaching human rights may "politicize" the school system.

During the 1994 round of this debate, Alfonso Bravo, then the co-ordinator of the Education Ministry's program, replied "If we want students to learn and live, as well as hear, about human rights, these must penetrate the whole school and not just one course." He added that the hardest part about implementing this program is how to train and prepare those who must teach it. Underlying the debate is the question, how can you teach human – and civil – rights, in a school system where they are so frequently trampled?

Claudia Dueñas's body has the soft, flowing curves of a woman who has just given birth and whose breasts are overflowing with nourishment for this new life. She hurries through the door of PIEE, the educational research institute where she works, and greets me warmly. She went to university in the years following the Cultural Association of the University, ACU. Older brothers participated; she knows the names of many who have been close friends to me; some of the events I witnessed reached her as legends.

Together with Abraham Magendzo, the director of PIEE, and two other people, Claudia has worked to move human rights from theory's dusty shelves to hallways stained by children's muddy feet. Perhaps more than anywhere else, the scars left by seventeen and a half years of military rule still distort relationships in the classroom.

"This is an issue that is deeply affected by people's own personal histories," she says. Her group, which is one of the most experienced in Chile, uses workshops with teachers and other educators to introduce human rights education.

"We find that our workshops bring together teachers who were fired for opposing the military regime, teachers who bit their tongues and said nothing, and people who worked with the regime, spying on their colleagues," Dueñas says. "First the group goes through a process of clearing the air. Then, they must build a new language for speaking of what has happened. Some teachers cry, others express terrible feelings of guilt, still others see themselves as heroes."

The sixty-hour workshops are led by professionals experienced in human rights, teaching and interpersonal relations. Thanks to careful preparation of the group dynamic, using games, dance, movement and physical exercise, along with conversation, most of the conflicts that arise can be resolved in an atmosphere of mutual tolerance and respect.

Each workshop, whether it bring together teachers, students or, increasingly, supervisors from the Ministry of Education, begins with the shuffling of a rather special pack of cards. Each person turns up a card and with it a question: What do human rights mean to you? Name three rights you consider important and tell us why you think they're important. What do you feel every day, when you enter your school?

"What good is teaching the Declaration of the Rights of Children, then sending students home to a beating?" Dueñas says. "Our approach views human rights as a prism that allows people to question their reality and search for solutions within an ethical framework." They also believe that genuine human rights education demands an active commitment. It is not just another subject that can be memorized and regurgitated on national exams.

"People's perception has evolved beyond the experience of the military years, to include women's and environmental rights," says Duenas, who points proudly to the case of a school in Concepcíon, six hours' drive south of Santiago. There, after studying human rights in class, students campaigned successfully for the city to build a wall, separating their playground from a neighbouring dump that had been spilling over into their space.

The educational research institute's (PIEE) human rights researchers, led by Abraham Magendzo, started thinking about the relationship between human rights and education during the late eighties. When the elected government replaced the military, their team expanded and joined up with human rights groups affiliated with the Catholic Church, Chile's largest. They have received crucial support from the National Corporation for Reparation and Reconciliation, set up in 1991.

The National Corporation for Reparation and Reconciliation replaced the Rettig Commission, carrying on the task of investigating accusations of human rights violations, but also searching for ways of implementing the Commission's recommendations regarding education. Its general secretary, Andres Domínguez, a lawyer, has dedicated most of his adult life to human rights. For many years, I used to visit him at the Chilean Human Rights Commission. Today, he supervises day-to-day work at the Corporation, writes books and dissertations, and teaches courses at the Catholic University and at the civilian police detectives' academy.

"Human rights education is based on several fundamental principles," Domínguez says. "The full development of the child's personality, learning as an apprenticeship in the practice of human rights, tolerance, non-violence, non-discrimination, and the child's need to belong and participate in society as an autonomous being."

Sometimes it is the parents themselves, trying to correct their own frustrations and achieve their own dreams through their children, who limit their children, he observes. The case of a youth, who didn't get a high enough score on national university entrance examinations to get into dentistry, haunts me. His score was high enough for agriculture, which was what he wanted to study, but his father had threatened to throw him out of the house and disown him, if he didn't get into dentistry. The young man committed suicide.

By 1995, with funding from the Ford Foundation, other foreign sources and the Chilean government itself, more than six thousand teachers had participated in human rights education workshops. A national network of experienced teachers existed and PIEE had expanded its workshops to include supervisors who are very highly regarded in the regions that they serve in the Education Ministry's special upgrading programs.

There are also programs for university professors and students. Attendance at a multi-disciplinary course on human rights, offered by the Catholic University in Santiago and taught by Andrés Domínguez and a colleague, has doubled from thirty to sixty. Students, who come from all disciplines, including engineering, teaching, agriculture and the arts, consistently rate it the best course on campus.

But today, as ever, perhaps Chileans are wiser than those who try to lead them. Andrés Domínguez cites a study by a citizen's group, Participa, which found that Chileans have three main fears: that the country's economic growth will stagnate, that this economic development won't include forms of personal development, that Chilean culture will remain mediocre and neglected. In the same study, almost one out of three thought that the lack of justice in human rights trials was the most serious weakness of Chile's new democracy.

On the home front, we've been plunged back into battle and are floundering around in a morass of doubt and guilt over Camilo's education. No library at the school, no public libraries with enticing rows of videos, picture books, encyclopediae with answers to every question you could imagine. No teachers steeped in the principles of humane, child-centred education, but rather the harsh reality of Chile's state-subsidized, municipalized schools. Camilo's latest teacher believes in values, the old-fashioned kind: obedience, short hair, godliness's next door neighbour. That's not enough any more, if it ever was.

The hunt is on, all over again. And all I come up with is another private school.

Thinking back over Camilo's five years in grade school, the muffled and declared conflicts between parents and teachers over what kind of an education our children are actually getting, I remain nostalgic for a public-school system that, for all its faults, taught me the languages and gave me the tools to build a reasonably happy, reasonably successful life in a country distant and different from my homeland. It included values, implicitly and explicitly taught: honesty, participation, tolerance, mutual respect. My experience in Chile has deepened my understanding of, and my commitment to, those values.

Resurrection is a mystery, a difficult and painful experience at best. "You can't take it with you," the old saying goes. But my education managed to come with me, brought me new life. I would like to think Camilo's will travel as well with him. But I'm not so sure.

Chapter sixteen

THE LITTLE RIFTS

ATACAMA DESERT/CHILOÉ 1993

de•vel•op•ment: n. The act of developing, the state of being developed,
a significant event, occurrence, or change. In music, the elaboration of a theme with rhythmic
and harmonic variations or the part of a movement in sonata form in which the theme is
elaborated and explored.
AMERICAN HERITAGE DICTIONARY

It is the little rift within the lute,
That by and by will make the music mute,
And ever widening slowly silence all.
ALFRED, LORD TENNYSON

In northern Chile, the world's driest desert holds some of its richest mineral deposits. Arid winds blow across twisted railway tracks and through the empty cabins which once housed thousands of nitrate miners and their families. Only at sunset do the faded colours deepen into vibrant shades of orange and pink.

The town of El Salvador sits in the middle of this desert, a thousand kilometres north of Santiago, halfway between the Pacific Ocean and the Andes mountains. Wide streets lined by boxy houses surround a central square, with basic stores, church, offices. El Salvador is strictly a company town and the company it belongs to is Codelco, the state-owned copper corporation. If it weren't for this, El Salvador might be a ghost town too.

For most of this century, copper was at the heart of debates about the nature of development and the role of foreign corporations in Chile's small national economy, yet the issue is barely raised in the nineties. Historically, Chile has depended heavily on mineral exports, mined by foreign corporations. A century ago, the nitrate mines fed small company towns whose workers were virtually slaves. When the market collapsed after World War I, those towns emptied, leaving the northern desert dotted with ghost towns, small, desolate reminders of the dangers of dependency.

Chile scrambled from sinking nitrates onto a copper lifeboat. A San Diego State University professor Brian Loveman calculates that American ownership of Chilean copper mines during World War II saved the US between US$100 million and 500 million, since it ensured prices for Chilean copper were kept down by the ceilings that the US imposed. Afterward, copper largely financed Chilean development, keeping taxes comfortably low, but it also brought constant political intervention from the United States.

Politicians of all stripes eyed the huge profits of American companies with growing disgust and, in the late sixties, the Christian Democratic government bought into major copper holdings. Two years later, a unanimous vote in Congress nationalized them. The American companies reacted violently and some contributed generously to campaigns that culminated in the 1973 military coup.

Today, people and parties who criticized foreign investment in the sixties travel the world singing its praises. In recent years, approved foreign investment has amounted to US$1 billion or more annually. The US continues to be the largest foreign investor, but in the nineties, Canadian interests have grown enormously, as have Japan's. More than half this investment has been in mines with names like "Blankets of Gold", "The Indian", "The Hidden One", which promise to repay hundreds of millions of dollars of investment in as little as five years. A quarter of this foreign investment went to services; smaller amounts to industry and construction.

The influx of foreign investment after 1990 has been widely interpreted as support for democracy. In 1990, Jay Taylor, general manager of Placer Dome Latin America, said that Placer Dome had decided to increase its investment in Chile because it saw military rule ending, bringing in an era of stable, democratic government. However, at the start of the new, elected government, Chilean entrepreneurs were more hostile, predicting economic collapse without Pinochet. Placer Dome and Cominco were the first to develop joint ventures with government mining companies. While local businessmen have complained about corporate taxes of 15 per cent, foreigners grin as they compare them to corporate taxes in developed countries, which average over 30 per cent.

Many foreign investors have opted to build plants according to the environmental requirements of their home countries, a wise move since Congress only approved an "Environmental Framework Law" in 1994, with strict enforcement hovering in a still rather nebulous future. Cities and state-run smelters remain among the worst polluters. In May 1993, some observers associated Chile's refusal to support a conservation area for whales to Chile's growing ties with Japan, although it changed its position under the Frei Administration in 1994. In three years, the number of Japanese companies operating in Chile doubled to more than fifty-five. Over two years, Japanese companies, large and small, invested US$700 million, more than they had in two previous decades, in everything from mines to energy, fish and forests. The Japanese increasingly see Chile as a stepping stone into Latin America and, wrote *The New York Times,* into the North American free trade area, a possibility that worries American authorities.

Codelco, the owner of the El Salvador mine and smelting complex, is probably the most concrete and lasting change achieved by the Popular Unity government. In July 1971, the Chilean Congress voted unanimously to nationalize copper companies owned by Kennecott and Anaconda. Five years later, the military regime approved a legal structure for Codelco.

Codelco is the largest copper corporation in the world. It represents about 12 per cent of the world market for copper and possesses 23 per cent of known copper reserves. It generates about one-quarter of Chile's exports, one-tenth to one-quarter of state revenue and more than a quarter of public investment. It contributes from four to ten per cent of the GNP annually, the equivalent of the top twenty US companies combined. Since nationalization in 1971, Codelco has supplied the state with more than US$21 billion, used to keep taxes down and to help finance health, housing and social programs. Thanks to a law decreed by the military regime, 10 per cent of Codelco's gross sales, around U$200 million dollars, goes directly to the Armed Forces. Normally, they use it to purchase weapons abroad.

During the 1993 celebrations of the "Day of Dignity", which annually marks the 1971 Congressional vote that decreed the nationalization of Chile's copper mines, Alejandro Hales, who was then the Minister of Mining, said, "There's no way Codelco is going to be privatized." Hales, who was also Minister of Mining during the first phase of nationalization in the sixties, dismissed privatization, "because I don't like it! This is a very good business and I like very good businesses. Codelco's income last year was almost $1 billion. Why should I privatize?" In 1995, the Minister of Mining in the Frei government, Benjamin Teplizky, also dismissed the idea of privatization completely, although Codelco is undertaking new joint ventures with private-sector firms.

And yet, privatization remains a hot issue for debate within the governing coalition of Socialists, Christian Democrats and small left and centrist political parties which took over from the military in March 1990.

Rising costs, the result of aging mines, dropping ore grades, overstaffing, inefficient administration and obsolete technologies, have led former opponents of privatization to consider it the key to saving the world's largest copper company from an irreversible decline. Fluctuating international copper prices and streamlining by other major producers, particularly in North America, threaten to leave the giant behind. While US copper production per man-year was double Codelco's in the eighties, it's now nearly triple. Codelco has not opened a new mine and won't until 1998. Attempts to do so in 1993 were foiled by the government's reluctance to spend US$400 billion on mining, rather than other items in the nation's budget.

"Codelco's owner is poor and has to choose carefully where it spends its money," says Jorge Berghammer, executive director of CESCO, a mining research institute. "Privatization might resolve Codelco's problems, but it wouldn't solve Chile's."

Jorge Berghammer says that the reorganization of Codelco is "in the spirit of nationalization. Reducing average cost levels to sixty cents a pound should be a national goal." Current costs hover around eighty cents per pound. "Privatization does not guarantee greater efficiency," he adds and proposes advancing rapidly "toward the modernization of property structures" instead.

Some proposals for solving Codelco's current problems resemble the "Chileanization" program carried out by the Frei government in the late sixties, in which the state bought 51 per cent of the North American copper companies' holdings. But supporters of mixed ventures say current proposals are different, because of changes in industry structure over the past thirty years. In the sixties, Chile was negotiating investment ventures with no property, no experience and limited know-how; today, it negotiates as the owner of a powerful corporation.

In fact, nationalization programs in Chile, and other developing countries, dealt a stunning blow to the powerful handful of corporations that once ruled the industry worldwide. A market crisis in the mid-eighties knocked several right out of the business and led to radical restructuring of survivors' operations. Ownership also changed when oil companies started buying into the industry.

Codelco's 20,000 workers, 17,000 of whom are represented by the powerful Copper Workers' Federation, strongly oppose privatization, but do accept the idea of Codelco developing new mines in association with private companies.

"We can't just copy what's happening abroad," said Federation president, Raimundo Espinoza, in 1994. "We have to find our own way of doing things. The thought of Codelco in private, foreign hands fills me with panic."

Ministers, Codelco executives, socialists and supporters of the former military government alike, all oppose outright privatization. But there's consensus that a structure which provides for more agile market and investment decisions and allows the sharing of risk would benefit the company and the country. Currently, the State gets all the profits, but must also absorb all the risks involved in new projects. Banks approve loans to Codelco because they're guaranteed by the State, not because of the quality of proposals.

A new Copper Law passed by the Chilean Congress in 1992 has opened the way to some significant changes, among them joint private-public sector ventures to exploit some of Codelco's reserves. More than fifty mining companies vied for the chance to buy 51 per cent of the El Abra mine, the first Codelco property to become available. A US/Canadian consortium won the bid in October 1993, but the Canadians later backed out, leaving Cyprus Amax and Codelco. Construction has gone ahead in 1995 and the mine is expected to enter production in 1996-1997.

The early nineties saw the copper, pulp, fishmeal and fruit industries worldwide engaged in a desperate race to outrun the recessions hitting major markets, including those most important to Chile: the US, Germany and Japan. While prices plummeted, Chilean producers gulped down lungfuls of their comparative advantages, ducked their heads and plunged on. They exported more by weight, so that even at lower prices total sales increased.

Eduardo Moyano, then head of the government's International Economic Affairs Department, said in 1994 that a key element in saving Chile from being sideswiped when other economies started to skid was evolving markets. "In 1990, our exports grew largely thanks to sales to the US and Europe," he says. "In 1991, it was Japan and Latin America. In 1992, it was Asian countries besides Japan, and the Latin American countries were also very important."

In 1992, Chilean products reached 155 countries, 26 more than 1990. Exporters were peddling their wares in more languages and across some surprising borders as well: shoes and Easter eggs to Russia; gears to Argentina; tires to Bolivia; cosmetics, car parts, engineering services and books to Central America. Trade has been the main force driving Chile's booming economy. Today, Chile does just over half its trade with its top five partners. In 1992, trade with the top ten increased from 8 per cent to 38 per cent, dropping in relation to Germany only, but Chile began to import more than it exported, creating deficits where surpluses had been the rule.

In the first nine months of 1992, overall exports increased 12.3 per cent, while imports rose almost double (25.6 per cent). Just over half those imports were consumer products and another 40 per cent were capital goods: vehicles, earth movement equipment, computers, heat exchangers, textile machinery, bottling machines, pumps, ovens, refrigerators and the like.

The Ministry of External Affairs predicted that the importance of value-added products would continue to grow and prepared a list of "Star Export products", about 10 per cent of total exports, whose sales increased at average rates of 30 to 40 per cent. Salmon topped their list, with sales up by half between 1991 and 1992, followed by wines, textiles and clothing, printed materials, frozen foods, candies, equipment, sea bass and cod.

Improved trade with other Latin American countries has also helped maintain the buoyancy of the Chilean economy. The Aylwin government initiated a series of trade and investment agreements destined to bring tariffs to zero in the case of Mexico (1996), Colombia (under negotiation, around 1998), Venezuela (1999) and Brazil (under negotiation).

Brazil and Mexico together produce more than half of Latin America's total Regional Product, but Brazil, which produces 38 per cent, imports only 15 per cent of the region's imports; while Mexico, with one-fifth of the regional product, absorbs one-third of imports. Trade with Argentina and Mexico doubled during the first two years of implementation of agreements with those countries and Jorge Marshall, Aylwin's Minister of Economy, predicted trade between Chile and Venezuela would double by 1996, thanks to a 1993 agreement.

"Latin America is opening itself up," says Eduardo Moyano. "It's recovering from the debt crisis and more countries are adopting a free trade policy. Chilean companies have more experience with an open economy. They know how to improve quality, cut costs. Chile imports cocoa, but nevertheless it's exporting chocolate. This is going to go on until other countries reach our level [of competitiveness]."

In the case of the Chile-Argentina agreement for Economic Complementation, overall trade increased while Chile's deficit dropped from close to US$400 million to under US$200 million between 1990 and 1992. However, increased trade with Brazil more than doubled Chile's deficit with that country in 1992.

Chilean exporters and industrial lobby groups viewed with interest Chile's participation in a free trade agreement with the US. The United States remains a major trading partner, although its relative importance declined slightly during the 1993 recession.

Trade agreements alone don't eliminate non-tariff barriers, particularly those produced by sanitation regulations, quotas and, increasingly, environmental concerns. This is particularly clear in the case of Europe, the destination for about one-third of Chilean exports. The overall value of Chile's exports to Europe has grown, but proportionately, the amount of trade with Europe has dropped for the past fifteen years.

New products, new technologies, new marketing techniques and increasingly new markets may set the pace for trade in the future, but traditional patterns still define the track. As other Latin American economies stabilize and complete the processes of technological innovation and opening to world trade, Chilean entrepreneurs have found themselves increasingly hard-pressed by their neighbours. Investment by Chilean firms abroad, especially in Argentina, and hypersensitivity to trends may help the Chileans maintain their current position. In 1994, the Frei government announced that they would make educational reforms a high priority, doubling spending on education from three to six per cent of the GDP, as part of the government's strategy to increase Chile's competitive edge on world markets.

"Chile must look at the world economy with a new kind of vision," said Alvin Tofler, an American economist, during a brief visit in April 1993. "It must seek new, increasingly specialized market niches, and it must add more value to its products.

"In the old concept of the economy, production was based on the repetition of a successful product. That formula's destined to die. The future is in innovation and modern business executives must accept innovators."

One reason that there was so little criticism of foreign investment and general economic policy during the nineties was that the economy was booming and was being heralded as a successful neo-liberal model. Driving southward from Santiago, the harsh rectangles of skyscrapers give way to orchards. Soon you're passing sparkling new packing plants, their driveways lined with rosebushes. In the foreground, the familiar logos of Dole, Unifrutti and other food companies flash by. Exponential growth in exports has made fruit a symbol of Chile's economic success.

As most countries struggled with recession, the Chilean economy grew an extraordinary 10 per cent 1992, an average of 6.5 per cent between 1984 and 1994, unemployment was hovering down around pre-coup levels of 4 to 6 percent, and real wages had risen steadily for the past three years. Inflation was under control and dropping, and foreign trade contributed half the country's Gross Domestic Product.

When the military seized power in 1973, it developed an economic policy which the press celebrated as Chile's "miracle economy" in 1975. Then recession hit. Economic advisers, called the "Chicago Boys" for their wholesale support of Milton Friedman's theories, experimented with massive changes to the economy in what has been called the world's largest social laboratory, a whole country.

In the early eighties, authorities reduced customs barriers, imports rose astronomically, and proponents celebrated a new "miracle". Then companies started to fold. Wages plunged and one out of three workers went jobless. The GNP dropped 14 per cent in 1982, and it took the next six years to return to pre-1982 levels. Nevertheless, the military continued a ruthless modernization program: laying off tens of thousands of workers, reducing bargaining rights and slicing social service and education budgets to the bone. As the private sector developed luxury private clinics, public hospitals couldn't afford to wash walls, keep toilets running, provide patients with sheets.

The military regime also privatized generally profitable public-sector corporations at bargain basement prices, using methods that were harshly criticized even by some of those who had supported the regime. Between 1985 and 1988, the government privatized thirty public companies, worth close to US$2.8 billion, among them a steel corporation (CAP) and a nitrate mining concern (Soquimich) that had previously been classified as strategically important. The State received an estimated US$1.25 billion in payment over the same period. Using three different kinds of calculation, one study concluded that the State lost US$600 million in privatizations in two years.

Buyers purchased half the steel corporation, CAP, which had earned profits of US$45 million in 1986–87 and was worth an estimated US$700 million, for US$18.5 million. Soquimich was privatized in 1984, with stocks sold at 20 pesos apiece; in 1988, they were worth 350 pesos each. General Pinochet's son-in-law, Julio Ponce Lerou, was president of Soquimich while it remained a state corporation, and carried on when it was privatized.

The Chicago Boys also developed a shrewd working agreement with the country's military rulers. With General Pinochet's explicit support, and over the strenuous objections of another Junta member, Air Force General Gustavo Leigh, they experimented with their model, but always with cautious parentheses around the military's own institutions. Aside from minor changes in the functioning of military arms factories, they made few efforts to apply their free-market principles to military institutions. Thus, while they slashed state expenditures on public health and created private health-care programs, the Armed Forces continued to run their own well-equipped private hospitals and provide their own medical services. While they trimmed ministry budgets, they didn't question the increase in defence spending. Nor did they protest when the military upped their slice of Codelco's income from a 10 per cent cut of net profits, to a 10 per cent cut of total sales. The defence budget leapt from US$777 million in 1973, to US$1 billion in 1974 and during the acute recession of 1982–83 was well over US$2 billion. In 1984, the budget for the CNI, the secret police service that replaced the notorious DINA after the Letelier killing, had reached US$14.3 million.

"In this aspect there was a non-aggression pact between the Chicago Boys and the military high commands to not interfere with each other. In this way, the disciples of Harberger and Friedman could experiment with changes in the Chilean economy without risking any political counterweight, and the military proceeded to carry out their repressive tasks without worrying about costs," wrote Manuel Délano and Hugo Traslaviña in their book, *La Herencia de los Chicago Boys* (*The Inheritance of the Chicago Boys*).

Yet the legacy from that period and the changes that followed are a far cry from the purely orthodox, free-market economy that enthusiasts sometimes describe. Pedro Saenz, an economist at the UN's Economic Commission for Latin American and the Caribbean (ECLAC), points to the continued importance of state ownership of Chile's largest copper mines. The military government had planned to privatize Codelco, but the effort failed due to opposition within its ranks, particularly from the Army.

"Thanks to taxes and profits, during the eighties, copper contributed between five and ten per cent of the Gross National Product, which has helped the government increase social expenditures and helped the model to work," says Saenz. "The influence of the private sector is larger than in the fifties and sixties; but this experience has led to a new and important role for the public sector," he adds. "This new equilibrium makes the Chilean model very special in Latin America."

In most countries, where exports are private and debt is public, the growth in exports would create a serious problem of balance of payments, but in Chile, when exports rose, they filled both private and *public* pockets.

Between 1990, when the first elected government replaced the military, and 1994, when it handed power over to its successor, the number of poor people who lived in overcrowded, flimsy, wooden shacks and ate mostly bread and tea, had dropped from 5 million to 4 million, as measured by both the government and the non-governmental organization, Programa de Economía del Trabajo (PET). But still Chile is a long way from its earlier levels of well-being. In 1970, only seventeen out of every one hundred Chilean households were poor; that grew to thirty-eight in 1987, and dropped to thirty-five in 1990.

"There's a problem of equity inside our society," says Jaime Ruiz Tagle, in charge of the think tank, PET. "This model doesn't consider the problem of equality, and a very strong intervention of the state is necessary to make sure that you are going to have a safer, saner society."

The old cliché about the rich getting richer and the poor getting poorer is truer than ever, although both the Aylwin and the Frei governments, which followed the military regime, have concentrated their efforts on reducing poverty, with some success. In 1968, the poorest fifth of the population received 7.6 per cent of the national pie, compared to the richest with 44.5 per cent. Nowadays, the poor chew on a thin 4.4 per cent slice, while the wealthiest fifth feast on more than half the pie.

"The richest 10 per cent earn about thirty times more than the poorest people," says Tagle, "so the socio-economic differences are very deep and will become deeper without strong social policies."

Manfred Max Neef, a Chilean economist, president of the Austral University in Valdivia, and one of the model's few critics, characterized this poverty as "the absence of an environment and the means necessary for a person to develop a life project. To be human is more than being a consumer. In Chile's economic model, you have people at the service of the economy, rather than the other way round."

During its years in office, from 1990 to 1994, the Aylwin government made some improvements. A tax reform increased spending on social services 40 per cent over three years, but Alejandro Foxley, its Finance Minister, admitted this was not enough.

"We've done as much as we could in the sense that we put all the extra tax revenues into health, education, youth training programs, housing for the poor." But the deficit, after seventeen years of slashing and neglect, was enormous and the government bureaucracy, mostly staffed by military appointees, both limits the impact of these programs and isn't efficient enough to correct regional disparities and reach target groups.

Ruiz Tagle says that traditionally the state has redistributed wealth and "that's not working at the moment" and he warns that the stability of the system depends on having "a stronger state in terms of control, social policy, environment and a lot of things. Our state isn't strong enough."

The military regime created a political system in which elected authorities have very limited powers. Pinochet's nine appointees to the thirty-five-member Senate can prevent the government achieving the two-third and three-fifth majorities necessary for reforms, while the electoral system ensures that, with a third of the vote, the parties who supported the military regime hold close to half the seats in Congress.

Max Neef has warned that Chile's integration into world markets is creating a dependency that could be dangerous, in spite of the diversification that others believed would provide a safety net. "We've already lost our self-sufficiency for food and we have situations like that in our 9th Region, which has the best pastures in Chile, but they're all growing eucalyptus because that's more 'profitable' according to market signs. But market signs," he warns, " are only valid in the short term and eucalyptus plantations are irreversible," since they leave the soil unfit for other vegetation.

Why, he asks, was Chile destroying the eco-system of one of the world's most extraordinary rivers, the Bío Bío, to build a hydro-electric dam? "We have a huge desert area, full of sunshine. Fifteen years ago, solar energy was expensive; now the costs have dropped enormously. Chile should be dedicating more to research that could benefit our country. Currently less than .1 per cent of the GNP goes to Research and Development."

Perhaps what goes on inside the country's sparkling new packing plants reveals the system's most serious flaws. There, and in the orchards that supply them, an estimated 500,000 temporary workers, mostly women, work twelve- to sixteen-hour days, six or seven days a week, on contracts that last as little as a week.

Because they work eight months at most, employers and authorities consider them "housewives, similar to students who work during holidays". Bernardo Reyes, of CEDAL, a non-government organization which works with the fruit handlers, spoke to me in 1993 about problems of working conditions within the fruit industry. "It's hard for them to recognize themselves as workers. They've only existed for eight years: they have no identity within our society.

"They spend an average of two hours a day travelling to and from work," he added. "Their children are left with a neighbour or a relative. Often the children end up alone. The rate of children with traumas due to the absence of their parents is very high." In 1993, employers, workers and government bodies began to sponsor day-care centres for some of these children.

The military government virtually destroyed a highly organized union movement. On September 17, 1973, the Junta banned Chile's national union organization, the CUT, and eliminated three-quarters of its affiliated federations and confederations. More than 2,200 union leaders, from 16 national labour organizations were fired from their jobs; 110 were killed and 230 were imprisoned. In 1978, the government banned more federations and 400 unions with 112,795 members, confiscating their goods. In 1973, 939,000 workers belonged to unions, close to 31 per cent of the workforce. By 1989, this had dropped to less than 500,000 (10.7 per cent).

Today, only 15 per cent of workers are protected by collective bargaining. Union leaders hit the headlines annually when they negotiate minimum wages with government and business officials, but there are few signs that they're reorganizing to handle problems like those in the fruit-producing sector. The government often doesn't have the resources to regulate industry, and Bernardo Reyes told me about a labour ministry official who does consulting for fourteen of the companies whose compliance he's supposed to regulate.

Occupational health hazards are rife. Chile still uses pesticides from the "dirty dozen" banned in most countries, and CEDAL studies found that safety procedures in the fruit industry are virtually unknown. Research in the Rancagua area south of Santiago, one of the main fruit-producing areas, indicates that birth defects have grown as exponentially as the fruit industry itself, with 93 per cent of the mothers of damaged babies having worked as pickers or handlers. One of General Pinochet's last actions before he left power was to eliminate therapeutic abortion, so women must continue their pregnancies to term and go through normal labour, or opt for an abortion and be liable for murder charges. One of the commoner birth defects in the fruit-producing areas is babies with no brains.

The salmon industry, non-existent twenty years ago, has become a symbol of the major trends in Chile's new, free-market economy. Between 1991 and 1992, sales jumped 58.4 per cent and producers predict that within five years they'll virtually double 1992 production to 100,000 tons of a total world supply of 900,000 tons. With a good reputation, imaginative marketing and the expansion of sales in the United States and Europe, that could situate them at the top of the pile. Or it might produce a glut.

Salmon helped consolidate Chilean exports to Japan, helped along by

Japanese ownership of one of the largest producers, Salmones Antártica. Special brand names commanded higher prices for Antártica's salmon, thanks to careful marketing and reliable delivery. High imports in 1992-93 allowed salmon producers to negotiate cheaper shipping rates to fly their fish up to the United States and hard lobbying stymied US attempts to impose quotas.

Producers have also focused on the specifics of market demand in Japan, Europe and the United States. This means careful handling of live fish until they're frozen; a preference for skilled manpower over machinery; special cuts for special markets; and so on. And they continue to lobby for a cross-industry campaign to increase fish consumption in the United States, where it is exceptionally low.

Nevertheless, some of those involved in the industry predict that by the turn of the century, mergers, closures, buy-outs and bankruptcies will reduce the 1993 level of eighty-seven salmon producers to fewer than a dozen, each with three or four main production centres, located at least eighty kilometres apart to avoid contagious diseases. The salmon industry, which many argue is exporting a value-added product that can promise sustained growth important income and genuine development, typifies the kinds of conflicts that economists don't notice and figures don't measure.

The way the industry has developed in the archipelago of Chiloé, a twenty-four-hour drive south of Santiago and one of the major salmon-producing regions, is an excellent example of the industry's shortcomings.

She sits on a wooden bench before the blackened slats of the walls of her two-room cabin. Beside her, huge pots of pork and water and a small teapot bubble cheerfully on the polished surface of an ancient wood-burning stove. Behind the stove, on a narrow wooden bench, gossip and giggle two young granddaughters, only half-listening to her stories. Her face is small and brown and wizened, with a sharp chin, black hair streaked with grey pulled back and sliding away down her back. She is the archetype of the old witch and her knowledge of traditional folk medicines and beliefs reinforces that image, as she tells us about the twenty-five illnesses you can get if you attract the Trauco's attention.

"He's a child," she says, with the singing accent of the gypsies, although she's never moved more than two hundred kilometres from Contuy, on the southern island of Chiloé, where she was born. "About the size of a two-year-old. And he wears a hat with a big round brim, and he sits high up on a big mountain trunk, and there he whistles. He whistles at anyone and if you look at him, he'll leave you in bad shape."

Or, she warns, he comes in a woman's dreams, to nurse and the woman feels ill. That happens and it's a dream, she says. If you dream of a baby who nurses at your breast it's a dream, but it really happens.

The Trauco throws twenty-five illnesses at his victim, each with its special remedy. To start, you must rub the patient with egg white and sugar, followed by garlic that is first scraped across the top of the stove. Sometimes that's enough for a cure, but if not, you must go to the mountains and find the right herbs.

She chants their names in Veliche, a language that's 10,000 years old: *eñuquín, huildín, manzanillón, lemulahuén, chaumamén, pelú* and the leaf of *rumaza de teñir* that is washed by the rivers. But for the remedy to work, you must go up the mountain early to cut the *pahueldín*, a vine as thick as the chimney of her wood-burning stove. First cut at the top, then the bottom, and then you must run, throwing ashes to cloud the Trauco's eyes so he can't follow you. Back in the kitchen you must carve the stick crudely with a knife and threaten it with the most dire of consequences if it won't cure its *enfermo*. You pass it through fire, you hang it over the stove, you menace it until it pees a litre of sap. This forms the basis of the remedy that's mixed with the herbs, then used to massage the patient and given by spoon. To complete the healing and protect the home, you cut four special bearded twigs from the seashore, you model four whistles from the *sargaso* shrub. You take four coals from the fire, four garlic cloves, eight grains of salt, a fistful of sand and distribute them among the four corners of the house. That way if he returns and tries to enter the house, he can't pass through the fire (from the coals); the deep pools of water (the salt) and the sand will distract him. He'll settle down to count the grains, until he gives up.

"He follows the weak," she warns. "For example, if I'm all worked out, I'm eating poorly, then of course he'll take me because of the weakness."

Almost three thousand kilometres south of the Atacama desert where copper and other minerals seem to dominate the future, at the last frontier between Chile's European-style civilization and the wilderness of its southernmost fjords and channels, the island of Chiloé struggles to cope with the implications of this new model for Chilean development. In these traditional farming communities with a strong indigenous influence, for more than a century the men have traditionally left for some-where else in order to seek survival, whether it be the northern mines or the sheep ranches of the Argentine and Chilean Patagonia even further south. And women like Rosa Huentén spend thirty or forty years planting and harvesting potatoes according to ancient designs, raising their children, their sheep and their pigs. Butchering, shearing, washing, spinning and knitting. Using reeds, they weave baskets or birds or images of the Trauco himself, and a host of his fellows, all figures from a mythology as rich as the Greeks, multiple and complex, vital and living still in the minds of old men and women like Rosa Huentén, in Contuy, on the island of Chiloé.

For most of the five hundred years since the Spanish Conquistadors claimed it for the crown, Chiloé has lived the typical boom and bust cycles of a small, marginal economy perched precariously at the edge of an empire. Early settlers thought they would find gold, but what they mostly found was hard work, impoverishment, and an uneasy partnership with the native people who had settled on the island centuries earlier. To this day, there is a large native population, of Huilliche, the southern strain of the Mapuche found on the mainland. Most of the islanders, called Chilotes, are a mixture of native and Spanish ancestors. The native languages, Veliche, Huilliche, and the now nameless language of a canoeing people called the Chono, who have long since disappeared, have quietly fused with settlers' seventeenth-century Spanish. Their words and phrases map the landscape with places and events, surreal and supernatural creatures, endless stories, jokes and legends. Together, language and landscape compose their memory.

The island's poverty and lack of resources won its inhabitants three centuries of neglect from the Spanish crown. In 1681, the King of Spain even received a letter suggesting that the Chilote people be moved northward to supplement labour shortages on mainland Chile, but the development of an industry to log the island's rich and rare timber reserves foiled that proposal. The Chilotes continued to survive by farming, particularly potatoes, sheep-herding and gathering shellfish along the generous shores of their inner and outer seas, and by producing their own woven cloths and knitted clothing.

In the early 1980s, a Japanese consortium's plan to clear-cut what remained of Chiloé's famous native forests for woodchips stirred enough controversy that its proposal was finally stopped. But, little by little, the government began to grant "concessions" – pieces of the island's scarce lakes and chunks of the inner sea that separates it from the mainland – to companies interested in farming salmon.

Chiloé's experience with the salmon industry exemplifies the shortcomings of the economic model, particularly when it comes to regional development. Salmon farming could potentially fit in well with the island's style of life and culture, but the way the industry has developed has hindered that process. While most of the country's main salmon companies run operations on the island, producing well over half the annual salmon harvest, their head offices remain in Santiago, where technical and administrative staff are hired. Taxes return to the nation's capital, forcing island authorities to beg, hat in hand, for funds to repair the dirt and gravel roads worn into bumpy strips by the fisheries' heavy trucks and to finance social and cultural programs. The wealth and development that the salmon companies have undoubtedly brought benefits a small minority, most of them outsiders who work in the companies' top posts, send their children to private schools, and pressure local services in such a way that they often bring price increases.

This progress, such as it is, does not take into account the area's extraordinarily rich culture, which is in danger of disappearing as the elderly who are conversant with ancient stories slowly die off and newer generations forget, influenced by television and an educational system that values neither their traditional mythologies nor their original languages. Independent writers, researchers, anthropologists, archaeologists and teachers try desperately to study and record the island's cultural wealth, as well as ensure that it doesn't become reduced to caricatures used to feed the tourist industry. But local government, with no tax base, has limited resources to finance the museums, galleries, local archives and study centres, perhaps even a much-needed university, and the salmon companies have shown little initiative in what could be an essential area of community relations.

In May 1993, John Koch, an American student, who was preparing his Master's thesis on the salmon industry, visited three of the island's fisheries, among them two belonging to the largest companies, Salmones Unimarc and Salmones Antártica. Both companies own salmon farms on lakes and in the sea, where they develop the salmon from eggs, to smolt, to adults in both lake and sea rafts and then run them through plants that employ as many as 450 workers at peak production, but far fewer the rest of the year.

Koch found that island employees of the *salmoneras* as they're called locally, earn less than U$100 a month, around the national minimum wage, but can expect full-time work for only four months of the year. The jobs available are the lowest in the processing hierarchy: machine operators in the plants, day workers or night watchmen on rafts or in hatcheries.

A 1989 survey by an island non-governmental organization, Opdech, revealed that the Salmones Unimarc processing plant had only one technician from Chiloé, Salmones Antártica none. Staff in these technical positions earned on average two-and-a-half times that of the ordinary workers. Gender discrimination was widespread, as were cases of sexual harassment, Koch found.

The fact that the jobs are seasonal makes unionization and thus collective bargaining virtually impossible, but it does allow Chilote employees to carry on with their usual farming and handicraft activities for the rest of the year. However, cultural and social conflicts have developed as the *salmoneras'* presence has driven up prices for housing rental and land purchasing, often beyond the Chilotes' capacity to pay.

The salmon companies fight bitter battles with local fishermen who fish in areas adjacent to rafts. When a raft breaks and the salmon escape, conflicts reach fever pitch, with the Chilotes often facing charges. Chiloé's fishing community relies on small rowboats and motor launches, which can only function in the protected waters of the inner sea.

But perhaps most serious is the suspicion, shared by Koch and many Chilotes, that their natural resources, their main food source and key elements in local beliefs, are becoming dangerously polluted. In March 1993, *El Candil de Chiloé*, a monthly journal issued by Opdech, published a comment by Onofre Millán, a twenty-eight-year resident of Lake Millán.

Before the arrival of the salmon company, "the water was crystal clear. The year the *salmonera* came, during the summer when the water is closed off [from the ocean], it looked turbid, dark and muddy. The second year the lake looked green ... and the whole area where the water flows [out of the lake] had about three inches of a greasy, green sediment."

In his visits and interviews, John Koch found that dead salmon were often buried illegally at night and that blood and guts were repeatedly dumped directly into the water, sometimes with bleach and other disinfectants. Human excreta was another problem, as some rafts are not equipped with bathrooms. But salmon feed is probably the most serious contaminant. Koch quotes Arturo Schofield, a fishery engineer who estimates that about 30 per cent of the food given fish, about 1.8 kilograms of waste food per fish, sinks uneaten to the bottom of lake or sea. For Salmones Unimarc, which produced 2.5 million fish last year, that would represent about 4.5 million kilograms of waste.

A drive along Chiloé's southern shoreline around the town of Quellón reveals an endless chain of salmon companies, huddled behind high barbed-wire fences. Often, administrators' homes are located within this isolated area rather than in touch with the surrounding community, an unwelcome reminder of the mining enclaves that once stirred so much hostility in the country's north.

Eugenio Tironi, the social scientist, mentions in *The Silences of the Revolution* Chileans' preference for "the values of sobriety, education and democracy" over "a country with a high standard of living, but large social differences". The economic model that the military and the Chicago Boys imposed at enormous cost has already created the second alternative. The president who replaced Patricio Aylwin at the head of the Chilean government is a dark-haired, bushy-eyebrowed businessman, Eduardo Frei, son of the Eduardo Frei who governed Chile from 1964 to 1970. His government, a smaller version of the coalition of Christian Democrats, Socialists and other parties that carried Aylwin to power, will make key decisions regarding the future of privatization and the other issues shaking Codelco. It will also establish economic, social, cultural and regional policies for the next eight years that will lay the foundation for Chile as one century fades into another.

While no one's disputing the virtues of foreign investment at the moment, the social problems which contributed to the debate over foreign ownership decades ago are more complex than ever, compounded by new awareness of environmental hazards. Public ownership of Codelco has helped to soften the impact of policies which devastated Chilean society under the military, but the issue of Codelco's future has been raised and the issue of foreign ownership will inevitably follow.

Interwoven with that debate will be the question of how the country's wealth is distributed now, versus how it should be distributed. With no military regime or secret police to silence dissenting voices, it seems inevitable that movements of workers and others, who are unable to achieve a comfortable livelihood, not for lack of their own efforts but because of the social priorities established by a regime that the majority rejected, will recur.

During the early years of the Aylwin government, national strikes by teachers and health-care workers highlighted the inconsistencies of the country's dominant social and economic policies. While polls indicate that a huge majority of Chileans consider quality health care a vital priority, with education not far behind, the economic system continues to privilege low taxes with a shrinking number of alternative sources of income for the state. A small proportion of Chileans earn so much they can afford luxurious cars and properties at prices that are high on an international scale, while the vast majority, including blue-collar workers and tradespeople, teachers, professors, health care workers, nurses, government employees, even professionals who are generally better paid, struggle to provide for their children something resembling the education, the health care and the other benefits usually associated with living in the twentieth century. Many remember enjoying these, as rights, in the past.

These conflicting forces have torn at the inner fabric of Chilean society for most of the country's existence, from its declaration of independence in the early 1800s. The refusal to negotiate these demands by a small but powerful group of decision-makers, be they landowners, industrialists or politicians or all three combined, has led to eruptions of violence throughout Chilean history, whether it be the great Mapuche rebellions of the late 1800s, the organizations of northern miners that culminated in massacres in the early 1900s or other disputes. Chile, like most less developed countries, has never successfully met this basic need to participate more than minimally in society's wealth and the well-being that it can provide, although it seems to have come closest in the late sixties and early seventies. The Frei government has made the elimination of poverty its first priority and it views economic growth as the only means to reaching that end. But the principles of equality that shore up a stable democracy require something more than simply raising the income of the poorest segment of the population. Unless the country faces this reality and seeks some resolution, it seems inevitable that the future will bring a repetition of past tragedies.

Three years ago, the main ore deposit at El Salvador began to run out and Codelco has had to scramble to develop new deposits and survive. Among the company's high costs are the local hospital, two schools, a supermarket, and community services that are necessary because the town exists solely to serve Codelco. A private company would just have shut the place down, turning it into a ghost town like so many of the nitrate centres before it. But for Codelco it's not so simple.

In recent years, the mine's local administrators have experimented with a new, heapleaching technology that can produce first-rate ore at around forty cents or less a pound. And they've carried out the exploration and the technical development necessary to make further mining of the area's reserves feasible, while reducing staff, and thereby related costs. They've also started to auction off some of the services in the town of the El Salvador that could be served by private firms.

The town's survival turns on the success of these measures. In the meantime, El Salvador could be viewed as either a last surviving edifice in the midst of the ruins of socialism, or as a milestone on the road to somewhere else.

Chapter seventeen

THE DRAGON PINCHOT

VALPARAISO/SANTIAGO 1915

Perfection, of a kind, was what he was after,
And the poetry he invented was easy to understand;
He knew human folly like the back of his hand,
And was greatly interested in armies and fleets;
When he laughed, respectable senators burst with laughter,
And when he cried the little children died in the streets.

W.H. AUDEN

"I've always been a good person, I greet ladies, I'm affectionate with children, I try to help the poor because I've been educated to have a human sensibility," he says, and adds, "I did everything I could, I gave this country peace, I avoided a war, I built houses and highways. I know that many will continue to judge me negatively, but I have the intimate conviction that I did my duty."

He was born in Valparaíso on November 25, 1915, the oldest of six children, with a stern, conservative mother and an often absent father. The family lived on the third floor of an old building that belonged to the Archbishopric, near the central square, the Plaza de la Victoria, where monuments celebrate Chile's victory over Peru in the 1879 war.

He attended the San Rafael seminar, until he was expelled for breaking some windows, and from then until he was eighteen he studied at one of Chile's oldest Catholic Schools, the Sacred Hearts. Friends recall him being a frequent visitor to the director's office, where he was reprimanded for participating in a stunt that burned out the school's electrical system or, more frequently, for his poor pronunciation in French. Like many, one of his old teachers never recalled anything negative about his former pupil.

"We all have faults, so he must have something, but frankly I haven't seen any. Friendship is precisely the contrary, don't you think? That there's no fault."

"He was an excellent son, a model," Monseigneur Augusto Salinas told me, in March 1987. "He was very disciplined at school, very obedient. He was never punished." And he added: "He was very correct, very friendly, very well-mannered, with a lot of good-will. In fact, there was never anything out of the ordinary about him."

He liked to race his friends, although he'd interrupt their play sometimes to go and assist the priest at mass. Father Santiago Urenda, the same director whose office he visited for disciplinary purposes, had a saying often repeated in the school: "The military and the priesthood are not careers for making a living, but rather vocations for serving God and the Fatherland."

He was a tyrannical older brother, watching carefully over his young siblings, particularly his sisters, screening every visitor.

In 1933, at seventeen, on his third attempt, he was accepted as a cadet at the Military School. From there he climbed steadily upward, serving a brief stint as commander of the concentration camp in Pisagua during the late forties, when President González Videla outlawed the Communist Party, which had helped him get elected. Later he would tell his former press secretary, Federico Willoughby, that there "he learned that [the Communists] were really a group without any moral principles, without any feeling of the country, any respect for human values." Then, as now, he was steeped in military pomp and ceremonies, the legacy of the Prussian instructors who formed the Chilean army in the late 1800s.

"Discipline and hierarchy are of utmost importance," says Raúl Sohr, a Chilean journalist who has specialized in military subjects. "You can't have those military virtues with deliberation in the Armed Forces. Even though there's a military government, people within the barracks and the Army canteens don't discuss politics. Barrack life is that and nothing else." Willoughby says that "when he was a young officer, what his captain or major or colonel said was the truth. There was no other truth."

He married and had three daughters and two sons. He specialized in a field called geopolitics, even produced a textbook called *Geopolítica de Chile,* first printed in 1968, reprinted in Argentina in 1978. "The reader will be surprised to find in these pages abundant quotations from Adolph Hitler, Haushofer and other supernationalist theoreticians who served the ideological postulates of Nazism, like Kjelen, Ratzel and Ritter ..." the blurb on the cover warns. For the author, "the state 'acquires in its composition a constitution similar to an amoeba', that is, the border will never remain stable but rather will grow by feeding on its neighbours, in this case Peru, Bolivia and Argentina."

During World War II, he followed both sides of the war, the way a doctor "studies a tumour and not the patient's ideology. We looked at the war strictly as a problem related to our profession as soldiers." Later he concluded that "Hitler made a mistake. Also he had the defect that he lost the war." He rejected the "brutality the Nazis used against the Israelites; but the blame isn't just Hitler's, but rather a group of dignitaries."

"I think that as an intellectual, he is a poor man really," Genaro Arriagada, a political scientist and leader of the Christian Democratic Party who spent many of the years that followed the coup studying and writing about Chilean and Latin American military institutions, told me in 1987. "I discovered a lot of plagiarism in one of his books. ... Besides, what he wrote was very naïve, things that were written at the beginning of the century by very small geopoliticians and some ideas of Haushofer, a Nazi geopolitician. Most recent books are a kind of justification of his very strange behaviour, before Mr. Allende. *The Final Day* has been written to prove that he was not a traitor."

Nevertheless, he continued his upward climb. By 1970, he was an Army general in command of a division. In 1973, when General Carlos Prats was forced to resign, he took over as Army commander-in-chief. Allende "offered [the post] to me and I just said: Thank you for the nomination. Knowing perfectly well that there would be a debacle, famine, that the country would disappear, be destroyed completely, but better to serve there, than quietly in my house."

Virginia Morales, who is better known as Moy de Tohá, was married to José Tohá, one of Allende's defence ministers. She remembers him then. "He was a very limited person in intellectual and cultural terms," she says. "The only subject he had really mastered or that really impassioned him was the military. He never had an opinion about anything else. But he balanced all this with a special warmth and an affection toward people. Above all, he struck me as a general who was willing to defend our democracy.

"We had a sort of friendship that wasn't deep but went beyond the natural and normal relationship of a minister with someone who worked under him." Her husband resigned as defence minister after troops surrounded the Moneda, the presidential palace, with tanks in June 1973. One by one, as Tohá said goodbye to the people he had worked with, they left the room until only two were left. "At one point he realized that José was waiting for him and he turned away from the window, his eyes full of tears. And he said [to my husband] 'I'll never forget your personality, your equanimity, and the respect that you have developed in this ministry. We're very sorry about your leaving.' I'm remembering more or less what José told me."

She also remembers that the day he was appointed Army commander-in-chief, other generals commented that he returned from the Moneda "more Allendista than ever". Legend has it that Allende worried about the fate of his loyal general up to the moment of his death.

"What we didn't take into account," Morales says, "was his capacity for betrayal. The possibility was put to him and he just happened to be Army commander-in-chief which is practically the head of the Armed Forces. So he ended up being head of the Junta. And then came power, corruption, ambition. But there was nothing to foresee that Pinochet would come to all that."

On September 11, 1973, soldiers arrested Tohá along with a group of supporters who had remained with Allende in the Moneda. The military government shipped him off to Dawson Island, near Punta Arenas where, according to the Rettig Commission report, military personnel subjected him to constant mistreatment and torture. Virginia Morales and Isabel Letelier together met with Pinochet to plead for their husbands' and others' lives and freedom. But as the months passed, Tohá's weight dropped from seventy-six to forty-nine kilos, although he was almost two metres tall. Finally, he was taken to the Armed Forces Hospital in Punta Arenas, then the Air Force Hospital and from there to the military hospital in Santiago, so weakened from starvation he could not move from his bed. Nevertheless, one day in March 1974, Virginia Morales received the news that her husband, José Tohá, had hanged himself and died.

Morales, with two small children, lost her job in the government women's secretariat. She accepted an invitation from the Mexican president and left Chile for Mexico, where she went to work on behalf of political prisoners. "I never really thought of leaving, but rather of seeking a bit of peace, to organize my ideas and figure out my future on the basis that I was going to be a woman alone. But I couldn't just go off looking for my own peace when there were so many wives and children of José's companions who were living through the same experience. So I worked on denouncing [what was happening] and that led the government to take away my passport." Finally, after thirteen years, with help from the UN and Amnesty International she was able to return to Chile in 1987.

And it was years after her husband's death that she had, with the help of letters from retired General Carlos Prats, figured out why the military singled him out for such savage treatment. "Pinochet couldn't leave José alive, because he would have caused him trouble. José knew him very well, knew very well the inner workings of the Armed Forces and the military apparatus. The whole time I thought nothing could happen to José. What an illusion! Because the military can talk to you if you're a woman, an unoffensive entity for them. And on the other hand they're squeezing the neck of the person who in their judgement is dangerous."

"We're tied hand and foot. We have to adapt to whatever His Majesty will concede to his subjects," Air Force General Gustavo Leigh told Monica González in 1984. General Leigh was in charge of the bombing of the Moneda on September 11, 1973, and from then on he battled with General Pinochet, trying to make him share the power conquered by the coup among the four members of the Junta. First, Pinochet prohibited their use of the presidential booth at the Municipal Theatre. A few days later, he decided they couldn't use the government's Castle Hill mansion in Viña del Mar.

General Leigh grappled with Pinochet for five years. "[The Army] is more powerful, it covers all of Chile. That's key. Based on that, Pinochet accumulated more and more power. That's how he softened up the other commanders-in-chief. We had some violent incidents. I fought with him to the end over his appointment as president of the republic," he told Monica González.

"I didn't leave willingly," he added. "I was stripped of my powers by force. On March 21, 1978 in El Bosque, in front of Pinochet, I asked for a scheduled transition with a chronological itinerary to return to the state of law within five years." Leigh lost. He left the Junta and the Air Force. Monica González describes him six years later, sitting in a heaterless office, trying to make a living as a real estate agent. After more than a decade of military government and eighteen months of protests, Leigh complained that "Chilean officers have superficial knowledge of the economy, of political organization, but they're not prepared to administer a country. The chain of command is so vertical that a subaltern can't give his superior negative information about his image."

He characterized Pinochet as having "unlimited ambition", a man who "systematically eliminates" anyone he considers a threat. The CNI, the main secret police organization, "responds directly to the orders of the Chief of State. ... Security organizations have the country covered with microphones, they control telephones, they have informants on every corner ... People are afraid to talk." Later he would add, "Before, we knew him for his unlimited ambition and his harshness. Now we know him only for his continual incoherencies and contradictions. What a sorrowful spectacle to be in the hands of this kind of governor!"

Pressured and upset by the protest movement, General Pinochet published in November 1983 a new book called *Política, Politiquería y Demagogia,* a scathing criticism of the vices of traditional politicians who were then regrouping in the Christian Democrat-led Democratic Alliance and a Socialist and Communist-led coalition known as the MOP. It is also a justification of his continued rule. Political activity requires a "profound vocation", he says, and he "has faith in the soul of the nation". As a military man, he's the ideal person to run the country.

"... In military life one lives, perhaps with more formal clarity than elsewhere, a permanent dynamic of commanding and obeying. Is any other activity any different? ... It may be a bit drastic to say it like this but, in life, the most useless person is he who doesn't know how to command or obey ... Everywhere there should be hierarchies and chains of command. And everywhere, as a result, there will be people with more or less capacity for being useful, according to their function," he writes.

Order is a key and far-reaching concept to the military man, and Pinochet epitomizes this, right down to the last detail of his personal routine. During his presidency, he got up every morning at 5:30, lifted weights, jogged, had one cup of tea, orange juice and unflavoured yogurt for breakfast. Even on weekends, his life was ruled by the clock. On Sundays he played with his grandchildren from one to one-thirty. On holidays he napped half an hour each day, swam ten minutes, walked fifteen and was always up at dawn. At ten every night he was in bed, where he would read history, philosophy, economy – for ten minutes. Then lights out.

Said Virginia Morales, "He's not a sensual man, one who enjoys reading a good book or seeing a good play, a good movie, listening to a concert. He's not sensual at the table either."

He has a vision though and he writes that even nature has seen the importance of basic order and hierarchy. "Planets observe an invariable order, one that permits the perfect functionality of the entire cosmic structure, which is a divine work. In other words, it is the Creator who places us before a reality of equilibrium, order and authority. And he shows us the enormous weight of his creation and its beauty. Because only that which possesses order is beautiful. That which has a relationship with a harmony, with limited functions is beautiful. And those functions are called hierarchies."

Dr. Juan Manuel Pérez, the psychiatrist, says, "I think Pinochet is probably the least free person in the world, because he's an absolute slave to an order which he did not even choose. Rather it was built around him, possibly from childhood. I think order is one of his supreme values, because without order he would disappear."

In Pinochet's view, the Communist Party is the incarnation of all that threatens his ordered world, and he believes that other political parties inevitably end up competing with and imitating the Communist Party, creating front organizations throughout society, particularly among unions, student and cultural organizations.

"I have repeatedly pointed out the danger threatening the free world of the growing expansion of Soviet, Communist Imperialism," he writes. "This is no obsession of mine, nor an idle accusation, pretext or slogan, but rather the absolute conviction, fully justified by events, that the appearance of Soviet communism profoundly altered the Western Democratic system, taking away all morality from the struggle to reach power. ...For the Muscovites, what happened in Chile was a tactical defeat within a great strategic battle to conquer the world."

Leadership of any party is "oligarchic", with a structure that is diametrically opposed to democracy, he argues. And they are all ruled from abroad. When he examines the internal workings of political parties he complained that a couple of votes could decide the rights of citizens. "In effect, only five or six hundred people, members of the party's oligarchic bureaucracy, have the power to resolve the living system of a whole people," he writes. He doesn't talk about why a four-man Junta should have a better chance of getting it right, although he does go ahead and provide his definition of democracy.

"The democratic system is that which understands that citizens desire a government open to their concerns, that gives them security and public order. And an authority that defends them from injustices, as well as sincerely worrying about the needs of the most destitute. Likewise, I think that the renewal of authorities should take place according to a calendar established constitutionally, and that enshrines citizens' right to participate."

He defines political struggle in stark black and white terms. "The intervention of transnational [political parties] and their ideological imperialism is another vice that distorts party 'democracy', exacerbating parties' action in the whole political struggle, turning the confrontation of ideas and programs into a true total war, that polarizes and destroys national unity, so necessary for the country's development."

The Armed Forces — he uses their full title here, that is, the Forces of Arms and Order — oppose this because "by definition and by oath, they are at the nation's service."

He accuses politicians of corruption for financial purposes and says that the "economic healing" that he has carried out has brought "moral healing" too. Morality plays a major role in Pinochet's verbal arsenal, although his definition of what is moral is always sketchy. An example: "Love for the land in which we were born is an unnegotiable moral imperative. It's something natural and inseparable, that could also be called virtue." Although he emphasizes that he is a practising Catholic and refers to God frequently, he often complains about the Catholic Church's intervention in national politics. "Give unto God the things that are God's," he would paraphrase, "and unto Caesar that which is Caesar's." One of Pinochet's sons is called Marco Antonio, and a grandson is Julius Caesar.

Discipline, he argues, like the military professor that he was for many years, is "the basic principle of respect for hierarchy. And, consequently, the obedience of those governed to those who govern." Anyone who continually questions what exists or "worse, permanently seeks justification for his unhealthy rebellion," is unsuited to participating in any social structure. "It's easier for man to let his appetites run away with him, than to control them," he warns. "And there the limits between what is order and what is chaos become cloudy."

As he fires out his criticisms he is strangely unselfconscious of how they reflect on his own government or how they might come back to haunt him. He criticizes the losers of elections for refusing to face their own defeat; five years later, once he and his advisers have recovered from losing the plebiscite, they declare it a victory, arguing that 44 per cent is an extraordinarily high percentage of the vote.

"Nevertheless," he writes in 1983, "you'll notice that this [hypothetical politician] who with impudence refutes an unrefutable fact is full of 'principles' and wordiness, behind which he hides attitudes whose intentionality does not exactly lead to the seal of the search for common good."

Pinochet ends his book *Política, Politiquería y Demagogía* on a note that echoes even more strangely, given subsequent events. Ten years after the coup, and five years before a majority of Chileans vote "No" to Pinochet's continuance in power, he writes: "I finalize saying that I fully recognize the idea written in universal history, that says that the great peoples are those capable of saying NO, when opportunism recommends the opposite. Chile already did so [on September 11, 1973]. And for daring to do so has had to pay a price. But history – sooner or later – will show that we are right. Our truth is the truth of the West. Of this West threatened by the intrinsically perverse forces of an enemy who seeks to implant itself therein. We defend the values of the spirit and of the faith. And I pray to God that He continues to give us the strength that He has given us, to resist attack ..."

Federico Willoughby, who served as General Pinochet's press secretary for three years after the coup, believes that Pinochet has won "a place in history, because he, with the movement in 1973, [turned Chile into] the single country in history that came out of the Soviet bloc." In 1987, when Willoughby and I spoke, he considered General Pinochet "a good friend, a good boss, a very human and warm person with a very deep knowledge of human beings. Also with a clear consciousness of power." To Willoughby, it was clear that Pinochet and other military officers felt they had "a sort of mandate to carry out a permanent defence of the country against the Communists."

He did, however, think that General Pinochet was exaggerating the Communist threat: "One thing is the [system in the] Soviet Union, but if we had a free election and the Communists voted, I don't think they would get more than 10 per cent." He was concerned about General Pinochet's "personalistic" style of government, and suspected that the General was perhaps misinformed about "the elements of the day-to-day life of his compatriots".

In our interview, Willoughby rationalized human rights violations by arguing that they occur every day, everywhere in the world, "because violence, perversion and crime are within human beings", but he felt that "at least there is a national consciousness" in Chile, and that this would begin to weigh more heavily on those making decisions. The solution, he said, was to "create a moderate environment, a free press, to have a congress where a representative will raise his voice and say these crimes have been committed".

By March 1987, Pinochet was feeling the pressure from people protesting on the streets and from increasingly ambivalent supporters like Willoughby. As he signed a bill legalizing political parties in Chile after a fourteen-year ban, he spoke with "the voice of a man who's exhausted. There are parts where he drags the words, he blurs, he can't read well, can't pronounce well," says Dr. Juan Manuel Pérez. "The only place with a bit of a shine is when he accuses the enemy of acting badly – he seems to like the letter "c" [giving it great emphasis], because it sounds like little explosions. I see a very tired, but terribly authoritarian person."

General Pinochet increasingly sees himself as a victim of misunderstanding and ingratitude, like Jesus Christ himself. "I have no doubt that Pinochet feels himself a Messiah," Dr. Pérez says. "The Messiah was the victim of misunderstanding by lesser beings, who were stupid or immature or whatever. He's said he feels the calling of a specific mission. In psychiatry, we call this an over-valued idea. It's an abnormal personality, that can become fanatic, without really going as far as hallucinating. But a Messiah can't resign."

Willoughby, while still an enthusiastic supporter of Pinochet's role in the "movement", thought, by 1987, that the time had come for him to step down. "The military have been very successful in many tasks but they're not being successful in creating a society that represents everybody's feelings and that will fit into the Western Christian model of democracy," he said. Within the year, Willoughby would join an independent committee supporting the Concertación for Democracy, the opposition coalition that would eventually replace Pinochet in government. When Patricio Aylwin took office, at the head of the coalition, in March 1990, Willoughby returned to the Moneda as press adviser to the minister responsible for communications. Pinochet expressed regret at having helped finance kidney transplants abroad that saved Willoughby's life.

I realized something essential about how the years of military rule had changed the Chilean army when I saw General Medina drive up, late and somewhat flurried, for our second interview. His rickety old Austin mini was quite a sight among the BMWs, Peugeots and Mercedes Benz in the parking lot of the National Academy of Political and Strategic Studies. Chilean history is full of officers, national presidents and even commanders-in-chief so frugal with the public budget (and their own) that they walked or took the bus to work. But the contrast between General Medina's vehicle and the Academy's official Mercedes Benz suggested that although he believes himself to typify the best army values, others have already changed those values.

Low wages fed a groundswell of discontent among Chilean officers for most of this century: a dissatisfaction that rumbled threateningly under a patina of Chilean democracy from the late fifties onward, erupting in the military siege of the Moneda, when it was still occupied by a Christian Democrat, Eduardo Frei in 1969. Four years later in June of 1973 officers staged a dress rehearsal for the coup against Salvador Allende. When it failed, they blamed the movement on monetary problems within the Armed Forces.

Chileans tend to speak of their democracy as having lasted a hundred years, or at least from the 1925 constitution onward. Yet there have been repeated breaks with that tradition, all noted as precedents by General Pinochet's supporters. A memorandum dated August 27, 1973, of the Direction of Army Operations, says that "the essence of the existence of the Armed Forces is rooted in the *survival of the nation*. This fact alone grants ... a moral authority over political parties, professional and/or religious associations, *when these have failed in carrying out their tasks of national importance*." Alvaro Pineda de Castro, a fan, underlines: "It's a fallacy to insist that the Armed Forces of a nation exist exclusively to defend its borders in the case of external war."

Aside from the civil war of 1891, Chile experienced a series of political crises with authoritarian solutions, usually supported or led by the military; in 1920, to depose and, in 1925, to restore Arturo Alessandri Palma, a home-grown Chilean populist; later, in 1925, with General Carlos Ibáñez, inspired by Mussolini and Spain's José Primo de Rivera; in 1931, with Ibáñez forced to resign, a series of governments tried to fill the vacuum, among them Colonel Marmaduke Grove, who installed a "Socialist Republic" that survived for ten days in 1932, and which was followed by a series of coups, after which, in October, Arturo Alessandri Palma returned to rule, purging the army, clamping down on unions and the press, and authorizing a massacre of students with Nazi sympathies, which is still commemorated by Chilean Nazis every September 5th.

For most of the military's most recent seventeen years in government, it was easy to see the country's rulers as a uniformed blur, carrying and using their weapons at will, functioning in the bustle of bright sunlight and in the silent empty streets after night curfew, arresting, kidnapping, torturing, making people disappear, making laws by decree, restructuring some of Chileans' most treasured institutions, rebuilding Chile itself in their own image.

But as the regime's hold weakened and opposition magazines were able to publish more investigative reporting, the shades of difference between the regime's military and civilian members and supporters became more apparent. Sometimes disagreement darkened into conflict, with the regime's critic leaving, temporarily or permanently, the sheltered fold of supporters for the rockier fields of the opposition or public silence. In 1976, the departure from the Junta of General Leigh, one of the coup's organizers, was the first sign of major cracks in the military government's edifice; they were quickly plugged.

After we had spoken about his arrest and torture during the coup, and his subsequent release and exile, retired Air Force Captain Raul Vergara reflected on the nature of the coup itself. Vergara believes that different coups were possible and that the one Chile experienced was not necessarily what most of those who initially supported a coup wanted or expected.

"There was a Christian Democratic option: officers who thought they had to end this story and that the president of the Senate, Eduardo Frei, should assume the government, call for elections and continue with the Christian Democracy and go back to what the country was before, in the sixties.

"Another option said that the world was heading leftward, so it was necessary to channel these good ideas, which had been prostituted by the politicians but weren't bad, and within this there were two wings, one the 'Peruvian' and the other that advocated not doing things by force, that there was a political action to bring together wills and that's what Allende was doing, [that] the people who seconded him were a disaster and there was political bartering which had to be eliminated.

"The other group – these were ideas more than anything – was Patria y Libertad ['Fatherland and Freedom', an ultra-right paramilitary organization], which included some commanding officers and is the only thing with structure and communication within the group. Because nobody knew what would happen. They manipulated the violence, assumed control within the coup and avoided any disparity in criteria through a very harsh repression, on the basis of inventing a supposed rebellion, weapons everywhere, so they had to unite and any arguments must come later.

"Afterward, there is the parallel line of command that guarantees that everybody does what they're supposed to. Later still, obviously the parallel forces of control are the DINA. So they start to build unity through complicity."

The sheer brutality of the torture by people who had eaten, partied and flown with Vergara ("sometimes I knew who it was just from the way they breathed") fed almost twenty years of meditation on the events leading up to his own arrest and what had made this possible. At first, he had thought that it was the stories – that he was plotting to kill them and their families – that turned interrogation sessions into brutal punishment. "There's also the whole military question in the background, inherent to soldiers, of acting with violence and imposing their will at any price."

But gradually, he realized that they did this for "two fundamental reasons, one to quickly mark and identify a group within the Armed Forces and the second, the need to separate with a line of blood the rest of civil society in such a way that any possibility of negotiations or cooperation was impossible and to create a sort of complicity.

"This was consciously done, with specific strategic goals. The repression against military officers played a role of intimidation inside [the Armed Forces] because it violated a fundamental principle, which is the hierarchical principle of the officer as untouchable. This created a lot of fear, because if you see that a general is being tortured, you think what will happen to me?

"There's no doubt that some people who didn't agree with what was going on had no alternative. They saw what was happening and often

AFTER THE FIRST DEATH

they had to demonstrate extra cruelty to avoid suspicion. There were people of principle who refused to torture and fell as a result."

Of all these possible coups, Chileans ended up with the "hardest". This ordinary man, with the gruff, friendly attitude of a *huaso*, a kind of country cowboy, did not possess an extraordinary intelligence, "but was very astute", said Genaro Arriagada in 1987, trying to explain how Pinochet consolidated his power. When the Junta initially took over, there was "a gentleman's agreement", General Pinochet announced at the time. "I don't plan to always direct the Junta. We'll rotate. Today it's me. Tomorrow it will be Admiral Merino, then General Leigh, then General Mendoza."

That agreement quickly and subtly changed. Although General Pinochet himself, and his official biographers, have him secretly planning the coup from the moment Allende reached the presidency in 1970, other generals and Admiral Merino, leader of the navy and a Junta member throughout the military government, tell a different story. In a televised interview in September 1989, Admiral Merino said: "In the Navy we had an organization called *"Plan Cochayuyo*, July 16, 1973", that was designed to fight any sort of subversion. It was anti-subversion." That plan eventually reached the desk of Salvador Allende where it received his approval. "The plan was [to fight] subversion, but ... the thing is when we put it into practice, on September 10th, around 6 p.m., I sent a message saying 'Execute Plan Cochayuyo without anti'."

A group of generals visited General Pinochet to inform him of the plan and insist that he take a clear position, for or against. "If he hadn't agreed, that would have been the end of it," Merino said.

Genaro Arriagada, in 1987, said General Pinochet used the Army's own structures to oust the generals who participated in planning the coup. "The most well-known authors of the coup were generals like Palacios, Arellano, Torres, Nuño. One was out within six months, another a year. After two and a half years not a single author of the coup remained inside the Army." Pinochet had begun to destroy any counterweight to his own authority within the country's "most extreme bureaucracy" where one's position in the hierarchy is definitive.

Raúl Sohr, the journalist and sociologist who has followed the military closely, said: "A number of generals were forced to resign. Others are dead. We know of at least four generals who suffered suspicious deaths."

For those who retired, there were perks because, "there's nothing as

sad as a general in retirement, with no uniform, without any power,"
said Arriagada. "But Pinochet was careful to offer any general who was
put out of the military a position as ambassador, university president or
president of a state enterprise."

By 1987, close to a third of Chile's ambassadors abroad and half the
university presidents were military officers, most of them retired. For years,
officers also ran the universities' television channels, along with Chile's
government-owned national television channel. They received their regular salaries, plus bonuses for the eternal States of Siege, States of Danger of Perturbation of the Internal Peace, and other States of Exception,
plus payment for services rendered in public and private corporations.

At 8.5 per cent of the Gross National Product, Chile's military expenditures were among the highest in the world, compared to Mexico with
0.5 per cent, Brazil under 1 per cent, the US with 6.5 per cent. Only fifteen countries in the world had higher military expenditures and most
were in regions threatened by or at war. The Chilean military was spending most of this money not on weapons or equipment, but on wages and
benefits. One-third of the country's military expenditures went to social
security, ensuring pensions that were ten to fifteen times those of equivalent civilian positions. "That is not corruption in terms of a person, but
in terms of an institution that appropriates such an enormous part of the
national wealth," said Arriagada.

And Raúl Sohr said: "In a country where 80 per cent of the population earns an average of 100 dollars a month and you have a general
earning US$3,000 a month, you could say there's an element of corrup-
tion or an extreme inequality of distribution of income."

Military intelligence played its role in controlling potential dissension
within the armed forces, long before it could take shape. "From the rank
of lieutenant onward, if they don't attend parties or official celebrations
even those where they can choose, well, they start to have problems
with their careers and they're marginalized from the Army very early
on," said Sohr. "Not to speak of colonels and generals ... all those who've
expressed different views from General Pinochet have ended up out of
the Army or worse."

Pinochet is a politician who on "exercising power, begins to see himself as a man of outstanding conditions, as a statesman, as beyond criticism because he is in a way very close to God. Pinochet's main corruption is in this sense," Arriagada told me in 1987. "How a stupid man, a

badly educated man, began to feel himself a hero, a brilliant statesman, a man appointed by Providence to develop his country."

The Rettig Commission concluded that some officers did not agree with the activities of the political police, at least in the early years. Nevertheless, the first secret police agency, the DINA, did as it pleased, thanks partly to its ability to keep many of its activities secret, and partly to many officers' sense that the ultra-left deserved the treatment that the DINA was meting out, combined with the justification that the Armed Forces were "at war". The warlike language of the political debate which preceded the coup, particularly left-party leaders' claims that they had well-trained and equipped parallel armies ready to defend the government, contributed to the consolidation of the DINA as "a necessary evil", said the Commission's report.

"We must also mention the fear that confronting the reality of the [DINA] group and its growing violation of fundamental rights might damage Chile's international prestige and its image," the Commissioners wrote. They found that Chilean officers, presumably "at war" with extremism, did not have "adequate knowledge of the laws and morality of warfare, for example, in terms of treatment of prisoners, torture, interrogatories, executions, trials in wartime, etc. This indicates insufficient studies of these subjects and could also have led to an inadequate focus ... in relation to human rights."

During the years that followed the civilian government's assumption of power, the Chilean courts have began to investigate the fraudulent bankruptcy of Alvaro Corbalán's transport company, millions of pesos the Army paid to General Augusto Pinochet's son, fat commissions on state insurance paid to one of his daughters and a son-in-law, an illegal finance company run by Army officers. Many Chileans questioned the presence of high-ranking military officers directing former state enterprises they had helped to privatize, at bargain prices.

In 1970, Chilean soldiers and police received 19.9 per cent of total funds paid out in state salaries in Chile. By 1985, they received 40.8 per cent. The price of upward mobility and higher salaries was a drop in the public's appreciation of the Chilean military. In July 1992, a Chilean research institute published a study indicating that 53.2 per cent of Chileans thought the military's participation in the previous government was the most important reason for their drop in prestige, while 71.8 per cent said it would have been better if they'd left the government in

1989, 91.6 per cent believed the military participated in human rights violations and 73.1 per cent believed those responsible should be sanctioned in some way.

"I'm leaving [power], very pleased with what I've done because I think the objective has been accomplished," General Pinochet told a *Mercurio* reporter, in the lead story on October 15, 1989. "My adversaries have abused me, that is to say, my political enemies, because adversaries and enemies are synonyms. They like to exchange words. Political enemies have woven calumnies around me that, frankly, history will take charge of cleaning up."

Unrepentant, he defended himself from "these delinquents who were expelled from the country", traitors because they spoke of hunger and killings in their homeland. Even foreign ambassadors stationed in Chile were forced to "inform negatively" because their ministries wouldn't accept positive information about Chile, he said.

Human rights violations, torture "those dreadful things you're telling me about, belong to the last century. The Inquisition, not now," he said in 1992, denying all knowledge of the disappearances and executions of potential opponents of the coup.

According to the Rettig Commission report, on October 7, 1973, Carabineros in the Isla de Maipo area near Santiago arrested eleven people one night in their homes, along with four in the public square. In 1978, the Catholic Church received an anonymous tip that the bodies had been found in an abandoned mine in the small town of Lonquén, near Santiago, and Judge Adolfo Bañados, who would later take on the Letelier case, began an investigation that ended with those responsible being amnestied under the 1978 law. This exchange, from Raquel Correa and Elizabeth Subercaseux's *Ego Sum Pinochet,* based on a series of interviews they did with General Pinochet in 1989, is typical of his response to concerns about human rights violations.

"Q: Do you know about what happened in Lonquén for example?

Pinochet: No, but I've read, and I think there may have been combat, a fight and it seems like those who fought didn't find anything better to do than put the dead into those kilns.

Q: Did you know, General, that those campesinos *were in their beds, inside their houses, and were taken out at night, in their underclothes, their mouths and noses stuffed with straw and they were thrown into the kilns and then covered with lime?*

Pinochet: Where did you get that story?

Q: It's in the trial.

Pinochet: Oh sure! The campesinos *weren't doing anything! I'm not justifying killings, but remember, in times of the Popular Unity a woman was raped in front of her children and then she committed suicide.*

Q: By the campesinos *of Lonquén?*

Pinochet: No! Others, but that's what these little angels that you paint like saints were like. As I'm telling you: they raped a woman before her children, to such an extreme that afterward she committed suicide. And Lieutenant Lacampetre: they killed him just to kill him. That's worth nothing.

Q: But in these cases, General, what's the right way to act? When you find the guilty of a crime like that, they're arrested, judged and punished under the law.

Pinochet: I told you: initially there were excesses. Some of my people were also killed, people who weren't fighting!

Like Augusto Pinochet's old teacher Monseigneur Augusto Salinas, the General's supporters tend to view him with unconditional love and awe. Some formed a kind of cult. When he survived the 1986 ambush, a slick, full-colour leaflet on shiny paper announced that the bullets tattooed the image of his patron saint on the car window: direct divine intervention. Some of his admirers even felt moved to write lengthy paeans.

In his book *Pinochet: Verdad y Ficción (Pinochet: Truth and Fiction)*, the author Alvaro Pineda emphasizes that he is not Chilean (he doesn't say what he is), a circumstance that guarantees the "objectivity of his testimony". In an early chapter, "The Man of Destiny", he introduces Augusto Pinochet, saying: "For this overwhelming task of material and moral rehabilitation of the nation was needed, not a politician – not even the best of them – but rather a Chilean with the style, manner and character of Augusto Pinochet Ugarte who, aside from being a soldier of undisputable prestige is a genuine *chilense*, with features and characteristics of his own, energy, sobriety, reserve, a sense of independence and self-confidence, a sagacious and at times long-suffering spirit, nerves of steel and a born organizer. Author of books and cultivator of Geopolitics and Strategy, from the first instant he revealed himself to be the man capable of directing the immense task of rebuilding the country."

The Armed Forces intervened in order to bring Chile into a new era, to create a different and modern country, with radically different habits, mentality, values and customs. In March 1974, Pinochet said, and Pineda quotes him, "it is not our intention to be a mere government of administration, nor a simple transition between two party governments such as the country has known in recent times. We have the responsibility for projecting our work toward the future, initiating a new era in the fatherland's history for the good of Chile and her sons."

Pineda tries to convince us, as Pinochet himself often did, that armies are the only "moral reserve in the midst of a crisis of profound dimensions. They can restore order, help to rebuild that which was about to perish and with disinterest and patriotism return to the people their faith in a better destiny."

Undoubtedly not all of the 44 per cent who voted for Pinochet identified with his plan for Chile, but a great many did. His "protected democracy" promised shelter from the kind of severe political crisis that preceded the coup, guaranteeing the right to "security". Many believed him when he said that only "under a regime of authority, fair and impersonal, that ensures order and tranquillity, can a people achieve development and well-being."

Key to Pinochet's concept of the new society he was trying to build was economic freedom, free enterprise, the free market, the inalienable right to property that is enshrined in the constitution and which is one of the principles that has helped to shield Colonia Dignidad from direct intervention. To a very large degree Pinochet succeeded. Chile was among the first, if not the first, country in Latin America to adopt open border economic policies and for the past eleven years the economy has boomed while the rest of the world has slipped into stagnation and recession. There are more Mercedes Benz and Jaguars and BMWs, in fact, more cars than ever before – more, in fact, than the country's often narrow, usually poorly paved or unpaved streets can handle; certainly more than Santiago's smog-choked atmosphere can absorb.

In spite of Alvaro Pineda's assertion, it is hard to be "objective" about Pinochet. Unless he is treated as the heroic saviour of his people, he tends to feel slighted. To this day, if human rights are mentioned, he becomes furious. He divides the world between black and white, enemies and friends, communists and true believers, much as Paul Schaeffer, the director of Colonia Dignidad is said to do.

"Power legitimizes oppression," Dr. Juan Manuel Pérez, the psychiatrist, said. During his seventeen-and-a-half year rule, Pinochet was neither a visionary nor a megalomaniac, he was neither a brilliant soldier nor a psychopath. He was the essence of the father or grandfatherly figure, almost a local version of the Pope, ever ready to convoke God and the Virgin's support for his cause. His supporters thought him stern, but fair; an affectionate man who would mete out harsh punishment to those who strayed. He reassured those Chileans who felt threatened by the reforms of the Frei and the Allende administrations. He terrified those who opposed him. He banned pornography, while security agents routinely raped women and men, sometimes in front of close family members. He eliminated therapeutic abortion, while hundreds of potential opponents were forced to disappear. He exalted Army hierarchy, while the secret service, the DINA, blew up his former commanding officer in Buenos Aires. He kept his soldiers out of politics and ruthlessly in line. He made many changes, but he also left some things unchanged, something he refused to recognize, most notably, the nationalization of Codelco in 1972, which his own generals refused to let him sell off to the private sector.

More than anything else, he was and is a very ordinary Chilean, profoundly influenced by the conservative values of his church, a man who has spent more than sixty of his almost eighty years within a social institution that is familiar to all of us by name, if not by intent, purpose, capacity, an institution that defines people's worth solely by their ability to give and follow orders, to fit in to existing social structures, with no misgivings, no criticism, no rebellion. In many ways, he was the antithesis of the questing era in which his career began to peak, the essence of all that was threatened by that questioning. A man of action, he seized the moment, cleaving indefinitely to power in a way even his supporters had not predicted.

Once he reached the top of his mighty institution and became the head of the state, it often looked as though he would never loosen his grip on power. The favourable reports of his own Praetorian Guard, as Federico Willoughby called them, fed his confidence and he fell into the delicate web of the plebiscite, a trap woven by his – finally – united opposition, allies who quietly felt the time had come for change, and by himself. Above all, it was a net of his own making, trimmed to his measure, carefully fashioned to ensure that he would never be any further from power than he chose.

"There's nothing so sad as a retired general," the saying goes. He has remained in power throughout the elected governments that followed him. The constitution that he created has enshrined his leadership of the Army until 1997, when he will be eighty-two years old. He has relinquished one of the pillars that supported his authority, the government, but the other, the Army, remains not only intact, but is virtually a state of its own, with its own laws, rulers and its own finances, thanks not only to the many properties it owns throughout the country but also an annual budget that Congress is obliged to approve virtually unchanged, and that includes such special tidbits as a fixed 10 per cent of the gross sales of the largest copper corporation in the world.

In August 1993, as Pinochet celebrated twenty-three years at the head of the Army, national newspapers focused on his plans for modernizing that institution. Now that he'd got Chile in order, he was going to start on the Army. In Chile today, "modern" usually means more technology. The Army, commanded by the oldest general in the western world, is scheduled to acquire new technology, to reduce its top-heavy upper echelons and, if Pinochet has his way, to permanently advise the president and Congress on subjects involving national development. What modernization will not mean, in all likelihood, is the inclusion of human rights education in Army curricula and a genuine reduction of the powers that have turned that Army into a fourth power in Chilean society, on a par with, and some would argue above, the presidency, Congress and the judicial system.

Virginia Morales de Tohá has said, "All human beings carry a small Pinochet in their soul; democracies are what stop this Pinochet from manifesting itself."

Chileans don't have to look far to find out who General Pinochet was, where he came from, the strengths and weaknesses that made him and his seventeen-year government possible, with all that it achieved, with all that it destroyed. Perhaps Ariel Dorfman says it best, in his novel *The Last Song of Manuel Sendero*, in the form of a children's bedtime story.

Some people say he came from outside, from up north. Others say he was born right there, that he was up in the mountains, sleeping, and that the people's arguing woke him up. Some others say he was made by taking a little piece of heart from every inhabitant of the land and that's why he was so strong. Because he had an eye, an ear, or a claw in every man, woman, and child. In any case, what is for sure is that he had the power to see everything. There wasn't a corner anywhere that his gaze didn't reach and his voice was so powerful and persistent, so evil, that it invaded everybody's thoughts and forced all the people to sing the same chorus.

... The people were all afraid, because they thought he was immortal. And because there was a rumour. A strange rumour. That whoever killed the Dragon Pinchot would first have to be dead himself.

Chapter eighteen

A ROOTED SORROW

PUNTA ARENAS 1890, 1993

Macbeth: Canst thou not minister to a mind diseas'd,
Pluck from the memory a rooted sorrow,
Raze out the written troubles of the brain,
And with some sweet oblivious antidote
Cleanse the stuff'd bosom of that perilous stuff
Which weighs upon the heart?
Doctor: Therein the patient
Must minister to himself.

SHAKESPEARE, MACBETH

In Punta Arenas, a tawny strand of beach stretches along the slate grey sea like a cat before a fire, the ocean splashed with silver, sombre greens and blues, the endless black fathoms of forgetfulness. The sea paints ordinary garbage with new meanings, revealing an inner threat or promise. Here it's broken glass mainly, the occasional cracked shell deserted by a dead clam or mussel, a purple jacket swollen with sand or water, so it looks like a human husk, abandoned among all the other broken things.

I stroll along a finger of salty water between the shore and a sandbar, wondering, What is it about the sea that rehabilitates the lost, changing this empty beige glove into a supple hand, open and appealing?

My husband, Patricio, and I are here, partly to work on a book, partly to write a chapter for a travel guide. We will travel the official tourist routes, along with the uncharted paths of memory. He is from Punta Arenas. This is his first trip back since the 1973 military coup. We start with a museum "opened by his Excellency, President of the Republic, don Augusto Pinochet, 1983".

Located in the small but luxurious mansion of the Braun Menéndez family, the museum contains an odd but telling collection. One room displays a rifle collection, an oil painting of an early settlement on the Straits of Magellan and a box of toiletries. A graph of "aboriginal and colonial populations" traces the evolution of the region's foreign immigrants and native peoples. While the yellow, red, blue and orange lines climb steadily, a bright green line – the native people – hits zero in 1946.

We put soft felt covers on our shoes and shuffle over the parquet floor into the main hall. A fleshy, middle-aged woman with carefully permed hair and a worshipful hush in her voice, guides us through the carefully preserved rooms, pointing out ebony tables from Italy, Louis XV walnut chairs, miles of brocade wallpaper, a glittering ballroom. Family photographs show fifty grandchildren, a total of three hundred descendants.

An oil painting gives us Sara Braun in a regal dress of purple satin. She donated the ornate main entrance to the Punta Arenas cemetery on the condition that she be the only person ever to use it. Even today, the main entrance remains sealed; ordinary mortals slip in through a side entrance.

The billiards room shares a wall with the bedroom where a painting of the Virgin and Infant Jesus piously stands guard over the bed. In the games room, back to back with the Virgin, a painting of a blonde woman gazes seductively down at the players. The neckline of her basic black dress plunges playfully downward, its fall broken by a red rose between the breasts.

We lunch with Carlos Vega and Elsa Barrida, surrounded by computers, a large colour television and shelves piled with papers and books of every vintage. A jar with a sprig of sarsaparilla leaves and transparent red berries stands on the table between us. She is both painter and publisher, slender and quiet with smooth skin and observant almond eyes. He has a round face with impudent, slightly protuberant brown eyes, dark hair frosted by suffering more than age. A journalist, he was arrested, tortured and imprisoned after the coup. Release brought the painful rebuilding of his career, with a shift toward printing and publishing when no newspaper would hire him. When we met, in February 1993, he was printing most of the region's writers and making both commercial and documentary videos. For more than a decade he has spent every spare moment digging and sifting through the region's past, turning up the bones, old weapons and feuds that many others would have preferred to leave buried.

Carlos showers me with papers describing how the main native groups of the region were hounded, hunted, poisoned and shot, mostly at the behest of the big landowners like the Menéndez Behety family. For one pound sterling per testicle or ear, hunters with nicknames like Red Pig made a decent living of one hundred pounds a year.

"The indigenous problem lasted five years," Carlos says, sarcasm twisting his grin.

Throughout lunch, the famous Punta Arenas wind howls and gusts and blows, banging at the roof and pounding at the four corners of the sturdy bungalow. Occasionally, it blasts open the door, hurtling across the room like an impetuous guest, determined to sit at our table.

Punta Arenas, the world's southernmost city, clings to the rocky bottom edge of America, just north of Antarctica, closer to Buenos Aires than Santiago, 3,100 km away. In 1842 the Chilean government sent a ship racing down the coast to claim the area, and it has perched uneasily at the edge of the nation's consciousness ever since. The straw-coloured steppes of Patagonia, most of which now belong to Argentina, stretch northward. To the south, the massive triangle of the island Tierra del Fuego looms on the horizon, echoed by the small blue silhouette of Dawson Island.

On November 1, 1520, Ferdinand Magellan discovered the strait. A steady trickle of explorers followed, naming coves "Last Hope", "Obstruction", "Disillusionment". In 1578, the Straits of Magellan witnessed Spain's efforts to keep the English corsair, Frances Drake, away from the treasures it was plundering from America. In later years, many tried to settle. Battered by storms, exhausted by hunger and the extreme cold, punished on the ever-present gallows, settlers died, their eyes fixed on the sea.

During the 1600s, the legend of the lost City of the Caesars enticed adventurers to explore southern fjords, in search of the mist-enthralled city whose streets were paved with gold and silver. Admiral Byron, the poet's grandfather, explored these shores in 1765; Cook passed through in 1769, concluding, incorrectly, that the native people of the region were cannibals. More scientific studies by the Spanish, under Antonio de Córdova, Alejandro Malespina and others, describe varied encounters with native groups during attempts to discover the City of the Caesars.

In the 1800s, whaling and sealing enterprises, travelling missionaries and scientific expeditions from England, Italy, Germany, Norway, the US and others investigated the region's botany, geology, zoology and pale-ontology. But not the people.

Today, scholars believe that five different native peoples roamed the channels and steppes and forests of the Magellan region for about 12,000 years. The Tehuelche or Aonikenk, the Ona or Selknam, and the Haush were landbound nomads, the lighters of the fires that gave Tierra de Fuego its name. The Yagan or Yamaná and the Alacaluf or Kaweshkar lived in their canoes and along the shellfish-rich coasts of southern Chile.

Between 1946 and 1953, a French anthropologist named Joseph Emperaire studied what remained of those who had survived thousands of years in the harsh landscape of the far south. The neat labels on his photographs give us names, ages and, inevitably, each year of death. The faces that gaze at or away from the camera are filled with sadness, anguish, shock. Only one round-faced, wide-mouthed mother smiles, while her son stares doubtfully past the photographer. Three naked children stand quietly on ice. Men and women weave baskets, mend shoes, shape canoes. They pose on beaches, the decks of ships, rock. Often they stand naked on snow.

In the "Mayorino Borgatello" Salesian Regional Museum of Punta Arenas, the Ona, Tehuelche and Yamaná have been reduced to a row of grinning skulls. An enormous calcium butterfly about two metres wide and several metres high, a whale's vertebra, sits quietly in a corner. Shell necklaces, arrowheads of crystal and blue, green and brown glass line shelves, along with eggs, birds and bones and something that looks like powdered chocolate used for drinks. To the original inhabitants, every animal had a meaning. The *telel*, or flamenco, was the north-east wind, the black-necked swan, an evil spirit.

Enshrined in the dusty rooms of the Salesian museum is one attempt, by missionaries of that religious order, to "integrate" surviving natives. The mission was supposed to solve a problem: the Ona, who had contin-ued to hunt and roam Tierra del Fuego as they had for thousands of years. The ranchers were upset about the Ona eating their sheep.

In *Los Nómades del Mar*, published in 1963, Joseph Emperaire writes that "Some of the Ona were massacred by order of the large sheep ranching companies ... The number of Ona who were murdered will never be known. Half a century later, persons and interests still at work maintain a wall of protective silence with respect to how these fortunes [were made]. However many Ona were massacred, be it a hundred or a thousand, this continues to be a monstrous blemish ..."

In 1890, the Chilean government gave some Salesian missionaries from Italy a twenty-year concession to Dawson Island to educate, care for and adapt indigenous people.

For five years, the Ona resisted all attempts at capture and only the Alacaluf people lived in the mission. Everyone over nine worked. The Punta Arenas museum is full of embroidered landscapes, rugs, altar cloths and lace "sewn by the Indians". A mission child has scrawled in round hand, a hundred times across a notebook's pages: "With the sweat of your brow, you will eat bread. With the sweat of your brow. ..."

"It's evident that putting the Ona on Dawson, in a sort of deportation camp, outside their territory and above all, out of contact with precisely those people they were supposed to be becoming adapted to, was at the very least a regrettable error," writes Emperaire. "They were trying to incorporate a native group into Chilean society and yet, paradoxically, they handed them over to Italian missionaries who had just arrived from Europe, who spoke no Spanish and used Italian among themselves."

A life-sized tableaux in the museum shows a textile workshop on Dawson Island. Perhaps a lightbulb has burned out, because night crowds the window behind a heavy, thick-jawed priest, while the other window offers pale daylight. A nun stands on his left. Between them, a native woman wearing a stiff leather skirt spins by a stove. For some reason, the lower half of her body is unfinished concrete. Near the foreground, another native woman hunches over her sewing.

The door stands ajar, revealing a luminous grey sky and the stark silhouette of a towering wooden cross. Around the cross, men and women stand with fallen arms, barely drawn faces, all turned toward the door, as if it led somewhere.

"In September 1911, the Dawson Mission's contract expired," says Emperaire. "The Mission had had over 500 Indians in its last years. The cemetery, which had to be enlarged several times, contained 800 graves."

Outside the museum, Punta Arenas hums with wind, sunlight defies clouds, printed and hand-lettered signs offer tours to the area's main sights. The tourist season is at its height, as are prices. Traditional sheep farms are thriving. Modern oil rigs dot the straits and salmon breeding has brought new income. In the Magellan Lawn Tennis Club a sign declares: "You can be a gentlemen without being a tennis player, but you can't be a tennis player without being a gentleman."

We pass a monument to the workers on the sheep ranches, the *ovejeros*. Later, Carlos Vega digs up a newspaper from October 18, 1944, and an interview with the sculptor's model.

"The Monument suggests the precise fate of our class," says Abel Oyarzún. "To shepherd a wealth that will never be ours, toward an unreachable destiny. Do you realize? The monument's shepherd walks forever, but never gets anywhere. The wind beats away at him implacably and he, we, just keep walking. Sometimes, life gets ahead of us and we enter the paths of the beyond."

Later, we take a bus, 254 kilometres northward through the rolling southern steppe to Puerto Natales. Until a few years ago, Puerto Natales was a sleepy, frontier town; now it too is a bustling tourist centre, offering services to travellers heading on to the area's main attraction, the Torres del Paine National Park.

We visit the park briefly, discovering a harsh landscape of rattling tufts of grass, prickly shrubs and a strange circle of mountains whose peaks of bare rock look like the mortal thrust of a gigantic bull's horns goring the sky. The colours are delicate and ever changing, straw, dark green and deep purples, the sky itself like the inside of a mussel's shell, deep blue, multiple shades of pearl.

At ground level, the soft earth offers infinite, delicate beauty, sterile turquoise lakes, purple clover, Queen Anne's lace, daisies, brightly coloured stones.

Returning to Puerto Natales we cross a grassy desert whose windmoulded cliffs look as though they're covered with fine beige velvet. A rider, small as the speck of dust on a camera lens, barely moves through the vast wasteland. The Andean peaks shrink behind us to the northeast, forming an ethereal blue silhouette.

How not to believe in the lost City of the Caesars? As the sun sets I can see splendid towers and turrets, unbreachable walls, ice glinting on the roofs of snowy palaces. I can almost hear the long strands of violin notes, see the golden brocades and marble floors, walls of polished wood.

Puerto Natales is buzzing with the activity of a seemingly endless collection of tour companies, offering visits to the park, local villages, the cave of the Milodon (mentioned in Bruce Chatwin's writings) and a boat ride to some glaciers, slightly north of Puerto Natales. We opt for the boat ride and head for the local dock at eight o'clock one morning. Heavy clouds stain sky and water a deep slate, with blue and purple highlights. Then the rising sun spills a sparkling, almost liquid light out of the clouds, over the water, splashing the black-necked swans and the old wooden fishing boats with brilliant yellows and reds and blues.

Our Captain herds a motley assortment of about fifty middle-aged and young sightseers from Chile, Argentina, the United States and Europe onto the boat. People with tickets get to sit in the cabin, while latecomers must choose between the windy, rainy deck or the airless hold. All morning, we chug northward along a channel, visiting cliffs where hundreds of cormorants nest, passing a small family of seals, one large and blond, another oily black, a third grey, with four pups virtually invisible against wet rock. Once these shores were covered with huge populations of seals, visited by whales, but this wealth quickly disappeared after the Europeans' arrival.

The cliffs tower above us like skyscrapers at night, solid black with foam spurting from their sides as if they had been wounded. A cobweb of green weaves itself across the grey hardness of rock, hanging downward as if to plot with the ocean below. Ahead, huge chunks of grey rock become mountains, black and implacable in the middle distance, the chain continuing its humped progress, visual echoes of each other, until the last one looks as if it is made of mist and the mist is more real than anything close by.

The Chono, the Alacaluf, the Yamaná canoed these fjords and bays, rocked children to sleep to the steady slap, whoosh, splash of their bailing, a quiet, constant song to keep you alert, to relive history or keep the coals alight in the bottom of their canoes made of boards sewn together to form the *dalca* or tree trunks hollowed out to create the *piragua*. Darwin would have passed through here, staring at these cliffs as I do, the slap of canvas and the creak of rigging in his ears. Like walls, the bluffs close in upon us, limit our course until we feel trapped by the ocean, condemned to navigate forever a small craft shut out by the stoney fortress of America.

Sylvia plants herself firmly before the window where her silhouette, pear-shaped and full, is plain to see and says, "I'm twenty-five kilos lighter than a few months ago. Then, I was extra large; now, I'm large. I told the doctor, at this rate, by the time I hit the box I'll be a medium!" She laughs merrily and I join in. She looks a long way from the grave, with wavy dark hair framing a smooth freckled face, lit by expressive blue eyes. Energetic, a four-year-old grandson in her care, she's on her way to fifty, although I would have believed her fifteen years younger.

She pulls out a fat folder, and unscrolls a rolled-up drawing. Before me to left and right, craggy mountains slope down into a small valley whose rounded edges are broken by a square palisade enclosing a series of neat, rectangular buildings. Internal fences separate some of these rectangles from others. Small wooden cubes perch on the mountain sides, surveying the scene. There's nowhere to escape to, as the Alacaluf and Ona learned a century before. And in 1974, the guards on Dawson Island held standard Army issue machine-guns. Punishment, torture, harsh physical labour and poor food became the rule, again.

Sylvia's folder contains other items: smooth, soapstone-like carvings like some I've already seen, hidden in my mother-in-law's drawers, brought out and polished like medals on special occasions. A clown face, drawn in bright colours, crisp clear lines. A birthday present, the inscription says, for Alexandra's ninth, signed by "the last ten prisoners".

We're visiting Sylvia and her husband, Daniel, an old friend of Patricio's family, back in Punta Arenas. An artist produced this sketch of the concentration camp on Dawson Island from Daniel's description. Patricio's father and both brothers were also imprisoned on the island, as were former ministers of the Popular Unity government, in a separate compound. Patricio hasn't seen Daniel in twenty years; this visit is almost a pilgrimage. They'll stay up all night, drinking, remembering.

For some Chileans, Patricio and Daniel will be remembering things that didn't happen. Before we left Santiago, a friend and colleague, who has studied the military, tells me of admirals who swear there was no torture, no harassment, no mistreatment on Dawson Island.

But in Aristoteles España's book, *El Sur de la Memoria (South of Memory),* the people of Punta Arenas tell another story. So does Patricio's brother Fernando. On October 10, 1973, he was sitting in an organic chemistry class at the university, when a group of civilians entered, shouting his name. "I stood up, I answered, that's me, and I thought to myself, my turn's come," he says. For ten weeks a team of thirty torturers routinely questioned Fernando and hundreds of others held in local regiments. The first time he was tortured was the worst, "it was so brutal because it was so unexpected.

"They took me from my cell around midnight. It was very cold, I was blindfolded, and they took me to Catalina Bay. All the way there, they threatened me with what they were going to do and when we arrive, they make me take off my clothes and start to beat me, without asking any questions. I think there are five, six. They make me run a lot. They throw me on the sand. I'm blindfolded. Naked. They make me run into the water, without my knowing it. They pull me shivering from the water. They throw me beside the fire, which burns. They make me put on wet clothes. They make me take them off. They make me run, while I run, they shoot. They put me in a box and ask about weapons. When I know nothing, they start all over again.

"Once I couldn't walk, they had to pull me out, because I'd been so beaten and was so cold. They started with electrical torture. I realized they were drunk."

Magda Ruiz, who was seventeen at the time of her 1973 arrest, speaks of being tortured on the Los Robles ranch belonging to the Menéndez Behetys, a branch of the family that donated the museum to the town, as does Ricardo Andrade, a student leader at the time of the coup. "We were staked out, that is tied down with some stakes like crosses. Beside me they were raping two companions, whose names I won't mention."

They made Marcos Barticevich sit naked on a broom handle, like "Caupolicán" [a Mapuche chief who died slowly as the stake passed all the way through his body]. Jorge Arriagada was unconscious for three days and blue from the blows. "We improvised some bottles to feed him milk and keep him alive. They'd broken his jaw, but wouldn't allow him to be taken to hospital."

José Cárcamo Barría, who had been National President of the Oil-workers Union, has never forgotten that "around seven every evening, a group of workers from [the] Tres Puentes [ranch] would watch and laugh as we were mistreated."

José Edison, who was sixteen, tells how a corporal who was making fun of his small size asked him what he wanted to be when he grew up: "And I said, 'what choice have I got but to work as an electrical transformer. After all the current that's gone through me, I can stand any voltage!'

We almost died of laughter ..."

Fernando remembers reaching Dawson Island in one of the last "shipments" of prisoners. "I knew my father and brother were prisoners but I hadn't seen them. They had managed to position themselves by the barbed wire and I saw them. It was a very special moment."

Life on the island settled into a routine of sorts that started with exercise and cleanup in the morning, followed by a light breakfast and hours of hard labour in the freezing cold, without proper clothes or tools. The food made him so sick that he eventually ended up in the hospital.

"I was tortured for singing a song by Victor Jara on Christmas Eve," he says. The island produced "an enormous feeling of isolation, of intense cold, wind, few sunny days. It was a prison, surrounded by water, with absolutely no escape. One of the great things was to be allowed to carve the stones: it relieved the stress and for some brought in some income." Until one day an officer decided that the implements used were dangerous weapons and carving was banned.

In June 1974, Fernando and another dozen or so of his companions were tried for "illegal association", although they had all joined the Communist Party when it was legal. He traded his sentence for exile, in Ireland, and did not return to rebuild his life in Chile until 1990.

Nelson Reyes, a student activist, was among the last of those to leave Dawson Island, in September 1974. A sergeant-major called him over and said: 'Let's close this once and for all, so that never in history will it open again,' and I noticed he was crying," says Reyes. "I gave him a carved stone, and he wished us luck.

On our last day Carlos Vega shows us a video interview with Virginia Choquintel, the last surviving Selknam/Ona. She was brought up by nuns in a mission similar to Dawson Island. Life meant study, prayer, work. At twelve years old, she started work as a housekeeper. She speaks no Selknam. "They offered to teach me the language and history, but I had problems," she says, admitting to nervousness and a little too much wine. She cries when asked how she feels about not having children. When she dies, she says, she doesn't want to be shut up in a box.

As we leave, Carlos slips a book into my hand. It is by a naval captain, Captain Humberto Palamara, an intelligence expert, and it's called *Etica y los Servicios de Inteligencia* (*Ethics and Intelligence Services*).

The book reveals no secrets, but lays out the ground rules for intelligence activities, within a framework of respect for human rights. It condemns political assassinations, disappearances, military participation in politics.

In the hustle and rush and thrust for progress that seem to characterize Punta Arenas, it seems absurd to worry about lost native lives or tortured leftists. Turn the page, forget the past is the message. Why care?

One reason to care leaps out from the pages of a Yamaná / English dictionary prepared in the 1890s, by Thomas Bridges, an English missionary. The word *Yamaná* means, or meant: "Human, pertaining to mankind, alive, sensible, not dead, sound living, in good health, humane, human, intelligible, that which can be well understood as human language."

With the suffix, *Yamana-ias,* it becomes "An honest or human hand, that is, a hand that is not like the talons of a hawk that robs and kills, such as becomes a man."

Yamana-n-kona, means "To be well on board, to be alive and well, to recover on board." *Yamana-n-gamata,* "He who was the least likely to die, dying, and the one expected to die, recovering. To escape, survive, when the rest die or are killed."

In our narrow, dogged way, we keep wiping off the face of the earth, not only native peoples, but whole ways of life that differ from high-tech, urban, market-driven societies. Life is so rushed and pressured that there is no time to think, so we eliminate those who do think, those who give us something to think about, those whose memory will later pain us when we think of them. What is a tourist, I have often wondered. Someone with no commitment to the place she or he visits, who expects to take something away while giving nothing in return? As European cultures have destroyed or imprisoned nomadic cultures, we have lost our ability to travel, to interact. We have become tourists in our own lives.

But they come back to haunt us. Many have tried to warn us across time. Wilfred Owen wrote from World War I, "I am the enemy you killed, my friend."

When we climb aboard our plane, we find ourselves surrounded by a crowd of youthful Naval officers in full uniform. Chile has been ruled by an elected government for three years now, so I try some conversation with the cadet sitting beside me but his tight jaw discourages this.

Later, my eyes stray across the aisle to a green-eyed officer, quietly reading a *Poetic Anthology* by the left-wing Uruguayan writer Mario

Benedetti. Benedetti's poems were often set to music and sung at *peñas* and protests during the regime. I wonder what sort of man this Naval officer is, reading poetry, that poet, in public. Is something changing? Will this officer rise to certain heights, reach certain conclusions, give certain orders which could save lives, change the course of a "war", or the history of a people?

I wish I knew the answers. Within a week of our return to Santiago, Naval intelligence raided Carlos Vegas's print shop, seized the computer diskettes and erased the hard-drive files. They confiscated all printed copies of Captain Palamara's book, *Ethics and Intelligence Services,* all, that is, except the one that sits on my desk, as I write this today.

The Navy expelled Captain Palamara and a military court martial tried him for revealing state secrets. He was convicted.

WHERE WE START FROM

SANTIAGO 1994–1995

What we call the beginning is often the end
And to make an end is to make a beginning.
The end is where we start from.
T.S. ELIOT, "LITTLE GIDDING"

I'm half-asleep when Cecilia phones to say that Ignacio is dead. This is expected, as if he'd been suffering from a long illness. I drop by to pick up the undertaker, who drives a long white fifties' station wagon, wears a long white dress and carries a long white package which I assume contains the tools of her trade. When we reach Cecilia's house, I hug Cecilia who gestures toward the room where Ignacio's body lies, and takes the undertaker off, to wash her hands I suppose.

The room is small and narrow and he's covered by a grey blanket. Ignacio is curled up on his side, a clear plastic tube still attached to one hand. As I watch, he seems to sigh or shudder. I look around for Cecilia, but another low murmur draws my eyes back to Ignacio. He rolls over and I'm thinking, absurdly, I didn't know dead people did this sort of thing, I hope it doesn't create too many problems for the undertaker. Then he sits up, plants his feet on the floor and tries very unsteadily to stand up. He manages, with my help, and together we stagger into the central hall. I think I call Cecilia, although the words have nothing to do with the emotion that shoots through me like a fountain.

343

He half sits, half collapses on the floor and all I can do is hug him, as the words "You're alive!" fly around my head in endless circles. I can feel the solid warmth of him, the blood pulsing under the skin. At this moment I don't know what he looks like, whether he's injured or scarred, indelibly, subtly marked. I only know the warmth of that hug, life's fingers supporting his bones, massaging his muscles, making him part of what is ours again. I can feel Adriana and Cecilia hugging too. For a moment I look into Cecilia's brimming eyes.

And then I wake up, confused, believing the dream at first, then piecing things together. But Ignacio wasn't disappeared, I think. He was shot and his body returned to his family after the usual red tape and examination at the morgue. I stood by his coffin before the funeral, watched his motionless face under glass.

Why have I suddenly tried to dream him back to life? Did I somehow dare to think that by defeating the regime and piecing a shattered society back together, the Chileans would bring back the dead and the disappeared? And if I feel this way about a friend, how must the survivors feel about their lost relatives as the years drag on, judges investigate, indict, only to watch the military courts take over, release all suspects and close their cases?

It's September and spring one more time. The yellow clusters of flowers on the *aromo* trees scatter again their fragrance on the breeze, the plum trees are blooming just as Pablo Neruda's poem had predicted and just as the University Cultural Association, ACU, had celebrated so often during its brief existence. Children are flying tissue kites and circuses are back in town. We go and see the National Circus of Cuba — no one is stopped at the border any more — at the large circular theatre that once housed the ACU's largest festivals. Nowadays, acrobats and ropewalkers and trapeze artists use safety nets, unlike a few years ago, when every performance could end in death.

September 11th rolls by and with it the twentieth anniversary of the coup. While many, from President Aylwin on down, have burned themselves at the stake of self-criticism, rising from the ashes with new commitments to democracy and human rights, others, like Corbalán, still "jailed" in an Army unit somewhere awaiting trial and Alejandro Medina, teaching as ever at the Army's academic institute, recognize no errors, ignore inconvenient facts. As marchers mourn and protest the coup,

Carabineros charge again and again with the water cannon, running over and killing an elderly man. A youth is shot and dies and demonstrators accuse the police of firing at peaceful crowds.

More than twenty years after the coup, there are 1,149 painstakingly documented cases of men, women and even children who disappeared after arrest, never to be heard from again. Another 600 cases are under investigation. Only 86 of the disappeared have ever been found; families received a parcel of bones and a few articles of clothing. Excavations in Patio 29 of the General Cemetery took place finally, in 1992. Anthropologists and specialists are still trying to piece together the faces of more than a hundred people, familiar to someone, somewhere.

The government has been reduced to haggling over interpretations of the 1978 Amnesty Law, in spite of electoral promises to repeal it. The military's supporters insist that the Amnesty law prevents investigation, while Aylwin and a growing number of judges interpret it to mean investigation first, then amnesty for specifically identified guilty persons.

Faced with trials in cases of alleged corruption and human rights violations, the Army has threatened violent action on several occasions. On May 28, 1993, the Army surrounded its downtown headquarters with élite troops in full battle gear, carrying grenade launchers and bazookas, just across from President Aylwin's offices in the Moneda, the same building that was bombed during the coup. The move, the Army said later, was simply to provide adequate security during a regular meeting of top generals. The truth, as the negotiations between Aylwin and Pinochet that followed clearly indicated, was that the Army had said jump.

Secret conversations between General Pinochet and Aylwin led to a series of unprecedented meetings between Aylwin and all generals of the Army, Navy, Airforce and the Carabineros. On August 3, 1993, Aylwin officially presented his proposals in a televised address to the country. They consisted of appointing ten to fifteen special judges dedicated exclusively to the investigation and resolution of roughly two hundred cases, involving no more than twenty military officers in active service. A special clause would also have guaranteed greater secrecy for those who testify and measures to protect the identity of the accused.

"We have information that there are military officers who would like to give information," said Andrés Domínguez, a lawyer working for the foundation that replaced the Rettig Commission, carrying on its work of investigating and ensuring some financial restitution for victims' relatives.

Domínguez, who has dedicated his life to human rights issues, believed the new measures would be a step in the right direction. In spite of the Army's pressures, the government did not extend the 1978 Amnesty, nor did it agree to draft a "Final Solution" Law formally closing all violations cases. In his 1993 speech to announce the agreement with the military, Aylwin said that "profound judicial and moral convictions" made either of these alternatives, used by authorities in Argentina and Uruguay, unacceptable.

"The Army's latest manoeuvre [on May 28, 1993] was a serious tactical error," Domínguez told me. "There we saw an Army using a criteria of low-intensity conflict to intervene in national politics. Even the right-wing parties didn't accept this, because if you accept it in this area, later you'll have to accept it in relation to the national budget, or because they don't like a particular Minister.

"The first time the Army acted this way [in December 1990] it had the support of the rest of the military. This time it acted alone. Next time it will be one isolated unit, rather than the whole Army."

Domínguez called the government's plan a "strategy to resolve this problem without sacrificing its principles" and predicted that Chileans would debate human rights for decades to come. But while some, like Domínguez, were relieved that the government avoided a Final Solution Law or an extension of the Amnesty Law, the relatives of the disappeared were bitterly disappointed. Police arrested twenty-four and two women received fractures, when they marched on the presidential palace in protest. Aylwin's proposals failed when he tried to push them through Congress, where both Pinochet's supporters and Socialist Party members voted them down.

"We feel that the government is trying to close these cases without uncovering the truth or doing justice," said Sola Sierra, whose husband, Waldo Pizarro is among the disappeared. "They've given the courts a green light to apply the Amnesty Law as quickly as possible."

At the end of 1994, two separate Appeals Court decisions ruled that, since Chile had signed the International Declaration of Human Rights, these international obligations, enshrined in the 1980 Constitution, took precedence over national laws and could, in effect, overthrow the Amnesty Law. However, the president of the Supreme Court, Marco Aburto, told me in an interview that the Supreme Court would probably uphold this principle but, since the Amnesty Law predated the Constitution, it should remain unchanged.

Throughout 1994 and 1995, relatives of the dead and human rights lawyers continued the Sisyphean task of attempting to achieve justice through the Chilean court system. Increasingly, judges applied Aylwin's interpretation of the Amnesty Law, that is, first they investigated and, once the culprits were clearly identified, specific people received the amnesty. The broadcast of the final appeals in the Letelier case on national television, to record ratings, in January 1995, effectively turned the case into a trial of the actions of the secret police during the military government. The final verdict, from five Supreme Court Justices, was expected for later in the year, with many, from the family's lawyers on down, seeing the Letelier case as the only possibility that those responsible for the repression will ever really see the inside of a jail.

In over eight years of public opinion surveys, CERC, the Centre for Studying Contemporary Reality, one of Chile's most prestigious public opinion pollsters, has found that two of every five Chileans fear the military may take power again.

The situation grew worse after May 31, 1995, when the Supreme Court convicted General Manuel Contreras, former head of the military government's secret police, and Brigadier Pedro Espinoza, his second-in-command, for the 1976 murder of Orlando Letelier and Ronni Moffit, in Washington. The Court sentenced them to seven and six years respectively in jail.

A government poll found that as many as 87 per cent of Chileans thought the officers should go to jail, but General Contreras disagreed and convinced enough of the Army's top echelon, including former military president General Augusto Pinochet, to produce a major conflict with the civilian government.

In June, the Army activated troops in three cities and moved General Contreras to the Naval Hospital in Talcahuano, south of Santiago. General Pinochet had initially said that the Army would respect the Supreme Court's decision, but later called the trial "unfair" and "stained by acute politicization". Tension slackened when the Army retired Brigadier Espinoza and packed him off to jail. But the conflict flared again in July, as newspapers published reports that Chile was on the verge of a coup. Media reported that General Pinochet had demanded an end to trials involving military officers in human rights violations and a full pardon for General Contreras, although the government later denied that the Army had asked for the pardon.

While General Contreras remained in the Naval Hospital, fighting transfer to prison through appeals, the Army pressured behind the scenes and publicly, even demonstrating outside the jail where Brigadier Espinoza is the sole inmate, to force the government to either strengthen the 1978 Amnesty Law or create a special law to end trials forever.

Camilo Escalona, president of the Socialist Party (SP), which opposed ending trials, said, "We're not going to change our position, even with a pistol held to our chests."

Public opinion polls showed three out of four people opposed the Amnesty Law. When the pro-military proposal hit the floor in Congress in August, Jorge Schaulsohn, president of the Party for Democracy, which belongs to the government, said, "There will never be an agreement for a law to end human rights trials," and added, "The right can cackle on all it wants and organize a major political offensive to drag the country into one, but their efforts will fail."

Nevertheless, by month's end, President Frei had presented three laws to Congress: to "speed up" human rights trials; to allow elected authorities to appoint and remove top generals; and to change constitutional and electoral laws, which currently allow pro-military political parties, with only 30 per cent of the national vote, to control Congress.

By 1995, government studies had concluded that 1.4 million Chileans, of a total population of 12 million, suffered from the abuse or loss of a family member as a result of the 1973 military coup. In August 1995, nurse Patricia Herrera, who coordinated a Health Ministry program for survivors in Santiago's west end, told me that the Army's support for Contreras had accentuated the traumas remaining from the military period.

"Since the Contreras conviction the number of consultations has skyrocketed," nurse Herrera said. Many health professionals blamed the regime at least partially for Chile's extraordinarily high rates of depression, tranquilizer dependency and other mental health disorders.

Although the rumours that Chile's Army might be planning a coup faded almost as quickly as they became known, the acute tensions between the civilian government and Chile's former military rulers remain, threatening the country's hard-won political stability and economic growth.

For the relatives of the regime's many other, less well known victims, even the conviction of General Manuel Contreras and General Pedro Espinoza, the director and assistant director of the secret police, the DINA, during the worst years of the repression, is simply not enough. They insist they want the Amnesty Law repealed. They want to know what happened to each and every one of their dead. They need to receive the remains and give them a decent burial. Chile is a profoundly Catholic country and the families cannot complete the mourning cycle, return to life themselves, without first completing the rites of death.

A quiet square in the General Cemetery awaits them. Beneath it, an empty crypt. Plaques bearing close to a thousand names cover one wall, along with the inscription from a poem by Raúl Zurita: "All my love remains here, fastened to these rocks, the sea and the mountains."

In a paper on "Justice and Human Rights Education During the Chilean Transition", a Chilean psychologist, Ana Cecilia Vergara, and her father, Jorge Vergara, a philosopher, trace the roots of human rights violations in Chile, starting from "the foundational violence of a conquest that was resisted by the Mapuche people" which "generated a long war that continued intermittently throughout the colonial period".

They recall how the first strikes of a nascent union movement in the early twenties met with fierce repression, exemplified by the massacre at the Santa María School in Iquique, where more than two hundred people died when the Army opened fire on a compact mass of men, women and children, unarmed strikers from the nitrate mines. Between 1932 and 1973, "almost all governments used selective and exemplary repression against peasants, *pobladores* and workers' issue-based union movements. In every case, the media published accusations and parliamentarian investigations were carried out, but those responsible for ordering and executing these actions went unpunished. Thus a tradition of impunity in relation to human rights violations was established and society became accustomed to such practices.

"The specificity of repression in comparison with other forms of control lies in its violent and traumatic nature," they remind us. "One part of this violence arises from the direct damage to the victims and the other stems from the psychological impact generated by human rights violations."

Just as Kika González concluded that the soldiers who had forced rats into her genitals were "depraved", society in general reacted by transforming the repressor into an abnormal person, labelling agents crazy, perverted or inhuman. Thus, "the rationality of their actions as part of a formal and bureaucratic machine could be denied. This also produced a sense of distance that reduced the shock of (re)discovering so much 'cruelty' in the human being."

The Vergaras note that first a minority of Chileans criticized the regime's violations. Then, as the 1982 recession created serious economic problems, "dissidents swelled to a majority and most of the country assumed the defence of human rights." However, in the mid-eighties, the opposition divided with the majority supporting the Christian Democratic-led Democratic Alliance, while the minority identified with left-wing parties and social sectors opposed to negotiating with the military government. Alliance leaders adopted what they called a pragmatic position, which held that truth, justice and restitution could not be completely achieved.

The Vergaras believe that as the opposition's political élite, rallying behind the Christian Democrats in the Alianza Democrática, gradually abandoned human rights demands, "it increasingly accepted the neoliberal economic model and the regime's political model as summarized by the 1980 Constitution ... Until the mid-eighties, the [vision of democracy] was broadly shared by most of the country and had a profoundly ethical and utopian base in which human rights were declared the fundamental nucleus. It was thought that a democratic transition without truth, justice and restitution for those suffering rights violations was not possible and would not guarantee the future."

However, as traditional parties gathered strength, political practice returned to old, élitist patterns and rights violations "ceased to be viewed as a grave problem to be resolved through the combined efforts of the entire nation". With the advent of elected government in 1990, General Pinochet's continued presence as head of the Army and the 1978 Amnesty Law saw courts forced to handle cases of human rights violations as if they were ordinary kidnappings or murders. The idea of state terrorism as "a rational system administered by a hierarchy" faded, and those responsible for violations faced trial, when they faced trial at all, as members of illicit organizations that happened to include members of the military and civilian state employees.

But "the fact that the Government does not play a direct role in most trials reinforces the image that these are problems limited to particular cases and victims," say the Vergaras. Within this framework, the way violations damage the whole fabric of society can more easily be ignored.

"The threshold of what is 'dreadful' or inconceivable has been reduced even further," they observe, "betraying the expectation that democracy would bring with it a return of people's ability to be shocked. Not even all rights-related murders are included in the public category of 'dreadful crimes', but only those whose extreme cruelty shocked the public. Thus the connection between the defence of human rights and the struggle to transform society according to more humanistic values is weakened: instead, we worry about relatively isolated events of a criminal nature."

Government spokesmen and the media tend to present justice as a threat, rather than an essential condition of democratic stability. Forgetting the recent past is presented as positive, while "to inform and testify about the damage it produced is to 'open wounds', closed by the passing of time. To want to judge those responsible is to 'seek vengeance', to be incapable of forgiveness," they add.

"Conflicts are perceived as destabilizing and threatening for a fragile peace and an unstable consensus, in spite of explicit statements that democracy is stable and solid. Chilean society seems unable to control its own aggression. In this context, political élites present themselves as responsible for 'taking charge' paternalistically, in order to protect democracy."

For the Vergaras, "impunity and insufficient truth and restitution are not simply the 'necessary price' for a difficult transition, but rather constitute factors functional to it. That is, these are conditions that favour the reproduction of existing power-structures."

Impunity smooths a return to the appearance of normalcy in relations between the elected civilian government and the powerful Armed Forces, even though the elected government clearly does not control the military or the police, as occurs in most democracies. Politicians reach agreements by avoiding the basic issues of what happened, who was responsible, and how they should be punished. The democratic government's inability to seriously challenge the political structures inherited from the regime limits its ability to make changes in other areas of Chilean society: the civil service, social programs, taxation levels, judicial reforms, and so on.

For the Vergaras, genuine reconciliation would require an explicit analysis of the trauma experienced during dictatorship, along with justice for the victims of state abuses. In contrast, what has happened in Chile "has some important similarities to the experience in postwar Germany. As is known, the judgements of human rights violations, along with the full clarification of what happened and restitution to victims, were both paralysed for international and internal political reasons."

They quote Theodor Adorno who warned that "the important issue is that unless the historic reasons that led to this disaster are explored 'unless the work of balancing our accounts with the past is taken seriously 'we run the risk of repeating the same historic cycle, as a 'compulsion for collective repetition'."

"Memory," they conclude, "exercises a therapeutic function that attacks the mechanisms of denial of a past that nevertheless continues to rule the present." The existence of this "open wound will maintain potential undercurrents of violence, injustice, oppression and misunderstanding in our society," even if Chile can avoid a return to overt authoritarian government. It will also "reinforce the sense that democracy is powerless when faced with the tangible power of forceful minorities ... It will constitute the end of the utopia of 'a homeland good for all' (Aylwin), and mean the success of the authoritarian project of 'changing Chileans' mentality' (Pinochet)."

It is September again and spring, one more time, four years after I wrote about Santiago's General Cemetery, not thinking it would become this journey. The interviews are done. The travelling is over, at least for now. I've finally finished reading the Rettig Commission Report, two volumes, nine hundred pages of names and lives torn from each other, an attempt to paste them back together. General Medina's vision, Captain Vergara's, Cecilia's, Laura Novoa's differ on many points. As much as was possible, the Rettig Commission brought visions together, the voices of people from different sides of the conflict that made the military government possible. It did what it could to produce a common, coherent version of what happened.

The Commission also tried to record what it meant for people, even years later, to have lost in this way someone they loved, as democracy slowly tried to put down roots again. "My twenty-five-year-old son loved his military career, he felt proud to serve his country," one mother told the Commission. Another said, "I had to explain to my five-year-old son that just as men kill animals and flowers, sometimes they also kill other men." And many others. "I still don't understand, he died when an extremist group attacked, while he was on guard duty in a *población*." "I discovered he'd died through the Civil Registry, no one had ever told us anything." "When my son turned seventeen, he had such a need to know where his father was, I said: Son, go to the cemetery, pick the most abandoned grave, care for it and visit it as if it were your father." "They gave me a closed and sealed coffin. I had to bury it alone in an hour. What if it wasn't him?" "Each time I see a madman or a vagabond in the street, I think he could be my husband; or that he may be somewhere, in those conditions." "They told me that he smoked his last cigarette with his hands in cuffs, trembling, he couldn't inhale it. It's that image that won't let me die in peace." "I want them to give him back to me, alive. I speak to him, it's as if I saw him. My mother's heart tells me he is somewhere." "I forgot how to live a normal life." "Each time I eat something good, I wonder if he might not be hungry." "Even if it's useless, I need to know why they killed him; what happened; what he was doing; how they found him. Anything that could let my mind rest." "We had nothing left, we'd lost everything in the search for him. A fortune-teller came to the Hotel Araucano, my mother sold the last thing we had and went with my little brother. She said not to worry, that my brother would be home for Christmas. My mother called us all, fixed the best meal ... he didn't come at Christmas or ever." "I was married on August 8th, by October 5th I was a widow." "My mom and dad never knew when I came or went. From eight years old on, I was alone. I felt I didn't exist for anyone. I don't blame them. Now that I have children, if I had to see one of them tortured and then go with him before he faced a firing squad, I couldn't be normal either." "Neither of my two daughters could have children after what they did to them when they searched our house." "When my brother disappeared, my father aged, went crazy. He died walking along the roads, shouting his son's name." "For a while I hated my husband, for having been involved in politics they killed him. I blamed him, I felt he'd chosen his ideals over his family." "Hatred is like a sickness and when you have hatred inside, you can't live." "Everyone was afraid and I'm still afraid. I think the whole town knows that we've come to talk to the Commission. Do you think that after this, something will happen to us?" "I'm afraid to wear a uniform, all I want is to retire." "My son was tortured in the study while I slept. How could my father's instinct not have warned me?" "They came by my house and asked for some chains to put on the truck's wheels; after, we heard that with these same chains they tied their hands." "I had been married such a short time, I never could fall in love again. I've tried to rebuild my life and I can't." "My brother-in-law was killed in Santiago, my husband was a prisoner on Dawson Island. In the meantime, we had to work and try to keep on living as if nothing had happened." "My daughter left home because she thinks we're all cowards because we still have relations with those responsible for my oldest son's death. It's because my other sons entered the Armed Forces." "When he disappeared I was left with eight small children. I got the three youngest a babysitter, my sister took the girl and the others stayed with neighbours and relatives. I worked as a live-in maid and each time I had anything I bought toasted flour and milk to take my children." "My brother went in voluntarily. Afterward we found his remains buried in a ravine." "After they took him away I spent ten days awake caring for my two babies, sure they'd come and take them away too." "The newspapers said they were terrorists and with that, everyone justified it." "The [agents] said he was still alive. When my mother remarried, they harassed her saying how could she do that when her husband was still alive." "I received this letter from the Commander of the Regiment. In it he says that if my husband doesn't return, in spite of being released, I must review in my conscience if we were really a good couple or not and if he might not have left with someone else. Now his body's appeared in a common grave." "After eight months they gave us a body that, according to the morgue, belonged to my father. We sat up all night with him. Just before the burial, Carabineros came with an order, saying there'd been a mistake, the body belonged to some other family. We had to give it back." "After they shot my father, the director called me and said: you're the daughter of a criminal and because of that you can't teach in this city any longer." "At school they told me, your dad was killed for being a politician. They called us the 'little extremists'." "We were a black night, we brought evil portents." "We are Christians. We believe in resurrection." "I never thought this could happen in Chile." "It scares me to think I'm as human as they are." "I don't want them killed the way they killed my father, but I don't want them loose on the streets either." "I don't want to have to hide any more. I want to shout to the world with pride that my father died for his ideals. I want society to understand once and for all that the children of the executed aren't a public danger." "I'm willing to pardon, but I need to know who I'm pardoning. If they would speak out, recognize what they did, they would give us a chance to pardon. It would be more noble if they did it like that." "I don't want vengeance, just peace, I want to rest and for that I need to know the truth."

I'm a fast reader, but it has taken me two-and-a-half years to finish the Rettig Commission Report. I find it too painful, end up trapped in a labyrinth of mourning the dead of others. This has been the hardest part about writ-

ing this book, the part I most wanted to leave behind, the most necessary part. Afterward I find my notes have poured out into Spanish: *If we
aren't capable of mourning these deaths and channelling this into real
help for survivors, then we have learned nothing, we are cowards, who
now that we have escaped the pit don't care about those we left behind.*

This will be the last time I have to revisit their voices filled with pain,
this will be my last attempt at exorcism, not because I have succeeded in
driving their histories out of my own flesh, but because I have learned,
at last, to live with them, to let them flow quietly on, part of my own
beating heart, my energy, my life.

I thought, as the new government assumed power, and all around me
I watched people leap into positions from which they had been barred
for the past seventeen years, as I heard new versions of recent history
that contradicted or distorted or made me doubt my own, as I tried to
lose the habits acquired under the regime, the caution on the streets,
mistrust, the endless rounds on protest nights, the phone ringing at three
a.m., I thought that it would be possible to travel, to think and write a
book and through that process shed the armoured patterns of that life. A
great many of those habits *have* disappeared, worn away by the gentle
friction of reality. The hardest to lose have been the illusions I har-
boured, the ones that sometimes were all that kept me going, the vague
image of some normalcy, once lost, on its way to being found.

Years have passed since Pinochet handed over part of his power,
since the first coup anniversary in democracy. Many cases are under
judicial investigation, many officers in active service or retirement have
stepped before the judges. Police have hunted down and the courts have
extradited civilian torturers who hid abroad for years. The military
courts have challenged many civilian judges' right to try these trials.
And won many. And promptly closed those trials down. A court order
bans coverage of Ignacio's and others cases. There is still hope that at
least in some key, symbolic cases, judges will find the courage to con-
vict, the Supreme Court to uphold, society to punish.

General Mario Morales Mondaca has come and gone as fifth in the
Carabineros' command, stunned, he said, when a judge indicted a group
of Carabineros for kidnapping and cutting the throats of three men in
March 1985. For Mario Morales Mondaca rushing between the classes he
taught and the courses he studied and reorganizing the accounting systems of his institution, it was relatively easy to avoid a confrontation

with his conscience. But, he admitted when we talked, he wouldn't necessarily have enjoyed the position he held, if it had been offered to him ten years earlier, when the regime was at its height.

"They say that after the battle, everyone's a general. If I look back at what was strictly Carabineros' area, undoubtedly I would have liked the possibilities of this position, but the truth is I don't know if in the conditions at that time I would have acted the same way as I do now. The conditions, the reality, the country's situation are different. Carabineros is a professional institution, and we always try to have our people act with professionalism and that means respect for human rights.

"I think I've been pretty successful in my professional life, and there's one thing I always tell my students, and one of the things that really makes me happy, is that after twenty-five years of service I never hit anybody, I never hit a prisoner and I never insulted a prisoner. And my concept of Carabineros has always been like this."

What have I learned? That an authoritarian government, sustained by repressive "security" services and widespread human rights violations, can exist in the most "civilized", the most "cultured" of countries. That the capacity for cruelty and murder lives within each one of us, to varying degrees. "Human" is no synonym for "humane", although we often comfort ourselves with that illusion. Perhaps it is at least an ideal to be sought. Dictators are both born and made: the raw material, the potential exists, in many ordinary people. So does the ability to stop them. Dictators and those they dictate to are an integral part of each other. One cannot exist alone.

When I set out on this book, I thought that by exploring this recent past, dissecting it, pinning the pieces to the page, I could somehow free myself. But exorcism cannot be carried out alone. No one alone can eliminate a Pinochet, or Franco, or Hitler, or whatever name he has, next time he bursts through the pages of history to threaten our present. It took Chile's political leaders sixteen years to figure this out, to bury their differences and unite around a single strategy. Today that unity is frayed but holds, as they try to build a new and somehow fairer society, using the flawed, imperfect materials provided by the past.

The Rettig Commission recommended five elemental changes that it believed were necessary if rights violations were not to occur again: the incorporation of international human rights norms into national legislation; judicial reforms to ensure the system guarantees respect for essential rights; a full commitment on the part of Armed Forces and police forces to functioning within a framework of respect for human rights; the creation of an institution that promotes and protects human rights; changes to constitutional, penal and trial norms to better protect human rights.

Every society has the potential for "modernization" in the sense that the sociologist Eugenio Tironi used it in *The Silences of the Revolution,* as "an emancipation from the factors which limit individuals and societies from guiding their own destinies". He adds: "to live and to grow, every society needs to be capable of integrating past and present, change and continuity, 'winners' and 'losers'."

Economic balance is essential because without it political stability is difficult. For individuals to foreswear murder as a solution, for social groups to foreswear violence as a political tool, they must have something important to lose. Tolerance of those who are different is also crucial. And a commitment to resolving conflicts through dialogue, within agreed upon rules that clearly exclude resorting to the use of weapons.

The Rettig Commission called democracy "the world in which members of society know how to meet each other and resolve everyone's problems in peace and freedom."

Sitting on the front steps of our house, enjoying the way the spring sun dapples through the budding filigree of acacia leaves, Camilo kicking a football against the low wall, I remember a conversation with my friend Joan in Toronto. We were talking about Canada's constitutional wrangling, all the little things that people worry about, that seem so small compared to the problems of people elsewhere in the world. "We worry about the minor details, who takes priority, whose rights are secondary to whose," she said. For those of us who don't manage huge business interests, who don't wield the power of a large and rich national government with a well-equipped Army, our salvation may be in the so-called petty details, small daily actions like voting, minor clauses, the individual judge who masters her or his own terror and makes the lonely decision.

Day by day, we teach our children not to throw stones at ducklings breeding on a nearby pond, not to bite each other, fight over their toys. To break down a lifetime's teaching, military instructors, the secret police also work collectively. Racism contributes to their task, that process of setting aside one group of human beings as somehow less than human, therefore less worthy of humane treatment. But not even the teachers know where those skills will lead each student, not to mention the society that taught him that they are worthwhile, even heroic.

We tend to believe, as L.P. Hartley once said, that "The past is a foreign country: they do things differently there." But in our headlong dash toward the future we sometimes end up running backward. Before we know it, the landscape has shifted, the meaning of our own words has been stolen away from us and replaced by substitutes we only partly understand, the soft humming of a folksong has become the drum-driven march of a military band. I have tried to sketch a rough map of this other land, for my children, for my friends, for the people who've shared their hopes and horrors with me, for you who read this. You can follow its designs or avoid them. In this we have a choice.

Ignacio's was among the thousands of cases that the Rettig Commission investigated in 1990. They concluded that he "had been executed by secret agents, belonging to the CNI", and that his death was "a violation of human rights". This made Cecilia and Lucien eligible for governmental compensation. With this assistance, they can live in the house they might have bought if Ignacio had still been alive. They have access to health care and Lucien will receive educational assistance throughout his schooling.

The Aylwin government's — and Ignacio's — legacy to Cecilia and Lucien is this modest, reasonably secure future, in a comfortable house she could never have bought alone. Month by month, she will pay off the mortgage with "Ignacio's money". Something endures of the impetuous man who needed to cuddle and be cuddled like a child, the dogmatic father who refused to let his son play with toy guns, the political activist whose convictions led him to fight the armed with arms. Ignacio remains an orderly grave in the General Cemetery, the moments we shared with him, the arguments, the wine, a ghost that steals through our dreams bringing unwarranted moments of hope.

Nothing can bring back the person he might have become, the arguments, the meals, the future we might have shared with him, alive. My dream was only a dream. Whatever his weaknesses or our strengths, our fumbling mistakes or his glowing moments of truth, he is just one of the many who were lost, the price we have paid and will have to keep paying, whether we have learned anything or not.

TIMELINE

The hunger for social change which swept most of the world during the sixties in Chile led to the electoral victory of the Christian Democrat Eduardo Frei (President of Chile, 1964-1970) on a platform of "Revolution in Liberty" and then, in 1970, when the Christian Democrats failed to fulfill their promises, the world's first election of a socialist government, formed by the Popular Unity coalition and led by a former Health Minister, Dr. Salvador Allende.

During its three short years in government, the Popular Unity successfully implemented many of the policies in its program, including the nationalization of Chile's most important resource industry, copper, by a unanimous vote of Congress. This move and other UP policies fed the already bitter opposition to it among US corporations (ITT, Kennecott, Noranda) and the Nixon administration. On September 11, 1973, the military, backed by the United States and a small band of Chile's monied families, seized power in what became one of the world's most brutal military coups.

In the years that followed, thousands were killed, hundreds disappeared, hundreds of thousands were forced into exile, and the entire country sank into a fear-fed inertia which at its worst made it look as thought the military might rule Chile for as long as it liked. Chilean exiles started to set up house (albeit temporary, with their bags always packed under beds, eternally prepared to depart for Chile at a moment's notice) in countries around the world and images of the mothers, sisters and daughters of the disappeared, defying police armed with bludgeons and automatic weapons, began to fill television screens and newspaper pages.

Led by the same copper workers who contributed to the destabilization of the Allende government in the seventies, massive national protests against the military regime exploded in May 1983 and continued on an almost monthly basis for two years. That movement won the support of the poor and middle-class professionals alike. The protest movement was essentially peaceful, but with Communist Party declarations supporting a policy of popular rebellion and the creation of a powerful armed resistance group, the Manuel Rodríguez Patriotic Front, the number of violent confrontation between students, *pobladores* and other groups on one hand, and police and soldiers on the other, increased.

In 1983, opposition leaders proposed a great national consensus around the voluntary resignation of the military regime, followed by a provisional government, the election of a Constituent Assembly, an emergency economic plan, the immediate restitution of social and political rights. The military government rejected the proposal and 18,000 troops occupied the city of Santiago for the next protest day. In 1985, the government again rejected a smaller proposal, the National Accord, in spite of the intervention of the Roman Catholic Church.

In 1986, doctors joined union, professional, native, women and student organizations to form the Assembly of Civil Society, which co-ordinated a two-day strike against the regime. The next year, when political parties became more active, the profile of union and other social organizations dropped. By 1988, Chile's fractious political parties had united to oppose the military in a plebiscite that was intended to rubber-stamp General Augusto Pinochet's presidency for eight more years.

The regime's opposition gambled on a longshot and won – in October 1988 they defeated General Pinochet in the plebiscite, and a year later their candidate, Patricio Aylwin, was elected president of Chile.

1810–1818 ~ Chileans battle for independence from Spain, under the leadership of General Bernardo O'Higgins and others.

January 1, 1818 ~ Chileans declare independence continuing a war with Spain that culminates in Chilean victory on August 20, 1820. Independence is traditionally celebrated on September 18th.

1831–1861 ~ Chile "authoritarian republic".

1861–1891 ~ Chile "liberal republic".

1879 ~ Chile goes to war with Peru and Bolivia.

October 1883 ~ Chile wins war with Peru.

April 1884 ~ Chile declares truce with Bolivia.

1880–1882 ~ Last major uprising of the Mapuche people, native to southern Chile, who maintained an independent territory throughout the Spanish Conquest.

Late 1880's ~ National policy encourages settlers of Swiss and German Catholic origin to establish farms and towns in southern Chile.

1891 ~ A brief civil war is fought by supporters of the reform-oriented national president and the conservative Congress, culminating in the suicide of President José Balmaceda.

1891–1924 ~ Chile "parliamentarian republic".

1925 ~ Chilean constitution establishes the country as a democratic republic, but chaos ensues as Arturo Alessandri, Carlos Ibáñez and other political *caudillos* (chiefs) battle for power. This constitution is not actually implemented until the early thirties.

July 26, 1931 ~ Ibáñez regime ends, defeated by popular protests on the streets and economic disaster in the wake of the 1929 crash.

1932 ~ A ten-day "Socialist Republic", led by Marmaduque Grove, goes down to defeat. Arturo Alessandri returns to power in the October elections.

September 3, 1948 ~ Gabriel González Videla's "Law for Defence of Democracy" outlaws the Communist Party which helped put him into power. He uses the northern village of Pisagua as a concentration camp for the first time, under Captain Augusto Pinochet.

September 4, 1958 ~ Jorge Alessandri crawls to power with 33,416 more votes than Salvador Allende.

1959 ~ Cuban revolution.

1960 ~ Clandestine intervention in Chilean politics by the United States, particularly the CIA, starts to grow exponentially.

1961 ~ A German religious group buys a farm and starts to build Colonia Dignidad, near Linares, southern Chile.

September 4, 1964 ~ Eduardo Frei, Sr., Christian democrat, elected president.

April 1966 ~ Scandal breaks out around a controversial German colony in southern Chile, Colonia Dignidad.

September 4, 1970 ~ Dr. Salvador Allende, elected president at the head of a coalition of left-wing political parties, including the Communist, Socialist, Christian Left and MAPU (a small Christian Left group that broke away from the Christian Democrats) parties. Allende wins with 1,075,616 votes to Alessandri's 1,036,278, only 39,338 more than his opponent.

September 12, 1970 ~ Agustín Edwards, owner of the *El Mercurio* newspaper chain that includes most of Chile's daily newspapers, meets with Henry Kissinger and John Mitchell in the morning; that afternoon, Nixon tells CIA and other advisers they must do everything possible to stop Allende's assuming power.

October 22, 1970 ~ General René Schneider, Army Commander-in-Chief killed during kidnapping, widely interpreted as a failed attempt to prevent Allende's taking power.

October 24, 1970 ~ Congress ratifies Allende's election, officially making him president of Chile.

November 3, 1970 ~ Allende officially becomes president of Chile.

July 1971 ~ Congress votes unanimously to nationalize Chile's copper companies.

September 11, 1973 ~ The Chilean military, led by Army Commander-in-Chief General Augusto Pinochet, seizes power in what supporters refer to as a "pronouncement"; the rest of the world calls it a *coup d'etat*. The four members of the governing Junta are: Augusto Pinochet Ugarte, Army Commander-in-Chief; José Merino Castro, Admiral, Navy Commander-in-Chief; Gustavo Leigh Guzmán, General, Air Force Commander-in-Chief; César Mendoza Durán, General, Director General of Carabineros. In 1978, a showdown with General Pinochet forced General Leigh out of the Junta and General Fernando Matthei replaced him. In 1985, General Mendoza was forced to retire, in the wake of scandal over the crime of the *degollados*, the kidnapping and killing of three Communist Party members, including a highly respected leader of the Teachers' Association and a human rights worker with the Catholic Church.

June 18, 1974 ~ The Dirección de Inteligencia Nacional, DINA, the military regime's first political police, officially created.

September 30, 1974 ~ A car bomb kills former Army Commander-in-Chief, General Carlos Prats and his wife, Sofía Cuthbert, in Buenos Aires, Argentina.

1975 ~ Australia detained wheat shipments to Chile to protest human rights violations. England made the renegotiation of Chile's foreign debt conditional to improvement in the political situations, particularly regarding human rights violations.

April 4, 1975 ~ Creation of Fasic, an interchurch committee for providing assistance to victims of human rights violations.

October 6, 1975 ~ A gunman fires on Bernardo Leighton, a Christian Democrat who has become prominent and crucial to the opposition's attempts to unify their efforts, and his wife, Ana Fresno, in Rome, Italy. They survive, but with crippling injuries.

January 1, 1976 ~ Vicaría de la Solidaridad, the Catholic Church's human rights department, created.

September 21, 1976 ~ A car bomb kills Orlando Letelier, a former Minister of Defence in the Allende government, who is also making significant strides toward unifying the fractured opposition to the military regime, and Ronni Moffit, in Washington, DC.

November 1976 ~ The number of detainees is significantly reduced, with the closure of most concentration camps set up after the coup.

August 13, 1977 ~ The DINA, Dirección de Inteligencia Nacional, the first secret police, headed by General Manuel Contreras, was dissolved and replaced by the CNI, Central Nacional de Informaciones.

January 4, 1978 ~ The military government holds its first plebiscite. Chileans are offered the chance to vote yes or no, to Chile. 75% vote in favour, "against the foreign attack". There are no voters' lists, no guarantees of basic civil rights.

April 19, 1978 ~ Decree Law 2,191, published in the Official Newspaper, declares an amnesty for the authors of crimes committed during the State of Siege, between September 11, 1973 and March 10, 1978, along with their accomplices. For years, the Amnesty Law prevented investigation of the crimes involving human rights violations. Under the Aylwin government, 1990-1994, a new interpretation becomes more widely accepted by society and many judges. Using this interpretation, courts investigate crimes involving human rights violations, up to the point where the culprit has been identified.

Amnesty then applies.

December 10, 1978 ~ The Chilean Human Rights Commission is formed.

June 4, 1979 ~ Kidnapping of Rodrigo Anfruns, the grandson of an Army officer, who fell afoul of the regime, when he investigated crime in the Post Office. The boy was found dead ten days later.

1980 ~ After five years of study, the Council of State presents a new draft constitution to the military Junta, which approves the text, and calls for its approval in a plebiscite, via decree Law 3,464, published in the Official Newspaper on August 11, 1980. The plebiscite is held a month later, on September 11th, the seventh anniversary of the coup. Again, the plebiscite was held during a combined State of Siege and State of Emergency, with civil liberties severely curtailed, no voters' lists and little opportunity for an opposition campaign. In one sweep, the plebiscite approves the Constitution and makes General Pinochet officially the President of Chile. The Constitution goes into effect on March 11, 1981. Twenty-nine transitional articles suspend many of the Constitution's general provisions. Most of these remain in effect until March 11, 1990.

January 1981 ~ The Communist Party's leaders in exile announce their support for armed struggle against the military regime.

1981 ~ Ongoing newspaper coverage of the Viña del Mar psychopath. Luis Gubler arrested March 3, 1982, then released. Two Carabineros are arrested.

February 25, 1982 ~ Tucapel Jiménez, a union leader who initially supported the military government, but then changed his mind and started to unify the opposition against it, is found murdered in his taxi.

May 11, 1983 ~ The Copper Workers Confederation organizes the first National Protest against the military regime. Two people killed.

June 14, 1983 ~ Second National protest against the military government. Copper workers strike, mass firings, leaders jailed. Four people killed.

July 12, 1983 ~ Third National Protest against the military government. Two killed.

August 11-12, 1983 ~ Fourth National Protest against the military government. 18,000 troops occupy Santiago. Twenty-five killed.

September 7, 1983 ~ CNI operations result in the killing of activists belonging to the Left Revolutionary Movement, MIR, in houses on Fuente Ovejuna and Janequeo streets, in Santiago. The name of CNI agent, Alvaro Corbalán, is mentioned in the press.

September 8, 1983 ~ Fifth National protest against the military government. Alianza Democrática is formed with Christian democratic leadership. Nine killed.

September 11, 1983 ~ Two die in conflicts related to the coup anniversary.

October 11-13, 1983 ~ Sixth National Protest against the military government. Four people die.

December 5, 1983 ~ A worker dies during protests against the government's Minimal Employment Programs.

December 14, 1983 ~ A nineteen-year-old youth is killed during a local protest on Santiago's southside.

March 27, 1984 ~ National Protest against the military government. Eleven die. The Rettig Commission considered this the eighth protest; Cavallo, Salazar and Sepulveda count it as the seventh.

May 1, 1984 ~ A sixteen-year-old high-school student dies during anti-government demonstrations to mark May Day.

May 11, 1984 ~ Ninth National Protest against the military government. An eighteen-year-old high-school student dies after being shot in the head from a passing car.

August 9, 1984 ~ A Day for Life, including anti-government protests, leaves one person dead.

August 14, 1984 ~ A local demonstration, in the Santiago *población*, Lo Hermida, leaves a seventeen-year-old dead.

September 4-5, 1984 ~ Eight die during the Tenth National Protest against the military government, among them, Father Andre Jarlan, a priest in the Santiago community La Victoria, shot and killed while reading his bible in the second-floor mission house.

September 27, 1984 ~ One man dies during an attempted land occupation in Puente Alto, a suburb of Santiago.

October 29-30, 1984 ~ A two-day National Work Stoppage, leaves nine dead. The former concentration camp in Pisagua, in northern Chile, is reopened and 239 prisoners taken during military operations in Santiago are held there.

January 26, 1985 ~ Two Carabineros face firing squad for their role in the psychopath's killings in Viña del Mar.

March 30, 1985 ~ Manuel Guerrero, a teachers' association leader, José Manuel Parada, a human rights worker, and Santiago Nattino, a little-known commercial artist, are kidnapped by DICOMCAR, the Carabineros' intelligence service. Their lifeless bodies are found a day later, their throats deeply slashed. Four others killed in "confrontations".

April 9, 1985 ~ During student demonstrations an eighteen-year-old university student, Oscar Fuentes, is shot and killed by Carabineros.

August 2, 1985 ~ General Cesar Mendoza resigns from the Junta, during demonstrations against the Carabineros for their role in the killing of the three men on March 30, 1985.

August 9, 1985 ~ During a second day for Life three people are killed.

August 25, 1985 ~ Parties forming the Democratic Alliance and the National Party sign the National Accord for Democracy, under the auspices of the Roman Catholic Church, in the hopes of beginning negotiations with the military government.

September 4, 1985 ~ Ten people die during another National Day of Protest against the military government.

November 6, 1985 ~ Four die during a Day for Social Mobilization.

December 1985 ~ Military government's rejection of National Accord (first expressed in news release, September 3) clear, as is its intention to carry on in power.

May 20 , 1986 ~ A university student dies during a Day for Democracy, organized to coincide with the International Assembly of Parliamentarians being held in downtown Santiago. The military take control of the city, cordoning off the entire downtown area.

June 13, 1986 ~ A young woman dies during student demonstrations against the municipalization of the education system.

July 2-3, 1986 ~ Two-day national strike called by the National Assembly of Civil Society. Two young people burned alive by military patrol; Carmen Gloria Quintana survives; Rodrigo Rojas dies. Seven others are killed.

August 1986 ~ Arsenals of the Manuel Rodríguez Patriotic Front discovered in Northern Chile.

September 4-5, 1986 ~ Two people die during anti-government demonstrations.

September 7, 1986 ~ Manuel Rodríguez Patriotic Front ambushes General Pinochet's convoy, killing five escorts. Unidentified civilians kidnap and shoot four regime opponents; a fifth escapes.

September 11, 1986 ~ A young woman dies in the Santiago community of La Victoria during demonstrations to mark the anniversary of the 1973 military coup.

March 6, 1987 ~ A newspaper boy is killed during International Women's Day demonstrations.

April 2, 1987 ~ One dies during an illegal land occupation.

April 1987 ~ Pope John Paul II visits Chile.

June 11-12, 1987 ~ Twelve people belonging to the Manuel Rodríguez Patriotic Front are killed during a military operation known as the Corpus Christi killings, Operación Albania or Elefante.

September 1, 1987 ~ The Autonomous Manuel Rodríguez Patriotic Front kidnaps Colonel Carlos Carreño. In December they release him in Brazil.

October 7, 1987 ~ Four people die during a National Work Stoppage.

March 8, 1988 ~ A coal miner dies during demonstrations to mark International Women's day.

April 28, 1988 ~ A student dies during a demonstration against the government's education policies.

August 30-31, 1988 ~ Four die during demonstrations against General Pinochet's nomination as the sole candidate for the plebiscite to be held in October 1988.

October 5, 1988 ~ General Pinochet loses the plebiscite, receiving 43.01% of the vote; 54.71% voted no. Two people die during demonstrations to mark the plebiscite.

December 14, 1989 ~ Patricio Alywin, Christian democrat, wins the elections with 55.17% of the vote, compared to Hernán Büchi (Pinochet's former Finance Minister) with 29.4% and Francisco Errázuriz with 15.43%. Aylwin heads a coalition including Christian Democrats, Socialists, Radicals, Party for Democracy (PPD), the Humanist and Green political parties.

December 15, 1989 ~ An Aylwin supporter dies, after being beaten by Carabineros.

December 29, 1989 ~ One person dies during anti-government demonstrations.

March 11, 1990 ~ Pinochet officially hands over power to Patricio Aylwin. The transition to democracy begins.

April 25, 1990 ~ The National Commission for Truth and Reconciliation, usually known by the name of its chairman as the Rettig Commission, begins investigations of human rights violations that ended in death or disappearance between September 11, 1973 and March 11, 1990.

December 19, 1990 ~ Army moves troops through Santiago, in clear threat to Aylwin government.

February 8, 1991 ~ The Rettig Commission presents its report on rights violations during the military government to President Aylwin.

May 28, 1993 ~ Troops in full battle gear surround the Army's headquarters, across the street from the Moneda, the presidential palace and the main seat of government. Aylwin initiates secret negotiation with Pinochet and produces the "Aylwin Law", which would eventually put a deadline on human rights-related court proceedings, among other provisions, but it fails in Congress due to opposition from the right and Socialist Party deputies in August 1993.

September 11, 1993 ~ Twentieth anniversary of the military coup.

March 1994-2000 ~ The second government of the Concertación for Democracy, the same coalition formed toward the end of the military regime, now headed by Eduardo Frei, Jr., a Christian democrat businessman, son of the president who ruled Chile 1964-1970, is sworn in, with Frei occupying the presidency. The Concertación for Democracy, now minus the Humanist and Green Parties, holds the majority in the House of Deputies, but is matched by supporters of the former military government in the Senate, thanks to eight Senators, appointed during the Pinochet government, under the provisions of the 1980 Constitution.

GLOSSARY OF
ACRONYMS AND NAMES

ACU. Agrupación Cultural Universitaria. University Cultural Association that brought together university faculty, students and staff, with an interest in culture and the arts, between 1978 and 1985.

Allende, Dr. Salvador. A member of the Chilean Socialist Party, Allende was health minister in Pedro Aguirre Cerda's government (1938-1941) and served several terms as a Senator. He ran for election four times, starting in 1952, and won by a small margin, of 1,075,616 votes over Jorge Alessandri's 1,036,278 votes, in the elections on September 4, 1970. On October 24, 1970, Congress ratified his election and he assumed power on November 3, 1970. He was overthrown and died when the military seized power on September 11, 1973.

Análisis. A monthly, at times weekly, magazine, known for its opposition to the military government, that began to publish in 1977 and folded in the early nineties.

Apsi. A publication that started as a newsletter and became a weekly magazine, known for its opposition to the military government, published from 1976 to the present.

Avanzada Nacional. An ultra-conservative political movement, formed by former CNI agent, Alvaro Corbalán, to try to build mass, popular support for the military government, during the late eighties, particularly around the time of the plebiscite on October 5, 1988.

campesino. A rural agricultural worker, often with no land of her or his own.

Carabineros. Chile's uniformed regular police. They are a nationally organized police force with a military-style hierarchy that includes a Commander-in-Chief, who participated in the four-man military Junta that ruled Chile from 1973 to 1990.

Cauce. A magazine that became known for both its opposition to the military government and its investigative journalism.

Central National de Informaciones. See CNI

CEPI. Comisión Especial de Pueblos Indígenas. Special Commission on Indigenous Peoples, created by the Aylwin government in 1990, to recommend new laws governing Chile's estimated 900,000 indigenous peoples of Mapuche, Aymara, Rapa Nui, Selknam, Yamana and other origins.

Christian Democrats. DC, Democracia Cristiana.

CNI. Central Nacional de Informaciones. The military intelligence group responsible directly to General Augusto Pinochet that carried out many of the military government's more violent operations. Created to replace the DINA in 1978; dissolved in January 1990, with most of its members being passed on to the DINE, the Army's Intelligence department.

Comisión Nacional de Pueblos Indígenas. See CEPI.

Comisión Nacional de Verdad y Reconciliación. See National Commission for Truth and Reconcilition.

Comisión Rettig. See National Commission for Truth and Reconciliation.

Comité Pro Paz. See Pro Paz Committee.

Corbalán, Julio. Also known as Alvaro Valenzuela. Real name, Alvaro Corbalán.

CORFO. Corporación de Fomento (Corportion for Industrial Development). Created by the government of Pedro Aguirre Cerda (1938-1941), to develop Chile's industrial base.

Corporación de Fomento. See CORFO.

Corporation for Industrial Development. See CORFO.

CP. Communist Party.

DC. Democracia Cristiana, Christian Democrats.

DINA. Dirección de Inteligencia Nacional. The military government's first centralized secret police agency. Decree Law No. 521 officially created the Dirección de Inteligencia Nacional, DINA, on June 18, 1974. Articles 9, 10 and 11 of the law were secret. They gave the governing military Junta the power to involve Army, Navy and Air Force Intelligence departments in DINA or DINA-type activities, including searches and arrests. Colonel Manuel Contreras, today a retired Army General, headed the DINA, which was dissolved and replaced by the CNI (see above) on August 13, 1977.

DINE. Dirección de Inteligencia del Ejército. The Army's Intelligence Department. It inherited many of the DINA's resources and personnel after the return of elected government.

Dirección de Inteligencia del Ejército. See DINE.

Dirección de Inteligencia Nacional. See DINA.

Don, doña, as in *don* Fanor or *doña* Delicias. A slightly archaic expression, used before a first name to show respect, much like Mr. in English, still used to mark social differences and other nuances in the Chilean countryside.

El Mercurio. Santiago's main daily newspaper, owned by the powerful Edwards family. It played an important role in the CIA's and other US agencies' campaigns to destabilize the Allende government between 1970 and 1973. Agustín Edwards owns *Las Ultimas Noticias* and *La Segunda* as well.

FPMR. See Frente Patriótico Manuel Rodriguez.

Frei Montalva, Eduardo. Elected president of Chile, on September 4, 1964 with 1,409,012 votes versus Allende's 977,902 and Julio Duran's 125,233, with support from women voters being decisive (Frei received 756,117 votes compared to Allende's 384,132 votes from women). He governed Chile from 1964-1970 and began the process of nationalizing Chilean copper properties, called the

Chileanization of Copper, that culminated in full nationalization, under the Allende government (1970-1973). Christian Democrat, died 1982.

Frei Ruiz-Tagle, Eduardo. Chilean President 1995-. Christian Democrat, son of previous president.

Frente Autónomo. See Frente Patriótico Manuel Rodríguez.

Frente Manuel Rodríguez. See Frente Patriótico Manuel Rodríguez.

Frente Patriótico Manuel Rodríguez. (Manuel Rodríguez Patriotic Front), the FPMR. An armed resistance group, formed primarily by members of the Chilean Communist Party, in early 1981, to oppose the military government. The Frente was responsible for a massive arms smuggling operation, discovered in August 1986 and for ambushing General Pinochet's convoy, in September 1986, killing five of his escort. In the late eighties, the Communist Party leadership withdrew its support for the Frente, and most of that organization continued to function under the name "Frente Autónomo", Autonomous Front. Between 1987 and 1990, the leadership was gradually decimated or returned to civilian life. The pro-military government media always referred to the FPMR as Frente Manuel Rodríguez.

Front. See Frente Patriótico Manuel Rodríguez.

General Bernardo O'Higgins. The illegitimate son of an Irishman and a member of Chile's southern gentry, he led the Chileans' war for independence and ruled the country for a short period after its victory, from 1817 to 1823, creating Chile's first Constitution in 1818. Political battling eventually forced him to abdicate on January 28, 1823 and he died without returning to Chile in 1842.

Hoy. A monthly magazine published by the Christian Democrats, from 1977 on.

Investigaciones. Investigations, Chile's civilian detective police force.

Investigations. See Investigaciones.

JAP. Juntas de Abastecimiento Popular. In 1971, the Popular Unity created a local food control and distribution system, known as the JAPs (pronounced haps). It consisted of a network of thousands of local committees, which helped government inspectors detect violations of price controls; they also distributed food baskets to poor and working-class neighbourhoods in response to the hoarding and speculation that followed the implementation of price controls. These JAPs quickly became a major point of conflict between the Allende government and its conservative opponents, including many officers in the Armed Forces.

La Cutufa. An illegal finance company associated with the CNI and Alvaro Corbalán.

La Epoca. One of two opposition daily newspapers to come to life during the last years of military government. Ownership was originally dominated by several prominent members of the Christian Democratic Party. *Copesa.* A consortium that also controls *La Tercera,* another Santiago daily, eventually bought into *La Epoca.*

La Moneda. See The Moneda.

La Nación. The government-run newspaper, a mouthpiece for the military government, 1973-1990, it has tried to maintain a more even course since then.

La Segunda. A daily, afternoon, newspaper, owned by *El Mercurio.*

La Tercera. A daily, morning newspaper.

Las Ultimas Noticias. A daily, morning, newspaper, owned by *El Mercurio.*

Law for Permanent Defence of Democracy. Passed in 1948 by the government of Gabriel González Videla (1946-1952), outlawed the Communist Party, striking almost 30,000 voters from an electoral register of 631,257 people. The law allowed authorities to purge the union movement, forced elected Communist Party members underground and resulted in massive firings of CP workers. Thousands were expelled from company-controlled towns and camps in the copper mines.

Left Revolutionary Movement. See MIR.

MIR. Movimiento de Izquierda Revolucionaria. A left-wing group inspired by the Cuban revolution, which opposed the Popular Unity coalition's program of profound social change through the ballot box. The MIR went underground in 1968, organizing armed actions in preparation for taking political power through insurrection.

Mercurio. See *El Mercurio.*

Moneda. See The Moneda.

National Commission for Truth and Reconciliation. Also known as the Rettig Commission. President Patricio Aylwin set it up in April 1990, to investigate human rights violations leading to death or disappearance that occurred between 1973 and 1990. Its members were Raul Rettig, Jose Luis Cea, Monica Jiménez, Ricardo Martin, Laura Novoa, Gonzalo Vial Correa, Jose Zalaquett. Its secretary was Jorge Correa Sutil.

National Renovation party. See Renovación Nacional.

Nguillatún. One of the Mapuche's most important ceremonies.

O'Higgins, Bernardo. See General Bernardo O'Higgins.

OS-7. Carabineros special élite, investigations section.

Partido Socialista. Socialist Party.

PC, Partido Comunista. Communist Party.

población, poblaciones. Poor working-class areas that surround most Chilean cities.

pobladores. The people who live in *poblaciones.*

Popular Unity, Unidad Popular. The coalition of Communist, Socialist, MAPU, Christian Left parties that supported Salvador Allende in the 1970 elections. Central to its program was the belief that revolutionary changes could be brought about via electoral politics.

Portales, Diego. One of Pinochet's heroes and models, Diego Portales was the key leader of the Conservative movement which dominated Chilean politics in the 1830s. Minister of the Interior, Foreign Affairs, the Army and the Navy, during the government of José Joaquín Prieto Vial (1831-1841), Portales created a Chilean Republic based on strong central government. He was gunned down in July 1838.

Pro Paz Committee. An ecumenical committee set up by Protestant and Catholic clergy, along with the Jewish Rabbi, to monitor human rights violations after the coup. It was forced to dissolve at the end of 1975. *Chile La Memoria Prohibida* details much of its history (see Books).

Radio Chilena. A key opposition radio station, owned largely by the Diocese of Santiago.

Radio Cooperativa. A key opposition radio station, controlled by the Christian Democrats.

Rettig Commission. See National Commission for Truth and Reconciliation.

RN, Renovación Nacional. National Renovation, a conservative, pro-regime political party, with some shades of disagreement and distancing from the old-line, military leaders.

Socialist Party. Partido Socialista.

Solidaridad. A magazine published by the Catholic Church's human rights department, the Vicaría de Solidaridad. *Chile La Memoria Prohibida* details much of its history (see Books).

SP. Socialist Party.

Special Commission on Indigenous Peoples. See CEPI.

Surnames. In Spanish, every one has two surnames, the first being the father's and the second the mother's, with the mother's being dropped in each succeeding generation and the father's, that is, the second last, being the one used most. I have tried to use primarily the name and (father's) surname throughout the book, but in some cases, where the name is extremely common, have used both surnames to distinguish between different personages.

TEMU. A musical workshop and group developed by students in the Faculty of Economics at the University of Chile during the late seventies.

The Moneda. Chile's presidential palace, the official seat of government.

TVN, Televisión Nacional or National Television. Chile's state-owned, national television channel.

TVUC. The Catholic University's television channel.

UDI, Unión Demócrata Independiente. The Independent Democratic Union. The most pro-Pinochet of the conservative political parties.

Unidad Popular. See UP.

UP, Unidad Popular. A coalition of socialists, communists and other left-wing parties, led by Dr. Salvador Allende, that reached power with his election to the presidency in 1970.

Valenzuela, Alvaro. Also known as Julio Corbalán. Real name, Alvaro Corbalán.

Vicaría de la Solidaridad. Sometimes referred to as the Vicariate of Solidarity, the Catholic Church's human rights department, set up in an old two-storey building beside the Santiago Cathedral on the Plaza de Armas. Cardinal Raúl Silva Henríquez took the decision to create the Vicariate in late 1975, after the Pro Paz Committee, an ecumenical group concerned about human rights violations, found it impossible to go on functioning, due to harassment from the military government.

Vicariate of Solidarity. See Vicaría de la Solidaridad.

SOURCES

Throughout the writing of this book I have relied heavily on my own files of clippings from the Chilean newspapers El Mercurio, Las Ultimas Noticias, La Epoca *and* La Nación *and from the magazines* Análisis, Apsi, Cauce, Hoy, *along with my experiences directly covering some of the events described herein, supplemented by personal interviews and conversations with political and military leaders, as well as people who are less well known. There haven't been many books published in English on Chile, but those that have, have been extraordinarily useful and I would like to extend special thanks to their authors, Harold Blakemore, Pamela Constable and Arturo Valenzuela, John Dinges and Saul Landau, Brian Loveman, Julio Faundez and Patricia Politzer.*

BOOKS

Arriagada, Genaro. *El Pensamiento Político de los militares.* 2d ed. Santiago: Editorial Aconcagua, 1986.

Arriagada, Genaro. *La Política Militar de Pinochet.* Santiago, 1985.

Atria, Rodrigo, Eugenio Ahumada, Javier Luis Egaña, Augusto Góngora, Carmen Quesney, Gustavo Saball and Gustavo Villalobos. *Chile La Memoria Prohibida (Chile: The Forbidden Memory).* 3 vols. Santiago: Pehuén Editores, 1989.

Bardini, Roberto, Miguel Bonasso and Laura Restrepo. *Operación Príncipe.* México City: Planeta, 1988.

Bengoa, José. *Historia del Pueblo Mapuche.* 2d ed. Santiago: Ediciones Sur, 1987.

Bengoa, José. *Quinquén, 100 Años de Historia Pehuenche.* Santiago: Ediciones ChileAmérica CESOC, 1992.

Blakemore, Harold. *Gobierno Chileno y Salitre Inglés 1886-1896: Balmaceda y el Norte.* Santiago: Editorial Andrés Bello, 1977. (Original English title: *British Nitrates and Chilean Politics 1886-1896: Balmaceda and North,* published by The Athlone Press, University of London 1974.)

Blancpain, Jean-Pierre. *Los Alemanes en Chile (1816-1945).* Santiago: Hachette, Ediciones Pedagógicas Chilenas, 1985. (Original title in French: *Les Allemands au Chili.)*

Bridges, Thomas. *Yamana-English Dictionary.* Ed. Dr. Ferdinand Hestermann and Dr. Martin Gusinde. Reprint: Buenos Aires: Azgier y Urruty Publicaciones, 1987.

Cárdenas, Renato and Carlos Trujillo. *Caguach, Isla de la Devoción.* Santiago: Editorial LAR, 1986.

Cárdenas, Renato, Dante Montiel Vera and Catherine Grace Hall. *Los Chono y los Veliche de Chiloé.* Santiago: Ediciones Olimpho, 1993.

Cayuela, José. *Laura Soto: Una Dama de Lila y Negro.* Santiago: Editorial Planeta, 1991.

Church Commission. *Covert Action in Chile, 1963-1973.* Staff Report of the Select Committee to Study Governmental Operations with Respect to Intelligence Activities. US Senate. December 18, 1975. (See Cristián Opaso below.)

Cohen, Gregory. *El Mercenario Ad Honorem.* Santiago: Arte Cien, 1991.

Constable, Pamela and Arturo Valenzuela. *A Nation of Enemies: Chile Under Pinochet.* New York: WW Norton & Company, 1991.

Cor:ea, Raquel and Elizabeth Subercaseaux. *Ego Sum Pinochet.* Santiago: Editorial Zig-Zag, 1989.

Dahse, Fernando. *Mapa de la Extrema Riqueza.* Santiago: Editorial Aconcagua, 1979.

Délano, Manuel and Hugo Traslaviña. *La Herencia de los Chicago Boys.* Santiago: Editorial Ornitorrinco, 1989.

Dinges, John and Saul Landau. *Assassination on Embassy Row.* New York: Pantheon Books, Random House Inc., 1980.

Emperaire, Joseph. *Los Nómades del Mar.* Santiago: Universidad de Chile publications, 1963.

España, Aristóteles. *El Sur de la Memoria.* Punta Arenas: Divina Ediciones, 1992.

Faúndez, Julio. *Marxism and Democracy in Chile. From 1932 to the fall of Allende.* New Haven: Yale University Press, 1988.

Foerster, Rolf. *Vida Religiosa de los Huilliches de San Juan de la Costa.* Santiago: Colección Cultura and Religión, Ediciones Rehue, 1985.

Gazmuri, Jaime, ed. *Chile en el umbral de los noventa.* Santiago: Planeta, Espejo de Chile, 1988.

Gemballa, Gero. *Colonia Dignidad.* Santiago: Ediciones ChileAmérica CESOC, 1990. (Original title in German: "Colonia Dignidad" Ein Deutsches Lugar in Chile.)

González, Mónica and Héctor Contreras. *Los Secretos del Comando Conjunto.* Santiago: Editorial Ornitorrinco, 1991.

Gutiérrez Lobos, Victor. *Los Presidentes de Chile.* Santiago: Gutiérrez Vidal y Cia. Ltda., n.d.

Herren, Ricardo. *La Conquista erótica de las Indias.* Buenos Aires: Planeta, 1991.

Honeywell, Martin, ed. *The Poverty Brokers: The IMF and Latin America.* London: Latin America Bureau (Research and Action Ltd.), 1983. (Especially chapter "The IMF and Monetarism in Chile" by Robert Carty.)

Huneeus, Pablo. *La Cultura Huachaca o el aporte de la televisión.* 19th ed. Santiago: Editora nueva Generación Ltda., 1991.

Huneeus, Pablo. *¿Qué te pasó Pablo?* 13th ed. Santiago: Editora Nueva Generación, 1990.

Koch, John. The Salmon Industry's Impact on the Island of Chiloé. Master's thesis, May 1993.

Latcham, Ricardo. *Manuel Rodríguez.* Santiago: Editorial Nascimento, 1975.

Lavín, Joaquín. *Chile Revolución Silenciosa.* Santiago: Zig Zag, 1987.

Leyton, Elliot. *Hunting Humans, The Rise of the Modern Multiple Murderer.* Toronto: Seal Books, McClelland-Bantam, Inc., 1987.

Loveman, Brian. *Chile: The Legacy of Hispanic Capitalism.* 2d ed. New York: Oxford University Press, 1988.

Magnon, CRO (Luis Alejandro Salinas and Paula Zaldívar Hurtado). *Humanos y Humanoides.* Santiago: Editorial Aconcagua Ltda., 1988.

Molina, Juan Ignacio. *Historia Natural y Civil de Chile.* Series: Escritores Coloniales de Chile. No. 10. Editorial Universitaria, SA. 1978.

Montecino, Sonia. *Madres y Huachos. Alegorías del mestizaje chileno.* Santiago: Editorial Cuarto Propio – CEDEM, 1991.

Montecino, Sonia. *Mujeres de la Tierra.* Santiago: CEM-PEMCI, n.d.

Mora, Ziley. *Verdades Mapuches de alta magia para reencantar La Tierra.* 2d ed. Temuco: Editorial "Kushe", 1990.

Muñoz Valenzuela, Diego. *Todo el amor en sus ojos.* Santiago: Mosquito, circa 1990.

Opaso, Cristián, ed. and trans. *Frei, Allende y la mano de la CIA.* Santiago: Ornitorrinco, n.d.

Otero, Edison and Ricardo López. *Pedagogía del Terror,* un ensayo sobre la tortura. Santiago: Editorial Atena, 1989.

Palamara, Humberto Antonio. *Etica y Servicios de Inteligencia*. Punta Arenas, Atelí Ltda., 1993. (All other copies were seized by naval intelligence, Monday, March 1, 1993.)

Pineda de Castro, Alvaro. *Pinochet: Verdad y Ficción*. Madrid: Iberia Editores SA., n.d.

Pinedo, Javier. Editor. *Chile: 1968-1988. Los Ensayistas*. Georgia Series on Hispanic Thought. Nos. 22-25. 1987/1988. Published yearly by the Center for Latin American Studies at the University of Georgia.

Pinochet, Augusto. *Política, Politiquería, Demagogia*. Santiago: Editorial Renacimiento, 1983.

Pohorecky, Adriana. *"Ignacio."* Book about her son, Ignacio Valenzuela. Santiago: 1990, 1991, 1992. Manuscript.

Politzer, Patricia. *Fear in Chile*. New York: Pantheon Books, Random House Inc., 1989.

Politzer, Patricia. *La Ira de Pedro y los otros*. Santiago: Planeta Espejo de Chile, 1988.

Prats, Carlos. *Memorias: Testimonio de un Soldado*. Santiago: Pehuén Editores Ltda. 1985.

Propper, Eugene M. and Taylor Branch. *Laberinto*. Santiago: Editorial Pensamiento Soc. Ltda., 1984. (Original title in English: Labyrinth.)

Rettig, Raúl, and others. *Informe Rettig: Informe de la Comisión Nacional de Verdad y Reconciliación*. Santiago: Joint publication of La Nación and Las Ediciones del Ornitorrinco, 1991.

Sanina, Kika. *Memoirs of Colonia Dignidad*. 1991. Manuscript.

Sierra, Malú. *Donde Todo es Altar: Aymaras Los hijos del Sol*. Santiago: Editorial Persona, 1991.

Simalchik, Joan. Part of the Awakening: Canadian Churches and Chile, 1970-1979. Master's thesis, March 1993.

Sohr, Raúl. *Para Entender a los Militares*. Santiago: Ediciones Melquiades, 1989.

Tironi, Eugenio. *"¿POBREZA= FRUSTRACION =VIOLENCIA? Crítica empírica a un mito recurrente."* Working Paper #123 May 1989. The Helen Kellogg Institute for International Studies. University of Notre Dame, Notre Dame, IN, USA 46556.

Tironi, Ernesto. *Es Posible Reducir la Pobreza en Chile*. Santiago: Zig Zag, 1989.

Tironi, Eugenio. *Los Silencios de la Revolución*. Santiago: Editorial la Puerta Abierta, 1988.

Valdivieso, Jaime. *Chile: Un Mito y Su Ruptura*. Santiago: LAR, Literatura Americana Reunida, 1987.

Varas, Augusto. *Los Militares en el Poder. Regimen y Gobierno Militar en Chile 1973-1986*. Santiago: Pehuén/FLACSO, 1987.

Various authors. *Chile en el siglo XX*. Santiago: Emisión Ltda, 1986

Verdugo, Patricia. *Los Zarpazos del Puma*. Santiago: Ediciones ChileAmérica CESOC, 1989.

Verdugo, Patricia and Carmen Hertz. *Operación Siglo XX*. Santiago: Las ediciones del Ornitorrinco, 1990.

Villalobos, Sergio. *Breve Historia de Chile*. Santiago: Editorial, 1983.

Wilhelm, Ernesto. *Voz de Arauco*. Temuco: Editorial Millantu, 1991. (The first edition was published in Gorbea, 1944.)

NOTES

Interviews are organized by book chapter titles. Those noted as "previous" are personal interviews done for articles in periodical publications between 1981 and 1994; others listed here were done personally, specifically for this book, and tended to be longer and more detailed. Interviews were carried out in Santiago, unless otherwise specified.

CHAPTER 1 ~ AFTER THE FIRST DEATH

1. Information on the killing of Manuel Guerrero, Jose Manuel Parada and Santiago Nattino, a crime known generally as the *degollados* (those whose throats were slashed) is from personal interviews and events which I witnessed in March 1985. Santiago Nattino was kidnapped on Thursday, March 28, 1985; Manuel Guerrero and Jose Manuel Parada were kidnapped during a police operation, supervised by a Carabineros helicopter, early in the morning of Friday, March 29, 1985, at the Colegio Latinoamericano de Integración, the school where Guerrero worked and Parada's children studied. Their lifeless bodies were discovered on the afternoon of Saturday, March 30, and their names announced, in the scene described here, after dark that same evening.

2. "dialogue with murderers": Estela Ortiz, outside the morgue. I recorded this scene including her reaction, for CBC "Sunday Morning," March 30, 1985. Other information about Estela Ortiz is from an interview with the author in 1986, published in *Student Lawyer*, USA, January 1987. Conclusions about the crime are based on coverge of the investigation in *Prensa Libre*, throughout 1985, the account in *Chile: La Memoria Prohibida*, volume III, p. 541-575, and information contained in Judge Milton Juica's lengthy summary and sentence, March 1994, which was provided to the press on diskettes. I attended the joint funeral of Jose Manuel Parada and Manuel Guerrero, on Monday, April 1, 1985.

6. I covered General Urzua's funeral for CBC "Sunday Morning," August 1983.

CHAPTER 2 ~ GOING TO ISLA NEGRA

Interviews: Going to Isla Negra: Juan Pérez, 20 May 92; Patricio Lanfranco, on several occasions, between 1979 and 1993; Diego Muñoz, 28 July 92; Cecilia Carvallo, 25 June 92.

11. "tree always blooms": Editorial, *La Ciruela*, August 1979.
11. "in that hour": Poem, *la Ciruela*, August 1979.
12. "Don't bother" Note, *La Ciruela*, August 1979.
12. "free expression and dialogue": Editorial, *La Ciruela*, August 1979.
12. "Neruda can't appear": Editorial, *La Ciruela*, August 1979.
13. "Auditorium is struck dumb": Article, *La Ciruela*, October 1979.
14. "What's the tell-tale word": Cartoon, *La Ciruela*, November 1979.
14. "fundamental feature of this Festival": Article, *La Ciruela*, November 1979.
17. "I'm no lord": Javier Garcá de Cortázar. *La Ciruela*, November 1979.
18. "in Anatomy class" and other comments: Juan Perez, interview with the author, 20 May 1992.
21. "Fine Arts Museum" and other examples of military actions against culture: *La Historia Oculta del Regimen Militar*, p. 168-176.
22. "not alive now" and other comments: Diego Muñoz, interview with the author, 28 July 1992.
25. Cecilia walked alone, and other information on Cecilia's life, compiled from interview with author, 25 June 1992.
28. "everything flowers": Pablo Neruda, *Para nacer he nacido*, p. 118, (my translation).
28. "In my city": song, "A Mi Ciudad", by Luis Pérez. Performed by Santiago del Nuevo Extremo. *La Ciruela*, June/July 1980.
29. "Goodbye": Poem by Eduardo Llanos, "Poesía, Concurso Literario Palabras para el hombre, ACU, 1981.

CHAPTER 3 ~ ESCAPES FROM PARADISE

General background information on German settlers to southern Chile, from Jean-Pierre Blancpain, *Los Alemanes en Chile (1816-1945);* on the Colony itself, from Kika Sanino's manuscript, listed under books; and Gero Gemballa's book, *Colonia Dignidad,* also listed under books. Gemballa's sources included many of the same people I have interviewed and articles I have consulted. He also had access to written reports by the Packmors and Baars to the German Ministry of Foreign Affairs. For details of his sources, see pp. 267-269 in his book. I have two file-boxes worth of coverage in newspapers of the Colonia, but have not listed individual articles here.

Interviews: Hector Taricco, 19 August 1991, Linares; Kika Sanino, 19 August 1991, Linares; Osvaldo Muray, 5 September 1991; Jorge Ovalle, 12 September 1991; Monseigneur Carlos Camus 19 August 1991, Linares; Francisco Cumplido, then Minister of Justice, 17 December 1990. Sergio González (previous by telephone).

Magazine articles that also contributed to my background knowledge, for this chapter were:

Original coverage in 1966:
"Policía Frustró Sensacional Rapto", by Osvaldo Muray Q. *Ercilla*, 23 March 1966. Santiago, Chile.

"Tras los Muros de la 'Dignidad'", by Erica Vexler, Osvaldo Muray, Juan Ehrmann and the photographer Heliodor Torrente. *Ercilla,* 30 March 1966. Santiago, Chile.

"La Colonia del Terror", by Erica Vexler, Juan Ehrmann and Osvaldo Muray Q. *Ercilla,* 6 April 1966. Santiago, Chile.

"La Larga Fuga de Wolfgang Müller", by José Pablo López. *Ercilla,* 6 April 1966. Santiago, Chile. On Müller's first flight.

"La Justicia Busca la Clave de 'Dignidad'", by Osvaldo Muray Q. *Ercilla,* 13 April 1966.

"Siembra de Dudas", by Osvaldo Muray and Daniel Galleguillos. Photographs by Bibí de Vicenzi. *Ercilla* 20 April 1966. Santiago, Chile.

"Wolfgang Müller: 'Solo contra Todos'", by Osvaldo Muray. Photographs by Bibí de Vicenzi. *Ercilla* 27 April 1966. Santiago, Chile.

"Diabólicos Métodos de 'Dignidad'", Ante Justicia Austríaca Denuncian. *Ercilla,* 4 May 66. Santiago, Chile.

"Tres niños Ponen Jaque a Dignidad". *Ercilla,* 4 May 1966. Santiago, Chile.

"Proceso a la Ingenuidad". *Ercilla,* 4 May 1966. Santiago, Chile.

"Extradición de Paul Schaeffer Pide Alemania". *Ercilla,* 11May 1966. Austria Pidió "Repatriación de los Wagner", p. 3. *Ercilla,* Santiago, Chile.

"Nueva Etapa en Proceso a Dignidad." *Ercilla,* 1 June 1966. Santiago.

Magazine articles covering post-coup activities of the Colony:

"Colonia Dignidad. Los otros Testimonios". *Hoy* No. 558, 28 March 1988. Santiago.

"Colonia Dignidad: Tortura y abusos sexuales". *Análisis,* 25 January 1988. Santiago.

"Colonia Dignidad: Informe Confidencial". *Análisis,* 21 December 1987. Santiago.

"Me estaba pudriendo en vida". *Análisis,* 1 August 1988. Santiago.

"Hablan sobrevivientes de Colonia Dignidad". *Análisis,* 16 May 1988. Santiago.

"Se Acabó la impunidad". Análisis, 11 February 1991. Santiago.

"La DINA en Colonia Dignidad". *Análisis,* 27 March 1989. Santiago.

"Colonia Dignidad: Sus días están contados". Análisis, 23 July 19 1990. Santiago.

"El retorno de los nazis chilenos". *Análisis,* 23 November 1987. Santiago.

34. Photograph of the two women is from "La Colonia del Terror", *Ercilla,* 6 April 1966.
35. "women's intuition" and other comments in this chapter: Hector Taricco, interview with the author, Linares, 19 August 1991.
36. "honest, hardworking Swiss": Benjamin Vicuña Mackenna, *Los Alemanes en Chile (1816-1945),* p. 34.
36-37. Information on German settlers in Chile, from *Los Alemanes en Chile (1816-1945).*
37. Arturo Maschke is mentioned in Gero Gemballa's book, *Colonia Dignidad,* and by Lutheran Bishop Helmut Frenz, General Secretary of the German section of Amnesty International, who once lived in Chile, in *Apsi* 234, January 11, 1988.
38. "a new group" Hector Taricco, interview with the author, Linares, 19 August 1991.
38-42. Accounts by Taricco, Sanino, Gemballa, *Ercilla.*
39-41. "without knowing her" and other comments: Kika Sanino, in her unpublished memoir.
42-43. Accounts of Müller's first flight based on information in Gemballa, *Ercilla,* especially "La Larga Fuga de Wolfgang Müller", by José Pablo López, 6 April 1966, and original newspaper accounts from that period, published in the local Chillan newspaper, *La Discusión.*
43 "Mr. Schafer began to scold": Hugo Baar, *Colonia Dignidad,* p. 134. "I can't forget": Hugo Baar, *Colonia Dignidad,* p. 136.

44. "visited their houses" and other quotes: Heinz Kuhn, in interview with Monica Gonzalez, *Análisis*, 14 August 1989, p. 33-37.

45. "Schafer surrounded the farm": Lotti Packmor, *Colonia Dignidad*, p. 145-147.

45. Congressional records: Congressional records, Session 12, Tuesday November 26, 1968 and Session 63 (Senate) March 5, 1968.

46. "a grand plot": Osvaldo Muray, in interview with author, 5 September 1991.

46. "the colony's image": Jorge Ovalle, in interview with author, 12 September 1991.

46-47. The Colony's ties with authorities are well documented in the media during the sixties, eighties and *Colonia Dignidad*, p. 216-218, especially.

47. "cuts and bruises": Luis Peebles, reported in several Chilean magazines, especially *Análisis*, 1 August 1988 and *Análisis*, 11 February 1991, as well as newspaper clippings.

48. "the guinea pig": Adriana Borquez, in the film, prepared by Jimmy Doran and Rapide Productions for Channel 4, England, circa 1990. Her testimony also appears in *Análisis*, 16 May 1988. I interviewed Sergio Gonzalez by telephone for a report to *The Times* of London.

49. "a certain number": Rettig Commission, *Rettig Report*, p. 469-470.

49. "doctor": Samuel Fuenzalida, *Análisis*, 21 December 1987. Schaeffer's story compiled using information provided by almost all the sources for this chapter.

50. "spiritual domination": Heinz Kuhn, *Análisis*, 14 August 1989, p. 33-37. "introduced by hammer blows": Hugo Baar, written testimony to Germany's Foreign Affairs Ministry, 2 April 1985, *Colonia Dignidad*, p. 130-136.

51. "I was twelve": Wolfgang Müller, *Ercilla*, 6 April 1966.

52. "heavy doses": Lotti Packmor, written testimony, 17 March 1985, Colonia Dignidad, p. 141-155.

53. "blank looks": *El Mercurio* report, 6 December 1987.

58. "lucid minorities": Erwin Robertson, "made to believe": Miguel Serrano, "classist racism": Gaston Soublette, *Análisis*, 23 November 1987.

59. Aylwin's speech, reprinted in *Colonia Dignidad;* also available in the Senate record, 28 February 1968.

CHAPTER 4 ~ PRONOUNCEMENTS

Interviews: General Alejandro Medina, 23 July and 3 August 1992; Captain Raúl Vergara, 24 July 1992; General Mario Morales, 21 July 1992; along with information from previous interviews with Genaro Arriagada, 16 December 1986; Moy de Tohá, 17 December 1986, Monseigneur Augusto Salinas, in Valparaíso, 21 March 1987; and Raúl Sohr, 17 March 1987, originally used for for CBC "Sunday Morning," 1987.

73-77. "At first they took me" and other comments: Captain Raúl Vergara, interview with author, 24 July 1994, Santiago.

80-81. "We came sweeping": General Alejandro Medina with author, 23 July 1992.

82-84. Rettig Report, p. 399-403.

CHAPTER 5 ~ THE RICH VILLAGE

All comments from interviews, unless otherwise attributed, and
Bengoa, José. *Quinquén, 100 Años de Historia Pehuenche* and *Historia del Pueblo Mapuche*.
Foerster, Rolf. *Vida Religiosa de los Huilliches de San Juan de la Costa*.

Herren, Ricardo. *La Conquista erótica de las Indias.*
Montecino, Sonia. *Madres y Huachos. Alegorías del mestizaje chileno.*
Montecino, Sonia. *Mujeres de la Tierra.*
Mora, Ziley. *Verdades Mapuches de alta magia para reencantar La Tierra.*

91. Panguipulli and other English definitions of Mapudungun terms are from *Voz de Arauco.*
92. "Until 1881": *Turistel SUR,* p. 105, 1994 edition. My translation.
92. "earth of man": Wetchemapu group, *Vida Religiosa.*
93. "How do you know": Cacique Calfunao, *Historia del Pueblo Mapuche,* p. 238.
93. Look, colonel": anonymouse Cacique, *Historia del Pueblo Mapuche,* p. 229.
94. "From then on": *The Meteor* (6 March 1869), *Historia del Pueblo Mapuche,* p. 208
94. "long and abundant": Luis de la Cuadra, *Historia del Pueblo Mapuche,* p. 239.
95. "Friend, I have suffered": Cacique Santos Quilapán, *Historia del Pueblo Mapuche,* p. 247.
95. "realizing impossible acts": José Bengoa, *Historia del Pueblo Mapuche,* p. 293.

CHAPTER 6 ~ OPERATIONS

Interviews: Interviews published in *La Nación, La Epoca, El Mercurio* and other newspapers. Interviews with Mariana Callejas and Michael Townley broadcast in BBC film, *The Assassin,* part of "The Inside Story" series, directed by Chris Olgiati, 1992. Testimony from Andrés Valenzuela, published in original interview by Monica González, 1986, and in the book cited above. Luz Arce's confession to the Rettig Commission as published in the magazines *Apsi* and *Hoy.*

97. "Statistics Show": reporter's question and reply from General Gordon, *El Mercurio,* December 4, 1983, *Humanos y Humanoides.*
97. "At first you cry": Andrés Valenzuela, *Los Secretos del Comando Conjunto,* p. 297.
98. "operations": Webster's *Dictionary,* 2nd Edition, p. 1253.
98. "networks of informants": Manuel Contreras, *Cosas* March 16, 1989, p. 30.
99. "Security services put": Juan Muñoz Alarcón's, *Cauce,* 17 September 1984.
100. "secret and above": Rettig Commission, *Rettig Report,* p. 450-452. DINA activities at home and abroad are from the Rettig report, pp. 450-451, 452, but are also well documented in books about and materials from trials in the US and Chile, to do with the Letelier killing in Washington in 1976, the attempted killing of Bernardo Leighton and Anita Fresno, in Rome in 1975, the case of Eugenio Berrios covered by *The Miami Herald, Newsweek* among others, in 1993, and other judicial investigations.
101. Osvaldo Romo's story: Dino Pancani. *La Nación.* 22 November 1992, p. 8-9.
102-103. "When I married" and other comments: Mariana Callejas, Interview with Odette Magnet, *La Nación,* 10 May 1992.
103. "Many officers found": Monica González and Lautaro Muñoz, *La Nación,* 14 June 1992, p. 4.
104. "How should I": Andrés Valenzuela, interview with Monica González, *Cauce,* 23 July 1985.
104. "They'd been living" and other comments: Andrés Valenzuela, interview with Monica González, *Cauce,* 23 July 1985.
105-108. "At one point" and other comments: Luz Arce, from her testimony to the Rettig commission, published in *Hoy,* 18 March 1991. *Apsi* also published a selection from her testimony.

108-109. "colleague of mine" and other comments: Andrés Valenzuela. *Cauce*, 23 July 1985.

110-111. Information on the killing of Tucapel Jimenez: from "El Asesinato de Tucapel Jiménez": *Chile La Memoria Prohibida*, p. 437-456.

113. "about sixty agents": Valenzuela. *Los Secretos del Comando Conjunto*, p. 268.

114. "a lousy father": Valenzuela. *Los Secretos del Comando Conjunto*, p. 296.

CHAPTER 7 ~ MURDER AMONG STRANGERS

Information on killings from press coverage during that period, as stated, and Cayuela, José. *Laura Soto: Una Dama de Lila y Negro*, particularly interview with former police detective Nelson Lillo.

González, Monica and Héctor Contreras. *Los Secretos del Comando Conjunto*.

Leyton, Elliot. *Hunting Humans, The Rise of the Modern Multiple Murderer*, including quote from Peter J. Wilson.

Interviews: Monica González, 17 May 1992; Juan Pérez, 20 May 1992.

117. "Murderer of strangers": Elliott Leyton, *Hunting Humans*, p. 281, 283.

119-120. "Father's anguished clamour" and other headlines: Coverage of the Anfruns case, *Las Ultimas Noticias*, (the Edwards' family morning tabloid), 4 -17 June 1979.

122-123. "Two unknown bodies" and other headlines: *Las Ultimas Noticias*, January to September, 1981, especially issues 16 March; 11, 12, 15, 16, 18, 23, 30 September; 12, 19, 21 January 1981.

124-126. Information on the crimes compiles from coverage in *Las Ultimas Noticias*, especially 6 March 1982 and *Laura Soto*, p. 73-111.

127. "names of detainees": Monica Gonzalez, *Los Secretos del Comando Conjunto*, p. 12-13.

127. "that little sore": Dr. Juan Manuel Pérez, in an interview with the author, 20 May 1992.

128 "individual who suffers": anonymous psychologist, *Las Ultimas Noticias*, 4 March 1982.

128. "strange personality": unnamed friends, *Las Ultimas Noticias*, 6 March 1982, Special supplement.

129. "There was no reason": Nelson Lillo, interview with José Cayuela, *Laura Soto*, p. 96.

129. "fifteen killings committed": Lillo, interview with Cayela, *Laura Soto*, p. 97.

129. "different strange affinities": Lillo, interview with Cayuela, *Laura Soto*, p. 98

129. "Intention of the crimes": Lillo, interview with Cayuela, *Laura Soto*, p. 100

129. "The method consisted": Lillo, interview with Cayuela, *Laura Soto*, p. 100

129. "the main author": Lillo, interview with Cayuela, *Laura Soto*, p. 101

130. "After we explained": Lillo, interview with Cayuela, *Laura Soto*, p. 80.

131. "Topp Collins is": headline, *Cauce*, 23 October 1984.

132. "What [the government]" and other comments this page: Monica Gonzalez, interview with the author, 17 May 1992.

134. "alienated men with": Elliott Leyton, *Hunting Humans*, p. 16.

134. "killing the failures": Leyton, *Hunting Humans*, p. 300.

135. "a single class": Leyton, *Hunting Humans*, p. 323.

135. "they are no freaks": Leyton, *Hunting Humans*, p. 2.

135. "profoundly conservative figure": Leyton, *Hunting Humans*, p. 10.

135. "when the dreadful": Dr. Juan Manuel Perez, interview with the author, 20 May 1992.

136. "anaesthesia that most people": unnamed mental health expert, *Hoy*, 31 March 1982.

CHAPTER 8 ~ IGNACIO

Interviews: Cecilia Carvallo, 25 June 1992; Adriana Pohorecky, 17 June 1992; "Eduardo", 6 May 1992; Monica González, 17 May 1992; along with information from previous interviews with Raúl Sohr.

Arriagada, Genaro. *El Pensamiento Político de los militares.*
Arriagada, Genaro. *La Política Militar de Pinochet.*
Bardini, Roberto, Miguel Bonasso and Laura Restrepo. *Operación Príncipe.*
Latcham, Ricardo. *Manuel Rodríguez.*
Pohorecky, Adriana. *Ignacio.* Manuscript about her son, Ignacio Valenzuela.
Sohr, Raúl. *Para Entender a los Militares.*
Verdugo, Patricia and Carmen Hertz. *Operación Siglo XX.*

140-142. Adriana's son and other information about Ignacio's youth based on Adriana Pohorecky's unpublished manuscript, *Ignacio.*
140. "I started high school": Eduardo (pseudonym), interview with the author, 6 May 1991, Santiago.
142. "He was enthusiastic": Unnamed economist, *Ignacio.*
143. "His clear eyes": Song by Patricio Manns.
144. "hills come alive": Ricardo Latcham, *Manuel Rodríguez*, p. 100.
144. "The coach sparkles": Latcham, *Manuel Rodríguez*, p. 107.
144. "no system, no constancy": Latcham, *Manuel Rodríguez*, p. 116.
144. "first sincere democrat": Latcham, *Manuel Rodríguez*, p.144.
145. "an opponent of the great minister's": Latcham, *Manuel Rodríguez*, p. 148.
145. "If you ordered": officer, *Manuel Rodríguez*, p. 209
145. "three days after the Cazadores": official communiqué, *Manuel Rodríguez*, p. 213.
146. "This is a war to the death": General Augusto Pinochet, *Apsi*, 8 January 1988.
146. "continuation of politics": Karl von Clausewitz, *Oxford Book of Quotations.*
146. "source of all arts": Colonel Romeo Barrientos, *El Pensamiento Político de los Militares*, p. 57.
146. "irregular in terms": Rettig Commission, *Rettig Report*, p. 108.
148. "a real possibility that the DINA": Hugo Rivas, *Los Secretos del Comando Conjunto*, p. 222.
148. "Army of the Shadows": Manuel Contreras, *Cosas*, 16 March 1980.
148. "destroy the [enemy's] military": Alberto Pollonia, *Cauce*, 26 May 1986.
148. "conquest of its vital zones": Orlando Saenz, *Cauce*, 28 August 1984.
149. "then the possible extremists": Ricardo Guzmán Bousquet, *Humanos y Humanoides*, p. 38.
151. "I fired many times" and other documents: Eduardo, in interview with the author 6 May 1992.
153. "punish the tyrant": José Joaquín Valenzuela Levy, *Operación Siglo XX*, p. 85.
153-156. The account of the ambush is based on my interview with "Eduardo" and Verdugo and Hertz, *Operación Siglo XX.*
156. "Because it failed" and other comments: Monica Gonzalez, in an interview with the author, 17 May 1992.
157. "Take Lucien and": Cecilia Carvallo, in an interview with the author 25 June 1992.
158. How the twelve were killed is pieced together from versions first published in *El Siglo*, April 1991, with leaked documents from the CNI, *La Nación*, May 17, 1992, a special report by the Chilean Human Rights Commission, prepared after the killings; and the

report of the Rettig Commission, published in April 1991. I visited the house on Pedro Donoso Street, where seven of the twelve reportedly died in a confrontation with the CNI, as the bodies were being removed. There were no signs that anyone had fired from within the house.

160. "a suicidal tendency": Genaro Arriagada, *El pensamiento de los militares*, p. 58.

160. "psychological catrastrophe": Arnold Toynbee, *El pensamiento de los militares*, p. 58.

160. "trusting too much": Arriagada, *El pensamiento de los militares*, p. 59.

CHAPTER 9 ~ SOWING THE WIND

Blakemore, Harold. *Gobierno Chileno y Salitre Inglés 1886-1896.*

Church Commission. *Covert Action in Chile, 1963-1973.* Staff Report of the Select Committee to Study Governmental Operations with Respect to Intelligence Activities. US Senate. From the edition prepared by Cristián Opaso, editor and translator. *Frei, Allende y la mano de la CIA.*

Dinges, John and Saul Landau. *Assassination on Embassy Row.*

Faúndez, Julio. *Marxism and Democracy in Chile.*

Loveman, Brian. *Chile: The Legacy of Hispanic Capitalism.*

Propper, Eugene M. and Taylor Branch. *Laberinto.* Original title: Labyrinth.

Interviews: Juan Pablo Letelier, 29 September 1992; Heraldo Muñoz, 21 October 1992 (Washington); Harry Barnes, 20 October 1992 (Boston); Laura Novoa, 25 July 1991. Fabiola Letelier, on several occasions for reports in the *Miami Herald,* 1993-1995. Interviews with Mariana Callejas and Michael Townley broadcast in BBC film, *The Assassin,* part of "The Inside Story" series, directed by Chris Olgiati, 1992. And interviews with Callejas and Townley, broadcast on Chile's National Television, August 1992.

164-167. Story of Juan Pablo Letelier, son of Orlando Letelier, a Minister in the Allende government. From an interview, 29 September 1992.

167. "What resulted in these years": Francisco Encina, *Chile: The Legacy of Hispanic Capitalism,* p. 133-134.

168. Figures on US investment from Loveman, p. 213.

169. Both Julio Faundez and Brian Loveman in *Chile: The Legacy of Hispanic Capitalism,* p. 255, use this figure for Chilean copper's subsidization of the American war effort.

169. "Chile is [a] key": Ambassador Claude Bowers, *Chile: The Legacy of Hispanic Capitalism,* p. 257.

169. Ambassador's cable, *Chile: The Legacy of Hispanic Capitalism,* p. 257.

169. "Law for the Permanent Defence" information: *Chile: The Legacy of Hispanic Capitalism,* p. 258.

170. "Credit to agriculture": Loveman, *Chile: The Legacy of Hispanic Capitalism,* p. 259.

170. "Most of all": Loveman, *Chile: The Legacy of Hispanic Capitalism,* p. 259.

171. "more than a billion dollars": figure from *Frei, Allende y la Mano de la CIA,* (Chilean edition of the Church Commission Staff Report of the Select Committee to Study Governmental Operations with respect to Intelligence Activities, US Senate, 18 December 1975.)

173. "noticed an intense change" and other comments: Laura Novoa, interview with author, 25 July 1991, in Santiago.

174. Information in this chapter on CIA and State Department activities and National

Intelligence Estimates, from Opaso, *Frei, Allende y la Mano de la CIA* (Chilean edition of the Church Commission Staff Report of the Select Committee to Study Governmental Operations with respect to Intelligence Activities, US Senate, 18 December 1975).

176. "You will agree, Mr. Ambassador": Richard Nixon, *Assassination on Embassy Row*, p. 42.

179. "gives me the creeps": Orlando Letelier, *Assassination on Embassy Row*, p. 59.

181. US figures for coup victims, from *Assassination on Embassy Row*, p. 71.

182. "at the beginning": unnamed agent, *Assassination on Embassy Row*, p. 126.

CHAPTER 10 ~ OF DWARVES AND GIANTS

183-185. Information on this international network was uncovered in both the United States and the Chilean courts investigation of the Letelier assassination, the Prats assassination, the attempted murder of Bernardo Leighton and Anita Fresno, during the late seventies and early eighties. In 1993, after elected government returned to Chile, the case of former DINA agent Eugenio Berrios, who worked with Michael Townley developing the lethal gas Sarin brought to light more information on the DINA's international network and its continued existence even after the DINA itself was dissolved and replaced by the CNI. Berrios himself disappeared, after a rather dramatic escape attempt, which was revealed in Uruguay in May 1993; I covered this story for both the *Miami Herald* and *Newsweek*, among other media.

185. "Goebbels, too, fought": Michael Townley, during an interview with the BBC filmmaker Chris Olgiati, in the United States in 1992. Broadcast on the BBC's "The Inside Story" series, as *The Assassin*.

186-188. Account of events compiled from *Assassination on Embassy Row* and *Labyrinth*. Both books provide highly readable accounts of the killings and the investigation that followed. Landau worked with Letelier at the Institute for Policy Studies, while Propper was the lawyer in the US Attorney's Office who participated in most of the investigation, including Townley's expulsion from Chile in April 1978.

189. "retreating ethical limits": Rettig Commission, *Rettig Report*, p. 45.

190-198. "I was born" and other comments in italics: Harry Barnes, former US Ambassador to Chile, in interview with author, in Boston, 20 October 1992.

199-200. Story of Juan Pablo Letelier compiled from an interview with author in Santiago, 29 September 1992.

CHAPTER 11 ~ LA VICTORIA

Lavín, Joaquín. *Chile Revolución Silenciosa.*

Tironi, Eugenio. ¿POBREZA=FRUSTRACION=VIOLENCIA? Crítica empírica a un mito recurrente. Working Paper #123 May 1989.

Tironi, Eugenio. *Los Silencios de la Revolución.*

Interviews: Maria Nélida Sánchez and her son Renato, 14 September 1992; along with information from previous interviews between 1983 and 1990, with Víctor Hugo Castro of La Legua, Rodolfo Seguel, then president of the Copperworkers Confederation, and regular coverage of news conferences with protest and political party leaders throughout this period.

201. "a married couple" and the rest of the oral history of La Victoria, in italics, through-

out this chapter, as told by Maria Nelida Sanchez, in an interview with the author in La Victoria, Santiago, 14 September 1992.

208. Figures on the protests compiled from report of the Rettig Commission, pp. 701-741.

208. "Death reached people": Retting Commission, *Rettig Report*, p. 709.

213. "The important thing" and other comments: Renato, in an interview with the author in La Victoria, Santiago, 14 September 1992.

215. "decade of English": Joaquín Lavín, *La Revolución Silenciosa*, p. 75.

215. "dramatic change in the world": Lavín, *La Revolución Silenciosa*, p. 11.

216. "vineyard boom": Lavín, *La Revolución Silenciosa*, p. 15.

216. "the export of blackberries": Lavín, *La Revolución Silenciosa*, p. 25.

216. "children from the población": Lavín, *La Revolución Silenciosa*, p. 83.

216. "massive book sales": Lavín, *La Revolución Silenciosa*, p. 85.

216. "children of Conchalí": Lavín, *La Revolución Silenciosa*, p. 112.

217. "The revolution which began": Eugenio Tironi, *Los Silencios en la Revolución*, p. 9.

217 "emancipation from the factors": Tironi, *Los Silencios en la Revolución*, p. 12.

217. "obsession for success": Tironi, *Los Silencios en la Revolución*, p. 10.

218. Increased povery figures: Tironi, *Los Silencios en la Revolución*, p. 29-33.

220. In a visit to Putagan, a small rural village near Santiago, before a plebiscite in 1988, women from a lace-makers workshop told me there would be cameras in voting booths and other attempts to control how people voted.

221. "a State of Law": Tironi, Working Paper, p. 28.

221. "a civilized, culture nation": Tironi, *Los Silencios en la Revolución*, p. 84.

221. "that won't awaken the violence": Tironi, *Los Silencios en la Revolución*, p. 84.

CHAPTER 13 ~ NGUILLATÚN

Interviews: José Bengoa, 8 August 1991; Dr. Francisco Rothhammer, 26 July 1991; Víctor Hugo Painemal, 20 August 1991, Temuco; Ernesto Meliñir, February 1992, Quinquén; roundtable conversation, 20 August in 1991, Temuco with José Maliqueo, José Cayupe, Dionisio Rapiman, Rosendo Huenuman, Ana Catrileo, don Gabino. Conversations with Adela Curaqueo, Helen Hughes, Fanor Castillo, Delicias Campos.

233. "ancient old man": Prayer, *Mujeres de la Tierra*, p. 135.

235. "Cadets, you are": I attended and these quotes are from material handed out to the audience that day, including the text of the speech.

235. "We don't know": Francisco Rothhammer, in an interview with the author in Santiago, 16 July 1991.

235. "a refuge and haven": Miguel de Cervantas, *La Conquista Erótica de las Indias*, p. 23.

236. "The symbolic vacuum": Sonia Montecino, *Madres y Huachos*, p. 59.

237. "I got involved" and other comments: Victor Hugo Painemal, in an interview with the author in Temuco, 20 August 1991.

238. "our race has lived abandoned": Manuel Alberto Panguilef, *Historia del Pueblo Mapuche*, p. 391-392.

239. "an effective alliance": Panguilef, *Historia del Pueblo Mapuche*, p. 401.

242-244. Information on the history of Quinquén from the press and Jose Bengoa's book, *Quinquén*.

244. "Just as a family gives": Mariela Vallejos, *La Epoca*, 6 March 1992.

CHAPTER 14 ~ ALVARO VALENZUELA/JULIO CORBALÁN

253. "My scale of values" and other comments by AC unless otherwise marked: Alvaro Corbalán, an in-depth interview published in three issues of *Cosas*, 22 December 1988-19 January 1989.

254-256. Information compiled from Manuel Salazar, Special Report, *La Nación*, 23 February 1991 and *La Nación*, Special report, 17 May 1992.

256-259. Alvaro Corbalán, *Cosas* Part I, 22 December 1988; Part II, 5 January 1989; Part III, 19 January 1989.

259. "This could well": Raquel Correa, *El Mercurio*, 28 May 1989.

261-264. Compiled from newspaper accounts in *La Nación*, 23 February 1991; *La Tercera*, 10 April 1991; *La Tercera*, 21 April 1991; *La Epoca*, 24 November 1990.

266-267. See especially, *El Mercurio*, Section D, 24 February 1991.

267. "treated with great respect": Patricio Roa Caballero, *La Nación*, 17 May 1992.

268. "I can only tell you.": Alvaro Corbalán, *La Epoca*, 19 May 1992.

268. "CNI agents will never pardon": Article, *La Nación*, 17 May 1992.

CHAPTER 15 ~ CAMILO'S FIRST DAY AT SCHOOL

274. Gustavo Hawes Barrios, "La Educación en Chile Período 1965-1985", p. 146, 150, from Los Ensayistas, Georgia Series on Hispanic Thought.

280. Los Desafios de la Educación Chilena Frente al Siglo 21, September 9, 1994 (Technical Commission's report to President Frei).

281-282. "The reconciliation remains pending" and other comments: Patricio Donoso, "El norte de la Educación, *La Nación*, 27 August 1993.

284. "If we want students": Alfonso Bravo, *El Mercurio*, 28 February 1993.

284-285. "This is an issue." Claudia Dueñas, in an interview with the author in Santiago, 10 January 1995.

286. "several fundamental principles": Andres Domínguez, interview with the author in Santiago, 9 January 1995.

CHAPTER 16 ~ THE LITTLE RIFTS

Cárdenas, Renato and Carlos Trujillo. *Caguach, Isla de la Devoción*.

Cárdenas, Renato, Dante Montiel Vera and Catherine Grace Hall. *Los Chono y los Veliche de Chiloé*.

Délano, Manuel and Hugo Traslaviña. *La Herencia de los Chicago Boys*.

Koch, John. "The Salmon Industry's Impact on the Island of Chiloé." Thesis.

Interviews: Rosa Huentén, 4 October 1993, Contuy, Chiloé. Previous interviews: Jay Taylor, 4 October 1992; Alejandro Hales; August 1993: Jorge Berghammer, Raimundo Espinoza, Eduardo Moyano, Manfred Max Neef, Bernardo Reyes, Bruno Behn (Salvador), Jorge Bande. Interviews contributed by Robert Carty, CBC "Sunday Morning": Pedro Saenz, Jaime Ruiz-Tagle, Alejandro Foxley, May 1993.

289. Comments from Jay Taylor, from an interview with the author, 4 October 1992.

291. "Codelco's owner is poor": Jorge Berghammer, in an interview with the author in Santiago in August 1993.

292. "We can't just copy": Raimundo Espinoza, in an interview with the author in Santiago in August 1993.

293-296. Figures from the International Economics Affairs Department.

293. "In 1990, our exports grew": Eduardo Moyano, in an interview with the author in Santiago in August 1993.

296. Figures from Délano and Traslaviña, *La Herencia de los Chicago Boys*, p. 50, 128, 20-21.

297. "Thanks to taxes": Pedro Saenz, in an interview with Robert Carty, CBC "Sunday Morning," April 1993.

297. Figures on distribution from *Revista de la CEPAL* (ECLAC), #48, December 1992, p. 38.

297. "There's a problem of equity": Jaime Ruiz-Tagle, in an interview with Robert Carty, CBC "Sunday Morning," April 1993.

298. "the absence of an environment": Manfred Max Neef, in an interview with the author in Santiago in August 1993.

298. "We've done as much": Alexandro Foxley, in an interview with Robert Carty, CBC "Sunday Morning", April 1993.

299. "housewives, similar to students": and other comments: Bernardo Reyes, in an interview with the author in Santiago in August 1993.

299-300. Figures on unionization from *La Herencia de los Chicago Boys*, p. 78.

300-301. My view of and information about the salmon industry is based on interviews done in April, October and December 1993 with Fernando Klimpel, then an executive at Salmones Antartica; Renato Cárdenas, a cultural researcher of Castro, Chiloé; staff of Salmones Yadrán, in Quellón, Chiloé. In December 1993, I visited the salmon rafts in Chiloé's inner sea, near Quellón, and salmon smolt farms on Lake Llanquihue and Lake Huillinco.

301-302. "He's a child" and other comments: Rosa Huentén, in an interview with Renato Cárdenas and the author in Contuy, Chiloé, 24 October 1993.

303-304. Information about the island of Chiloé is the result of four years of visits and research, that began as part of the work for my poetry collection, *Medusa's Children*, (Coteau, 1993) and has gone on from there.

304-306. Koch's work is from his unpublished Master's thesis (See Books).

CHAPTER 17 ~ THE DRAGON PINCHOT

Interviews: Previous interviews for CBC "Sunday Morning" (and others) in 1986-87, with Genaro Arriagada, 16 December 1986; Virginia Morales (Moy de Tohá) 17 December 1986, Raúl Sohr, 17 March 1987, Monseigneur Augusto Salinas (Valparaíso) 21 March 1987; Dr. Juan Manual Pérez 24 March 1987; Federico Willoughby, 16 December 1986. Interviews specifically for this book took place with General Alejandro Medina, 22 July and 3 August 1992, Captain Raúl Vergara, 24 July 1992. Interviews with General Pinochet from books listed above, and in the newspaper *El Mercurio*, along with regular coverage of his speeches, etc.

Aside from the books listed in the bibliography, a number of magazines have published feature profiles outlining details of General Augusto Pinochet's life. For this chapter, I have used a number of these for background: "Rasgos Psíquicos del General", by Pablo Azócar, *Apsi*, 24 February 1986; "Augusto Pinochet", *Revista del Domingo, El Mercurio*, 3 February 1974; "1986: El Balance de Pinochet", interview by Blanca Arthur, *El Mercurio*, 28 December 1986; "Presidente Augusto Pinochet", *Cosas*, 29 September 1988; "Como es este hombre", *Que Pasa,* 2 July 1987; "La práctica de las leyes políticas vendrá en la segunda etapa", *Que Pasa,* 24 April 1986; "El Pinochet Oculto", by Rodrigo de Castro, *Análisis,* 6 May 1991; "Pinochet Cumple 19 Años", by Maria Eugenia Camus, *Análisis,* 19 August 1991; "Pinochet y el León", by Ignacio González Camus, *La Nación,* 20 September 1992; Pinochet, Part I, "De los soldaditos de plomo al golpe de Estado", by *Apsi* staff, 29 August 1988 and Part II, "De las gafas oscuras a los rezos en La Moneda", 5 September 1988; "Los Bienes de la Familia Pinochet", by Monica González, *Análisis,* 30 October 1989; "El Poder Oculto", by Monica González, Maria Olivia Monckeberg, Patricia Verdugo, *Análisis,* 27 July 1987; "Se rompe la confianza", by Marcia Scantlebury, *Análisis,* 22 January 1990, "Los Negocios de La Familia", by Patricia Verdugo, *Apsi,* 1 June 1992, "Las Púas del Bunker", by Nibaldo Fabrizio, *Apsi,* 16 October 1989.

Interviews published in the Chilean media with some of General Pinochet's current or former colleagues have also been useful, especially: Admiral José Toribio Merino, interviewed by Raquel Correa on Channel 13, 28 September 1989, published in *La Epoca,* 1 October 1989; General Gustavo Leigh, interviewed by Monica González, *Cauce,* 28 June 1984; Mónica Madariaga (his cousin and former Minister of Justice), interviewed by Monica González, *Análisis,* 10 December 1985; Orlando Sáenz (one of the main organizers of the 1973 coup), interviewed by Mónica González, *Cauce,* 28 August 1984; General Agustín Toro Dávila, interviewed by Elizabeth Subercaseaux, *Apsi,* 2 June 1986; General Sergio Poblete, interview by Felipe Pozo, *Análisis,* 3 July 1984; Federico Willoughby, interviewed by Maria Eugenia Camus, *Análisis,* 28 October 1991.

Other documents: "La grabación del golpe" (The recording of the coup), *Análisis,* 24 December 1985; "Los negocios del clan cívico militar", by Edwin Harrington and Monica González, *Análisis,* 13 May 1986; "Prats, General Demócrata", by Cecilia Allendes and Pamela Jiles, *Análisis,* 27 March 1984; and General Pinochet's official Curriculum Vitae, April 1982.

And, of course, there were also the years I spent covering his official speeches, his occasional conversation with the foreign press, and interviewing his supporters on the street, in offices and campaign headquarters.

309. "I've always been": General Augusto Pinochet, *Ego Sum Pinochet,* p. 156.
310. "We all have faults": Monseigneur Augusto Salinas, in an interview with the author in Valparaíso, 21 March 1987.
310. "group without any moral principles" and other comments: Frederico Willoughby, in an interview with the author in Santiago, 16 December 1986.
310. "Discipline and hierarchy": Raúl Sohr, in an interview with the author, in Santiago, 17 March 1987.
311. "studies a tumour": General August Pinochet, *Ego Sum Pinochet,* p. 39-41.
311. "I think that as an intellectual": Genero Arriagada, in an interview with the author in Santiago, 17 December 1986.
311. "very limited person": Virginia Morales, in an interview with the author in Santiago, 16 December 1986.
312. "I just said: Thank you": Pinochet, *Ego Sum Pinochet,* p. 73
313-314. "We're tied hand" and other comments: General Gustavo Leigh, in an interview with Monica González, *Cauce,* 26 June 1984.

314. "perhaps with more formal clarity": General Augusto Pinochet, *Política, Politiquería, Demagogia*, p. 16.

315. "Planets observe an invariable order": Pinochet, *Política, Politiquería, Demagogia*, p. 70.

315 "the least free person": Dr. Juan Manuel Pérez, in an interview with the author 24 March 1987.

315. "the danger threatening": Pinochet, *Política, Politiquería, Demagogia*, p. 25.

316. "The democratic system": Pinochet, *Política, Politiquería, Demagogia*, p. 34.

316. "Love for the land": Pinochet, *Política, Politiquería, Demagogia*, p. 115.

316. "give unto God": Pinochet, *Política, Politiquería, Demagogia*, p. 59.

316. "the basic principle.": Pinochet, *Política, Politiquería, Demagogia*, p. 69.

316-317. "worse, permanently seeks": Pinochet, *Política, Politiquería, Demagogia*, p. 70.

317. "appetites run away": Pinochet, *Política, Politiquería, Demagogia*, p. 70.

317. "who with impudence refutes": Pinochet, *Política, Politiquería, Demagogia*, p. 74

317. "I finalize saying": Pinochet, Política, *Politiquería, Demagogia*, p. 119

318. "because violence, perversion": Federico Willoughby, in an interview with the author in Santiago, 16 December 1986.

318. "voice of a man" and other comments: Dr. Juan Manuel Pérez, in an interview with the author in Santiago, 24 March 1987.

319. "the essence of existence": memorandum dated 27 August, Director of Army Operations. Pinochet: *Verdad y Ficción*, p. 100-107.

320-321. "Christian Democrat option" and other comments: Captain Raúl Vergara, in an interview with the author in Santiago, 24 July 1992.

322. "I don't plan": General Augusto Pinochet, *Apsi*, 5 September 1988.

322. "Execute Plan Cochayuyo": Admiral José Toribio Merino, in a televised interview with Raquel Correa, transcript published in *La Epoca*, 1 October 1989.

323. Figures on military expenditures from Genaro Arriagada, in an interview with the author, 16 December 1986.

323-324. "How a stupid man" and other comments: Genaro Arriagada, in an interview with the author 16 December 1986.

324. "mention the fear": Rettig Commission, *Rettig Report*, p. 451-458.

324. Figures for salaries and public opinion polls from Raúl Sohr's column, *La Epoca*, 1991.

325. "those dreadful things" and dialogue on human rights violations: Pinochet in *Ego Sum Pinochet*, p. 117-123.

329. "some people say": Ariel Dorfman, *The Last Song of Manuel Sendero*, p. 426, 427.

CHAPTER 18 ~ A ROOTED SORROW

Bridges, Thomas. *Yagan-English Dictionary.*
Emperaire, Joseph. *Los Nómades del Mar.*
España, Aristóteles. *El Sur de la Memoria.*
Palamara, Humberto Antonio. *Etica y Servicios de Inteligencia.*

Interviews: Fernando Lanfranco, 12-16 March 1993. Conversations with Carlos Vega and Elsa Barrída, Sylvia Barrías, February 1993.

334-337. The history of the Salesians and Dawson Island appears in Joseph Emperaire, *Los Nómades del Mar*, pp. 74-76.

338. "I stood up": Fernando Lanfranco, in an interview with the author, 12-16 March 1993.
339. "We were staked": Ricardo Andrade, *El Sur de la Memoria*, p. 177-181.
339. "around seven": José Cárcamo Barría, *El Sur de la Memoria*, p. 61-66.
339. "an electrical transformer": José Edison, *El Sur de la Memoria*, p. 67-75.
340. "he was crying": Nelson Reyes, *El Sur de la Memoria*, p. 165-172.

CHAPTER 19 ~ WHERE WE START FROM

Interviews: Andrés Domínguez, often between 1983-1995, Sola Sierra, 1983-1993; Cecilia Carvallo, 25 June 1992; General Mario Morales, 21 July 1992.

345-346. "We have information" and other comments: Andrés Domínguez, in an interview with the author, August 1993.
349-352. Ana Vergara and Jorge Vergara, "Justice, Impunity and the Transition to Democracy: a challenge for human rights education", published as an article in *The Journal of Moral Education*, Volume 23, Number, 1994, The Norham Foundation, Oxfordshire, UK.
352-354. "My twenty-five-year-old son" and other comments in this section: unnamed witnesses speaking before the Rettig Commission, *Rettig Report*, p. 766-786.
356. "after the battle": General Mario Morales, in an interview with the author in Santiago, 21 July 1992.
357. "an emanicipation from": Eugenio Tironi, *Los Silencios en la Revolución*, p. 12.

INDEX

Abril, 31

Aburto, Marco, 346

Aburto Panguilef, Manuel, 238–39

Acevedo, Ana María, attempt to interview Alvaro Corbalán, 261–62

ACU, 11–17, 21–22, 24, 25, 27, 28

    role of, in life of students and artists, 30–33

    Theatre Festivals, 13–14, 16–17

    what happened to activists after, 32–33

Adriana, 139–40, 141–42, 163

agrarian reform, 243

agricultural workers, 299–300

agriculture, 299–300

    export-oriented, 216

Aguirre, Isadora, 16

Aguirre Cerda, Pedro, 168

Alacaluf, 334, 335, 337

Alegria Mundaca, Juan, 111, 267, 268

Alessandri Palma, Arturo, 168, 320

Alessandri, Jorge, 170–71

Allende government, 65–66. See also Popular Unity

    threat to US interests in Chile, 177

Allende, Dr. Salvador, 7, 141, 170

    buried in Viña del Mar, 124

    concern for Pinochet, 312

    funeral, 7

    suicide, 147, 149–50

    support for, 173–74, 175

Alliance for Progress, 171, 174

Alvarez Santibáñez, Federico, 265

Alzamora, Cecilia, 110

Amauta, 31

American aid, 171. See also United States

American control of Chilean copper, 168

American influence, xx

American investment in Chile, 168, 169

American ownership, 289

Americans, died in the coup, 181

Americas Watch, 194

Amnesty International, 53, 59, 194

    help for exiles, 313

Amnesty Law, 115, 162, 281, 325, 345, 346, 347, 348

Anaconda, 170, 173, 290

Análisis, 122

Anfruns, Rodrigo, murder of, 119–21, 125, 127

Aonikenk, 334

Apsi, 122

araucaria fruit, 238

araucaria pine, 226, 241

    protection of, 243. See also logging

Araucarian Federation, 238–39 See also Mapuche

Arce, Luz, 105–108, 109–10, 115–16

Argentina, 294

Armed Forces

    income from copper, 290

    Marxist infiltration of, 66

Army

    a state of its own, 329

    formed by Germans, 37

    threats, 345, 348

    tradition of repression, 349

    values, 62–63, 64

Arrau, Claudio, xxi

Arriagada, Genaro, xx, 146, 160, 322–24

opinion of Pinochet, 311
Arriagada, Jorge, 339
art, effect of the coup on artistic activities, 21–22
Atacama desert, xix, xx, 167
Atacameños, 237
Australia, xxv–xxvi
Avandada Nacional, 255–56, 257, 261
    roots in nazism, 256
Aylwin government, 307
    and Mapuche, 240
    lack of credibility, 222
Aylwin, Patricio, 6, 59, 88, 162, 236, 270, 345
Aymara, 237

Baar, Hugo, 43, 44, 47, 50, 55
Bachelet, General Alberto, 73
barbarism, humanity's capacity for, xxi
Barnes, Harry, 190–98
Barón Jiménez, María Josefa, 264
Barrida, Elsa, 332
Barros, Alejandro, 263
Barros, Pía, 32
Barros Ortiz, Air Force General Diego, 21
Barticevich, Marcos, 339
Becerra, Miguel, 54
Bengoa, José, 93, 237, 238, 240
Berenguer, Carmen, 32
Berghammer, Jorge, 291–92
Binet, Ramón, 25
Blancpain Jean-Pierre, 36–37
Bohle, Luisa, 124, 131
Bolivia, xix, 94, 167
Bornand, Rosemarie, 265
Bórquez, Adriana, 48
Branches and Leaves Workshop, 17
Bratti, Guillermo, 108–109
Bravo, Roberto, xxi
Brazil, 294
British influence, xx
British investment in Chile, 167–68
Büchi, Hernán, 6
Bunster, Cesar, 153
Bussi Hortensia, 124
Byron, Admiral, 333

Cabrera, Ester, 158
Calfunao, Cacique, 93
Callejas, Mariana, 101–103, 116
Camilo, 10, 270, 271–72
Camus, Albert, 115
Canada, xxiii
    and refugees, xxiii–xxiv
    attitude towards Chile, xxvii
    compared to Chile, 357

Confederation des syndicats nationaux, xxiv
External Affairs, Department of, xxiv–xxv
foreign policy, xxiii–xxiv
interest in, 139
investment, 289–90
reaction to the coup, xxiv
religious persecution in, 54
Canadian Association of Latin American Studies, xxiv
Canadian Association of University Teachers, xxiv
Canadian Centre for Victims of Torture, xxv
Canadian churches, xxiv, xxv
Canadian Labour Congress, xxiv
Cánovas, Judge José, 2
Capri, 31
Carabineros, 78, 98, 125–26
    and Colonia Dignidad, 41
    convicted of murder, 355–56
    helped by CIA, 182
    involvement in executions, 83
    involvement with death squads, 129, 131
Cartagena, 27–28
Cárcamo Barría, José, 339
Carevic, Captain Raúl, 105
Carreño, Colonel Carlos, kidnapped, 159
Castro, Fidel, 171
Catholic Church, xxii, 24, 178
    and Colonia Dignidad, 53, 54
    and corporal punishment, 66
    human rights department, 109
    refuge for victims, 254
Cauce, 122, 126, 137, 152
Cayuela, José, 128–29
Cayupe, José, 245
Cecilia, 25–27
CEDAL, 299, 300
cemetery closure, 7
censorship, 14, 21–22, 118, 127
    authors banned, 21
    books banned, 21
    movies banned, 21
CEPI, 236–37, 239–40, 244, 245
Cerro, 173
Certa, Judge Carlos, 115
CESCO, 291
Chacón, Juan, 105
Chicago Boys, 295, 296, 297, 306
childhood, 9–10, 357–58
children
    abused, 52, 280, 285
    effect of the coup on, 8. *See also* relatives of
        the disappeared
Chile
    a cemetery, 7–8
    a symbol, xx

Chile *(continued)*
  armed forces, low wages, 319
  attitudes to immigrants, 36
  banking, reform of, 168
  biology of its people, 235–36
  British investment in, 167
  child abuse, 280, 285
  class structure, xx
  culture, xxi, 15, 23
  dependence on copper, 167
  economy, 152, 168
  geography, xix
  history, xx
  human cost of protest, xxvii
  independence, xx, 93–96, 172
  liberal democracy's failure, 61
  life in, xviii
  Nazis, 57, 58
  perspective on "America", xxvii
  politics, 143
  society, polarized, 177
  values, 306
  war with Bolivia and Peru, 94, 167.
    See also copper
Chileanization, 173, 175
Chileans in exile, 85
Chiloé, 301, 302, 303
Chilotes, xx, 303
Christian Democrats, 122, 159–60, 178, 183
  party re-emerges, 205
  reforms of education, 274
  support for coup, 88–89
  weakened, 174
Church Commission, US Senate, 171, 176–77, 181, 182
CIA, 190
  foreknowledge of coup, 182
  helped DINA, 185
  intervention in Chile, 174, 176, 177, 178–79
  personnel involved in chile, 171
Civic Neighbourhood, 71–72
civil disobedience, 152–53, 162
civil law, not applied, 148
civil war, 149. *See also* war
civil war of 1891, 319
CNI, 98, 253, 264
  agents testify against Corbalán, 267
  dissolved, 262
  formation of, 187
  murders of FPMR members, 158
  special unit within, 268
coalition governments, 169, 170, 222, 306
Codelco, 175–76, 288, 290–92, 296–97, 306, 308
  payments to Santa Barbara Transport, 265
Cohen, Gregory, 32
coigüe trees, 226

Colina, Coño, 104
Colonia Dignidad, 34, 35–56, 37–61
  a sect? 54
  and the Chilean Navy, 55
  arms, 55
  colonists, xx
  escapees, 43–44
  German Embassy, 60
  investigation of, 38–41, 45–47, 59
  like Germany of the 30s, 56–57
  Nazi sympathizers, 56
  protected by Chilean legal system, 59
  protected by conservative Chilean society, 58
  relations with the governments of Chile, 46–47
  security, 41, 45, 55
  suspension of charitable status, 59–60
  tax fraud, 59
  torture at, 47–49
  training agents, 99
  violates labour laws, 59
Columbia, 293
Comando Conjunto. *See* Joint Command
Cominco, 289–90
commission for reparation, 345–46. *See also* Rettig
  Commission
Communism, an enemy, 66
Communist Party, 149, 159–60, 161
  and FPMR, 150, 156, 157
  and González Videla, 310
  leaders, disappeared, 100
  outlawed, 169
Communist youth, 22, 140–41, 142, 148, 150
concentration camp, 20. *See also* Dawson Island
Concertación [coalition government], 222
Coñoepán, Venancio, 238
Conquest, xviii, xx, 92, 94
  natives resisted, 231, 234
conservatism, xxi
Constitution
  of 1925, 168
  of 1980, 218, 346
constitutional democracy, xx
Contreras, Colonel Manuel, 55, 98, 100, 107, 182,
  185, 187, 281, 348
  sentenced, 347
Contreras, Héctor, 98, 115
Contreras Maluje, Carlos, 148
Cook, Captain, 333–34
copper, xix, 167–69, 184–85, 188, 289–92.
  See also Codelco
  British investment in, 167
  mines, American ownership of, 169
  nationalized, 171, 289, 290
Copper Law, 292

Copper Workers' Confederation, 150–51, 189, 292
  strike, 202
Corbalán Castillo, Alvaro Julio, 253–68, 344
  See also Alvaro Valenzuela, Santa Barbara
  Transport Company
CORFO
  formation of, 169
  initiatives of, 170
corporal punishment in education, 66, 283
corporations, mixed, 173
Corvalán, Luis, 150
coup, xvii, 141, 146, 187, 322
  anniversary of, 344–45
  break with democracy, 143
  effect on families, 201
  effect on pobladores, 211–12
  ideological foundations of, 189
  personal description, 19–20, 141–42
  results, 181
  United States involvement in, 178
courts, pro-military, 187
cruelty, xviii, xxi
Cuatro Alamos, 22
Cuba
  aid from, 87
  changing attitude towards, 344
  training in, 151
Cuban exiles, 102, 185, 187
Cubillos, Hernán, 187–88
cueca, 26
CUSO, xxiv

Dawson Island, 15, 74, 181, 333
  mission on, 335
  prison, 338
day-care, 276
de Córdova, Antonio, 334
de la Cruz, María Olga, 263, 264
de la Parra, Marco Antonio, 32
death
  the effect on others, 8
  rites of, 349
death squads, 128, 129, 131
deaths of exiles, 100
del Rosario Pinto, Maria, 155
democracy, 172, 280–81, 357
  experience of, 72
  in crisis, 86
  role of ACU in, 31–32
  support for, 289
  tradition of, 197, 198, 319
Democratic Alliance, 205
democratic opposition, 196
detainees disappear, 107

detention, 73–75
Díaz Eterovic, Ramón, 32
DICOMCAR, 98
  blamed for Guerrero and Parada murders, 256
dictators, xix
DIFA, 98
DINA, 98–100, 148, 182, 184, 253, 324
  above the law, 100
  active at Colonia Dignidad, 49
  agents of, 101–16
  desertion from, 99
  prisoners join, 107
  radio, 100
  work abroad, 100, 182
DINE, 253
Dinges, John, 182
disappeared, 19, 22, 99, 100, 105, 116, 147, 345
  at Colonia Dignidad, 49
  relatives of, xxiii, 109, 116, 219, 346, 347,
    348–49
Domínguez, Andres, 286, 345–46
Donoso, Patricio, 281–82
Dorfman, Ariel, 21, 329–30
Doukhobors, 54
Drake, Sir Frances, 333
DuBois, Padre Pierre, 212, 213–14
Dueñas, Claudia, 284–85

economic changes, 215–18
economic controls, 170
economic policies, United States influence on, 188
economy, 295. *See also* copper, poverty, salmon,
  trade
  Chicago Boys, 295, 296, 297, 306
  foreign investment, 289, 290, 306
  Friedman, Milton, 188, 295, 297
  neo-liberal model, 295
  recession, 292–93, 295–97
  research and development, 299
  under the military government, 306
Edison, José, 339–40
"Eduardo", 140–41, 149–50, 154–55, 158–59
education, 307
  and military values, 70
  corporal punishment in, 66, 283
  drop-out rate, 280
  human rights, 281
  importance of, xx–xxi
    to General Medina, 66
    to Mapuche, 238, 246, 248
  in Canada, 269–70
  in Chiloé, 304
  influenced by Germans, 37
  integral, 23

education *(continued)*
  private schools, 274, 276
  privatization, 275
  public schools, xxi
    in Canada, 287
    in Chile, 273-74
  reforms, and trade, 295
  system in crisis, 274-76, 278
Edwards, Agustín, 118, 177-78
  family ownership of newspapers, 204
Edwards, Paula, 32
El Mercurio, 14, 21, 174, 186, 204, 284
  defends Colonia Dignidad, 53-54
El Salvador, 288, 290, 307-308
el gato Sepúlveda, 19
electoral system, 6
Emperaire, Joseph, 334-35
Engineering, Faculty of, 22-23
engineers and writers, 32
England, xxvi
Enríquez, Juan, 158
Environment Framework Law, 290
environmental hazards, 306
Ercilla, 34, 41, 50, 53, 56, 57
Escobar, Elizabeth, 158
España, Aristoteles, 338-39
Espinoza, Colonel Pedro, 187, 281, 348, sentenced, 347
Espinoza, Raimundo, 292
executions, 109
  members of MIR, 83
  members of the Socialist Party, 83
exiles, 31, 170, 174, 181, 183, 228, 340
  internal exile, 106
Eyzaguirre, José María, president of the Supreme Court, 2
Eyzaguirre, Nicolás, 15

Fatherland and Freedom, 101, 185, 321
fear, 149-50, 159, 272-73
  in Chile today, 286-87
  of new coup, 347
Fernández, Rolando, 263, 264
Fernández Dittus, Lieutenant Pedro, 279, 281
Fine Arts Museum, 21
fish farming, 300-301, 304-306
fisheries, 216
flag, honour to, 70
Flores, Carol, 104, 108
foreign investment, 289, 290, 306
FPMR, 97, 139, 142, 149, 159, 161
  abandoned by Communist Party, 156
  actions of, 151-52, 152-53
  ambush on Pinochet, 154-56
  anthem, 154
  demonstrations, 197

effect of, 162-63
failure of, 160-61
founding of, 150
influence of, 195
members disappear, 268
origins of, 145
use of history, 145
Frei, Eduardo, 280, 306, 307, 348
Frei Montalva, Eduardo, 38, 65, 171, 173, 178, 319
Frente Autónomo, 156
Frente Patriótico Manuel Rodríguez. *See* FPMR
Fresno, 100
Friedman, Milton, 188, 295, 297
Front. *See* FPMR
frontier, Chilean, 90, 302
frontier, psychological, 37
Fuenteovejuna Street, operations, 111-14, 253, 255
Fuenzalida, Samuel, 49
Fuerzas Populares Rebeldes Lautaro, 153
funerals, 4-5

Gajardo, Enrique, 124
Gallardo, Miguel Rodríguez, 108
García de Cortázar, Javier, 17
Gemballa, Gero, 46, 58-59
General Cemetery of Santiago, 1
Geneva Convention, 148
German community, attitudes of, 37
German immigrants, xx
German influence in current affairs, 37
German schooling, 35
German settlers, 36-38
German support for Colonia Dignidad, 55
Germany Embassy, relations with Colonia Dignidad, 46
Germany, 168
ghost towns, 288, 289
Gloria Quintana, Carmen, 193, 279
González, Kika, 349
González, Monica, 98, 115, 117-18, 119, 121-22, 123, 126-27, 132, 133-34, 137-38, 156, 160-61, 162
González, Sergio, 48-49
González Apablaza, Delia, 125, 130, 131
González Meneses, Alvaro, 223
González Videla, Gabriel, 169, 310
Gordon, General Humberto, 255, 256
graves, mass, 3, 345
Grove, Marmaduke, 239, 320
Gubler Díaz, Luis Eugenio, 126, 128, 129, 130
Guerra, Julio, 158
Guerrero, Manuel, 1-2
  murder of, 115, 256
Gullén Zapata, José Mario, 264
Guzmán, Jaime, 6-7

Haig, General Alexander, 178, 185
Hales, Alejandro, 291
Hales, Jaime, 110
Hauch, 334
health care, 278–79, 307
health hazards, occupational, 300
Heghme, Jecar, 7
Helms, Senator Richard, 178, 193–94
Hennings, Erika, 105
Henríquez, Wilson, 158
Herrera, Patricia, 348
Herrera Echegoyes, Mariana, 126, 130
Hertz, Carmen, 156
Hess, Rudolph, tribute to, 57
Hitler, xviii, 311
Hofer, Pati, 25
Hopp, Dr. Hartmut, 54
Horman, Charles, 181
How to Read Donald Duck, 21
Hoy, 122, 136
Huelén [Santiago], 9
Huenuman, Rosendo, 246
Huerquehue National Park, 226
Huife Hotsprings, 231
Huilliche, xx, 303
human, xviii, xix, xxvi, 341, 356
human rights, 5, 109, 188, 193, 194, 197, 341, 346
    a basic value, 281
    actions, 85
    an issue in the plebiscite, 219
    Catholic Church human rights department, 109
    education, 284–87, 341
    groups, 24
    lawyer, 110
    monitoring of, xxv
    trials, 348
    violations, 149, 281
        roots of, 349–50
        victims of, 187, 254
    workers, 99
Human Rights Commission, 286–87
humane, xviii, xix, xxvi, 356, 358
Hutterites in Canada, 54

Ibáñez del Campo, Carlos, 72, 170, 273, 320
Ignacio, 5–6, 26–27, 138–40, 142, 358
    and the Front, 156–58
    death of, 161
immigration, 36
income disparity, 307. *See also* poverty
informants, 98, 99
informers, on the regime, 127
Inostroza Martínez, Jorge, 125
Inquisition, xviii, xxii

Interchurch Committee on Chile, xxv
Inter-Church Committee on Human Rights in Latin
    America, xxv
Inti Illimani, xxi, 22
Investigaciones, 41, 98, 121, 125–26, 131
    involved in torture, 223
invisible enemy, 148
Isla Negra, 26, 27–29
Italian fascists, 103
Italy, 100

JAP [Popular Supply Boards], 65, 73
Japan, 293, 300, 303–304
Japanese investment, 289, 290, 303
Jara, Eduardo, 110
Jara, Victor, xxi, 3–4
Jarlan, Padre André, 212
Jiménez, Tucapel, murder of, 110–11, 131, 267, 268
Joint Command, 98, 253
joint ventures, 291–92
Jordán, Judge Servando, 110
José Domingo Cañas, 107
journalists
    foreign, 111–12
    under the coup, 21
judicial investigations, 2, 110, 115, 132, 324
    of Letelier and Moffit murders, 186
    of military, 345–46
    of the disappeared, 98–99
Junta, supported by United States, 187, 189.
    See also military government
justice system, 149
    breakdown of, xxi
justice, 287, 351

Kemmerer Mission, 168
Kendall, Donald, 177–78
Kenecott Copper, 173, 290
killed by the coup, 147
killed, 181
killers, 137
Kissinger, Henry, 176, 177, 178
Klein-Saks Mission, 170
Koch, John, 304–306
Kuhn, Heinz, 43–44, 51, 53

La Ciruela, 11–13, 17, 23
La Cutufa, 265, 266
La Epoca, 139
La Nación, 137
La Segunda, 21, 204
La Tercera, 122, 204
La Victoria, 169, 206–207, 208, 210–11, 212, 221,
    224–25

Lagos, Ricardo, 6
Lagunas Alfaro, Fernando, 124–25, 130, 131
Lamliate, Andrés, 243
Landau, Saul, 182, 185
Lanfranco, Fernando, 338–39, 340
Lanfranco, Patricio, 9, 15–16, 17, 24–25, 28, 331
Larrea, Miguel Angel, 32
Las Ultimas Noticias, 118–19, 122, 204
Latcham, Richard, 144–45
Laureani, Fernando, 107
Lautaro, 161, 234
Lavín, Joaquín, 215–17
Law for the Permanent Defence of Democracy, 169
laws, re: indigenous people, 240
legal system compromised, 188–89
Leigh, General Gustavo, 111, 152, 320
    opinion of Pinochet, 313–14,
Leighton, Bernardo, 100, 132, 184
Letelier, Isabel, 312
Letelier, Juan Pablo, 164–67, 199–200
Letelier, Orlando, 100, 103, 132, 173–74, 184, 187, 200, 281, 347
    Ambassador to the United States, 176
    arrested, 180–81
    assassination, 166, 197–98
    exiled, 166, 183
    Minister of Defence, 179
    Minister of External Affairs, 179
Leyton, Elliott, 134, 135
Lillo, Nelson, 128, 129, 130
Linares, 34
Linares, Bishop of, 35
Lindemann, Wilhelmine, 34–35, 39–41, 61
literacy, xx–xxi, 23
Littín, Miguel, xxi
Llanos, Eduardo, 29–30, 32
logging, 241, 243–44, 303
Loveman, Brian, 169, 289

Magellan, Ferdinand, 333
Magendzo, Abraham, 284, 285
Magni, "Comandante Tamara", Cecilia, 153
Malespina, Alejandro, 334
Maliqueo, José, 245
Maluenda, María, 5
Manns, Patricio, 145
Mapuche, xx, 36, 37, 235, 237, 239, 247, 248. *See also* native people
    and tourists, 90–91
    ceremonies, 236, 239
    deeded land, 242–43
    discussion of future, 245–47
    healing, 232
    last rebellion, 242

participation in Chilean society, 238
struggle against the conquest, 92–96
survival, 234
tactics, 94–95
territory, 231
values, 95
Mapudungun [Mapuche language], 96
Marchenko, Miguel Krassnoff, 103
Martínez, Liliana, 111
maté, 241–42
Matta, Roberta, xxi
Matthei, Air Force General Fernando, 7
Max Neef, Manfred, 298, 299
Mayoraz, Isabelle, 155
MECI, 283
media
    attitude towards justice, 351
    credibility, 204
    interpretations of protests, 204
    involvement in the coup, 178
    lies after the coup, 147
    role of, 135, 136–37
    view of natives, 245
Medina Luis, retired General Alejandro, 62–69, 80–81, 90, 344
    acted to prevent war, 146–47
    army values, 319
    attitude towards Rettig Commission, 85–86
Meliñirs, 240, 242–43, 244
Melivilu, Franscisco, 238
Mena, General Odlanier, 187
Mennonites, 54
Merino, Admiral, history of the coup, 322
Merino, Marcia Alejandra, 105
Mertins, Gerhard, arms dealer, 55
Mexico, 293
militarism, 160
military
    action, 80–87
    allegiance to the constitution, 178
    control of the country, 68, 81
    control of the media, 118
    coup's purpose, 135
    expenditures, 323, 324–25
    intelligence, 323
    pensions, 323
    rescued the country, 89
    race, 235
    support of Allende, 69
    values, 69–70
    virtues, 310
military government, 188–89, 320
    economy, 306
    effect on families, 15

retaliations against protesters, 204, 206
mining, xx. *See also* copper, nitrates
  joint ventures, 289–90
MIR, 6, 7, 18, 19, 65–66, 141, 161
  leaders, 100, 113, 255, 268
  disappeared members, 100, 105
  target of the coup, 149
Miranda Carrington, Sergio, 256
missionaries, to the natives, 334, 335
Mistral, Gabriela, xxi
Mitchell, John, 177–78
modernization, 217
Moffit, Ronni, 100, 103, 184, 187, 281, 347
Moneda, 18, 67, 72, 73, 78
Montealegre, Jorge, 32
Montecinos, Sonia, 236
Moraga, Marcial, 155
Morales, Luis, 125
Morales, Virginia (Moy de Tohá), 312, exiled, 313,
  opinion of Pinochet, 311–12, 315, 329
Morales Anabalón, Guillermo, 130
Morales Moncada, Mario, 77–80, 355–56
Morel, Isabel, 173
Moreno Avila, Juan, 154
Moyano, Eduardo, 293, 294
Müller, Juan, 35
Müller, Wolfgang, 41–43, 44, 51, 56, 60
Muñoz, Diego, 22–25, 32
Muñoz Alarcon, Juan, 99–100, 116
Muray, Osvaldo, 46, 56–57, 59
musical workshop, 26

National Commission to Modernize Education, 280
National Corporation for Reparation and Reconciliation, 285
National Protests, 151, 189–90, 202, 205, 206,
  207, 208–209, 212, 214
National Security, 189, 274–75
National Stadium, 4, 99
National Union of Students [Canada], xix, xxiv, 15
nationalization of copper mines, 289, 290
native people, 90–96. *See also* Chillotes, Mapuche,
  Ona, Selknam, Yamaná
  and workers, 239
  arts, 250
  Atacameño, xx
  beliefs, 301–303
  claims approach to problems, 244–45
  Diaghuita, xx
  languages, 91, 93, 302
  poverty, 236
  Punta Arenas, 332, 333
  survival, 248
  Tierra del Fuego, 333–34

nature, concern for, 247
Navarro, Esteban, 32
Navarro, Heddy, 32
Nazi values in Chile, 57, 58
Nazis in Latin America, 56, 57, 58, 61, 320
Neghme, Jecar, 268
negotiations with the military regime, 159, 162, 205
Nélida Sánchez, Maria, 169, 203, 205, 206–207,
  208, 210–11, 212–13, 221–22
neo-liberal model, of economy, 295
Neruda, Pablo, xix, xxi, 2, 4, 11–13, 27, 28,
  169–70
  Neruda banned, 21
New Song Movement, 22, 228
news, 118–19, 122–23. *See also* Agustin Edwards, media
newspaper ownership, 118
Nguillatún, 234, 236, 238, 239, 240–41, 241–42,
  248–49, 251–52
Nicaragua, inspiration for FPMR, 157
nitrates, xix, 167, 288, 289, 296
Nixon, Richard, 176, 177, 178
Nobel prizewinners, xxi
Noguera Palacios, Oscar, 125
North American attitudes towards Latin America, xxvii
North American free trade area, 290
Novoa, Laura, 172–73, 174–76, 180, 188, 189
  reaction to the coup, 179–80, 183–84
Nueva Imperial, 247–48
Núñez Bories, Eduardo, 264

O'Higgins, General Bernardo, 143, 145
Ona, 237, 334–35
Onofre Jarpa, Sergio, 205
opposition news, 122
Ortiga, 31
Ortiz, Estela, 2, 5
Orwell's *1984*, 122
Ovalle, Jorge, 46, 47, 111, 152
Oxfam-Canada, xxiv
Oyarzún, Francisco, 102

Pacific War of 1879, xix, 94
Packmor, Georg, 43, 55
Packmor, Lotti, 43, 44–45, 51
Painemal, Victor Hugo, 237, 238
Palamara, Captain Humberto, 340–41, 342
Palma Ramirez, Adolfo, 108–109
Panamerican Highway, 35, 90
Panguipulli, 81–84, 91
Parada, Jose Manuel, 1–2, 131, 256
  murder of, 115
Parada, Roberto, 14, 16
Parra, Angel, 22
Parra, Isabel, 22

Parra, Nicanor, 21
Parra, Violeta, xxi, 22, 228
Patria y Libertad. *See* Fatherland and Freedom
Peebles, Luis, 47–48
Pehuenches, 237–38, 240, 243, 244. *See also* Mapuche
Pellegrin, "José Miguel", Raúl, 161
Peñailillo, Irene, 105
pensions, military, 323
Pérez, Juancho (Dr. Juan Manuel), 15, 17–20, 30, 32–33, 127–28, 133, 135–36
    opinion of Pinochet, 315, 318
Peru, xix
    war with, 94
PET, 297–98
physical abuse of prisoners, 106–107
physical abuse of students, 66, 283
PIEE, 284–85, 286
pine plantation, 216. *See also* araucaria pine
Pineda de Castro, Alvaro, 319
    praise for Pinochet, 326–27
Pinochet, General Augusto, xix, 6–7, 65, 126–27, 143, 196, 218–19, 234–35, 273, 345
    ambush of, 151, 153–55
    an ordinary Chilean, 328
    and democracy, 146, 316
    and Manuel Rodriquz, 144
    and the CNI, 313
    appointments to Senate, 298–99
    attitude towards resisters, 98
    biography, 309–9
    commander of detention camp at Pisagua, 170, 310
    concept of new society, 327–28
    critical of Democratic alliance, 314
    critical of Supreme Court, 347
    denies knowledge of torture and disappearances, 186, 325–26
    DINA, 100, 187
    disposed of military opponents, 322–23
    government, 66
    hands over ribbon of office, 270
    helped by CIA, 182
    ideology, 311
    need for order, 314–15,
    opinion of Communists, 146, 315–16
    incarnation of O'Higgins, 145
    signature campaign, pro-, 256, 265
    swears to uphold the constitution, 179
    values, 316–17
    view of foreign journalists, 112
    worked for Allende, 311–12
Pizarro, Isabel, 265
Placer Dome, 289–90
plebiscite (1988), 6, 89, 152, 160, 199, 218–20, 221

poblaciones, 203, 204, 205, 206–207, 209–10, 214, 217–18, 220
pobladores, 220, 221
police
    agents speak up, 116
    corruption of, 132–33
    secret, 99–100, 132, 136–37
political crises, 319–20
political instability, 168–69
political parties legalized, 318
Polloni, Lieutenant-Colonel Alberto, 148
pollution, 290, 305–306
Ponce Lerou, Julio, son-in-law of Pinochet, 127, 296
Popular Unity government, 18, 71, 134–35, 141. *See also* Allende
Portales, Diego, 145
post office, 127
poverty, 218, 220, 236, 297–98, 307
Prats, General Carlos, 100, 132, 178, 179, 184, 313
prisoners
    become informants, 105
    treatment of, 104. *See also* human rights, torture
private schools in Chile, 274, 276
private sector, 296
privatization, 296, 297
    of education, 275
    of mines, 291
protests, national, 136, 150, 151, 152, 189–90, 202, 205, 206, 207, 208–209, 212, 214, 220, 221, 346
    middle class participation in, 278–79
psychopath murders, 124–26
psychopathology, 128, 129, 133–34, 136, 137
public schools, xxi
    in Canada, 287
    in Chile, 273–74
publishing, 21
Puerto Natales, 336–37
Punta Arenas, 331–37

Quilapa, 22
Quilapán, Cacique Santos, 95
Quilapayún, xxi
Quinquén, 236, 238, 239, 240, 242, 243, 244
Quiroz, Patricia, 158

racism, xxi, 357
    Chilean Nazism, 58
Radio Chilena, 122
Radio Cooperativa, 122
radio stations, 21
Rapa Nui, 237
Rapiman, Dionisio, 245–46, 247
Rauff, Walter, 57
recession, 292–93, 295–97

relatives of the disappeared, 109, 116, 219, 346, 347, 348–49
research and development, 299
resistance, armed, to the Junta, 150
Rettig Commission, xxvi, xxvii, 6, 82–84, 99, 100, 146–47, 149, 189, 208–209, 279, 281, 286, 312, 325, 358
a record of what was lost, 352–55
findings, 115–16
on the military, 324
recommendations, 356–57
violent deaths, 99
Revolutionary Communist Party, 18
Reyes, Nelson, 340
Rivas, Hugo, 147–48
Rivera, Ricardo, 158
Riveros, Ana María, 125
Roa Caballero, Patricio, 267
Rodriquez, Manuel, 143–45. See also FPMR
Rojas, Rodrigo, 4, 193, 279
romería, 2, 7
Romo, Osvaldo Enrique, 100, 103, 105, 108, 116
Rosalía, Doña, 246–47
Rothhammer, Dr. Franscisco, 235
Rovekamp, Walter, 53
Rozas, Jorge, 14
Ruiz, Catalina, 25
Ruiz, Magda, 339
Ruiz Tagle, Jaime, 297–98

Saavedra, Colonel Cornelio, 91, 92, 93, 94–95
Saenz, Pedro, 297
Sagredo, Jorge, 126, 130–31
Salesians
mission, 334, 335
Museum of Punta Arenas, 334
values, 69
salmon, 216, 300–301, 304–306
salmon farm workers, 305
Salmones Antártica, 301, 304–305
Salmones Unimarc, 304, 304–305, 306
Salvadores de Castro, Evita, 105
Sanchez, Isabel, 25
Sánchez Muñoz, Dr. Alfred, 124, 131
Sandanista army, exiles fighting in, 151
Sanino, Kika, 35, 38–41, 59, 60
Santa Barbara Transport Company, 261, 264, 265, 266, 267
Santiago, xix
changing, 214–15
occupation of, during the coup, 67–68
founding of, 9
Huelén, 9
Santiago del Neuvo Extremo, 28, 31

Santigáñez, Margarita, 125
Sarin, 102
Schäfer, Paul, 42, 43, 45, 49–53, 57, 61
principles of, 50
Schaulsohn, Jorge, 348
Schmidt, Hermann, 42, 54
Schmidt, Ursula, 34–35
Schneider, General René, attempted kidnapping of, 178
Schneider doctrine, 65, 178
school drop-out rate, 280
secret police, 99–100, 132, 136–37
security forces, 98
Seewald, Gisela, 43
Selknam, 237, 334, 340
Senate, 6
September 11, 1973, 62, 67–69, 73, 77–79
number killed on, 147
serial killers, 134, 135
Serrano, Bruno, 32
sexual abuse
of children at Colonia Dignidad, 43, 44, 51
of prisoners, 103, 106, 339, 349
shadow army, linked with Italian fascists, 185
shadow war, 148, 162, 163
cost of, 149
SICAR, 98
SIFA, 98, 104
silence, 202–203
broken with democracy, 272
in schools, 280
Silva, Ricardo, 158
Silva Silva, Andrés, 82–83
SIN, 98
Skinner, B.F., 279–80
social problems, 306
social services, 298
Socialists, 159–60
government, xix, xx
leaders, disappeared, 100
Sohr, Raúl, 322, 323
Solidaridad, 24, 122
Soublette, Gaston, 58
southern Chile, rural, 226
State Bank, 68
State of Siege, 127, 148
state ownership of copper, importance of, 297
State, role of, 71
steel, 296
Stern, 55
Strätling, Erich, 46
Strauss, Franz-Joseph, 54
strikes, 307
student activists, 23–24
student organizations, 32

Suco, xxiv
survivors, 344, 348. *See also* relatives of the
disappeared

Taricco, Hector, 35, 38–40, 45, 52, 53, 59, 60
tax reform, 298
taxes, 290, 307
Taylow, Jay, 289
teachers, 277, 358
abuse children, 277
training, 274, 282–83, 284–87
tear-gas bombs, 203, 205, 212, 213, 270–71
Tehuelche, 334
Téllez, General Indalicio, 235
Temuco, 91–92, 96, 237
Teruggi, Frank, 181
Thauby, Claudio, 107
Theberge, James, 189, 190, 191
Tierra del Fuego, 333–34
Tinquilco, life in, 226–28, 230
Tironi, Eugenio, 217–18, 306
Tofler, Alvin, 295
Tohá, José, 311, 312
Topp Collins, Carlos, 126, 130–31
Toro Dávila, Augustín, 235
Torres, Oswaldo, 31
Torres del Paine National Park, 336
Torres Silva, General Fernando, 156, 159
torture, xxi, xxxii–xxiii, 19, 74–76, 84, 105, 110,
115, 223, 265, 321–22
by the state, 135
on Dawson Island, 338–41
results of, 147
revealed, 219
sanctioning of, xxii
to train agents, 104
torturers, xvii, 116, 137
tourism, 336–37, 341
tourists, 90, 231
Townley, Michael, 101–103, 116, 185–87
trade, 292–94
agreements, 292, 294
North American free trade area, 290
partners, 292–94
Trauco, 301–302
trials, for human rights violations, 350–51, 355
trust, lack of, in governments, 223–24
truth, telling, 112

UNICEF, 280, 282
union leaders, 99
unions
Copper Workers' Confederation, 150–51, 189,
202, 292

destroyed by military government, 299–300
strikes, 307
Workers Federation of Chile, 239
United Nations
and human rights in Chile, xxvi
condemnation of Chile, 149
help for exiles, 313
United States
and salmon, 301
anti-US sentiments, 171
economic assistance, 170
investment in defeat of Allende, 174
opposition to CORFO, 170
policy for Latin America, 171
policy towards Chile, 168–69, 188
relations with Chile, 171
training Latin American countries, 189
University of Chile, xx
Faculty of Economics, 71
university activities, 13
Urrutia, General, 96
Urzúa, General Carol, 6

Valdivia, Pedro de, xix–xx, 9, 92, 234
Valencia, Manuel, 159
Valenzuela, Alvaro, 108, 113–14, 116, 254.
See also Alvaro Julio Corbalán Castillo
confesses, 127
testifies, 114–15
Valenzuela, Andrés, 103–104
Valenzuela, Ignacio, 257
Valenzuela Levy, Commander "Ernesto",
José Joaquín, 151, 153–54, 156, 158
Valparaíso, 15, 124
value-added products, 293, 301
values, 175
Chilean, 271
military, 69–70
private education, 276
US, and Chile, 198
Vanguardia Nazionale, 103
Vargas Bories, Jorge, 264–65, 266
Vega, Carlos, 332–33, 340–41, 342
Veliche, 302
Venegas, Roxana, 125, 131
Venezuela, 294
Ventura, Jaime, 125, 131
Venturelli, Pepi, 18
Verdugo, Patricia, 156
Vergara, Air Force Captain Raúl, 69–77, 84–85
opinion of the coup, 320–22
Vergera, Ana Cecilia, 349–52
Vergara, Jorge, 349–52
Vicariate of Solidarity, 109, 122

Villagra, José, 105
Villagrán, Alvaro Vallegos, 49
Villarrica, 90, 92, 95, 96, 231
Viña del Mar, 123–24
violence
 during popular unity, 141
 escalating, 161
 of Chilean society, 307, 349
von Clausewitz, on war, 146

war
 a character in this book, 145–46
 an excuse for detentions and disappearances,
  83–84, 86
 as viewed by FPMR, 155
 goals of, 148
 language of, in the military, 324
 one-sided, 147
 shadow war, 148, 149, 162, 163
 talent for, 235
Washington, 100
Weibel, José, 127
Wenderoth, 106–107, 109
whales, 290
Whole Earth Council, 244–45
Willoughby, Federico, 310, 317–18, 318, 319
Wohri, Franz, 44
Wohri, Teresa, 44
women
 in ACU, 25
 in the Mapuche community, 246
words, actual to describe what happened, 112
words, changing meanings, 97–98
workers
 agricultural, 299–300
 health hazards, occupational, 300
 mining, 292
 salmon farm, 305
Workers Federation of Chile, 239
World University Service, xxiv
World War I, importance of Chile in, 168
World War II, 169
writers, 32

Yamaná, 237, 334, 337
Yamaná language, 341
Yugoslav immigrants, xx

Zúñiga, Franscisco, 265, 266

The body text and display titles in this book are set in Rotis Serif and Rotis SemiSans respectively. Created in 1988 and digitized by Agfa in 1989, the Rotis family of typefaces was designed by German graphic designer/typographer Otl Aicher. Rotis was designed in four forms: Sans Serif, SemiSans, Serif and SemiSerif, and is notable as a highly polished, exceptionally legible design with a very distinct and contemporary style.